Egerton Ryerson and His Times

Egerton Ryerson and His Times

edited by
NEIL McDONALD and ALF CHAITON

Macmillan of Canada

Canadian Cataloguing in Publication Data

Main entry under title:
Egerton Ryerson and his times

ISBN 0-7705-1706-4 bd.   ISBN 0-7705-1707-2 pa.

1. Ryerson, Egerton, 1803–1882—Addresses, essays, lectures.
2. Education—Canada—History—19th century—Addresses, essays, lectures.
I. McDonald, Neil, 1937–   II. Chaiton, Alf, 1949–

LA411.7.E44 / 379'.71   C78-001531-2

27,114

*This book has been published with the help of a grant from the Social
Science Federation of Canada, using funds provided by the Social Sciences
and Humanities Research Council of Canada.*

*Illustrations courtesy of
Ontario History of Education Collection, OISE Library*

Printed in Canada for
The Macmillan Company of Canada Limited
70 Bond Street
Toronto, Canada
M5B 1X3

Errata
On pages v and 59, the title of the essay and
author's name should read:
  "The Moral Foundation of Egerton
  Ryerson's Idea of Education,
  Albert F. Fiorino".

Contents

CONTENTS

For Jennifer, Trevor, Jill, and Michael—our children.

Undoubtedly, Egerton Ryerson is the most prominent name in Canadian educational historiography. Ryerson's name was synonymous with educational developments in Canada for much of the nineteenth century. Over the past decade, a reassessment of "the Ryerson era" has been taking place. New interpretations of Ryerson's work and influence, fresh insights into well-worked areas, and new thrusts into hitherto unexplored areas have all been part of this reassessment. Much of this work, however, has been done in relative isolation, due primarily to geographical considerations, and also because the opportunities for sharing ideas and assessing trends are limited. Therefore, it was thought that a national conference, bringing together for the first time historians of Canadian education and those interested in the field, was particularly desirable.

The context for this gathering was the centennial of Ryerson's retirement from the post of superintendent of education for Ontario. To commemorate this event an invitational symposium was organized with the theme "Egerton Ryerson and His Times". It was held at the Ontario Institute for Studies in Education (OISE) in Toronto, on February 19–21, 1976, with Neil McDonald as Chairman and Co-ordinator. This volume is the result of that conference.

The response to the symposium in terms of interest was little short of overwhelming. Consequently, the accumulated list of obligations is long, and in highlighting the efforts of a few, others, whose co-operation and encouragement were greatly appreciated, must unfortunately be omitted.

Few such public gatherings can take place without financial assistance. The Ryerson symposium was not an exception. The Canada Council was particularly generous. With the Council's contribution the participants were aided in travel and accom-

PREFACE

modation for the duration of the symposium. The Department
of History and Philosophy of Education at OISE and the Department of Educational Foundations at the University of Manitoba
provided funds to help in necessary organizational work. Trevor
Wigney and Keith Wilson, chairmen of those departments,
were especially helpful. A special debt is owed to June Armstrong, head of the Conference Office at OISE. Her efforts on
behalf of the symposium were unstinting. Linda Baynham is
to be thanked for her work on this manuscript, which required
a great deal of skill and patience.

For a variety of reasons a number of presentations could not
be included in this volume. We are grateful to Keith McLeod,
Gerald Craig, Alf Chaiton, J. Donald Wilson, and Marina Robinson for their contributions. A number of other participants
agreed to act as moderators of sessions, respondents to papers,
and/or readers of papers for those who could not attend. These
include Willard Brehaut, Ian Winchester, Heather Lysons,
J. A. Riffel, T. R. Morrison, Eric Ricker, Marvin Lazerson,
Seymour Wilson, and Clifford C. Pitt.

The final session of the symposium was a round-table discussion entitled, "Canadian Educational Historiography:
Future Directions". This session provoked stimulating debate
on a topic of obvious interest to delegates. A panel of five helped
begin the discussion: Hugh Stevenson, Marvin Lazerson,
T. R. Morrison, Michael Jackson, and Ian Winchester. Their
comments were greatly appreciated and brought a fitting
conclusion to a very successful symposium.

The editors of this volume also wish to express their gratitude
to Virgil Duff, of Macmillan. His encouragement and positive
direction were both helpful and necessary. Finally, to our wives,
Angela and Sarah, whose patience and understanding helped
us get this volume to press by freeing us from other responsibilities.

Neil McDonald

Egerton Ryerson and His Times

I Introduction

Canadian Educational Historiography: Some Observations*

MARVIN LAZERSON

In the history of childhood, the family, and social service institutions, the nineteenth century, as Alison Prentice and Susan Houston have recently suggested, was the century of schooling. Government interest and involvement in the promotion and management of schools significantly increased, as did the willingness of parents and other adults to make the schools the prime agency for the formal education of the young.[1] The essays in this book probe the dimensions of that process in mid-nineteenth-century Upper Canada. They examine the dramatic expansion of schooling, the growing attention to organization, the complex interaction between state compulsion and individual choice, and the elaboration of educational philosophies that marked the first great wave of educational reform.

Lest readers assume too easily that this book is simply about schools, let me hasten to add that the essays which follow blend educational history with new and significant insights into topics of continuing concern to Canadian social and cultural historians: the influence of English and American institutions on Canadian culture, the nature and impact of the Rebellions of 1837, the complex relationship between the Anglican establishment and religious voluntarism, the response to immigration, the influence of Ontario on western Canada, and the shaping of public service institutions. Essays by Albert Fiorino and Goldwin French reveal the religious basis of nineteenth-century Canadian society. In particular, they show how the commitment to a Christian public-school system that was religious and non-sectarian and that educated youth to "a life of Christian citizen-

*I wish to acknowledge Neil Sutherland, George Tomkins, and J. Donald Wilson for their helpful comments on an earlier draft of this essay.

3

ship" reflected fears of social disorder and a search for new standards of public behaviour. These shaped the moral values taught and the organizational structure of public education.

In all this Egerton Ryerson looms large. Neither the mythic hero of traditional historiography nor the villain of an oppressive bureaucratic tradition, Ryerson stands out as the most articulate, politically active, and sometimes inconsistent spokesman for common schools. His activities were not *sui generis* however, and much that he accomplished, J. Donald Wilson shows, was based on developments before 1844. By the time he retired as chief superintendent of schools in 1876, most of his innovations had also occurred in the United States and Western Europe, and must therefore be seen as part of a larger process of modernization. Ryerson's role, as historians are coming to understand, was both to help build a new system and to accommodate to social trends over which he had little control. What is intriguing about Ryerson, then, is the complex interaction between individual and small-group political decisions and the underlying economic and social transformations affecting mid-nineteenth-century Upper Canada.

Perhaps most striking to the reader of this book will be the insights and materials on issues which for too long have been neglected by social and educational historians. A number of these are worth examining for the themes that emerge, and are of immense importance to historians, current policy analysts, and the lay public.

It now seems clear that the expectation that the school would act as an agent of political socialization was crucial to the origins and expansion of a common-school system. In the cauldron of mid-nineteenth-century social change, pressure to systematize the process of integrating people more effectively into the community intensified. Increasingly, the more traditional agencies of socialization—families, denominational churches, and local communities—were criticized, often for being unstable and needing supplementation. Growing social complexity required more threads to bind individuals and groups together. As Neil McDonald points out, educational reformers turned to formal schooling as a sometime supplement, sometime surrogate for family, peers, and localities; they saw their roles as "public educators", to use Alison Prentice's phrase, both in the sense of articulating a provincial identity within the British system and in socializing the young to that identity.

The content of that socialization included a commitment to a

Christianity that could accommodate most Protestants, to Canadians as loyal subjects of the Queen, and to social class harmony within a hierarchically ordered society. There was no real conflict between Britain and Canada, between Protestantism and morality, or between social classes. As Ryerson put it in 1845, his goal was "to impart to the public mind the greatest amount of useful knowledge based upon, and interwoven throughout with sound Christian principles, but to render the Educational system . . . the indirect but powerful instrument of British Constitutional Government".[2]

The goals and content of political socialization had enormous consequences for the shape and structure of public education. James Love suggests that the desire to create a centralized, Christian, British-oriented, socially harmonious educational system after the 1837 Rebellions led to strictures on who should teach, how they should be certified, what textbooks to use, and the power of local authority to make such decisions.. More broadly, the search for harmony within the educational system was itself beset by conflicts between local and provincial authority, Reformers and Tories, and Irish Catholics and Irish (Ulster) and non-Irish Protestants. These conflicts dominated mid-nineteenth-century politics, and they substantially affected the schools.

The expectations of socialization had other consequences. They brought to the fore the problem of school attendance, and the conflict between schooling and work, and they raised the spectre of compulsion. The essays by Ian Davey, Susan Houston, and Harvey Graff establish that school enrolment and regular attendance were central if socialization was to be successful. Whereas the late nineteenth and early twentieth centuries found Canadians asking what should be done with those who came to school, the dominant mid-nineteenth-century concern was to get them there. Without regular attendance, there would be illiteracy and no common moral code, and thus continued social disorganization and criminality. Attendance was necessary, moreover, to justify the increasingly elaborate organizational and training mechanisms that had become central to public education.

Regular attendance at school also raised questions about who should pay for the education of all social classes and about mixing social classes. Did Upper Canadians really want the poor to sit alongside the respectable? Even more, regular attendance conflicted with the most basic rhythms of work, the seasonal adaptations of rural areas, the erratic labour markets in the cities, and the need to take work whenever and wherever it was available. And, the demand that children attend regularly quickly became tied to the question of compulsion—the right and necessity of the state intervening in the educational choices of families and individuals. Here was one of the great dilemmas: how to make compulsion under state authority an acceptable operating principle in a society that professed "the self-conscious anti-statist and individualist colouring of . . . mid-Victorian liberal convictions".[3]

One way out of that dilemma was to view different cultural values, irregularity and transiency in the work force, intemperance, crime, and lack of school attendance as rooted in immorality rather than in social conditions. With immorality defined as the problem, reformers could seek an expansive school system that emphasized the teaching of a common moral code. "By mid-century," Harvey Graff notes, "the school was more than ever before seen as the vehicle required to replace the family and church in giving moral instruction."[4] Learning correct behaviour would mean the elimination of the social problems that so concerned some Upper Canadians.

These expectations for schooling were essential to the creation of educational bureaucracies and the emergence of particular styles of educational leadership. On the one hand, there were personal attributes, ideological viewpoints, and actions of the charismatic leaders, and on the other, the press was for a bureaucratic structure that stood outside and above the actions of individuals. During the Ryerson years these two styles, as Alison Prentice reveals, were essentially mixed. It is almost impossible to separate Ryerson the person from Ryerson the superintendent, yet by the time of his retirement, it was clear that the bureaucratic mode had become dominant.

That mode was not limited to schools, nor were its consequences solely concerned with education. As Robert Gidney and Douglas Lawr argue, the Ontario Department of Education was "one of the earliest ventures of the state into the daily lives of its citizens".[5] The establishment of public schooling joined a traditional policy of government economic development, the changing provision of welfare services, and the founding of asylums and other institutions to provide the blocks that built the modern liberal state. Moreover, questions internal to the educational structure were shared in countless ways by other governmental and private agencies: how to assure accountability, how to identify the lines of communication, how the process of decision-making was to be arrived at. These questions touched the heart of the newly emerging corporate institutions in Canadian society. How all the parts fit together, the relationships between public and private policy, and between corporate and individual decision-making, are not yet clear, but the essays in this book are a major step in that clarification.

Having probed some of the major themes (and readers will undoubtedly find more), what does it all come to? Are there lessons here for those concerned about the present? As a historian, I raise these with some hesitancy. The past's utility is limited in the interpretation of current events, yet the themes that emerge in this book are suggestive of contemporary policy. For one, it is clear that nineteenth-century assumptions and decisions have powerfully influenced the shape of today's schools. The bureaucratic turning inward of Ontario's Department of Education after 1876 described by Robert Stamp, and the unevaluated application by western Canadians of procedures adopted elsewhere described by Alan Child, suggest continuities in our assumptions and practices.

It is also important to understand that our educational system was and continues to be tied to politics. In its origins, Neil McDonald writes, the common-school system was designed to "support a political system about which there was to be no serious examination or questioning".[6] The consequence of that was that critical analysis of either politics or the social system was not encouraged in the schools. In effect, when such questioning emerges, as has happened recently, the schools are accused of malfunctioning, and we are caught in a box wherein social criticism is labelled poor schooling.

Of interest too is the extent to which the social problems of the nineteenth century were displaced onto the victims. Their lack of morality, their unwillingness to work, and their propensity to delinquent behaviour were at issue. This displacement enhanced the role of both education and punishment. On the one hand, educate to correct values; on the other, punish those who fail to learn the lessons. And yet, as is clear for the nineteenth century and should be clear today, school problems that are based on the social structure and the material conditions of people's lives will not be solved by educational reforms.

Finally, these essays suggest we should be wary of cultural chauvinism. Schools that coerce socialization into one set of cultural values have too frequently been hidden by the myth of the mosaic. A multicultural society is, at best, a tenuous experiment. Its success depends not on the dominance of one set of ideas or of any particular institution, but on the ability of different groups to retain the values they cherish while still sharing in the material rewards the society offers. To the extent that an institution like the school denies those multiple values or serves to close off opportunity, it has done us a disservice. That too is a message this book sends.

These, then, are a few of the policy implications I find in the historical essays presented here. Other readers will certainly disagree with my assessments and find different meanings, but that is what makes this book so exciting. It is good history, filled with possibilities for a thoughtful reappraisal of Canadian education past and present.

NOTES

1. Alison L. Prentice and Susan E. Houston, *Family, School, and Society in Nineteenth-Century Canada* (Toronto, 1975), p. 1.
2. Ryerson quoted in this volume by Neil McDonald, "Egerton Ryerson and the School as an Agent of Political Socialization", n. 38.
3. Susan E. Houston, "Social Reform and Education: The Issue of Compulsory Schooling, Toronto, 1851–71", in this volume.
4. Harvey Graff, "The Reality Behind the Rhetoric: The Social and Economic Meanings of Literacy in the Mid-Nineteenth Century", in this volume.
5. Robert D. Gidney and Douglas A. Lawr, "The Development of an Administrative System for the Public Schools: The First Stage, 1841–50", in this volume.
6. Neil McDonald, "Egerton Ryerson and the School as an Agent of Political Socialization", in this volume.

The Pre-Ryerson Years*

J. DONALD WILSON

In the history of Upper Canada there is a striking similarity between the development of the state and the evolution of education. Both grew out of a virtual wilderness. Large-scale settlement began in 1784 with the coming of the Loyalists; the first English school was established at Kingston in 1786. The province officially came into being in 1791 with its governmental structure set forth in the Constitutional Act of that year. Seven years later the first land grant for the support of grammar schools and a university was proclaimed. In 1812 the very existence of Upper Canada as a British colony was seriously threatened as the region became the major battleground of the War of 1812. With this storm successfully weathered the government passed in 1816 an important act creating a system of state-supported common schools. This act marks the beginning of state acceptance of responsibility for the education of the masses.

The late 1820s brought to both education and the state a period of change and instability. Some of the social and economic factors which contributed to the passage of the Great Reform Bill in Britain, the election of Andrew Jackson in the United States, and the abolition of slavery in the British Empire were also present in Upper Canada. The province had its proponents of British radicalism, Jacksonian democracy, and liberal humanitarianism, but it had its Tories too. The result was conflict in both the educational and political spheres. Dr. Charles Duncombe's report of 1836 calling for a revamped educational system fell victim to the intense unrest prior to the

*Previously published in J. Donald Wilson, Robert M. Stamp, and Louis-Philippe Audet, eds., *Canadian Education: A History* (Scarborough, 1970).

1837 uprising led by William Lyon Mackenzie. Although neither Duncombe's report nor Mackenzie's rebellion bore immediate fruit, both were to play their part in later developments. The rebellion contributed to the decision to send Lord Durham to The Canadas, and his report led in turn to the attainment of responsible government signalled by the summoning of Baldwin and LaFontaine to form a government in 1848. Many of Duncombe's recommendations were later utilized by Rev. Egerton Ryerson, the province's first superintendent of education. Ryerson was responsible for drafting two significant school acts, one in 1846 which established the basis for the system associated with his name, and the other in 1850 which laid the groundwork for free and universal education in the province. Thus, by mid-century, the flourishing colony had attained both responsible government and the basis for free schooling for all.

FORMATIVE INFLUENCES

Education in Upper Canada was essentially influenced by four main factors: geography, colonialism, the religious affiliation of its inhabitants, and the structure of government.

Environmental Factors

Education in English Canada, like other aspects of English-Canadian society, has been moulded largely from the melting together of two forces—one British in origin, the other North American. As much as anywhere else, this phenomenon is apparent in the development of Upper Canada where, from the very origins of the colony, the two influences contended with each other for supremacy. Both sides had their proponents. Lieutenant-Governor John Graves Simcoe strove to make Upper Canada a model British colony, while individuals such as William Lyon Mackenzie were convinced that Upper Canada had much to learn from the American Republic.

The struggle between British and North American forces can perhaps best be seen in the outlook of the United Empire Loyalists. Although not the first white settlers of Upper Canada, they were the first to come in any numbers. The first explorers of Ontario were two Frenchmen, Etienne Brûlé and Nicholas Vigneau, in 1610. During the seventeenth and eighteenth centuries clusters of French Canadians settled around Fort

Frontenac on the site of Kingston, at Fort Detroit, and also at Sault Ste. Marie and Rouillé (Toronto). At the fall of New France in 1760 there were a few hundred French-Canadian families living in the present territory of Ontario.[1] Twenty-five years later, as the Loyalists entered, there was still a distinct French presence in the region.

Driven from their homes by revolutionaries or prompted by a desire to continue to live under the British Crown, approximately 6,000 Loyalists had settled in Upper Canada by 1786. The majority installed themselves along the Niagara River and the north shore of the upper St. Lawrence and about the Bay of Quinte. These settlers, many of humble origin, came from New England, New York, and Pennsylvania. On the surface every Loyalist vehemently upheld British institutions; after all, had he not left his home or been forced to do so for just this reason? Deep down, however, the Loyalist was conditioned by the society he had come from—a society based not on privilege and class, but on democratic and egalitarian principles born of the frontier and the New World. In short, he was an American.

Most of the Loyalists who came to Upper Canada were small farmers. Consequently, as a group, Loyalists cannot be said to have been in the forefront of the movement for common schools. A few, however, who came from a cultured background, upheld the value of learning. They were accustomed not only to locally supported non-denominational schools, but also to institutions of higher learning, for in the Thirteen Colonies, prior to 1776, there were no fewer than nine universities and colleges stretching from New Hampshire to Virginia. To their great disappointment, they found not one English grammar school in either Upper or Lower Canada, much less a university. It is not surprising then that one of the first Upper Canadian Loyalist memorials to Lord Dorchester, the Governor General of British North America, concerned the matter of education. Upon the instigation of the Hon. Richard Cartwright, a prominent Kingston merchant, the document was drawn up in 1787. It lamented the deplorable state of education for the children of Loyalists and requested "a school in each district . . . for the purpose of teaching English, Latin, Arithmetic and Mathematics".

The concern of some Loyalists about proper education for their children was almost immediately reinforced by an influx of post-Loyalists (often erroneously called "late" Loyalists), many of whom upheld the same view of education. Paradoxically, while Lieutenant-Governor Simcoe sought on the one hand to make of Upper Canada a British bastion in North America, he was forced at the same time to launch a campaign to attract "true New England Americans" as colonists. Determined to create a "vigorous colony" he realized the impossibility of achieving this goal on the basis of 10,000 inhabitants, including both Loyalists and non-Loyalists. His most pressing need was an increased population. Because of Britain's involvement in the French revolutionary wars and Irish preference for emigration to the United States, the latter became the only country from which settlers could readily be procured. Consequently, prospective American settlers were attracted to Upper Canada by the offer of free land grants.

In pursuing this immigration policy, Simcoe was, of course, challenging his own desire to establish a "British country". Regardless of the obvious suitability of Americans to frontier conditions, they nevertheless had American ideas of republicanism and democracy, which were anathema to the concept of the ideal state held by Simcoe and the Executive and Legislative councils. The "levelling spirit" was not long in making its appearance. As early as 1792 the Surveyor General, David W. Smith, warned: "Our House of Assembly for the most part have violent levelling tendencies which are totally different from the ideas I have been educated with. The neighbouring states are too often brought in as patterns and models which I neither approve nor countenance."[2] The influx of American settlers was such that by 1812 an American traveller in Upper Canada could estimate that four-fifths of the population were post-Loyalist Americans.[3] A more recent authority suggests that in four of the eight districts into which the province was administratively divided, American immigrants outnumbered all other inhabitants two to one.[4]

Concern about American influence generally focused on education, specifically the role of American teachers and textbooks. There were many American teachers in Upper Canada before the War of 1812, particularly in the rural areas since the town-centred grammar schools provided for by the act of 1807 were usually staffed by Anglican clergymen from Great Britain. Most of the Americans were little more than adventurers who moved from place to place wherever they could gather a few students in return for room and board and, if they were lucky, a few shillings. Despite their intellectual and occasionally moral deficiencies, the American teachers gave many children the only instruction they ever received. Their efforts, however, aroused strong criticism from some quarters. One prominent resident complained of the activities of two American schoolmasters in his neighbourhood north of York: "They use all their efforts to poison the minds of the youth by teaching them in Republican books. . . . Youths educated in such books will by and by have the privilege of voting members for our own assembly and filling the House with their own kind, and when that is the case what may the governor and council expect but trouble."[5] Another contemporary account refers to "books . . . imported from the United States [which] are completely calculated to train up our children as citizens of the Republic, and to divert them from every affection and respect for the parent country."[6]

Whether in the United States or in British North America, the frontier seemed to spawn a common pragmatic philosophy of education. Education, it was held, should be practical so as to solve everyday problems. A premium was placed on immediate action rather than theory. In the face of practical needs, a certain scepticism, if not contempt, existed for book learning, academic training, and intellectual pursuits. As a short-term resident in Upper Canada observed, "As soon as the young hero attains his seventh or eighth year, he is provided with an axe, instead of a primer."[7]

Under the circumstances it is not difficult to see that if education were to be accepted at all, it must lean towards the practical. Rev. John Strachan, master of the fine grammar school at Cornwall (established in 1803), and later bishop of Toronto, saw this need early. He realized that many of his students would not enter university or the professions. Their stay at common or grammar schools would in most cases be short, necessitating a broader, more practical course of instruction than the traditional classical curriculum with its heavy emphasis on Latin and algebra. "Their parents," Strachan pointed out to his Scottish mentor in 1806, "are anxious to get them introduced to business and they can seldom appreciate the advantage of a liberal system of education."[8] In *A Concise Introduction to Mathematical Arithmetic for the Use of Schools*, which was the first school text published in Upper Canada in 1809, Strachan underlined the need for practical arithmetic.

The Upper Canadian's practical attitude towards education persisted throughout the nineteenth century. A well-known incident that occurred in 1831 emphasizes the same point. A group of citizens from York and vicinity, including Robert Baldwin who later inaugurated responsible government, urged

Lieutenant-Governor John Colborne to revise the classical course of study at prestigious Upper Canada College so as to better equip the students "for discharging with efficiency and respectability the scientific and other business of Tradesmen and Mechanics."[9] But the Lieutenant-Governor remained unmoved in his conviction about the validity of classical education for all "sons of gentlemen". The question of classical as opposed to practical or technical education persisted into the twentieth century.

Colonialism: The English Example and the "Simcoe Tradition"

Influence on Upper Canadian education stemming from the English example is best identified with the colony's first Lieutenant-Governor, John Graves Simcoe. A graduate of Eton and Oxford and a strong supporter of the established church, Simcoe was a typical Tory. The impact of his views on education allow us to speak of a Simcoe tradition in Ontario education which lasted long after his departure. Simcoe's attitude, which was subscribed to by the Church of England, favoured proper education for the select few—"The Children of the Principal People of this Country", as Simcoe put it[10]—who would eventually become the country's leaders. For the rest, Simcoe held that "such education as may be necessary for people in the lower degrees of life . . . may at present be provided for them by their connections and relations."[11] Simcoe believed that the resources of the colony should be concentrated on the education of the few rather than spread thinly over the population as a whole. In conformity with this view of education, he stressed the establishment of classical grammar schools and a university in the colony's capital. For Simcoe, educational institutions were an essential feature of the official British system of a close interrelationship between church and state.

Despite Simcoe's determined efforts to foster grammar schools and a university to prepare the future ruling class of the new colony, no significant advances were made during his day. Secretary of State Henry Dundas persisted in his view that schoolmasters in the elementary subjects would satisfy present needs; advanced students could go to Quebec, Montreal, or Nova Scotia to further their education. He summed up his refusal to consider a university for Upper Canada by asserting, "the Country must make the University, and not the University the Country."[12] Interested parents were therefore forced to depend on itinerant teachers or private schools, such as John Stuart's in Kingston (from 1786) and John Strachan's in Cornwall (from 1803), for the education of their children.

All Simcoe's efforts were, however, not in vain. He did succeed in obtaining government support for two grammar schools, and in 1797, a year after his departure from Upper Canada, the colony's Legislature sent a petition to George III requesting a land grant to provide for a grammar school in each district and a university in the capital. The next year authorization came for setting apart 540,000 acres of land for these purposes, and the Executive Council dutifully set aside ten townships and parts of two others. Unfortunately the land-grant system for the support of schools proved relatively ineffective in Upper Canada. Good land was still readily available and cheap, so there was little demand for the school lands which were sold for higher prices.

The years following the land grant of 1798 were marked by a lack of public action in the field of education. From 1800 to 1803 no mention was made of education in the Upper Canada Legislature. However, the next year the Assembly formed a committee to investigate the administration of public affairs in the province. The report presented by the committee contained a resolution recommending that "seminaries for the education of the youth are highly necessary in this province."[13] The first concrete step was taken in 1807 with the passage of the District Public (Grammar) School Act. This Act, which remained in force with slight modifications until 1853, provided for the establishment of a grammar school in each of the eight districts of the province. (Actually only three schools were immediately opened and four more before the outbreak of war in 1812.) The teacher of each school was to receive from the provincial treasury £100 to be supplemented by fees charged to the pupils. This was the first example of acceptance by the Legislature that the duties of the government included educating the young, even though in this case it meant only some of the young.

The district schools, as they were called, were firmly in the Simcoe tradition of establishing schools for the "sons of gentlemen". Because of the distance between the schools and the outlying regions of each district, together with the high tuition charges, only the children of the well-to-do could afford to attend. A petition from the Midland District (Kingston area) in 1812 made the point that "instead of aiding the middling and poorer classes" the Act of 1807 merely "casts money into the lap of the rich".[14] Even at that, the expense of fees, books, and board and lodging was almost equal to that incurred by sending children out of the country for their education, mainly to the United States, "where a more extensive course of instruction may be had. . . ."[15] It was ironic that sons of gentlemen of the colony were sent to the United States for higher schooling despite the establishment of schools intended to foster the British tradition.

Another exclusive feature of the early district schools was their denominational character. The schoolmasters were invariably Church of England clergymen or laymen. Later on, the presence of Church of Scotland clergy and laity as district schoolmasters became commonplace. It was rare, however, to find a Methodist or a Baptist teacher in a grammar school. Grammar schoolmasters were, wherever possible, chosen from candidates who had been to university or held a degree; Methodist and Baptist clergymen normally did not. Masters, therefore, were usually members of the English or Scottish churches.

Despite the efforts of the Assembly to alter the act, the Lieutenant-Governor and the Executive and Legislative councils upheld the schools as constituted. Their virtual independence remained unaltered since the Lieutenant-Governor who held effective control did not attempt close supervision and the Assembly had no control whatsoever over them. One important result arising from discontent over the district schools was the move to set up private academies for both elementary and secondary education. Such institutions were established at Bath and Newcastle in eastern Upper Canada in 1811, and in 1815 the Midland District School Society was created. The Bath Academy under the direction of the "experienced preceptor", Barnabas Bidwell, who had been a college tutor in Massachusetts prior to his arrival in Upper Canada, was to gain a favourable reputation throughout the colony. Among its graduates were several notable political figures, including Peter Perry, Christopher Hagerman, and Marshall Spring Bidwell. The Midland District School Society was incorporated by an act of Parliament "to collect funds for primary education".[16] The growth of private, local educational institutions, a characteristic of American education, was thus duplicated in Upper Canada.

Religious Affiliation of Inhabitants

Successive religious denominations were destined to play an important part in moulding educational institutions in Upper

Canada. The Church of England, backed by the various lieutenant-governors and councils, contended that all education should be controlled by the state and administered by the established church. Although the Church of England was not officially designated as the established church by the Constitutional Act of 1791, it assumed that it was and acted accordingly. That education should be conducted by the church was never seriously questioned in the early years of the nineteenth century. But that the control of education should rest in the hands of one denomination, the Church of England, was quite another matter, especially since most Upper Canadians were not Anglicans. The Church of England, therefore, found itself obliged to fend off the attacks of the other religious denominations which firmly opposed its monopolistic position. The most bitter assaults came from the Methodist church which commanded a great deal of support, especially in the rural areas of the province. Here the emotionalism of the rousing camp meeting and the personal contact of the "circuit rider" held greater attraction for the pioneer farmer than the ritual and aloofness of the "established" church.

Anglicans, Presbyterians, and Catholics held Methodists and Baptists in great suspicion. Their clergymen, it was argued, were barely literate, although Ryerson's intellectual competence disproved that contention. However, it was true that many of their preachers were American-born or trained and in the political sphere some were associated with the reform cause. Herein lay the basis of Anglican and Tory suspicion. As one Victorian has put it, they were accused of being "disguised agents of republicanism".

Structure of Government

A final major influence on education in Upper Canada was the structure of government with the appointed bodies, Lieutenant-Governor, Executive Council, and Legislative Council, usually contending against the elected Assembly on matters affecting education. An illustration of the tenacity with which each group held to its opposing views in regard to education is the debate over the District Public (Grammar) School Act of 1807. The schools established as a result of this act were modelled on English schools and were not well attended for reasons already stated. Yet efforts on the part of the Assembly to repeal the act and replace these schools with less exclusive ones were continually blocked by the Legislative Council. The Assembly was unable until 1816 to push through a bill providing a modicum of state support for a system of common or elementary schools.

Another issue between the councils and the Assembly concerned the disposition of the Clergy Reserves. The Constitutional Act stipulated that land equal to one-seventh of Crown, or public, lands granted was to be set aside "for the Support and Maintenance of a Protestant Clergy". For years the last phrase was taken to mean the clergy of the Church of England. It is not surprising that this privileged position enabled the Church of England to attain a degree of power much in excess of the actual number of its colonial adherents. The conservative ruling groups, eventually known as the Family Compact, felt the full favour of Anglican power, especially when its employment was required against the palest evidence of radicalism among the mass of the people who were, generally speaking, non-Anglicans. Reformers, who held the balance of power in the Assembly for brief periods, sought to dissolve the Anglican control of the Clergy Reserves either by dividing the proceeds from the sale of the land among all the major religious denominations or alternatively by putting the entire proceeds into much-needed public services such as roads and schools. Such proposals as the latter made allies of Catholics, Presbyterians, and Anglicans, because although the Catholic Church and Church of Scotland were opposed to Anglican pretensions to exclusive jurisdiction over the reserves, they feared even more a system of secular education erected from the proceeds of their secularization.

SCHOOLS AND TEACHERS BEFORE 1812

As mentioned earlier, the United Empire Loyalists generally valued the importance of education. The unwillingness of the government in Quebec to support the establishment of schools with public funds led the settlers to set up private schools where their children could receive the education they considered essential. It is little wonder then that the first English school in what was not yet designated Upper Canada was opened in 1786 in Kingston, a major Loyalist settlement. (The first French school had been opened in the same location at Fort Frontenac, 110 years earlier.) The teacher of the English school was the resident Church of England clergyman, Rev. John Stuart, himself a Loyalist.

While Stuart stands as representative of one category of early schoolteacher, Rev. John Strachan might be considered representative of another group, the English- or Scottish-born schoolteacher. Strachan was born in Scotland in 1778, son of a quarryman. Through personal effort and scholarships he was able to attend King's College, Aberdeen. After graduating he studied divinity at the University of St. Andrews, but remained there only three months. While earning a living as a teacher, he aspired to a university post in Scotland, but when he failed to attain one he gave careful consideration to an offer he had received in 1799 to teach in Upper Canada. The invitation came from the Hon. Richard Cartwright, a legislative councillor and prominent Kingston businessman, and his business associate, the Hon. Robert Hamilton. The offer was to teach up to twelve children for £80 a year plus travelling expenses on a three-year contract. The possibility of a government academy which might become a university may have been mentioned, but the likelihood of Strachan's being offered a university appointment in Upper Canada, as he later contended, seems very remote indeed. Lieutenant-Governor Simcoe had envisaged a university in the colony's capital, but both Hamilton and Cartwright knew by this time that, despite the land grant of the previous year, no definite steps had been taken to create one. Twenty years after his arrival in Kingston, Strachan claimed he would have gone home if he had had the money, but since he had signed a teaching contract, even that seems unlikely.

While teaching a small group of children, Strachan was becoming acclimatized to his new surroundings. Thanks to Cartwright he moved in the best circles in Kingston as well as in Montreal where he was befriended by the wealthy McGill family. (He later married Andrew McGill's widow and influenced James McGill's decision to bequeath £10,000 and his Burnside estate to the formation of McGill College.) Strachan was continually impressed by the fact that people of any account in Upper Canada were members of the Church of England; in fact, the Presbyterian system, which he had studied at St. Andrews, was not much in vogue. Moreover, although the Church of England had not been specifically mentioned in the Constitutional Act as the established church in Upper Canada, it was certainly treated as such. Though his father was a member of the Episcopal Church of Scotland, Strachan was raised by his mother as a Presbyterian and thus was familiar with the notion of an established church. He was also familiar with the opinion of important theologians of the Church of Scotland who held the doctrinal differences between their church and the Church of England to be slight. The differences in their forms of church government (presbyterian *versus* episcopal) were overridden by the fact of their establishment in each case. All considered, Strachan decided to stay on in Upper Canada and to become a Church of England clergyman. He was prepared for ordination by Rev. John Stuart. Ordained in 1803, he was appointed missionary to Cornwall. There he also found time to open a grammar school for boys.

According to the American traveller Michael Smith in his *Geographical View of Upper Canada*, there were only three private schools in the province before 1812 teaching Latin and Greek. Strachan's school was one of them, and became so well known and highly regarded that students came from Lower Canada to the east and from as far west as York. The list of graduates resembles a *Who's Who* for Upper Canada. Many of his students appear again twenty years later as prominent members of the Family Compact among whose ranks Strachan himself was numbered. A partial list would have to include John Beverly Robinson, his most brilliant pupil (Chief Justice of Upper Canada, 1829–62), Peter Robinson (Commissioner of Crown Lands and founder of Peterborough), William Robinson (leading landowner at Newmarket and one of the commissioners of the Canada Company), Archibald McLean (Robinson's successor as Chief Justice), Sir James B. Macaulay (Chief Justice of Common Pleas), and the Boultons (leading Toronto officials, lawyers, and landowners).

With emulation and competition as the basic tenets of his pedagogy, Strachan quickly gained a reputation as an outstanding teacher. He apparently was not unaware of his success or of the social status of his students. He once remarked in a letter that "almost all the young men of eminence in both provinces have been my pupils and have for me to this day [1824] the attachment of children."[17] Nor was he averse to using the eminence of his former pupils to bring him more power and influence. To his confidant, Dr. James Brown, the clergyman of Dunino, the Scottish village where Strachan began teaching, he wrote in 1808: "Bye and bye my pupils will be getting forward, some of them perhaps into the House and then I shall have more in my power."[18]

In 1812 Strachan moved from Cornwall to York where he became missionary at York and schoolmaster of the Home

District Grammar School. Because he played a prominent role at the time of the American assault on York during the War of 1812, Strachan soon emerged as a figure of political importance while remaining the most prominent clergyman and teacher in the colony. His first love, however, was teaching, a task he continued to perform five and a half days a week until his resignation in 1823 when he assumed his duties as president of the General Board of Education. Including his teaching years in Scotland, Strachan had taught continuously for almost thirty years.

Another category of pioneer schoolteacher in Upper Canada was the American-born or "American by influence". One such person was Richard Cockrell, who opened a school in Newark (now Niagara-on-the-Lake) in 1796 and then moved to Ancaster to establish another school. Although his name is virtually unknown today, Cockrell appears to have been one of the outstanding pioneer schoolmasters. "An excellent mathematical school", was Strachan's description of Cockrell's school.[19] Among his first students was William Hamilton Merritt, whose father was so pleased with Cockrell he sent his son after him to Ancaster to continue his schooling.

Born in England, Cockrell spent a brief period in the United States. This gave him a basis for comparison with the schools of the new colony which led him to put on paper his *Thoughts on the Education of Youth.*[20] This was the first book on educational theory and practice published in English in North America, preceding by thirteen years the first such effort in the United States.[21] According to Dr. J. J. Talman, this pamphlet, published in Newark in 1795, was the first non-governmental publication in Upper Canada, preceded only by Simcoe's speech at the opening of the Legislature and the laws passed by the first and second legislatures.

Cockrell's *Thoughts* reveals some very modern views on such aspects of education as discipline and pedagogy, but one of his major points of concern was the deplorable state of the teaching profession in Upper Canada. To improve this situation, Cockrell recommended adoption of the American practice of examining teachers, which was not as widespread as he supposed. Thus the first non-governmental publication in Upper Canada applauded American practice and urged its emulation in the new province. It thereby established a pattern that has continued to the present day.

In spite of teachers like Cockrell there was no great demand ιor elementary schools before the War of 1812. Grammar schools were considered more advantageous and attention was concentrated on them. The general populace was more concerned about clearing the land than "learning". Nevertheless, an American traveller records a total of twenty-three schools in Norfolk County alone. Another estimate places the number of private schools in operation by 1816 at close to 200. These were supported partly by subscriptions and partly by fees that usually amounted to one dollar per month per student.[22] The education available in these schools, conducted mostly by itinerants, many of whom were "Yankee adventurers", was limited. There were no regulations affecting curriculum, admission requirements, graduation, or attendance. The reason for the dismal state of elementary education before 1812 is simply stated by Michael Smith: "The greater part of the inhabitants of Canada are not well educated for as they were poor when they came to the province, and the country being but thinly settled for a number of years, they had but little chance for the benefit of school."[23]

EARLY ATTEMPTS AT COMMON-SCHOOL EDUCATION

Historians have long recognized the War of 1812 as an important watershed in the history of Upper Canada. Up to the outbreak of war, parts of the province, particularly west of York, were settled largely by Americans. Indeed, had it not been checked by the war, the process of Americanization begun in Simcoe's time might have reached the point where Upper Canada would soon have become virtually an American colony. The war, of course, reversed this trend. Lord Bathurst, the secretary of state for war and the colonies, sent specific instructions to the governors of The Canadas to refuse the granting of land "to subjects of the United States and . . . to prevent their settling in either of the Canadas."[24]

Another factor at work to change the political complexion of the province was the departure during the war of some settlers who held sentiments favourable to the American system of government. In place of the American immigrant came, in the mid- and late 1820s, an influx of British settlers who embossed on the province a British and conservative character which it was to retain for decades. In the wake of the war, loyalty to the Crown was matched by an equal measure of anti-Americanism. Immediately following the close of the war, the battle over whether education should be designed for the classes or the masses, the few or the many, was joined once again. The opposing viewpoints were best represented by the Legislative Council on the one hand and the Assembly on the other. The former clung, largely from fear that a system of common schools could only be established at the expense of grammar schools, to its conviction that the latter were the most advantageous institutions of education in the colony at the moment. The Assembly, for its part, continued its pleas of pre-war days for a modification of the Act of 1807 and for the introduction of a system of common schools for the "middling and poorer classes". The Assembly's main opposition to the district schools arose from their exclusive nature and their expense to parents. Instead they wanted common schools maintained wherever needed throughout the province rather than confined to the district town. This way students could reside and work at home while attending school part of the day. Few people outside towns could afford the cost of private education or the district schools; fewer still could afford to do without their children's labour at home.

Common School Act of 1816

The Assembly's agitation on the question of district schools finally bore results. A select committee on education was set up in February 1816, and three weeks after its formation a bill was drafted proposing the extension of common-school education throughout the province. After passing through both houses the bill was quickly enacted. The Common School Act of 1816 was of tremendous significance in the educational development of Upper Canada. Its passage constituted a compromise between the Assembly and the Legislative Council, for the Council consented to it on the condition that the district grammar schools would remain undisturbed. Despite this concession, it was a triumph for the Assembly and marked the first evidence of recognition of the state's responsibility to ensure facilities for the education of the common people.

The Act of 1816 was based upon the principle of local option. If the residents of any town, village, or township desired a school, the act enabled them to hold a public meeting to decide the question. If twenty students could be collected the government would make an annual grant of £25 to help pay the salary of a teacher. But there was no government grant to build or maintain the school; money for this purpose had to be raised by voluntary subscription. The effective administration of the school remained highly decentralized too. Local school matters were to be attended to by three popularly elected trustees whose duties included the hiring and firing of teachers, making rules for the operation of the school, choosing textbooks or making no stipulation on texts, and collecting fees from parents, usually $2 to $3 per quarter. All decisions were subject, however, to the approval of the District Board of Education comprised of five members appointed by the Lieutenant-Governor.

The hiring of teachers was not left completely in the hands of local trustees. An important clause in the act stipulated that all teachers must be natural-born subjects of Great Britain or have taken the oath of allegiance. Such a provision was intended to be an effective means of curbing the practice of hiring American teachers with their "pernicious" ideas and "deleterious influence". This measure was not a new idea. Similar efforts dated back to 1799 when it was government policy "to exclude [from Upper Canada] schoolmasters from the States lest they should instill Republicanism into the tender minds of the youth of the Province."[25] The provision in the 1816 act against Americans was thus in the tradition of earlier measures.

Despite its significance as the first recognition of public support for elementary education in Upper Canada, the Act of 1816 nevertheless had its defects. Many parents found it difficult, even impossible, to pay the fees required to supplement the legislative grant. A year after the bill's passage Robert Gourlay, Ontario's first educational statistician, calculated that the average cost of student fees for common schools was about $10 per pupil annually.[26] This was more than some parents could afford. A second weakness lay in the unsystematic apportionment of the annual legislative grant: some school districts had money they never granted, while others could have used more than they received. In some districts, there was also an unnecessary duplication of schools because of the provision in the act for the establishment of a school wherever twenty students wanted to attend. Moreover, the elected trustees, charged with the appointment of teachers, were often careless in their choice. Finally, there was not much financial incentive for the common-school teacher. While £100 was contributed from public funds towards the salary of the grammar-school teacher, the amount allowed for the support of his common-school counterpart was only £25. Four years later even that was halved. By 1833 a select committee of the Assembly could report that in some districts no more than £4 or £5 was being given to any one teacher. In comparison, an ordinary craftsman would earn £75 a year. It is not surprising then that in those days, as J. G. Althouse remarks, "a teaching post was commonly regarded as the last refuge of the incompetent, the inept, the unreliable."[27] Despite regulations to the contrary, school boards were often forced to hire transient Americans who alone were willing to take on such a poorly paid job.

Pioneer Schools After 1815

In the days before a centralized elementary school system was established in Upper Canada by Egerton Ryerson, any room in a suitable building often served as a classroom until a separate building could be constructed. Sometimes houses were rented, but public meeting-houses, halls, churches, and even old taverns were commonly used. When a separate building was erected, it followed the same design as the simplest pioneer homes. Made of rough-hewn logs, it usually measured about fourteen feet by sixteen feet with a low ceiling. A fireplace would assume a prominent place in the building. Pupils were normally required to supply a set amount of firewood each month during the winter as well as their basic tuition fees. The school benches, arranged around three sides of the room, were constructed of planks supported by simple legs. Crude writing desks to be used by the older pupils accompanied the benches. Ranged about the centre of the room the younger children sat on low, backless and deskless benches. In the centre was the "crack" which the pupils were to "toe" when reciting their work.

Other than the teacher's desk there was rarely any furniture in the room—no apparatus (when Strachan requested some scientific apparatus for his school in Cornwall it required an act of the Legislature and three more years to acquire it), no maps, no blackboards, in short, no teaching aids. The quill pen, however, was present and prominent in the pioneer school. Writing was stressed, often for as long as two hours daily, and in the early days students practised using poor ink on poor quality paper or birchbark. Innovations such as slates and blackboards appeared after 1820 and steel pens after 1840.

Pedagogy remained unchanged; individual rather than group instruction was the rule, but more often, lessons were assigned and recitations heard with little or no explanation. The impact of the Pestalozzian movement with its emphasis on the needs of the child rather than on the subject matter was not felt in Upper Canada until the second half of the century.

Textbooks posed a special problem. Where they existed, they were always in great variety. There was no such thing as a standard textbook. Each pupil would bring to school whatever he could put his hands on, and if he had no textbook, he would count on sharing someone else's. David Mills, the one-time federal cabinet minister, recalled that as a child in Kent County in the 1830s, the only textbook he possessed when he started school was an American edition of *Cobb's Spelling Book* and that there were only two geographies for the whole class, Olney's and Woodbridge's, both American. Mills's case underlines two features of textbooks in pioneer schools—their scarcity and their Americanness. "The scarcity of books," a contemporary observer noted in 1824, "in the country parts of Canada is nearly as great as that of pineapples on the summit of Snowdon."[28] The "baneful influence" of American teachers and textbooks has already been noted. American textbooks, warned an article in the Kingston *Gazette* in 1815, "teach us to hate the government that we ought and are bound to support; to revile the country we are bound to love and respect; and to think that there is nothing great or good, generous or brave, anywhere to be found but in the United States."[29]

Various legislative efforts were made to improve the textbook situation. The Common School Act of 1816 authorized the district boards of education to spend certain amounts in the purchase of textbooks, but since the legislation remained permissive, little came of it. Eight years later, the Common School Act of 1824 provided for a small grant to purchase books for religious and moral instruction. This was the first attempt to provide free textbooks, but on such a limited scale that it made little impact. The solution lay simply in the publication of Canadian books. Some attempts were made in this direction as early as 1824 when a few books were printed cheaply at a press in Lanark County near present-day Ottawa. Five years later Alexander Davidson of Port Hope completed the first copyrighted book in Upper Canada, a speller entitled *The Upper Canada Spelling Book*. That the number of Upper Canadian printed schoolbooks was increasing by the 1830s can be verified by an examination of the advertisements for them in local newspapers.

In addition to formal schools there was in Upper Canada a system of indentured apprenticeship for orphans, abandoned children, or those whose parents were unwilling or unable to look after them. The Courts of Quarter Sessions, a contemporary form of local government, could bind a child as an apprentice up to twenty-one years of age, provided the consent of the Justices of the Peace was obtained. In one case in 1817, the master was obliged to provide his six-year-old apprentice "with sufficient wearing apparel and victuals and teaching him or causing him to be taught, to read and write and at the expiration of his apprenticeship to furnish him with two suits of wearing apparel, a Yoke of Oxen worth Fifty Dollars with a Yoke and chain."[30] It is difficult to say how common this sort of apprenticeship was in the colony, but the legislation providing for it in 1799 may be termed the first truly educational legislation in Upper Canada.

JOHN STRACHAN: COUNCILLOR, CLERIC, EDUCATOR

The Plan of 1815

John Strachan's early career as a teacher and clergyman in Kingston and Cornwall has already been outlined. He arrived in York at an auspicious time coinciding with the outbreak of the War of 1812. Strachan's assumption of leadership during the American occupation of York led directly to his appointment to the Executive Council in 1815 and to the Legislative Council five years later.

Following the close of the war one of Strachan's first acts was to submit to General Gordon Drummond, president of the Executive Council, a report on education. Dated 26 February 1815, the report was in essence a comprehensive plan for education in the province. Strachan called for the creation of a system of common schools to provide basic education for the children of all inhabitants; an improvement and extension of the existing grammar schools; a superintendent or board of education under whom control of elementary and secondary education would be centralized; and the establishment of a university for the youth of all denominations.

Many of Strachan's ideas concerning common-school education are readily discernible in the Common School Act of 1816, drafted by a committee of which Strachan was a member. The most notable omission and one that Strachan deplored was the rejection of centralized control. The Assembly's opposition to a central body administering education is not difficult to comprehend. First, it feared that a centralized system would be tailor-made to the wishes of the Church of England and thus facilitate its gaining the same control over the common-school system that it already possessed over the district grammar schools. Second, the small population—slighty over 95,000 in 1816—strung out over more than 500 miles, in addition to the poor communications, could hardly be expected to make any central control effective. Proof of this can be seen in the inability of the General Board of Education a few years later to make any progress as a central body supervising education in the province. A third factor concerned the scarcity of both teachers and textbooks. Without these basic tools of education effective central control was imposible.

In Upper Canada it took another two decades for the situation to change. By the mid-1830s the population was approaching 240,000 and communications were much improved. Not only did the number of roads increase but so did the possibility of travelling over them. The Rideau and Welland canals were then in operation. Textbooks, some even published in the colony, were more readily available. Teachers were also more numerous, and there was talk of establishing normal schools for the training of more. Local autonomy, established by the Act of 1816, continued. Central control of education awaited the answer to an important political question: which house of the Legislature was to be supreme, the appointed Legislative Council or the elected Assembly? Lord Durham's report contained the answer which was to be worked out in the next decade. The result was the erection of a highly centralized system which has remained to the present day.

With respect to grammar schools, Strachan was instrumental in persuading the Legislature to pass in 1819 an important amendment to the Grammar School Act of 1807. The amendment provided for an annual public examination of each school, annual reports to be made to the Lieutenant-Governor, and provision for tuition-free education for ten students from poorer families at each of the eight grammar schools. The last was a special point with Strachan who considered that grammar-school education should be extended beyond the sons of gentlemen to all children who showed promise. In fact, had it not been for the objection of the Legislative Council, Strachan might have succeeded in securing tuition-free grammar-school education, an aim he had revealed in 1815. Here again the

influence on Strachan's thinking of his democratic Scottish
background is apparent.

Strachan, Maitland, and Monitorial Schools

In the meantime, the replacement in 1818 of Lieutenant-
Governor Francis Gore by Sir Peregrine Maitland served to
raise Strachan's fortunes, as he quickly gained Maitland's
respect and admiration. Maitland's ten-year term of office marks
the heyday of the Family Compact, that group of men who, Lord
Durham charged, through its influence in the Executive Council
"wielded all the powers of government". Strachan was so much
the leading figure in this group that he has sometimes been
referred to as the province's first unofficial prime minister.
From this new-found power base as a confidant of Maitland
and leader of the oligarchy, Strachan experienced the most
successful years in his career as a politician and educationist.
Surrounding himself with many of his former pupils, such as
as John Beverly Robinson and George Herkimer Markland,
Strachan managed to cut an unmistakable swath through
Upper Canadian affairs.

One of Maitland's first actions was an attempt to establish
Dr. Andrew Bell's system of monitorial schools throughout the
colony. Unlike the Lancasterian schools, Bell's system was
based on the teaching of Church of England doctrine. The
attempt to create a monitorial-school system was assisted by
the passage in 1820 of a new common-school act that neutralized
the gains of the Act of 1816 by reducing the total annual legislative grant from £6,000 to £2,500. Maitland tried to allay public
concern by saying he believed the same benefit could still be
provided by the reduced grant. Such a statement was patently
false, as Strachan himself revealed the year before when he
affirmed the necessity of three times as much provincial revenue
to carry out the provisions of the Act of 1816. Under Church of
England auspices, the monitorial system was not only intended
to rival the non-denominational common schools created by
the Act of 1816, but to counteract dangerous American influences which persisted despite official countermeasures. Maitland
believed the system would "instruct all the youth of the province to the exclusion, not only of American masters, but of
their republican apparatus of Grammars and Lesson books;
all of which are studiously composed with a view to instilling
principles into the pupil's mind unfriendly to our form of

Government."[31] To alleviate these dangers the masters were to come from England.

Strachan, too, was pleased with the "National Schools" as they were sometimes called in reference to the society which operated them in England (The National Society for the Promotion of the Education of the Poor in the Principles of the Established Church throughout England and Wales). Not only did they provide a cheap means of educating the masses, but more important in Strachan's view, they included religious instruction in accordance with the tenets of the Church of England. For Strachan, religious instruction was an essential ingredient of education, for "knowledge if not founded on religion is a positive evil."[32]

Despite Maitland's plan to open schools similar to the one at York in every town of Upper Canada, monitorial schools proved a singular failure in the province. Not only was the Bell system with its Church of England bias unacceptable to the vast majority of Upper Canadians, but also the Assembly vigorously opposed the schools which appeared to them as an attempt to circumvent their triumph, the common schools. Both factors contributed to the abandonment of the plan to establish more monitorial schools throughout the province, although the York school, known as the Upper Canada Central School, continued in operation until 1844. The Assembly then set about assuring the retention of the common schools by obtaining passage of the Common School Act of 1824. This act also made provision for Sunday schools for children unable to attend the daily common school, and made available government grants for Indian education. Prior to 1824 direct support for Indian education had come from the King and missionary societies.

General Board of Education

Disappointed by the avoidance of a centralized authority over education in the Act of 1816, Strachan's efforts in this area were finally successful in February 1822 when Maitland submitted to the Colonial Office a plan for a General Board of Education recommending Strachan as president. A year later the board was constituted with Strachan in the position he felt his due along with five other members all of whom were former pupils or close associates of his. The board was charged with supervising school lands and finances, controlling teacher ap-

pointments, and choosing textbooks. At last Strachan was in
a position to mould a system to his liking, free of the vagaries
of the political arena. However, because of his insistence that
education come under the control of the Church of England,
the General Board proved unpopular and bore the brunt of
attacks from the growing ranks of Reformers who objected to
Tory and Anglican dominance. Strachan himself soon after
turned his attention to higher education. His alleged avarice
and ambition came in for fresh assaults at this time, led by the
young upstart William Lyon Mackenzie, who made ample use
of his newspaper, the *Colonial Advocate*. Moreover, the Assembly was displeased that the board was responsible not to the
Legislature but to the Executive Council. It was not surprising
that the Assembly finally succeeded in persuading the Colonial
Office to dissolve the board in 1833. Thus Strachan's long-term
plan for a national system of education was crushed. For their
part, the Reformers were unable to agree upon a suitable
replacement for the despised General Board, whose functions
for the time being were transferred to the Council of King's
College.

University of King's College

In higher education Strachan ultimately achieved a limited
triumph. Like Simcoe before him, Strachan had early recognized
the value of a provincial university as a means of attaching the
colonists more firmly to conservative principles and the mother
country; as a vehicle for training needed native clergy; and
as a way of removing the necessity for parents to send their
children for advanced training to the United States where,
according to Strachan, they learned "little beyond anarchy in
Politics and infidelity in religion".[33] Originally his plan was to
establish a college in Lower Canada where "the French and
English Youth might associate, become attached and imbibe a
love for the British Government."[34] By 1820 he was thinking in
terms of a university for Upper Canada and with the backing
of Maitland he went to England in 1826 to seek support and
a charter for the university.

Although Strachan's original plan for a university made no
provision for religious tests or qualifications for either students
or professors, by 1826 his views appear to have been changed
by extenuating circumstances. Both the Colonial Office and the
Archbishop of Canterbury, concerned about the rising tide of

liberalism at home and on the continent, were convinced that Strachan's measure was too liberal in its lack of stipulations for religious tests or qualifications. This did not conform at all to the established Oxford and Cambridge example. Another important source of opposition to Strachan's plan was the powerful but conservative Society for the Propagation of the Gospel (SPG), which securely held important colonial purse-strings. Consequently, in order to ensure financial support from the Church of England, Strachan spoke of the university as a "Missionary College" whose main function would be to train Anglican clergymen. Another feature on which the Colonial Office insisted was that the office of president of King's College should be held by the archdeacon of York. Strachan wanted these offices to be separate because he quite correctly foresaw the bitter reception this provision would receive from his enemies at home now that he had just been named archdeacon of York. The one major concession which he managed to retain from his original plan was that the professors, excluding members of the Divinity School, did not have to be Anglicans except those who would be appointed to the College Council. They did have to be university graduates, however, and if they came from England, as Oxford or Cambridge graduates, they would be Anglican. Graduates of Scottish universities were likely to be Church of Scotland adherents. Similarly no religious tests were to be imposed on students who wished to take a degree, except for those in divinity.

The "sectarian tendency" of the proposed institution, especially in its governing council, was abundantly clear and this fact did not escape the notice of the opponents of Strachan and Church of England domination of higher education. William Lyon Mackenzie referred to it as "one of the most obnoxious chartered institutions on earth".[35] Such was the popular clamour for revocation of the charter that the Colonial Office decided to reverse its steps. Instead of proceeding with the establishment of the college, it threw the problem into the hands of the colonial Legislature to solve. This course of action proved impossible since the Assembly and Legislative Council were unlikely ever to agree on changes.

The arrival in 1828 of a new Lieutenant-Governor, Sir John Colborne, cleared the air somewhat. Colborne, who proved to be an outstanding administrator, immediately waded into the maelstrom, and drawing upon his recent experience as governor of Guernsey where he had re-established Queen Elizabeth

Grammar School, he reminded the colonists that what they most required at the moment was not a university but a good preparatory school modelled on the English classical school. Promptly and over Strachan's objections, Colborne set out to establish such a school in York. The result was Upper Canada College, founded in 1829 and partly financed from the university endowment.

Never one to avoid a fight, Strachan continued to battle for his university. The picture brightened in 1837 when some measure of liberalization was achieved in the 1827 charter. In fact, in the summer of that year it looked as if the doors of King's College would open. However, the tense situation preceding the rebellion precluded such a development. Strachan's hopes were further dampened two years later when Lieutenant-Governor George Arthur's investigations into the financial administration of King's revealed that £13,000 of college funds could not be accounted for. Joseph Wells, the College bursar and a close associate of Strachan, was so seriously implicated that he was dismissed. Strachan was one of the friends to whom Wells had extended "loans" from the College treasury. The whole affair served to delay for another four years the opening of King's and further undermined Strachan's position.

Finally in 1843 King's was opened, due in part to the concern of Lieutenant-Governor Charles Bagot. By this time both the Presbyterian Queen's College in Kingston and the Methodist Victoria College in Cobourg had been functioning for over a year. But King's College's days were numbered. The appointment the next year of Egerton Ryerson, an old foe of Strachan, as assistant superintendent of education for Upper Canada marked the beginning of a new era in education in the colony. The administration of both common and grammar schools was to be placed firmly in the hands of the government. A similar secularization was afoot in higher education as well. In 1849 King's College, to Strachan's horror, was secularized and became the University of Toronto. Anticipating this turn of events, Strachan had resigned the presidency of the College the previous year. Then at the age of seventy-two, he sought and obtained a charter for a new university, Trinity College, a thoroughly Anglican institution, which was opened in Toronto in January 1852. This was the only segment of Strachan's comprehensive system first enunciated in 1815 that he managed to salvage. His work in the field of education was essentially ended by 1851 although he lived for another sixteen years.

EFFORTS AT REFORM IN THE 1830s

Measures in the Assembly

The year 1830 ushered in a decade of activity in the Assembly directed towards educational reform. The period was one of intense ferment; educational change was in the wind although actual legislative reforms were not to appear until the next decade. And educational change was needed. According to John Strachan, in 1826 there were only 300 boys in eleven grammar schools and 7,000 pupils in 350 common schools throughout the entire province.

—Hostility between the two branches of the Legislature has usually been held as the main obstacle to change in the 1830s. It is true that the Assembly had little objection to introducing school bills based on American models, whereas the Council, upholders of the British tradition, normally felt obliged to amend or veto such bills. It is also true, however, that the Assembly was not united in its thinking about what type of educational system would be best for the colony. Although the Reformers were quick to point to American models and to draw from them those aspects which suited their purposes, such as popularly elected educational officials and schools with no denominational influences, they conveniently disregarded those essential features which were unfamiliar or unpopular in Upper Canada. Central among these features were local taxation to pay for education and acceptance of a centralized educational authority such as a superintendent. The promotion of such ideas was left to acknowledged Tories like John Strachan and Mahlon Burwell of the London District. Both these men recognized the intimate connection between an efficient system of schools and a proper scheme of finance and control. The Reformers, consciously or otherwise, tended to overlook these unpleasant facts and resorted, as Ryerson did, to accusing schemes like Burwell's of making the common school a "mere engine of the Executive".[36] The Reformers could rail against the failings of the Tories, but the fact remained that the common-school system of the colony could never attain the development it did in the United States without considerable financial support. Under the circumstances, one wonders whether the Reformers were simply using education as a handy weapon to clout the Tories about the head.

Amid the agitation and concern over education in Upper

Canada, a rash of school bills were introduced in the Assembly in the 1830s. Among the politicians who introduced these bills, three names stand out. All three were much removed in make-up from the fiery editor, William Lyon Mackenzie. Two of them, William Buell, Jr., of Brockville and Mahlon Burwell of the London District, proposed alternative ways of organizing and financing common-school education. Buell, in a bill presented in 1831, favoured local control of a system financed by provincial grants. Burwell, in a series of bills presented in 1832, 1833, and 1837, proposed a "Provincial Board of Educational Commissioners", crown-appointed with supervisory powers and control over local management of schools through crown-appointed district boards. Financing would be based on local tax assessment similar to the New York system. While calling for local control, Buell's bills had opposed local taxation on the nineteenth-century liberal principle that taxation of persons who had no children or whose children were not in school was an infringement of personal liberty. For his part Burwell, who had a long record of interest in education dating back to 1814, saw the need for some compulsion from two viewpoints: not only would compulsory taxation alleviate problems in school finance but also it would encourage parents, who otherwise would keep their children at home to save money, to send their children to school. Thus the unhappy state of education in the province would be doubly improved.

The views of Egerton Ryerson in this controversy are worth noting. He gave his whole-hearted support to Buell's bill. On Burwell's bill of 1833, he expressed support for the plan of financing education by taxation on the value of assessed property. However, the proposal to remove education from the political arena by retaining control of the schools in the hands of the executive branch of government, he argued, served to centralize control of the common school in the hands of the executive. It is ironic that, as superintendent of education for the province a decade or so later, Ryerson himself succeeded in making the office of superintendent responsible to the Executive Council rather than to the Legislature.

The third educational promoter was Charles Duncombe, an American-born doctor who, prior to taking up residence in Burford, west of Hamilton, had conducted the first medical school in Upper Canada, the St. Thomas Dispensatory. In 1835 the Assembly sent him to the United States to observe the systems of education to be found there. (He was also charged with examining the operation of lunatic asylums!) During the last months of 1835 and the first of 1836 Duncombe visited Lexington, Cincinnati, Baltimore, Philadelphia, Boston, New York, and Albany. Generally speaking, he reported favourably on what he saw, although he had little praise for the school system of some states. New York State's system impressed him the most, a fact reflected in a common-school bill he presented to the Legislature in 1836. In urging central control through a provincial superintendent and voluntary taxation of rateable property, Duncombe's bill came close to duplicating the New York Act of 1812. In fact it was argued in the Legislative Council, in opposition to the bill, that it was "nearly, if not altogether, a transcript" of New York school law.[37] The defeat of the bill was, however, prompted not only by fear of creeping republicanism, but also by concern that the proposed system was beyond the means of provincial revenue.

Although Duncombe's ideas suffered a setback in the short run, many of his proposals reappeared in the next decade and foreshadowed school legislation up to the Act of 1871. Local assessment, elective school boards, regular inspection of schools, curriculum changes, female education, female teachers, proper teacher training to improve teaching standards, prescribed textbooks, and religious instruction of a non-denominational nature with stress on Christian morality—all became accepted policy during Ryerson's tenure of office between 1844 and 1876.

The Rebellion and Aftermath

The Rebellion of 1837 and the unsettled atmosphere that preceded and followed it interrupted efforts for educational reform. The aftermath of the rebellion was marked by a strong reaction against all things American, a mood reinforced by the activity of the Hunters' Lodges which triggered in 1838 a series of American patriot invasions into Upper Canada. Bitter anti-Americanism was reflected in all aspects of Canadian life, not the least of which was education. Post-mortems were avidly conducted on the rebellion and numerous diagnoses suggested. For example, Robert Baldwin Sullivan, the president of the Executive Council, concluded that the main cause of discontent was the proximity of the United States and the extent of the spread northward of the American ideas of democracy and republicanism. American teachers and textbooks were held up as one of the prime forces in the spread of American ideas in

Upper Canada. In a report to Lieutenant-Governor Arthur, Sullivan laid the blame for disaffection on the deleterious influences of American schoolbooks.

Ryerson even went so far as to state in an 1847 report to the Assembly his belief that an inquiry would disclose that "in precisely those parts of Upper Canada where the United States schoolbooks had been used most extensively, there the spirit of the insurrection in 1837 and 1838 was most prevalent."[38] For Lieutenant-Governor Arthur the main deficiency was the absence of strict surveillance and direction of education resulting from a lack of centralization. It was probably this situation which contributed to the "madness of allowing Americans to be the instructors of the Youth of the Country".[39] Within a decade Ryerson had set the stage for the replacement of American textbooks by the Irish National Readers, established a normal school to train teachers, and taken a major step in the Act of 1846 towards the creation of a centralized educational system.

In his famous report, Lord Durham underlined the need for educational reform in The Canadas. In Upper Canada he spoke of the lack of schools "even in the most thickly peopled districts", and how those existing were "of a very inferior character". The more remote settlements, he added, were "almost entirely without any [schools]".[40] The McCaul committee, headed by the first president of the University of Toronto and appointed in 1839 by Lieutenant-Governor Arthur to investigate the state of education in the province, concurred with Durham's findings. Out of a population of 450,000 in 1838 the report found 800 common schools with close to 24,000 pupils. It was estimated that only 55 to 60 per cent of school-aged children attended school. In the thirteen district grammar schools there were only about 300 students, a figure roughly comparable to that reported in 1826. Durham predicted that educational progress would derive from two sources: emulation of American advances in education and "the establishment of a strong popular government [which] would very soon lead to the introduction of a liberal and general system of education."[41]

The criticisms put forth in Durham's report and the substantial recommendations of the McCaul committee might have been expected to lead directly to improvements in Upper Canada's educational system. However, in the aftermath of the rebellion and the troubles which followed, jails, court-houses, and roads received primary consideration when it came to appropriating public funds. The Act of Union in 1840, following hard on the heels of the committee's report, also played a part in postponing implementation of its recommendations. But Durham's prediction proved indeed an accurate one. Shortly after the creation of a united Canada in 1841, the Common School Act of that year ushered in a series of measures culminating in the Act of 1871 that firmly established the "liberal and general system of education" of which Durham had spoken.

THE ACT OF UNION

Education was one matter requiring the urgent attention of the first parliament of united Canada when it met in Kingston in June 1841. Governor Lord Sydenham was determined to act immediately in this area, not only to alleviate the deplorable state of education, but also to devise a unified school jurisdiction for both provinces. Solicitor General Charles Day introduced a bill "to make further provision for the establishment and maintenance of common schools throughout the Province", that is, in both Canada East (formerly Lower Canada) and Canada West (formerly Upper Canada). The act, which was an important part of a larger scheme to create a cultural union of the new province according to Lord Durham's recommendation, was rendered unworkable by the fact that each section of the union had evolved over several decades quite distinct educational structures which were felt best to serve the needs of their respective populations. Nevertheless a genuine effort was made to arrive at provisions in the act which would allow its acceptance in both regions. The crucial clause in this regard was Section XI which made the famous provision of "separate schools" without once mentioning the term. It provided that "any number of inhabitants of a different faith from the majority in [either] township or parish might choose their own trustees", and "might establish and maintain one or more schools" under the same conditions as other common schools.[42]

The conditions surrounding the inclusion of the separate-school clause are worthy of note. Contemporary accounts indicate that the clause was added in the committee stage.[43] That the committee consisted of seven more members from Canada East than from Canada West has often been alluded to as the reason for the inclusion of the clause in question. However, of the fourteen members from Canada East, only four were French Canadians and the most forthright appeals for separate schools came not from Roman Catholics but from Protestants. Of the thirty-nine petitions sent to the committee, only one was made by a Roman Catholic, the rest requested the use of the Bible as a textbook in the schools. The bulk of these came from Church of England and Presbyterian clergymen disturbed by the absence of any mention of religious education in the common schools. The predominant view among Protestant petitioners was perhaps best expressed by the Hon. William Morris, a spokesman for the Church of Scotland, when he warned that "if the use by Protestants of the Holy Scriptures in their schools is so objectionable to our fellow subjects of that other faith, the children of both religious persuasions must be educated apart."[44] John Strachan, fresh from numerous setbacks over King's College, plunged into a determined campaign to ensure the creation of a system of separate, publicly supported Church of England schools. For him there was no alternative but to fight the practice of "imitating the irreligious scheme of our [Amercian] neighbours",[45] and he remained true to his commitment until his death twenty-three years later.

Roman Catholic claims to separate schools in Canada West were soon registered. Roman Catholic schools had been functioning in Upper Canada for many years. The first such school, using French as the language of instruction, had been opened at Fort Frontenac in 1676, and in 1786 Abbé Dufaux had opened in his parish of Sandwich (Windsor area) a school staffed by two female teachers sent from Quebec by Mgr. Hubert. The first English Catholic school was established in 1804 at St. Raphael's in Glengarry County, between Cornwall and the present Quebec boundary, in an area settled by Roman Catholic Highland Scots. The prime force behind the movement for English Catholic education was Father Alexander Macdonell who became bishop of Regiopolis (Kingston) in 1826 and a legislative councillor five years later. Because of his sympathy for the conservative and anti-American views of the Family Compact, Macdonell managed to gain financial support for his ventures from official quarters and a free hand just as the other denominations had in an era characterized by many private schools supported by voluntary subscriptions and fees. The Act of 1841 in effect gave legal sanction to these schools fostered by Macdonell.

Other features of this act, while perhaps less controversial, also merit attention. One was the delegation of basic decision-making powers to elected township commissioners. This provision not only marked an acceptance of the American elective principle, but also a victory for the advocates of a provincial system such as was proposed by William Buell, Jr., a decade before. A centralized provincial system such as Mahlon Burwell had advocated in the 1830s was not accepted until five years later. A major defect of the act was its dependence upon an efficiently functioning municipal system. Although Sydenham saw to it that a system of municipal government was established, the people had not yet learned the lesson of local self-government; nor had they grasped the idea that they would have to pay for education. Unwillingness to accept this need called into question for another decade or two the extent of popular commitment to education, an essential ingredient of an adequate common-school system.

Another provision of the Act of 1841 was the appointment of a chief superintendent of education for the entire province with assistants in Canada East and Canada West. Robert Jameson, the vice-chancellor of Upper Canada from 1837 to 1854, was appointed to the senior post that lasted until it was abolished by the Act of 1843. Rev. Robert Murray, a Presbyterian minister from Oakville, became assistant superintendent for Canada West until relieved of his post in 1844 and replaced by Egerton Ryerson, who was elevated to superintendent two years later.

The failure of the School Act of 1841 led to its repeal by the Common School Act of 1843, sometimes known as the Hincks Act after its sponsor Sir Francis Hincks, receiver general in the first Baldwin-LaFontaine ministry. In this, the first school bill sponsored by Reformers to become law in the history of Upper Canada, the principle of separate schools, which was accepted in 1841, was continued. The term, "separate schools" was actually used in the provisions of the act that became the basis of all subsequent laws governing separate schools in the united province. A decentralized school system, a second feature of the Act of 1841, was also continued in the Hincks Act. In this regard, one scholar has noted that this act marked "the zenith of liberal, American . . . influence on Upper Canadian legislation" affecting education.[46]

In contrast, Ryerson's Common School Act of 1846 inaugurated a centralized, provincial system of a type that had long been advocated by conservative Upper Canadians, such as John Strachan and Mahlon Burwell. Ryerson's school system was much more highly centralized than that of either New York State or Massachusetts, the two American states most often referred to by nineteenth-century Upper Canadian educational reformers. It was so successful, however, that a century later a distinguished Canadian historian could point to the extreme centralization of the Ontario school system of the 1950s and label Ryerson as the villain of the piece.[47]

NOTES

1. Arthur Godbout, "Les Franco-Ontariens et leurs écoles de 1791 à 1844", *Revue de l'Université d'Ottawa* XXXIII (1963), 246.

2. Quoted in Fred Landon, *Western Ontario and the American Frontier*, Carleton Library, No. 34 (Toronto, 1967), p. 128.

3. Michael Smith, *A Geographical View of the Province of Upper Canada* (Philadelphia, 1813), p. 62.

4. E. A. Cruikshank, "Immigration from the United States into Upper Canada, 1785–1812", Thirty-Ninth Convention of the Ontario Education Association, *Proceedings* (Toronto, 1900), p. 275.

5. Graham to Hon. W. D. Smith, 28 March 1802, State Books of Upper Canada, Public Archives of Canada (PAC), Vol. C: 194.

6. *Montreal Herald*, n.d., Hodgins Collections, Public Archives of Ontario (PAO).

7. Edward Talbot, *Five Years' Residence in the Canadas* (London, Ont., 1824), p. 96.

8. Strachan to Brown, 13 July 1806, Strachan Papers, PAO.

9. Quote from a petition to the Lieutenant-Governor of York, July 1831, in J. George Hodgins, ed., *Documentary History of Upper Canada, 1791–1876* (28 vols.; Toronto, 1894–1910), II: 29.

10. Simcoe to Bishop Mountain, 30 April 1795, as quoted in E. A. Cruickshank, ed., *The Correspondence of John Graves Simcoe* (Toronto, 1923–31), III: 349.

11. Ibid., I: 143.

12. Dundas to Simcoe, 12 July 1792, ibid., IV: 319.

13. Journals of the Assembly of Upper Canada, 27 February 1805, *Ontario Archives, Eighth Report, 1911* (Toronto, 1912), p. 46.

14. Hodgins, *Documentary History* I: 77.

15. Ibid., pp. 269–70.

16. 55 George III, c. 18.

17. Unsigned letter of Strachan to Bathurst, 7 June 1824, quoted in J. D. Purdy, "John Strachan and Education in Canada, 1800–1851" (PHD thesis, University of Toronto, 1962), p. 72.

18. Strachan to Brown, 9 October 1808, Strachan Papers, PAO.

19. *Christian Recorder*, April 1819; Hodgins, *Documentary History* I: 55.

20. Richard Cockrell, *Thoughts on the Education of Youth* (Newark, 1795). Reproduced in Toronto by the Bibliographical Society of Canada in 1949.

21. Joseph Neef, *Sketch of a Plan and Method of Education* (Philadelphia, 1808).

22. Smith, *A Geographical View*, p. 44.

23. Ibid., p. 63.

24. William Wood, ed., *British Documents of the Canadian War of 1812* (Toronto, 1920–23), III, Part I, 509.

25. Smith, *A Geographical View*, p. 44.

26. Robert Gourlay, *Statistical Account of Upper Canada* (London, 1822), I: 354.

27. J. G. Althouse, *The Ontario Teacher, 1800–1910* (Toronto, 1967), p. 5.

28. Hodgins, *Documentary History* I: 195.

29. Kingston *Gazette*, 19 September 1815, quoted in F. F. Thompson, "Reflections Upon Education in the Midland District, 1810–1816", *Historic Kingston* XI (1962), 19.

30. G. P. de T. Glazebrook, *Life in Ontario: A Social History* (Toronto, 1968), p. 101.

31. Maitland to Bathurst, 4 January 1821, PAO, C.O. 42/336, pp. 3–4.

32. Strachan to J. S. Sinclair, 23 May 1840, Strachan Letter Book, 1839–1845, PAO.

33. "Report on Education", 26 February 1815, in G. W. Spragge, ed., *The John Strachan Letter Book: 1812–1834* (Toronto, 1946), p. 78.

34. Strachan to the Marquis of Wellesley, 1 November 1812, Strachan Letter Book, 1812–1827, PAO.

35. *Colonial Advocate*, 11 October 1827, quoted in M. Fairley, ed., *The Selected Writings of William Lyon Mackenzie, 1824–1837* (Toronto, 1960), p. 94.

36. *Christian Guardian*, 15 January 1834.

37. J. G. Hodgins, *Historical Education Papers and Documents Illustrative of the Education System of Ontario, 1792–1853* (Toronto, 1911–12) I: 62.

38. Canada, Journal of the Assembly V: Appendix B.B.

39. Arthur to Bishop Mountain, 18 December 1838, quoted in C. R. Sanderson, ed., *The Arthur Papers* (Toronto, 1943), I: 465.

40. G. M. Craig, ed., *Lord Durham's Report*, Carleton Library, No. 1 (Toronto, 1963), p. 101.

41. Ibid., p. 72.

42. Statutes of Province of Canada, 4 and 5 Vict., Chapter 18, Sec. xi.

43. F. Hincks, *Reminiscences in the Life of Sir Francis Hincks* (Montreal, 1884), p. 69.

44. J. G. Hodgins, *The Legislation and History of Separate Schools in Upper Canada* (Toronto, 1897), p. 18.

45. Strachan to J. E. Small, 11 December 1844, Strachan Letter Book, 1844–1849, PAO.

46. M. J. Duncan, "American Influences on Ontario's Elementary School Legislation, 1836–1850" (MA thesis, University of Rochester, 1964), p. 197.

47. F. H. Underhill, "So Little for the Mind: Comments and Queries", *Transactions of Royal Society of Canada*, third series, XLVIII (1954), Sec. II, 18.

II Dimensions of Ryerson's Thought

Egerton Ryerson and the Methodist Model for Upper Canada

GOLDWIN S. FRENCH

As befits an age of arduous endeavour, the history of Upper Canada is peopled with mythic figures. To many, except the serious historian, John Strachan, William Lyon Mackenzie, Robert Baldwin, and Egerton Ryerson stand out in heroic relief as the friends or enemies of progress and the people. In retrospect, one can see more clearly that each cherished a vision or a model of the shape which Upper Canadian society should attain. Each of these models had a measure of validity, but some were more utopian than others. In the end the articulate design of John Strachan was rejected as were the inchoate aspirations of William Lyon Mackenzie. Both Baldwin and Ryerson were more closely attuned to the limitations and the potentialities of their world and had a greater degree of success in translating their objectives into reality. Thus, Ryerson has become enshrined as the champion of religious and civil liberty and the founder of Ontario's educational system, a system complacently described in 1876 as "the best in the world"![1]

In our time, no one, except a few Anglicans, believes that Ryerson thwarted Strachan's noble plan for the development of Ontario's schools and universities, or that persons of Ryerson's ilk were somehow unreliable, and dangerous. Few would denigrate Ryerson's accomplishments. One should note in passing, however, that in education Ryerson built on foundations for which John Strachan was largely responsible, and that, whatever his intentions, Ryerson's work "bears witness to the pervasive influence of attitudes susceptible to the promises of an educational solution to social problems. . . . The development and internal elaboration of the public school system would provide the middle class with their main strategy for meeting the problems of their changing society."[2] Even so, the significant fact is, that despite Ryerson's monumental writings on many subjects,

45

and the books written about him, he remains a myth. It should be our aim now to begin disentangling the man from the myth and to acquire a more comprehensive grasp of his objectives. During this process, we may begin to discern that Ryerson was a complex and ambivalent character whose values were potentially far more radical in some respects than those of Mackenzie, and much more akin to those of Strachan than either man recognized at the time.

Recently, Reginald Whitaker has written: "Religion of one sort or another is a glue that holds Canadian history together, helping to shape everything from racism to radicalism."[3] C. B. Sissons maintained that "political motives were secondary with [Ryerson]. The primary and dominant motive of his life was religious."[4] To Robin Harris, "Ryerson was a Christian, first, last, and all the time; his religious principles were his first principles. He was, of course, a particular kind of Christian, a Methodist, and he subscribed fully to the doctrines of that Church."[5] But, if one accepts that Ryerson was an important example of the religious man and specifically, the Methodist in action, surely one must begin by trying to understand the origins and the qualities of his belief, a task that students of Ryerson have carried out superficially.

To the contemporary historian who mistakes religious pluralism for secularism and for whom the limits of reality are humanly intelligible if not wholly visible, the world view of early nineteenth-century Methodism is both absurd and incomprehensible. Moreover, he is likely to classify it as an emotional, simplistic form of Christianity and thereby to underestimate the continuing influence of John Wesley over its ongoing life. In reality the Methodism to which the young Ryerson subscribed was largely untouched by the intellectual revolution of the eighteenth century, and to the perceptive literate convert such as he was, it was still the religion of Wesley.

At the outset, Egerton Ryerson was affected simply by the religious concern of his three elder brothers, all of whom would precede him into the Methodist ministry in Upper Canada. "In the end," he recounts, "I simply trusted in Christ, and looked to Him for a present salvation . . . . I henceforth had new views, new feelings, new joys, and new strength."[6] On his twenty-second birthday, he entered upon his ministerial vocation. An obsessive student, he must have plunged willingly into the course in practical divinity which all probationers were required to take. The core of this program was Wesley's sermons, evidently supplemented in his case by extensive reading in Wesley's other works and in those of Adam Clarke and Richard Watson, Wesleyan scholars in Ryerson's generation. That Wesley's words entered deeply into his consciousness is evident in his editorial writings, his reliance in old age on Wesley's authority, and in such simple remarks as, "I think Mr. Wesley's advice indispensably necessary, 'to rise as soon as we wake'."[7] Hence, one may properly ask: What were the important elements in the Wesleyan legacy which Ryerson acquired in the first years of his career?

Despite the clarity and the general consistency of his words and actions, Wesley was much misunderstood in his own time and has been the object of some controversy in the present. The contours of the political and religious battleground on which he stood are now more visible, and the nuances of his position are more intelligible and more evident than they would have been to Ryerson and his contemporaries. But the evidence suggests that the essential elements of Wesley's outlook were grasped clearly by Ryerson. He, unlike the modern student, shared albeit imprecisely, Wesley's theological and philosophical presuppositions, and thus entered his world readily and sympathetically. In Wesley's mental universe he would have perceived four significant concepts: the primacy of Scripture over reason, a belief in a dynamic and uninhibited providence, the Christian life as a form of secular monasticism, and a curious synthesis of conservative and critical attitudes towards the political and social order.

In the eighteenth century and later, Methodist theology was categorized as a theology of experience and thus open to the perversions of emotionalism and self-delusion. Wesley's motto was: "At any price give me the book of God! I have it: here is knowledge enough for me. Let me be *homo unius libri* .... In His presence I open, I read His book; for this end, to find the way to heaven ... And what I thus learn that I teach."[8] Of course, Wesley's understanding of Scripture was influenced by his wide reading and especially by his fondness for the Anglican homilies, but his theology remained ultimately biblical. For him, "experience is not sufficient to prove a doctrine which is not founded on Scripture",[9] nor does experience alone prove anything, but on occasion may confirm a statement derived from Scripture. On the other hand, Wesley preached the doctrine of assurance, namely, that the believer would share "an outward impression of the soul whereby the Spirit of God

directly witnesses to my spirit that I am a child of God . . .",
which in turn would be validated by the transformed life of the
individual.[10] In this, however, Wesley was making an assertion
about the work of God, not about the significance of experience.
Moreover, the claim that the Spirit is at work must be sustained
not by personal testimony, but by changes in attitudes and
behaviour capable of being assessed by one's peers. The corol-
lary of this biblical orientation was a strong antipathy to the
rationalism of the *philosophes*. Locke alone was acceptable to
Wesley, who discerned "a deep fear of God and reverence for
his word" in his "Essay on Human Understanding".[11] Indeed,
the fundamental basis of Wesley's teaching was a reaffirmation
of the traditional Christian description of reality as a realm in
which the power of God is at work continuously within the
limits defined by Scripture, shaping the characters and the
destinies of men and society.

Wesley differed sharply from many religious people of his
generation in his conviction that the Holy Spirit is a dynamic
and untrammeled force in human affairs. For him the notion
of providence as a first cause, the rather easy-going platitudes
of many of his Anglican brethren, and the Calvinist doctrine of
election, were either erroneous or deficient. On the contrary,
he insisted especially that "the doctrine of predestination is not
a doctrine of God" but one which destroys "the comfort of
religion" and inspires "contempt or coldness towards those
whom we suppose outcasts from God". To undermine our "zeal
for good works" in this way was to present "God as worse than
the devil".[12] Grace, Wesley affirmed, is "free in all and free for
all".[13] It is a gift of the Spirit which opens the way to heaven,
but it may be accepted or rejected by every man, either at the
outset or along the road to eternity. He added that the poor had
"a peculiar right to have the gospel preached unto them", as did
"the unlearned", since "God hath revealed these things unto
unlearned and ignorant men from the beginning."[14] In effect,
the Spirit works unceasingly for and among men, to make them
aware without distinction that there is a road to salvation and
to assist them along it.

Wesley was persuaded utterly that his mission in the world
was to diffuse his understanding of "the way to heaven" and to
help those who responded to move faithfully along this road.
In essence, he believed that, although men are corrupt, grace,
the gift of an immanent Spirit, enables each of us "to choose
and do good as well as evil".[15] By divine power, the repentant

man experiences the new birth by which the image of God is restored in his soul. But, this is the beginning, not the end of the Christian life, for the crucial task of the believer is to strive for perfection or holiness in this present existence. Wesley insisted further that, although one could relapse into wickedness, one could achieve holiness in this life, a doctrine which scandalized his contemporaries and has baffled many subsequently. By this he meant, "that those who unreservedly trust in Christ for salvation have only one allowable ideal which they can set before themselves. . . . In the serious Christian life there is no room whatever for conscious trifling with known temptation in the heart or for continuance in known compromise in conduct." The Christian can and ought to expect that he will secure the "divine gift of an undivided heart" or conscience, which will be exemplified by devotion and by the quality of his conduct.[16]

Believing as he did, that the Christian's goal is to strive for mastery over all wilful wrong, Wesley founded not a church, but a religious society whose spirit was that of "married and secular monasticism".[17] The life of the individual Methodist was to be a standing rebuke to the human desire for security, comfort, praise, and honour. He was to do "no harm", to avoid "evil of every kind", to do "good . . . of every possible sort and as far as is possible to all men", and to participate in "all the ordinances of God".[18] To assist him in this difficult endeavour, the members of the society were "to watch over one another in love", a task that was committed to the classes in which Wesley's adherents were grouped.[19] In effect, the Methodist was to live in the world and to endure all its temptations, since there is no room in the divine plan for two kinds of Christians, the cloistered specialist and the conventionally moral man. The mark of the serious Christian is the intensity of his awareness of the moral perils of existence, and of his determination to effect a qualitative change in his moral perceptions and actions, especially in his relationships with others. His persistence in this process is alone made possible by divine support; in the end, "without holiness no man shall see the Lord."[20]

As Wesley recognized, his advocacy of the doctrines of universal grace and Christian perfection could have led not only to spiritual renewal, but to secular revolution. This formidable possibility was nullified by the manner in which he exercised authority, and by his contradictory teaching on social and political issues. The form of church government was for him a matter of expediency, but in the Methodist polity Wesley was advised but not governed by his brethren. His power, he believed, had been conferred upon him by Providence; those who did not wish to acknowledge it were free to leave the Methodist connection. He took care before his death to convey his authority collectively to the so-called "Legal Hundred" of selected ministers who sought with some success to function as a group episcopate. Similarly, Wesley enjoined his followers "honour and obey all in authority".[21] He described himself as a Tory, that is one who "believes God, not the people, to be the origin of all civil power."[22] The Christian elector should vote "for the man that loves God", or failing that, "for him that loves the King". If "a man does not love the King, he cannot love God."[23] Nonetheless, "as all others owe allegiance to the King, the King himself oweth allegiance to the Constitution."[24] "Loyalty," he concluded, "is with me an essential branch of religion .... There is the closest connection, therefore, between my religious and political conduct...."[25]

Significantly, however, Wesley was a strong advocate of civil and religious liberty. He emphasized that Methodists "do not insist on your holding this or that opinion" or "impose any particular mode of worship", which in his view was true "liberty of conscience".[26] His goal was to destroy wickedness and bigotry, by which he meant "too strong an attachment to or fondness for our own party, opinion, Church and religion".[27] His opposition to slavery drove him to state that "liberty is the right of every human creature as soon as he breathes the vital air; and no human law can deprive him of that right which he derives from the law of nature."[28] But, fearful of the social implications of his theology, Wesley did not become an advocate of natural rights and thus avoided a serious confrontation with his own inconsistency.

To put the matter succinctly, Ryerson imbibed from Wesley's writings a version of the Christian message that was theologically conservative, immensely demanding, and intensely other-worldly, and yet deeply relevant to the human condition in its concern for the individual and for the serious pursuit of moral improvement. Behind the Methodist façade lurked an affinity for egalitarianism and the basis for a profound leavening of the social order, tendencies which were held in check by Wesley's respect for the political system and by the ease with which evangelical Christians can mistake selfishness for charity.

The manner in which Ryerson applied this complex creed which he espoused so thoroughly and so faithfully was shaped by his upbringing, his education, and by the circumstances of Upper Canada. Although Ryerson was raised on a farm and had but a modest exposure to formal education, he should not be seen as the poor boy who has done well. In reality his social connections were with the Tory ruling group in the province; it was his Methodism and his clerical status which barred him from preferment for so many years. His family were imbued with an awareness of their Loyalist origin; hence for them loyalty to the British connection, the monarchy, and the constitution was axiomatic. It was natural and inevitable that Ryerson's father and two of his brothers should have served in the War of 1812. That Loyalism was ingrained in Egerton Ryerson was amply demonstrated by the publication of his magnum opus, *The Loyalists of America and Their Times*,[29] and by his fiery reaction to the Fenian raid in 1866: "The feeling which I had when a boy during the American war from 1812 to 1815 seems rekindled in my heart . . . . I said I would go myself if required . . . . My hope & prayer is that they [the Fenians] may receive such a lesson on their first attempt as will forever prevent a repetition of it."[30] As the son of Colonel Joseph Ryerson, former High Sheriff of Norfolk, Ryerson was led insensibly to accept at natural the social hierarchy of Upper Canada. Although highly independent, he was never unaware of the distinction between the classes and the masses, and showed no disposition to challenge the social structure as such. Moreover, the conservatism of his surroundings was reinforced by his reading. He "took great delight in 'Locke on the Human Understanding', Paley's 'Moral and Political Philosophy', and 'Blackstone's Commentaries', especially the sections of the latter on the Prerogatives of the Crown, the Rights of the Subject, and the Province of Parliament."[31] His early writings, especially, contain frequent references to Paley and Blackstone, clear testimony of the impact of their traditional ideas on his political outlook.

Although he was a man of immense energy and determination and had by his own efforts acquired a considerable fund of knowledge and literary skills, the Ryerson who on March 24, 1825, decided "to travel in the Methodist Connexion and preach Jesus to the lost sons of men"[32] was without fully realizing it at a cross-road in his life. His social background, his political convictions, the simplistic attitudes of his brethren, and his own sense of unfitness for his calling, all pointed either towards "a position in the Church of England" and "other advantageous attractions with regard to this world", or to an uncomplicated concern for the welfare of souls. In the end he made a different choice. He concluded, "earthly distinctions will be but short; but the favour of God will last forever. . . . My heart is united with the Methodists, my soul is one with theirs. . . . I believe them to be of the Church of Christ."[33] He would never cease from preaching to the sons of men from within the Methodist community, but the scope and character of his mission were to undergo a dramatic alteration. The discrimination which the Methodists suffered made him aware of the growing tensions in Upper Canadian society and impelled him to define his role in a broader perspective. In so doing he was influenced and limited by his social environment, his understanding of Wesley's teaching, and by his overwhelming conviction that "the diffusion of Christianity is the most important subject that can engage the attentions of men."[34]

Between 1825 and his appointment in 1844 as superintendent of education for Canada West, Ryerson served variously as an itinerant minister on circuit, missionary to the Indians, editor of the *Christian Guardian*, informal adviser to Sydenham and Metcalfe, and principal of Victoria College. From 1829 until 1844 he was almost continuously involved in controversy, either as an editor or pamphleteer, and as such he earned a measure of notoriety and misunderstanding. His formidable skill as an advocate which, under other circumstances, would have secured him a great reputation at the bar, led him into disputes seemingly far removed from his proper function and endangered his own spiritual well-being. Out of his inner anxiety and the outer turmoil which he helped to generate, emerged, albeit in bits and pieces, his definition of the values which would inform Upper Canadian society of the direction in which it should grow.

Upper Canada in the 1830s was a heterogeneous collection of settlements whose inhabitants were intent upon the satisfaction of their material needs and the elimination of social and political discrimination. Ryerson did not challenge directly their preoccupation with improvements, and the emerging gospel of progress. Rather, as a minister and writer he stressed, as did John Strachan, the primacy of the Christian tradition as the foundation and the norm of the social, political, and cultural order. For him this implied acceptance of the ultimate insignificance of human existence, and recognition of "the presence and power of God the Holy Ghost",[35] not simply in the church, but in the whole life of the community. Knowledge was derived from inspiration and reason. Society was under judgment and direction; hence the moral quality of beliefs and actions must be scrutinized in the light of Scripture and the quest for holiness. In practice this could and did produce an affinity for censorious restrictions and the denigration of cultural growth, but to Ryerson, the Christian society would be characterized by constructive discipline and a determination to explore the practical meaning of charity in human relations, an attitude often obscured by emotionalism and sectarian controversy.

Ryerson was convinced that the second essential attribute of the good society for Upper Canada was the achievement of civil and religious liberty for all its members. In his later years he asserted proudly that Methodism was "the first and most effective promoter of civil and religious liberty for the entire country".[36] One need not dispute the claim here. The important fact is that Ryerson believed, as did Wesley, that the right of all citizens to equal rights and privileges before the law, and to freedom of conscience, was based directly upon Scripture: "Before these fundamental and sublime truths of revelation— God our Creator and all we, His children; Christ our Redeemer, and all we His redeemed . . . how are all mankind, and every man, enfranchised with the rights of an equal freedom and dignified with the grandeur of more than angelic glory!"[37] He continued: "The doctrine of universal equality before the law was the natural result of the doctrine of universal equality before God in both creation and redemption. . . ."[38] Moreover, every man has an "undeniable and inviolable right of private judgement in all matters of religious faith and duty . . . . Religion being a spiritual system of inspired truth, must be promoted only by moral and spiritual influences, and not by the coercion of civil government. . . ."[39] The inferences which the young Ryerson drew from these truths encompassed much of his work as a controversialist in the 1830s.

The disputes in which Ryerson was involved were exceedingly tortuous, as was his reasoning on occasion, but his principal arguments are clear and consistent. Every religious denomination, he believed, should for its own health and for the good of society be dependent only on its members for sustenance. If ministers were "to trust in the arm of the flesh" they "will in respect to their simplicity, their innocence and their usefulness draw their last breath",[40] an assertion which was fully con-

firmed in his view by the history of the Church of England in
Britain and Canada. Rather, "the latitude of Canada never was
designed to wear the shackles of an ecclesiastical or literary
despotism . . . . Our Chief Magistrates must . . . deal alike with
all . . . and be no respecters of persons."[41] In practice this
meant that the clergy of all denominations should have equal
rights and privileges. Thus, Ryerson fought vigorously to deprive the Church of England of its privileged position in Upper
Canada. In so doing, he was seeking the separation of church
and state as institutions, but he did not intend to free the state
from moral judgment or to imply that the state should not take
thought for the moral content of education. Perhaps equally
important was his implicit attack on the existing system of
patronage, part of whose justification was the alleged social
and political reliability of Anglicans and Presbyterians in contrast to the potential disloyalty of so-called Dissenters. "The
executive obloquy and disabilities which still . . . deprive the
Methodists and others of privileges extended to another portion
of the same compact is an infringement and absolute outrage
upon the very first principle upon which every free government
is founded."[42] Civil liberty meant simply that every citizen
should have an equal opportunity to deploy his talents in his
own interest or in service to the state. Religious liberty meant
freedom of conscience and freedom for the churches, but it
also meant for him that a clear distinction must be drawn
between religious and political opinions. Mr. Wesley, he noted,
"gives the right hand of fellowship to those who differ from
him on many points . . . . The discipline of the church does not
authorize us to become the judge of another man's political
opinions—the church is not a political association."[43] The
"undoubted constitutional right of individual judgment and
discussion on political matters [must be] fully understood and
mutually acknowledged by all."[44]

Undoubtedly Ryerson was much more interested in religious
teaching and the church–state controversy than in political
issues as such. His political opinions were none the less clearly
articulated and formed an important ingredient of his model
for a provincial society.

In one so conscious of the egalitarian dimension of the Gospel
and so involved in bitter controversy, an effort to work out the
political implications of the doctrines of equality and civil
liberty might have been expected. Ryerson was induced, however, by other considerations to formulate a cautious political

philosophy which was distinctive in application rather than in content. His social background, Wesley's teaching, which was infused with "a kind of natural affection for our country, which we apprehend Christianity was never designed to root out or to impair,"[45] and his fondness for Paley and Blackstone led him to defend without hesitation the British connection and the established political order. "I am opposed to the introduction of any new and untried theories of government. . . . I assume that this country is to remain a portion of the British Empire, and view every measure . . . in reference to the well-being of the country in connexion with Great Britain. . . . In civil affairs I take my stand upon the established constitution of the country. . . ."[46] But, Ryerson, as Wesley, did not assume that the constitution was based simply upon a human contract:

> Civil Government itself, we believe, is based on the principles of Christian morality; and to the binding obligations of social compact, in every properly constituted Government—such as ours—is added the authoritative voice of Divine Revelation. Therefore, "to resist the power is to resist the ordinance of God". . . . The same Bible that gives the magistrate his authority, limits it by saying, he is to be a "minister of God—for Good." On the other hand, while the Bible tells the subject that he should obey magistrates . . . it also tells him that his obedience has limits . . . . From these brief and hasty observations two inferences follow. 1. That the civil authorities are derived from God, and every Christian is bound to obey them. 2. That the rights peculiar to a subject are also secured by the Supreme Being, and every Christian is at liberty to maintain them.[47]

The practical conclusions which Ryerson drew from this mixture of biblical, contractual, and traditional concepts were very significant. There was no necessity to seek changes in the constitution, not only because of its basis, but because the balance of the system must be preserved. To infringe upon the prerogative of the Crown was "a blow at the liberty of the subject";[48] equally, to exalt or to misuse the prerogative, as happened in Upper Canada, was to undermine the loyalty and the obligation of the subject to the established order. The proper business of all branches of the government was to ensure that the rights of all parties to the compact were upheld. The Christian had a peculiar obligation to ensure that all public issues were examined on their merits and were not misrepresented to serve party and factional interest. He should never forget that the opponents of the state—those who remind it of its obligation to uphold the rights and privileges of all—can be the defenders of its real values.[49] Ryerson's political writings and actions in the 1830s were intended to exemplify his concern for the maintenance of harmony in the political system and his conviction that this could be best accomplished by assessing the moral implications of all social and political issues in the light of his conception of civil and religious liberty. Government should be conducted by those who have the true interest of the community at heart. Partyism and faction were degrading and divisive, and if permitted to flourish, would reduce Upper Canada to the sad state of a democratic society.

Believing as he did that educated people are the "best security of a good government and constitutional liberty", that ignorant people will become "the slaves of despots and the dupes of demagogues", and that "sound learning is of great worth even in religion; the wisest and the best instructed Christians are the most steady and may be the most useful",[50] Ryerson was certain that Upper Canada should become an educated society. It required "a system established by Acts of our Provincial Legislature—a system on an economical plan—a system conformable to the wishes of the great mass of the population—a system promoted by the united efforts of the laity and clergy—a system in . . . which the different bodies of clergy will not interfere—a system which will bring the blessings of education to every family."[51] Instruction in the schools, he insisted, would be "but a sounding brass and a tinkling cymbal when not founded upon and sanctified by the undefiled and regenerating religion of Jesus Christ."[52] The original description of Upper Canada Academy doubtless embodied his ideal: "A place of learning where the stream of educational instruction shall not be mingled with the polluted waters of corrupt example; where the pupils will be guarded against the infection of immoral principles and practices—where a good English and classical education may . . . be acquired—where the rudiments of the several Sciences will be taught—where scholars of every religious creed will meet with equal attention and encouragement . . . ."[53] This early statement reappears more succinctly in his first report as superintendent of education, in which he sought to lay "the basis of an Educational structure . . . as broad as the population of the country . . . the whole based upon the principles of Christianity, and uniting the combined influence and support of the Government and the people."[54]

Such in broad outline were the principal ingredients of Ryerson's model for the development of Upper Canadian society. In the primacy he accorded to the Christian religion, the maintenance of the British connection, and the balanced constitution, it was a highly traditional design, but these elements were coupled in principle with his determination that Upper Canada should become a community in which every man would be recognized as a person entitled to full civil and religious liberty, to equality of opportunity, and to the kind of education which would fit him for his role in life. He sought as well to persuade Upper Canadians to see themselves as one people, with distinct interests and needs. Above all perhaps, he wished to ensure that his society perceived itself as under judgment, in the sense that the moral implications of public policy and public acts would be the subject of critical scrutiny in the light of the Christian worth of the individual and the Christian obligation to avoid evil and to do good.

Not surprisingly, given his humanity and the contradictory influence on his own position of tradition, class, and religious conviction, Ryerson did not develop the radical dimension of his beliefs. To many he appeared to be, and indeed he was, an inveterate, inconsistent, and often self-righteous advocate of denominational or other interests, a judgment which in moments of introspection he did not dispute. He remains, none the less, a formidable figure, not so much for his accomplishments, as for his strenuous determination to bring together and to apply the Christian tradition and the British inheritance in the shaping of Upper Canada. His devotion to the public interest, as he defined it, was his way of fulfilling Wesley's injunction to seek after holiness in this life.

NOTES

1. Quoted by R. M. Stamp from the New York *Tribune*, in his manuscript "Education in Ontario, 1876–1976".

2. Susan E. Houston, "Politics, Schools and Social Change in Upper Canada", *Canadian Historical Review* LIII, No. 3 (September 1972), 271.

3. Reginald Whitaker, "Mackenzie King in the Dominion of the Dead", *Canadian Forum*, February 1976, p. 7.

4. C. B. Sissons, *Egerton Ryerson: His Life and Letters* (2 vols.; Toronto, 1937–47), I: 3.

5. R. L. McDougall, ed., *Our Living Tradition*, third series (Toronto, 1959), p. 255.

6. Egerton Ryerson, *The Story of My Life*, ed. J. George Hodgins (Toronto, 1883), pp. 25–26.

7. Ibid., p. 53.
8. E. H. Sugden, ed., *The Standard Sermons of John Wesley* (London, 1931), II: p. 31.
9. Ibid., II: 352.
10. Ibid., I: 207.
11. *The Works of the Rev. John Wesley, A.M.* (London, 1872), XIII: 455.
12. *Works of Wesley*, VII: 376–83.
13. Ibid., VII: 373.
14. Quoted in B. Semmel, *The Methodist Revolution* (New York, 1973), p. 32.
15. Sugden, *Sermons of Wesley*, III: 218.
16. R. Davies and G. Rupp, eds., *A History of the Methodist Church in Great Britain* (London, 1965), I: 186.
17. Ibid., p. 187.
18. Ibid., pp. 192–94.
19. Ibid., p. 192.
20. J. Telford, ed., *The Letters of John Wesley* (London, 1931), V: 264.
21. Semmel, *The Methodist Revolution*, p. 56.
22. Telford, *Letters of Wesley*, VII: 305.
23. Ibid, IV: 271–72.
24. Semmel, *The Methodist Revolution*, p. 60.
25. L. Tyerman, *The Life and Times of the Rev. John Wesley, A.M., Founder of the Methodists* (New York, 1872), I: 441.
26. N. Curnock, ed., *The Journal of John Wesley* (London, 1909–16), VII: 389.
27. *Works of Wesley*, V: 490.
28. *Works of Wesley*, XI: 79.
29. Egerton Ryerson, *The Loyalists of America and Their Times from 1620 to 1860*, (2 vols.; Toronto, 1880).
30. C. B. Sissons, ed., *My Dearest Sophie: Letters from Egerton Ryerson to his daughter* (Toronto, 1955), pp. 85–86.
31. Ryerson, *The Story of My Life*, p. 27.
32. Ibid., p. 39.
33. Ibid., p. 41.
34. *Colonial Advocate*, 11 May 1826.
35. E. Ryerson, *Canadian Methodism; Its Epochs and Characteristics* (Toronto, 1882), p. 82.
36. Ibid., p. 129.
37. Ibid., p. 131.
38. Ibid., p. 133.
39. Ibid., p. 138.
40. *Christian Guardian*, 23 January 1830.
41. Ibid., 26 December 1829.
42. Ibid., 3 July 1830.
43. Ibid, 9 May 1838.
44. W. Harvard to R. Alder, 28 April 1838, *Records of the Wesleyan Methodist Missionary Society*, Microfilm, Reel 19, United Church Archives.
45. *Works of Wesley*, XIII: 229–30.
46. *Christian Guardian*, 11 July 1838.
47. Ibid., 21 November 1829.
48. Quoted in McDougall, *Our Living Tradition*, p. 257.
49. *Christian Guardian*, 8 October 1831.
50. Ibid., 23 April 1831.
51. *Colonial Advocate*, 14 August 1828.
52. *Christian Guardian*, 21 November 1829.
53. Ibid., 6 November 1830.
54. J. George Hodgins, ed., *Documentary History of Education in Upper Canada, 1791–1876* (28 vols; Toronto, 1894–1910), VI: 142.

The Moral Education of Egerton Ryerson's Idea of Education

Foundation

ALBERT F. FIORINO

In *Report on a System of Public Elementary Instruction* Egerton Ryerson closes his "Prefatory Letter to the Provincial Secretary", the Hon. Dominick Daly, with the following statement: "I have 'borrowed from all [all sources documented in the report] whatever' appeared to me to be 'good', and have endeavoured to 'perfect', by adapting it to our condition, 'whatever I have appropriated'."[1] In making this prefatory statement, Ryerson distinguished between what he considered to be good and what he judged as appearing to be good in the various sources he documented in the report; that is, a distinction between the logical and the historical roots or sources of his conception of education. Thus, what he considered to be good (implying a value judgment) acted as the criterion for determining what to borrow from others. Ryerson clearly implies that the selection of his sources in the report was determined by what he conceived "good" to be, which was the good of man, especially as "good" was effected by education. Consequently, his conception of education cannot be fully appreciated except in relation to his view of the good of man, that is, in relation to the moral dimension of his thought.

The distinction between logical and historical roots or sources is effectively accentuated by Professor Carl Becker in his classic work *The Heavenly City of the Eighteenth-Century Philosophers*. There, in his discussion of the influence of David Hume's *Dialogues Concerning the Nature of Religion* on contemporary thinkers, Becker makes it a point to criticize what he considered to be a naive notion of historians about culture, which views the transfer of ideas from one writer to another "as if it were no more than a matter of borrowed coins . . . to note, for example, that Mr. Jones must have got a certain idea from Mr. Smith because it can be shown that he had read

59

Mr. Smith's book; all the while forgetting that if Mr. Jones hadn't already had an idea, or something like it, simmering in his own mind he wouldn't have cared to read Mr. Smith's book, or, having read, would very likely have thrown it aside, or written a review to show what a bad and mistaken book it was."[2]

Aristotle writes to the same effect in the first book of his *Nicomachean Ethics*. There he states: "each man judges well of things he knows, and of these he is a good judge. And so the man who has been educated in a subject is a good judge of that subject, and the man who has received an all-round education is a good judge in general."[3] In other words, man judges in accordance with what he already knows. It follows that the process by which an individual judges what knowledge he should further appropriate to himself is determined by what he knows. The latter can be termed the principle of appropriation or the logical roots of one's acquired knowledge, and the former, the origins of the knowledge appropriated, the historical roots or sources, to indicate simply that the ideas are derived or borrowed from others, either living or dead.[4]

Thus, in the case of Professor Becker's example, it may be possible for Mr. Jones to have borrowed certain ideas from Mr. Smith or Mr. Brown, or perhaps, from a reading of a general intellectual history of Europe. However, it is also possible, and most likely, that what motivated Mr. Jones to borrow from these sources was the logical connection he perceived to exist between his own ideas and those contained in these sources.

In his prefatory statement, Ryerson does nothing more than to give particular expression to the views expounded by both Aristotle and Becker. He acknowledges his indebtedness to the authors of whom he availed himself in the development of the report and implies that what motivated him to borrow from them was the logical affinity that appeared to exist between their educational ideas and his own.

In the *Report of 1846*, Ryerson makes a further distinction between principles and means, or policy. This distinction constitutes the underlying logic of the organization of the report. Thus, in Part 1, Ryerson sets out to define education and to elaborate the principles upon which the system of education of Canada West was to be founded, and in Part 2, he describes the "machinery" which, he hoped, would facilitate the realization of these principles. For Ryerson, this "machinery" referred to that body of educational policy covering a host of items such as the nature of the schools, teachers and teacher training, the kinds of textbooks to be used, the control and inspection of schools by the government, and the role of the individual and the public in the cause of education.

Ryerson's second distinction, which can also be documented in several of his other writings, discloses not only an educator who was very much concerned with founding a system of education for Canada West on what he believed to be sound principles, but also provides, together with the first distinction, a very useful model by which to examine systematically his educational thought. For if there is a reason why previous students of Ryerson's thought have neglected to analyse the relationship between his educational ideas and his moral philosophy, it is, perhaps, due to their failure to perceive the relevance of these two distinctions. Consequently, a truly well-balanced assessment of Ryerson's personal contribution to both the theoretical and practical developments in Canadian education has not been attained.

But a further analysis of these two distinctions is not what is intended here since this has already been done elsewhere.[5] At the same time, neither an assessment of Ryerson's personal contribution to Canadian educational thought nor a systematic presentation of all his educational ideas will be attempted, regardless of how desirable these might be. However, with the two distinctions noted above as a point of reference, it will become the principal aims of this article, first, to examine the main features of Ryerson's moral thought (particularly, though not exclusively, as it is developed in writings preceding 1846), then to show briefly the logical connection between his moral principles and his "idea of education" (a phrase used here to denote especially the definition of education and the principles proposed in the *Report of 1846*), and, last, to situate Ryerson's ideas historically by suggesting probable sources of his moral views. It is hoped that this analysis will contribute to a greater appreciation of Ryerson, his concerns, and his efforts exerted towards the cause of nineteenth-century Canadian education.

THE MAIN FEATURES OF EGERTON RYERSON'S MORAL THOUGHT

Like many orthodox English divines of the eighteenth century, Egerton Ryerson maintained the view that a moral theory, developed solely on rational foundations, is not sufficient in itself to justify and produce moral conduct. Thus, he made the claim that moral theory becomes a viable norm for human conduct only when it is integrated in and grounded on the all-encompassing truths of Christianity.[6] In the same editorial, Ryerson goes on to distinguish between two schools of thought on moral instruction. The first is that of thinkers who expounded some version of natural law theory. According to Ryerson, this school of thought recommended a restricted Christian morality based on the nature and fitness of things, "its own excellence—its influence upon individuals and society—its adaptation to the constitution of human nature and the relations of men—as manifested to be the will of God."[7] Ryerson found this purely rationalistic means of deriving the will of God unacceptable and inadequate for providing the kind of moral knowledge required in order to achieve moral rectitude in conduct.

Ryerson recognized and adhered to a second school of thought which, he contended, went a step further than the first. It not only outlined what moral conduct involved, but also unveiled the very cause of man's immorality. In addition, it showed man the way to happiness by directing him to the Gospel of Jesus Christ and by predisposing him to the workings of the Holy Spirit, thus "effecting the destruction of the love of sin, and directing the whole affection of the soul to virtue and to God."[8] There is no doubt that Ryerson was of the opinion that little success could be achieved if moral instruction were restricted to the mere consideration of the prescriptions of reason. For Ryerson, success could be attained only when moral norms were treated in relation to a Christian anthropology. Indeed, it can be stated that for Ryerson (reiterating a commonly accepted view of early nineteenth-century Wesleyan Methodists) moral science is synonymous with a Christian morality in which the ultimate rule of moral obligation is not reason but the will of God as expressed in the Scriptures. "Christianity furnishes the only authoritative and unerring rule of moral action."[9] The reason for this is that the moral principles provided by Christianity are divinely revealed and their truth rests on the veracity of God himself, who is Truth.

It is this notion of moral science which served as the basis of Ryerson's later work entitled *First Lessons in Christian Morals; For Canadian Families and Schools*. In its preface, he writes:

"I have, at once, assumed the truth of Christianity and the
authority of the Holy Scriptures, and have endeavoured to present the subjects in harmony with the views of all religious
persuasion who receive the BIBLE as the rule of their faith
and practice, and Jesus Christ as the only foundation of their
hopes of eternal life."[10] Thus, he defined Christian morals as
"those principles and duties which Christianity teaches".[11]
Accordingly, in this book, he makes the will of God, as revealed
in the Scriptures, the only sure foundation of moral obligation.
"The rule or standard by which human conduct ought to be
regulated is undoubtedly the will of God."[12] That the will of
God be assigned such an absolute role to play in human affairs
is supported by Ryerson for the following reasons:

> *First,* Because the will of God is, and must be, like himself,
> holy, just and good. *Second*, Because He is the Creator and
> Upholder of the universe, and must, therefore, be the Supreme
> Governor. . . . *Third*, The will or command of God is the rule
> of conduct to the highest orders of intelligent beings. The
> inspired Psalmist says, 'Bless the Lord, ye his angels, that
> excel in strength, *that do his commandments*, hearkening unto
> the voice of his word'(Ps. 103. 20). Our Saviour said, 'My meat
> is to do the will of him that sent me, and to finish his work'
> (John: 4. 34).[13]

Consequently, Ryerson concluded, the same rule of conduct of
the angels and that which guided the actions of Jesus Christ
himself, should be the highest standard by which all human
conduct ought to be regulated.
   Ryerson succinctly defended this conception of moral science
in "Advantages of Religion to Society". In this article, he main-
tains explicitly that the predominant and underlying principle
of human desire and action, and that of the Christian religion,
is one and the same, namely, "man's preservation and happiness".[14] However, he argues that, although the end is the same,
there exists a wide difference with respect to the means and
objects by which this end is attained. According to Ryerson,
this difference can only be reconciled through revelation, which
teaches man "the true objects and the true way to happiness".[15]
It teaches man that his ultimate end consists of the "enjoyment of God—the adorable and only source of all excellence
and happiness"; and the sole means by which to attain this end
is obedience to the will of God, which, for Ryerson, is synon-

ymous with the evangelical expression "receiving Christ Jesus as our wisdom, and righteousness, and sanctification and redemption".[16]

In his early writings, Ryerson's emphasis was on the theological dimension of man's end. Hence, he described this end almost exclusively in relation to a future existence in the hereafter. Nevertheless, he also believed that man can attain a certain degree of happiness here on earth which provides man with a taste of what God has in store for him in the next life. This view reflects the Wesleyan Methodist doctrine of Christian perfection as a process and a transformation that can begin to occur in this life.

Ryerson outlined his conception of earthly happiness in his work *First Lessons in Christian Morals*. There, after refuting in bold scholastic fashion the different views maintaining that happiness consists in riches, pleasures of the senses, power, or exemption from labour and toil, he defines happiness as "a state of mind and heart irrespective of outward circumstances".[17] This idea of happiness included the following elements: moderation and reasonableness in life-expectations, the exercise of the social and benevolent affections, the exercise of both mental and bodily faculties, the formation and maintenance of good habits, good health, and a life lived in relation to God himself—"the primary and ever-living spring of true happiness is the Being of all possible perfections and blessedness; and the consciousness of His favour and conformity of heart to His image of righteousness and true holiness, must be the highest state of enjoyment, as well as of honour, to which any human being can be exalted in this life."[18]

Thus, it can be said that, for Ryerson, happiness (what he considered the good of man) is attainable in some measure during this life. This is possible through a Christian morality, which offers man both the means and the objects of realizing his end. This is a key notion in Ryerson's thought since it was in relation to what he conceived to be man's end (the "good") that he defined the role of education and the function of his system of public instruction. However, in elaborating an educational philosophy based on this conception of moral science, Ryerson made two basic assumptions which would find little support in today's pluralistic society: first, he assumed that all men needed Christianity as the means to true happiness; and, consequently, he assumed that any system of public instruction should be grounded on Christian principles.

The tenability of these two assumptions was further reinforced for Ryerson by his firm conviction and belief that only Christianity could fulfil the gigantic task of improving the human condition. Only Christianity recognized, what he believed to be, the essential nature of man as being that of a moral agent, that is, one possessing moral feelings and the faculty of conscience.[19] According to Ryerson, God has implanted man with the power to judge right from wrong, "has stamped upon him a *moral* condition and character, and invested him with a *moral agency* and responsibility".[20] It follows, Ryerson reasoned, that since it is man's moral feelings which are depraved, his moral condition and character which are debased, and his moral guilt and alienation which fill this world with much misery, the only valid solution to the human condition must be a moral one.[21]

Moreover, Ryerson contended that it is only Christianity that possesses the true view of man as a being far removed from his original state of righteousness and holiness, having an unrelenting propensity to evil, "blind, ignorant, wandering out of the way with his mind wholly estranged from God", his Creator.[22] Only Christianity teaches the transformation of man's will to do good works and persevere through the power of God's grace.[23] Only Christianity, through the Gospel of Jesus Christ, gives man access to this regenerative power.[24] In addition, he constantly reiterates in his early writings, it is the Gospel of Jesus Christ that provides man with a plethora of extraordinary means by which to strive towards perfection: "wisdom to instruct him, mercy to pardon, grace to sanctify, power to strengthen him,—enlightening his understanding, awakening his conscience, subduing his will, renewing his heart, regulating his passions, expanding his prospects and hopes to a far more exceeding and eternal weight of glory."[25]

Consequently, the ultimate solution to the human condition that Ryerson preached was none other than that of early nineteenth-century Wesleyan Methodism: the "Gospel of the grace of God, as the only means of regeneration and happiness to the world of mankind".[26] Ryerson described the goal of Wesleyan Methodism as the "salvation of sinners . . . to make men Christians,—Christians in heart and life, in temper, word and work,—Christians, such as the Bible describes, such as love God with all their hearts, and their fellow creatures of mankind as themselves."[27] This is the highest man can aim. Ryerson hoped that if the goal of Wesleyan Methodism were realized in practice all kinds of transformation would result over the face of the earth: every human soul would become the dwelling place of the Holy Ghost; Christianity would be professed throughout the world; halls of legislation would become places of "sweet counsel"; all educational institutions would become infused with wisdom from above; all forms and creations of art would be dedicated to the glory and honour of God; God would become the centre and focus of all the sciences; and love would constitute the "sacred and inviolable bond of nations".[28]

A CHRISTIAN MORAL PHILOSOPHY, THE BASIS OF EGERTON RYERSON'S IDEA OF EDUCATION

It becomes quite clear from a consideration of Part One of the *Report of 1846* that Ryerson's idea of education was essentially the result of a discursive process by which he determined, in the light of his moral principles, what he thought to be the best educational philosophy that should rest as the foundation of the system of public instruction in Canada West. The numerous sources which he documented in the report simply gave form to educational insights that he already possessed. A brief examination of the idea of education that Ryerson systematically elaborated in the report and which he treated in some of his earlier writings will strongly confirm this thesis.

In the report, Ryerson presents the following definition of education: "By education, I mean not the mere acquisition of certain arts, or of certain branches of knowledge, but that instruction and discipline which qualify and dispose the subjects of it for their appropriate duties and employments of life, as Christians, as persons of business, and also as members of the civil community in which they live."[29] Hence, in the report, Ryerson viewed education as a means of qualifying and disposing the educand to a life of Christian citizenship. In other words, he understood education as a means of realizing the end for which man was created.

This practical role of education is also accentuated by Ryerson in a lecture he delivered in 1841 at the opening conference of the Upper Canada Academy (soon to be known as Victoria College). His text begins with the following observations on the nature of education:

Education is the elevation of a thinking animal into a reasoning, active, beneficent and happy intelligence; the culture and ripening of the seeds of reason, judgment, will, and the affections, into a teeming harvest of virtue, enterprise, honour, usefulness and happiness. The object of education, rightly understood is, first, to make youth good men—good members of universal society; secondly, to fit them for usefulness to that particular society of which they constitute an integral part—to form their principles and habits—to develop their talents and dispositions in such a way, as will be most serviceable to the institutions under which they live, and to the interests of the country in which they dwell.[30]

So as to leave no doubt in his audience's mind about his view of education, he goes on to make it very explicit that, for him, "Education is a means to an end; and ought, throughout the process of its acquirement, to be connected with the end proposed," namely, to make "youth good men", and to make them diligent, useful members of civil society.[31] By this Ryerson certainly intended that education should assume as its fundamental task the realization of a society in which all of its members reached or were in the process of attaining a certain degree of physical, intellectual, and moral maturity. Within Ryerson's scheme of things, this implied making education a handmaiden to the Christian religion by sharing the grandiose object of helping man attain happiness in this life and the next.

It was from this conception of education that Ryerson derived the five educational principles of his system of public instruction which he elaborated in his report.

Ryerson's first principle of his system is that it should be universal, particularly "in respect to the poorest classes".[32] He argues that since the rich can easily look after their educational needs, the poor are the ones that deserve special attention by government.[33] For this reason, he adopted the position that no educational system should be restricted to any particular class, but should include the whole of society, especially the poor.[34]

Ryerson developed a more cogent argument for universal education where he grounds the right of every human being to an education on the will of God, who decreed, through the Scriptures, that it is not good for man to be without knowledge. He writes: "The Divine Author of mind has said, 'for the soul to be without knowledge is not good' [Prov. 19: 2].[35] This

inspired apothegm is of universal application—from the mon-
arch to the peasant—and clearly recognizes the *right* and *duty*
of educating the mass of the people;—yes, of imparting knowledge to every human soul."[36] If it is God's will that every human
being have knowledge as a prerequisite for the attainment of
happiness, therefore, he concludes: "Education . . . should be
indiscriminately and universally diffused among the people; it
is the equal right and interest of all classes; and is sanctioned
by the authority and example of God Himself" (referring here
to God's example in educating the Hebrew nation through his
divine revelations).[37] Consequently, it should be the duty of government to make provision for the education of all classes of
society.[38] "It is the divine birthright of every national being
whose intellectual powers are capable of intellectual development, and by the obligations of imperative duty should every
parent, guardian and ruler, secure it to the rising generation.
Thus is one generation depending upon another."[39]

Hence, the principle of universal education is ultimately
based on God's will, which intends it as a help to man in his
quest for happiness. Succinctly phrased, Ryerson's argument
in support of this principle runs as follows: since knowledge
is an essential requirement for the attainment of human happiness, and since education is a means of acquiring this
knowledge, therefore, it is also God's will that all men have
the opportunity of reaping the fruits of education, as a way of
securing for themselves happiness in this world and the next.

The second principle of Ryerson's system of education is that
it should be practical. He was firmly convinced that any form
of education which is primarily concerned with the diffusion
of knowledge without any consideration for its application
does not deserve to be called education.[40]

Ryerson's basic argument in support of this second principle
is based on the premise that the very end of man's being is
practical.[41] For this reason, he argues, "every step, and every
branch of our moral, intellectual, and physical culture should
harmonize with the design of our existence."[42] However, in
adhering to this view, he also wished to underline his contention that man is a special kind of agent, one that is called to a
life of virtue, usefulness, and happiness.[43] Now, since education
is a means to these goals, it follows that "the end of every part
of . . . education is *practice*."[44] This was Ryerson's way of stating that the fundamental object of education is the well-being,
prosperity, and happiness of man; that a sound education is

a vehicle for preparing the educand for a life of virtue, usefulness, and happiness, the same key elements of his Christian moral philosophy.

No other principle expresses any better the affinity between Ryerson's conception of moral science and his educational philosophy than his third principle, that a system of education should be religious and moral. By "religion and morality" he meant the general system of truth and morals taught in the Scriptures.[45] Thus, steadfast to his belief that neither the social happiness nor the welfare of man could be procured through either ideological or institutional changes or by any other secular means, Ryerson placed Christianity and its morals at the base of his system of education. "Christianity is the foundation and only efficient *cause* of every valuable improvement in the condition of men—that the inestimable blessings of education . . . are among the effects of Christianity . . . ."[46] He believed that only a Christian education is consonant with the objects of a truly practical system of public instruction—one that would infallibly direct the educand towards the attainment of happiness in this life and the next.

A system of education should acquaint the educand with the several branches of elementary knowledge, among which reading (which included spelling), writing, and arithmetic held first place for Ryerson.[47] By this fourth principle, Ryerson understood that if a system of education is to be practical, then it should acquaint the educand with those elementary branches of knowledge which will enable him to grow in virtue and wisdom and thus become an asset not only to himself but also to his fellow man. In the *Report of 1846*, he also lists the following subjects under this principle: grammar, geography, linear drawing, music, history, natural history, natural philosophy, agriculture, human physiology and mental philosophy, civil government, political economy, and Christian biblical instruction.[48]

He painstakingly points out that all these subjects are practical, that is, they are intended for man, a practical being, to help him realize the end for which he was created. He writes: "Every topic is *practical*—connected with the objects, duties, relations and interests of common life. The object of education is to prepare men for their duties, and the preparation and disciplining of the mind for the performance of them. What the child needs in the world he should doubtless be taught in school."[49]

The above passage provides a key to a deeper understanding of this fourth principle. Since, for Ryerson, the object of education is to prepare men for the performance of their duties in life, it follows that any system of public instruction should acquaint the educand with those branches of fundamental knowledge which he requires in order to fulfil this object. Moreover, viewed in this light, the principle goes beyond the list of subjects noted by Ryerson in the report, and applies to all curriculum planning at all levels of education. In other words, Ryerson's fourth principle is not restricted to the level of elementary public instruction, but equally applies to secondary and post-secondary curriculum planning.

Thus, it can be maintained that in proposing this fourth principle Ryerson had a twofold purpose. First, he wished to isolate those branches of elementary knowledge which would best equip the educand for a virtuous and useful life. Second, in proposing this fourth principle he intended to postulate the broader principle that a system of education, regardless of the level, should prepare the educand for a moral and fruitful existence by instructing him in that body of knowledge with which he should be acquainted for the realization of these ends. As is the case with the other principles of his system, the underlying premise of his fourth principle is the end of man as set forth in his moral philosophy.

His fifth and last educational principle is that a system of public instruction should promote the development of both the intellectual and physical powers of man.[50] This principle certainly reflects the conception of earthly happiness that Ryerson outlined in *First Lessons in Christian Morals*, in which he describes happiness as consisting, at least in part, in the exercise of both the mental and bodily faculties. Moreover, this principle is also logically related to Ryerson's moral philosophy by way of the end education shares with the latter, namely, the happiness of man in this life and the next. Thus, it can be argued that since man is a being who possesses both intellectual and physical powers whose actualization is necessary for the realization of his end, it follows that it is one of the objects of education to develop and cultivate these powers, not only with a view to promoting man's earthly happiness, but also with a view to assisting man in achieving happiness in the hereafter.

Hence, it is evident that the main features of Ryerson's moral thought permeate and constitute the logical roots of his idea of education. They were to his educational principles, as he would have put it, "what the tree is to the fruit—what the fountain is to the streams which proceed from it—what the sun, in the solar system, is to the planets which revolve around it."[51] As such, they could also be viewed as having constituted the underlying practical philosophy of the system of education for which Ryerson was the chief superintendent for over thirty years.

THE PROBABLE HISTORICAL SOURCES OF EGERTON RYERSON'S MORAL THOUGHT

As has been maintained above, Ryerson espoused a Christian moral philosophy in which the ultimate rule of moral obligation is the will of God as expressed in divine revelation. Considering that, as a young man, he had enthusiastically read *The Principles of Moral and Political Philosophy* by William Paley and later, as principal of Victoria College, included this work as the standard text on the subject, it would not be unreasonable to suppose that Ryerson derived his conception of moral science from Paley.[52] This supposition is further sustained by Ryerson's numerous references to Paley in many of his *Christian Guardian* editorials and other published discourses. Like Ryerson, Paley did view the Scriptures, the expression of God's will to man, as the basis of moral obligation. He thus defined virtue as "the doing good to mankind in obedience to the will of God, and for the sake of everlasting happiness",[53] a definition which he borrowed from Edmund Law.[54] However, unlike Ryerson, Paley also contended that the Scriptures are not specific enough on all moral questions, but provide only general rules for the direction of man's conduct.[55] Indeed, he maintained that the Scriptures do not teach any new rules which man, by his use of reason, could not discover by himself.[56] Eventually, for Paley, the Scriptures do not so much reveal a body of norms about human conduct as they provide the necessary motivation for moral action. It is only in this sense that the Scriptures are the basis of moral obligation which Paley described as "an inducement of sufficient strength, and resulting, in some way, from the command of another", with everlasting happiness promised to those who do God's will being the motive, and the command being that of God.[57] Now, since the Scriptures are too general in their prescriptions and their value lies primarily in providing a strong inducement to moral conduct, Paley resorted to "the light of nature" as a means of determining God's will.[58] He understood "the light of nature" to mean reason enquiring into the "tendency of an action to promote or diminish the general happiness" of mankind which God wills, an end that is confirmed by the beneficial purposes for which all the contrivances of nature are designed.[59] Thus, what may appear at first a possible source of Ryerson's conception of morality turns out to be, upon closer examination, its antithesis, subordinating divine revelation to reason, a view quite in line with the Lockean tradition, but certainly not acceptable to the Wesleyan Methodism of Ryerson's day. A good case could be made, as is done elsewhere, that Ryerson's thought in general does tend towards utilitarianism and that this tendency finds its roots in Paley's ideas.[60] However, in Ryerson's thought, Paley's utilitarianism is screened, though somewhat unsuccessfully, by Wesleyan-Methodist teachings in which the Scriptures are not merely an inducement to moral action, but have a predominantly positive role to play in man's existence. The Scriptures, for Ryerson and early nineteenth-century Wesleyan Methodism, are not simply a motivational force for conditioning man to live a moral life, but constitute the only source of true moral knowledge and the means by which man can achieve this end.

If Paley was not his source, from where did Ryerson derive his conception of moral science? In view of the fact that Ryerson was a staunch Wesleyan Methodist, a probable answer can be given to this important question. It can be strongly suggested that a major source of Ryerson's moral ideas was none other than Richard Watson, a leading spokesman of early nineteenth-century Wesleyan Methodism whose *magnum opus*, *Theological Institutes*, was required reading for every aspirant to the Methodist ministry at that time. A brief examination of Watson's views, that he set forth in this work, reveals a close affinity between his ideas and those of Ryerson.

Watson elaborated his conception of a Christian moral philosophy in "Part Third" of his *Institutes*. There he contends that in the Scriptures, and especially in the Gospel, one can find the most complete and perfect expression of the moral law. For this reason he maintained, as Ryerson did, that, "All attempts to teach morals, independent of Christianity, even by those who receive it as a Divine revelation, must, notwithstanding the great names which have sanctioned the practice, be considered as a mischievous tendency . . . ."[61] In support of his view, Watson gives several reasons. First of all, to disassociate Christianity from the teaching of morals is an implicit admission that man, through reason alone, can discover, "the full duty of man toward God and toward his fellow creatures".[62] Secondly, this disassociation would imply a deficiency in Christian morals.[63] Moreover, since, for Watson, most moral systems owe much of what is of value in them to Christianity, a substitution of a secular system for Christian morals constituted a displacement of the perfect with the imperfect.[64] In addition, Watson insists in his *Institutes*, that the teaching of morals without reference to Christianity diverts the attention from the law of God, with its sanctions, as the basis of moral obligation, to what, he considered, inferior considerations such as "fitness, beauty, general interest, or the natural authority of truth, which are all matters of opinion."[65] However, a more practical reason for deploring the separation of morals from Christianity in teaching, was his fear that this would result in a completely different process by which morality among men would be promoted from the means prescribed by God himself in the Gospel.[66] He feared morality would be promoted by other purely secular and rational means. "They [those promoting morality apart from Christianity] lay down the rule of conduct, and recommend it from its excellence *per se*, or its influence upon individuals, and upon society, or perhaps because it is manifested to be the will of the Supreme Being, indicated from the constitution of human nature, and the relations of men."[67] On the other hand, Watson stressed that Christianity does more for man. In the same spirit exhibited by Ryerson in treating this topic, Watson writes:

> But Christianity rigidly connects its doctrines with its morals. Its doctrine of man's moral weakness is made use of to lead him to distrust his own sufficiency. Its doctrine of the atonement shows at once the infinite evil of sin, and encourages men to seek deliverance from its power. Its doctrine of regeneration by the influence of the Holy Spirit, implies the entire destruction of the love of evil, and the direction of the whole affection of the soul to universal virtue. Its doctrine of prayer opens to man a fellowship with God invigorating to every virtue. The example of Christ, the imitation of which is made obligatory upon us, is in itself a moral system of action, and in principle; and the whole revelation of a future judgment brings the whole weight of the control of future rewards and

punishments to bear upon the motives and actions of men, and is the source of that fear of offending God, which is the constant guard of virtue when human motives would in a multitude of cases avail nothing.[68]

Thus, for Watson, God's sanctions do have a role to play in sustaining the moral order. However, it would seem that this role is secondary in relation to the redemptive dimension to which Christianity raises morality and in relation to the certitude of moral norms it provides through revelation. Unquestionably, the latter also represented Ryerson's view of the matter.

As was the case for Ryerson, Watson maintained that the ultimate basis of moral obligation is the will of God. But unlike Paley, who based moral obligation on the will of God as collected from expediency, Watson held that the will of God is the source of moral obligation in virtue of the relation man, as creature, bears to God, as his Creator.[69] Apart from the specific commands God may issue to man, man's obligation to obey Him rests, according to Watson, primarily on the relation of dependence that man, as created, stands in in relation to God as Creator. He writes to this effect: "If a creature can have no existence, nor any power or faculty independently of him; and if it have no right to employ its faculties in an independent manner, the right to rule its conduct must rest with the Creator alone; and from this results the obligation of the creature to obey."[70] In other words, God's revelation and commands presuppose this relation of dependence between the creature and the Creator. Man should obey because he is essentially a creature, a being created by God, who, in his goodness, cannot but will "what is upon the whole best for his creatures".[71] In refuting Paley's position, Watson contended that making the will of God as collected from expediency the basis of moral obligation leaves the whole question to be determined by mere opinion as to whether "an action be upon the whole good; and gives a rule which would be with difficulty applied to some cases, and is scarcely at all applicable to many others, which may be supposed."[72]

That Ryerson took Richard Watson's criticism of utilitarianism seriously is not evident in his early writings. However, a look at his later work, *First Lessons in Christian Morals*, discloses a critique of utilitarianism which is quite similar to that of Watson. There he writes:

From this connexion between bad actions and bad consequences, may be inferred the will of God that we should avoid
such actions; and from the good consequences following many
good actions, may be inferred the will of God that we should
perform such actions. Such is the teaching of natural religion;
but how uncertain, inefficient and feeble is the voice of such
teaching? What parent would leave his children to learn his
will and their duty from observing the consequences of their
conduct? What government would leave its ambassador at any
foreign court to infer his duty from his knowledge of the
character and views of the government that sent him, or from
considering the consequences of his acts?[73]

In the light of the above considerations, two conclusions can
be drawn. First of all, William Paley did not influence Ryerson's
moral thought as greatly as one would be led to believe from
a superficial reading of Ryerson's writings. Secondly, it would
seem highly probable that a major source of Ryerson's moral
ideas was the author of the *Theological Institutes*, Richard
Watson.

If that is correct, how is one to explain Ryerson's extensive
usage of Paley's ideas in many of his writings? Moreover, how
is one to interpret his inclusion at Victoria College of Paley's
work on moral and political philosophy as the standard text
in this field?

In reply to the first question, it may be stated that, lacking
any formal training in philosophy, Ryerson failed to use his
sources critically. A careful reading of Paley's work would have
disclosed to Ryerson that the moral principle of utility under-
lies all of Paley's thought, and especially his political philosophy
to which Ryerson was particularly drawn with respect to some
of its aspects.[74] Consequently, the same criticism that both he
and Watson level against Paley's principle of utility applies
equally to all of Paley's ideas. It would appear that Ryerson
did not realize this connection. His failure to do so caused him,
in several places throughout his writings, to run together ideas
which stemmed respectively from irreconcilable premises.

Ryerson's inclusion of Paley's work on moral and political
philosophy in the curriculum of Victoria College can be explained by two other probable reasons. First, Paley's work was,
during the first half of the nineteenth century, a standard text
in this field at Cambridge and other universities.[75] This must
have surely impressed Ryerson. Second, Paley designed the

presentation of his material with a view to exciting the curiosity of the student in examining ethical questions.[76] This pedagogical aspect of Paley's work must also have motivated Ryerson to use it as a standard text.

Closely connected with Ryerson's moral thought is his view of the importance of Christianity in all human affairs. In his discussion of this theme, Ryerson does not document any specific authors. This view of Christianity, being so popular with divines in seventeenth- and eighteenth-century England, became quite often the central theme of many a sermon. Consequently, he could have derived many of his ideas on this question from a multiplicity of sources. However, a few authors could be suggested here as possible historical sources on the basis that Ryerson was acquainted with their works and did, on different occasions, avail himself of their ideas.

In discussing the importance of Christianity to all human endeavours, Ryerson wished to underline its beneficial influence on man's life and destiny. This same theme can be found expressed in Richard Watson's writings and, of course, it pervades all the sermons of John Wesley.[77] It is also the object of a discourse by Archbishop John Tillotson on "The Advantages of Religion to Societies", an essay with which Ryerson was definitely acquainted.[78] Another writer with whom Ryerson was acquainted, Dr. Hugh Blair, a professor of rhetoric and belles lettres at the University of Edinburgh, developed the same theme in a sermon entitled "The Importance of Religious Knowledge to Mankind".[79] There he discusses the benefits to mankind of religious knowledge in general, and of Christianity in particular. He writes:

> The doctrine of Christianity is most adverse to all tyranny and oppression, but highly favourable to the interest of good government among men. It represses the spirit of licentiousness and sedition. It inculcates the duty of subordination to lawful superiors. It requires us *to fear God, to honour the king, and not to meddle with them that are given to chance.* Religious knowledge forwards all useful and ornamental improvements in society. Experience shows that, in proportion as it diffuses its light, learning flourishes, and liberal arts are cultivated and advanced. Just conceptions of religion promote a full and manly spirit. They lead men to think for themselves; to form their principles upon fair enquiry, and not to resign their conscience to the dictates of men.[80]

These same ideas are reflected in a sermon entitled "The Influence of Christianity on Civil Society", by the Right Reverend George Horne, whose sermons Ryerson read.[81] Lastly, the theme runs through Thomas Chalmers, whose writings upon practical divinity Ryerson admired as a young man.[82]

In discussing doctrinal questions, in particular his conception of man, one would naturally have expected Ryerson, an ardent Wesleyan Methodist, to refer occasionally to John Wesley's *Explanatory Notes Upon the New Testament* or to his *Standard Sermons*, which, in 1763, Wesley made the Methodist doctrinal standards.[83] That was certainly not the case. The only significant reference Ryerson made to Wesley is in his *Christian Guardian* editorial introducing a series of articles on sanctification.[84] There he inserts several short excerpts from one of Wesley's sermons on Christian perfection, wherein Wesley contrasts Adamic with pre-Adamic man, and points to the transformation that takes place to the latter as a result of the redemptive merits of Jesus Christ.[85]

The only source which he documents in his treatment of the nature of man in his sermon on "Wesleyan Methodism in Upper Canada" is the book, *Methodist Doctrines and Rules*.[86] However, his conception of man could also have been nurtured by other sources. Richard Watson's *Theological Institutes*, which includes a systematic and soteriological analysis of the nature of man could be proposed as one such source.[87] Likewise, some of the works of Dr. Adam Clarke, another leading spokesman of early nineteenth-century Wesleyan Methodism, could be noted as probable sources. In particular, special mention should be made of Clarke's short work entitled "Clavis Biblica", which consists of a list, with a brief commentary, of the principles of the Christian religion; and, of course, his voluminous commentary on the Bible, which contains a similar list of principles as one of its appendices.[88] Finally, Ryerson includes an excerpt from Laurence Kean's defence of Methodism in a work entitled *A Plain and Positive Refutation of Reverend Samuel Pelton's Unjust and Unfounded Charges*, in which the author clearly enumerates and explains the fundamental doctrines of Methodism.[89] Thus, there was no scarcity of sources of which Ryerson could have availed himself with respect to this question. And he was certainly acquainted with the ones listed above.

Viewed in relation to the probable historical sources of his moral thought, Ryerson's idea of education can be described as the offspring of a Christian practical philosophy whose end is the salvation of all mankind. The application of this philosophy to the field of education could not have been too difficult a task for Ryerson since his conception of education was not only shared by many eminent educators of his day, but also by the authors who have been designated in this article as probable sources of his thought.

Ryerson's educational philosophy also reflects a widespread movement within Protestant Christianity, and within Wesleyan Methodism in particular, to oppose and retard the secularizing trends of the times that were rapidly changing the attitudes and values of eighteenth- and nineteenth-century man. This concern is certainly evident in the apologetic literature of the period and, of course, finds expression in the scripturally based, authoritarian, practical philosophy expounded by such writers as John Wesley, Richard Watson, and Adam Clarke. Seen in this light, Ryerson's idea of education constituted an essential part of this Christian crusade designed to counteract the rationalistic tendencies of the age and thus to promote Christianity as the only efficient solution to the human condition.

NOTES

1. Egerton Ryerson, *Report on a System of Public Elementary Instruction* (Toronto, 1847), p. vi. Hereafter cited as *Report of 1846*.
2. Carl Becker, *The Heavenly City of the Eighteenth-Century Philosophers* (New Haven, 1932), pp. 72–73.
3. Aristotle, *Nicomachean Ethics*, Book I, Chapter 3.
4. The terms "roots" and "sources" are used interchangeably throughout this article.
5. Albert Fiorino, "The Philosophical Roots of Egerton Ryerson's Idea of Education as Elaborated in His Writings Preceding and Including the Report of 1846" (PHD thesis, University of Toronto, 1975), pp. 54–76.
6. Egerton Ryerson, editorial in the *Christian Guardian*, 18 January, 1832, p. 116, c. 3.
7. Ibid.
8. Ibid.
9. Ibid.
10. Egerton Ryerson, *First Lessons in Christian Morals; For Canadian Families and Schools* (Toronto, 1871), p. iii.
11. Ibid., p. 9.
12. Ibid., p. 60.
13. Ibid., p. 60–61.
14. Egerton Ryerson, "Advantages of Religion to Society", an editorial in the *Christian Guardian*, 16 July 1834, p. 142, c. 3.
15. Ibid.
16. Ibid.
17. Ryerson, *First Lessons in Christian Morals*, p. 90.
18. Ibid., p. 93.
19. Egerton Ryerson, "Wesleyan Methodism in Upper Canada", a sermon preached before the Conference of Ministers of the

Wesleyan-Methodist Church in Canada, in Toronto, 18 June 1837, p. 2.

20. Ibid.
21. Ibid.
22. Ibid., p. 16.
23. Ibid.
24. Ibid.
25. Ibid.
26. Ibid., p. 2.
27. Ibid., p. 3.
28. Ibid., p. 3–4.
29. Ryerson, *Report of 1846*, p. 9.
30. Egerton Ryerson, "The Kind of Education which Canadian Youths Require; and Hints to Them for Its Attainment", Victoria University Archives, 1841, p. 50b.
31. Ibid., p. 50d.
32. Ryerson, *Report of 1846*, p. 20.
33. Ibid.
34. Ibid.
35. Cf. Adam Clarke's rendition of the same proverb in his work *The Holy Bible. With a Commentary and Critical Notes* (6 vols.; New York, 1854), III: 755, c. 1.
36. Egerton Ryerson, "Education of the People—Upper Canada Academy", an editorial in the *Christian Guardian*, 7 May 1834, p. 102, c. 3.
37. Ibid.
38. Ibid.
39. Ibid.
40. Ryerson, *Report of 1846*, p. 20.
41. Ibid., p. 21.
42. Ibid.
43. Egerton Ryerson, "The Principal's Inaugural Address", written on the nature and advantages of an English and liberal education, and delivered at the opening of Victoria College, Toronto, in 1842, p. 15.
44. Ibid.
45. Ryerson, *Report of 1846*, p. 22.
46. Egerton Ryerson, "Only Means of Improving Mankind", an editorial in the *Christian Guardian*,

13 March 1830, p. 130, c. 3.
47. Ryerson, *Report of 1846*, p. 63.
48. Ibid., pp. 63–148.
49. Ibid., p. 145.
50. Ibid., p. 52.
51. Ryerson, "Only Means of Improving Mankind", p. 130, c. 3.
52. See the places indicated in the following works by Ryerson in support of this supposition: *The Story of My Life*, ed. J. George Hodgins (Toronto, 1883), p. 26; *Canadian Methodism. Its Epochs and Characteristics* (Toronto, 1882), p. 315. See also the *Christian Guardian*, 6 May 1840, p. 109, c. 1, where the inclusion of Paley's works as standard texts at Victoria College is noted.
53. William Paley, *The Principles of Moral and Political Philosophy* (New York, 1867), p. 26.
54. Edmund Law, "On Morality and Religion", prefixed to his translation of William King's *Essay on the Origin of Evil*, fifth ed. (London, 1781), p. liv.
55. Ibid., pp. 35–36.
56. Ibid., pp. 13–14. See also "Evidences: A View of the Evidences of Christianity", in Paley's *Works*, new ed. (1 vol.; Philadelphia, 1857), pp. 329*ff*.
57. Ibid., p. 34.
58. Ibid., p. 37.
59. Ibid. To this effect he writes: "therefore . . . God wills and wishes the happiness of his creatures. And this conclusion being once established, we are at liberty to go on with the rule built upon it; namely, 'that the method of coming at the will of God concerning any action, by the light of nature, is to inquire into the tendency of that action to promote or diminish the general happiness.'"
60. Fiorino, "Philosophical Roots of Ryerson", pp. 222–25, 240–44.
61. Richard Watson, *Theological*

Institutes, ed. J. M'Clintock (2 vols.; New York, 1851), I: 473.

62. Ibid.

63. Ibid.

64. Ibid.

65. Ibid.

66. Ibid., pp. 473–74.

67. Ibid.

68. Ibid.

69. Ibid., p. 477.

70. Ibid.

71. Ibid.

72. Ibid.

73. Ryerson, *First Lessons in Christian Morals*, pp. 62–63.

74. Fiorino, "Philosophical Roots of Ryerson", pp. 120–24, for an examination of Ryerson's dependence on Paley's ideas in developing his position on religious establishments.

75. J. D. Morell, *An Historical and Critical View of the Speculative Philosophy of Europe in the Nineteenth Century* (New York, 1853), p. 267; see also M. L. Clarke, *Paley: Evidences for the Man* (Toronto, 1974), pp. 127ff.

76. Paley, *Moral and Political Philosophy*, p. v., wherein Paley describes his pedagogical approach.

77. Watson, *Theological Institutes*, p. 474. See also id., "The Influence of Revealed Truth Upon a Nation", in his *Sermons and Sketches of Sermons* (2 vols.; New York, 1845), I: 473–81.

78. John Tillotson, "The Advantages of Religion to Societies", in his *Works* (10 vols.; Edinburgh, 1772), I: 70–81. This sermon is the basis of Ryerson's article bearing almost exactly the same title in the *Christian Guardian*, 16 July 1834, p. 142. (See n. 14.)

79. Hugh Blair, "The Importance of Religious Knowledge to Mankind", in his *Sermons* (5 vols., new ed.; London, 1818), I: 397–426. See Ryerson, "The Princi-

pal's Inaugural Address", p. 11, as a confirmation of Ryerson's acquaintance with Blair's writings.

80. Ibid., p. 401.

81. George Horne, "The Influence of Christianity on Civil Society", in his *Discourses* (3 vols.; London, 1824), III: 193–213. Ryerson makes special reference to this work on his discourse "Civil Government: The Late Conspiracy", (Toronto, 1838), p. 6.

82. For example see Thomas Chalmers, "On the Advantages of Christian Knowledge to the Lower Orders of Society", in his *Sermons and Discourses* (2 vols.; New York, 1848), III: 340–44. See Ryerson, *The Story of My Life*, p. 42, for an acknowledgment of Ryerson's admiration of Chalmers' writings.

83. John Wesley, *The Journal of the Rev. John Wesley*, ed. Nehemiah Curnock (8 vols.; London, 1910), VIII: 335–41, wherein may be found the Model Deed drafted in 1763 by Wesley, stipulating these works as the doctrinal standards of Methodism.

84. Ryerson, "Editorial", in the *Christian Guardian*, 30 January 1830, p. 85, c. 2–c. 3.

85. Ibid. The excerpts are taken from Wesley's Sermon LXXVI, "On Perfection", in *The Works* (London, 1872), VI: 411–23.

86. Ryerson, "Wesleyan Methodism in Upper Canada", p. 16.

87. Watson, *Theological Institutes*, I: 3–87.

88. Adam Clarke, "Clavis Biblica", in *The Preacher's Manual*, which also includes "Letter to a Methodist Preacher", and four other discourses by Thomas Coke (New York, n.d.), pp. 56–67; id., *The Holy Bible*. VI: 1068–70.

89. See the *Christian Guardian*, 3 June 1832, p. 121, c. 1–c. 4.

Egerton Ryerson and the School as an Agent of Political Socialization

NEIL McDONALD

The way in which people acquire political orientations has been the subject of considerable research in recent years. The vast inventory on political socialization, dating particularly from 1959 with the publication of Herbert Hyman's *Political Socialization*,[1] is ample proof of academic interest in this area of study. Basic to these studies is the belief that political behaviour is learned. Historically, this belief has long been held by both seekers and holders of political power. The minds of youth have always been viewed as a key to political loyalty and social stability. As Jack Dennis has recently pointed out, "A standard general hypothesis in this connection is that the earlier the person adopts a given set of political orientations, the less likely it is that these orientations will be eroded later in his life."[2] The regime that leaves this process to chance risks social and political chaos. According to David Easton and Robert Hess, "no system can attain or remain in a condition of integration unless it succeeds in developing among its members a body of shared knowledge about political matters as well as a set of shared political values and attitudes."[3] Two basic assumptions, therefore, emerge from the literature. First, that children can early acquire basic knowledge, values, and attitudes which influence their future behaviour as citizens and political actors; and second, all political regimes accept pre-adult political education and learning as a necessary prerequisite to their survival.

In this area of research there is considerable emphasis on socializing agents. A distinction is made between primary agents, namely the family and peer group, and, secondary agents, among which the school is assigned high priority. The former agents are classified as primary because of their "highly personalized and relatively unstructured" relationships, while the latter represent "more formal and impersonal" relationships.[4] It is believed that family and peer group have greater influence than the school in inculcating and changing beliefs and attitudes. However, it is also recognized that the difficulties inherent in bringing about change in beliefs and behaviour through manipulation and control of primary agents are nearly insurmountable. As a consequence, secondary agents, such as educational institutions and mass media, are more attractive to individuals or groups seeking to control or manipulate political loyalties and values.[5] Secondary agents, in a sense, are used to counter what are often viewed as the negative influences of primary agents.

This writer contends that these basic assumptions and beliefs concerning the political socialization of future citizens were an integral part of the thinking of early nineteenth-century educators. The writings, addresses, and activities of Egerton Ryerson, examined in the historical context of his times, serve as a useful focus to investigate this contention. The following, therefore, is an examination of Ryerson's belief in the public school as an effective agent of political socialization, and a consideration of the implications of this belief in its application.

The late 1830s and 1840s in The Canadas were years of severe social, economic, and political stress. Ryerson was no mere observer of these conflicts, but was often deeply immersed in them. Becoming convinced that mass support for the established political system was in fast decline, as people became increasingly alienated from their rulers, he advocated special measures to encourage loyalty to properly constituted authority. An editorial that followed in the aftermath of the rebellions of 1837 and 1838, and his direct involvement in the constitutional crisis precipitated by Governor Metcalfe in 1844, provide two significant but typical examples of Ryerson's early thinking on these matters.

In 1838, five years after he had abandoned the reform movement, Ryerson wrote a long editorial in the *Christian Guardian*. Intended as a statement of editorial policy, it was, in effect, a revealing personal statement of his political beliefs. He claimed that in "civil matters" he could not remain "neutral" as an editor, for the compelling reasons that, "I am a man, am a British subject and a professing Christian, and represent a British community."[6] Recent events had made it abundantly clear to him that contemporary decisions were crucial to the future development of the colonies. The task of rebuilding the "foundation of our government" was to begin in earnest now that "the last whisper of rebellion is to be silenced in the land."[7] In his view these foundations must be built on the unmistakable assumption that The Canadas were to remain part of the British Empire. With clear reference to the various preferences of the reformers for democratic and republican institutions, or responsible government, he wrote that decisions with respect to the form of government must not be rationalized on the grounds of "abstract political theory" but "in reference to the well-being of the country in connection with Great Britain."[8] Categorically declaring his opposition to "the introduction of any new and untried theories of government", he claimed to be on firm ground in his orthodoxy because it was based upon, "the established constitution of the country, as expounded in royal despatches, and illustrated by the usage of the British Parliament, British courts of justice and the common law of England."[9] Significantly, he expressed his regret that the province had not already developed "an efficient system of general education" which could be harnessed to other agencies to assist "in the noble, statesmanlike and divine work of raising up an elevated, intelligent, and moral population."[10]

A few years later Ryerson became a central figure in the crisis precipitated by Governor Metcalfe's refusal to consult his Executive Council prior to making appointments to government posts. Emotions were raised to such a pitch over this issue that Ryerson expressed the fear to his brother John, that "he could see nothing in prospect but a renewal of the scenes of 1837 and 1838, only on a larger scale."[11] Ryerson's subsequent support for Metcalfe unquestionably helped the Governor survive the 1844 crisis. The overwhelming victory of the government at the polls at least indicated that the patriotic cry of loyalty and order dinned into Upper Canadian ears by successive governors and their supporters still evoked sufficient emotion to rally the faithful around the flag. This assurance must have given no small pleasure to men of Ryerson's persuasion. The knowledge that loyalty had to be stirred up and brought to the surface at times of crisis, however, made the occasional victory less sweet. It was disturbing for the loyalist to be reminded that people were not fixed in their convictions to the point that they could be relied on to choose always the safe and tried path to political stability. Recent events were painful reminders of the precarious instability of the people's views. During this period Ryerson wrote to Metcalfe: "In the present crisis, the Government must of course be first placed upon a strong foundation, and then must the youthful mind of Canada be instructed and moulded in the way I have had the honour of stating to your Excellency, if this country is long to remain an appendage to the British Crown. The former without the latter will only be a partial and temporary remedy."[12] Again, Ryerson unequivocally declared his belief that the future stability of the state depended in no small measure on the success or failure of government efforts to mould and influence the minds of the youth. The obvious remedy was a system of mass education since he equated civil disorder and disloyalty with ignorance. He wrote that "the one was the legitimate parent of the other,"[13] and that "the increase of ignorance is the evening twilight of civil freedom."[14] It is not surprising, then, that he should consider formal education an effective antidote to political and social disintegration. Such a plan as he envisaged was destined to make Canada West "the brightest gem in the Crown of her Britannic Majesty".[15] Moreover, Ryerson had long argued that there was a certain urgency to the task.[16] As indicated above, he was keenly aware that the foundations being laid in the 1840s would most likely become permanent. There was little time to lose if the "sentiments and feelings of the population" were to be guided in the proper direction. Those who presently had the opportunity "to establish our institutions" and the "system or form of government" would not be afforded a second chance.[17] It would appear that the rebellions of 1837 and 1838, and the crisis of 1844 merely underlined his conviction about the absolute necessity of this task, as well as a determination to play some part in it.

The tenor of these comments hints at the reason for the education post having such strong appeal to Ryerson. It was perhaps best expressed by a contemporary Methodist clergyman and noted author, John Carroll, who wrote: "The Doctor's ambition has not lain in the direction of coveting office, but . . . in the direction of influencing public opinion on those questions and measures the carrying of which he deemed to be for the good of the church and the country; and it was when an office furthered these objects that he showed any care to obtain it."[18] Ryerson believed the education office could be used as an effective instrument to help abolish the differences and jealousies among the peoples of the new united province, while at the same time promoting agreement on those "great principles and interests" which all should share in common.[19] He also believed that this task, although enormous, could be accomplished in time by writing, speaking, and strictly controlling books and literature made available to the public at large, but particularly to youth. Moreover, he was persuaded that the leisure time afforded by the "not onerous duties" of office could be used with even greater profit in the interests of the state: "to prepare publications calculated to teach the people at large to appreciate, upon high moral and social considerations, the institutions established amongst them; and to furnish, from time to time, such expositions of great principles and measures of the administration as would secure the proper appreciation and support of them on the part of the people at large."[20] Clearly, from the outset, he saw the office of superintendent in a political context extending far beyond the parameters of his commission to structure a system of public education. The position, at least from this perspective, handily complemented the much needed task of creating and strengthening loyalty to Crown and country in the mass of the population by exploiting to the limit the ordinary channels of propaganda; a task not beyond the proven ability of a speaker, writer, and polemicist of Ryerson's talent and experience. To his own satisfaction he was convinced that his writings and personal influence had already demonstrated the power to manipulate and control public opinion. He described himself to Governor Sydenham, for example, as "a sort of break-water" whose vigilance and sound advice had checked the destructive excesses of party conflict.[21] Prior to the Metcalfe affair he told his brother that the only hope to assure the decision in favour of the Crown lay in the intervention of "some enlightening, healing agency".[22] From a somewhat pretentious letter he wrote a few days later to the Governor's civil secretary, J. M. Higginson, there is little doubt that he perceived himself as that agency. It read, in part:

> It has been alleged by both my friends and enemies, that . . . I have not hesitated to face in succession the united press of each of the two ultra-parties in Canada, and succeeded in each instance to reduce them from a large majority to a small minority. . . . My life having been bound up with the two great principles of constitutional monarchy on the one hand,

and civil and religious principles in Canada on the other, all who really desire such a government, without regard to the domination of a party . . . seem to think the Governor-General will succeed if I have resolved to espouse his government.[23]

If he saw himself as one who could define and shape political attitudes and beliefs among the wider public, *a fortiori*, his expectations and confidence were greatly increased with regard to the political socialization of the province's youth.

After Ryerson's views were made known to a "much impressed and pleased" Metcalfe, the Governor expressed the wish that Ryerson "could be induced to give them public effect."[24] Metcalfe's difficulties with his Council and subsequent election delayed Ryerson's formal appointment to the education post. To Ryerson, however, this delay merely proved the need for the appointment. Every such civil disturbance added force to his position, as was so clearly evident in correspondence prompted by his first educational tour of Europe, and his subsequent report to the Legislature. The latter detailed the system of education he considered appropriate to the social and political development of Upper Canada, but in the former he revealed to Metcalfe's secretary his criteria for accepting or rejecting particular aspects of the various systems he observed. Predictably, these criteria strongly reflect the concerns already raised in this chapter. An interpretation of these observations and conclusions, however, becomes more meaningful and significant when examined, albeit briefly, against the background of contemporary Europe.

The Europe that Ryerson travelled in 1845 was still coping with, what Hobsbawn has called, the "dual revolution—the French Revolution of 1789 and the contemporaneous [British] Industrial Revolution".[25] The political, economic, and social changes generated by these two revolutions were heralded as the beginning of a new age of progress, in that "human life faces a prospect of material improvement to equal the advance of man's control over the forces of nature."[26] A close analysis[27] of the social and political structure of Europe during the 1840s, however, reveals that the shibboleth of "progress" must be interpreted in a narrow and special sense. The traditional social pyramid had not become inverted; forming the massive solid base, as always, was the peasant. Slave trading was even more lucrative, and serfdom, even if on the decline, had by no means disappeared. At the top one still found, in large measure, the old landed aristocracy, except in countries of direct peasant revolution like France. The only change was in their source of wealth, from property to industrial investment; hardly a substantive change of any consequence to those at the other end of the scale. A new bulge in the pyramid might be noted by the sudden increase of the "middle classes" and those who imitated their standards of living and style of life. The working class, of course, grew more quickly than all the others, but even their growth was negligible compared to the total population, and even more significant, as a class they were as yet unorganized.

The change that had occurred in the political structure of Europe is particularly relevant. Monarchy was still predominant but it was monarchy with a difference. By the 1840s most of the European kingdoms could now be described as constitutional monarchies. Much of the change could be directly attributed to the 1830 revolution which "introduced moderate liberal middle class constitutions—anti-democratic but equally plainly anti-aristocratic—in the chief states of Western Europe."[28] The triumph of the moderates entailed compromise along the way, which was "imposed by the fear of a mass revolution which could go beyond moderate middle class aspirations."[29] The notable example was the fall of the Bourbons in France. In July 1830, Charles x, gravely underestimating the political temper of the country, attempted a coup reminiscent of the days of the *ancien régime*. This attempt to return France to absolutism was immediately and successfully resisted at the barricades. The country was not declared a republic because the insurgents, unsure of their strength, considered it inopportune. Instead, a compromise was reached when Talleyrand proposed the Duke of Orleans as a candidate for the throne. Louis Philippe represented a compromise of the monarchy and the revolution.[30] Hans Kohn writes: ". . . Louis Philippe mounted the throne, no longer king of France by the grace of God, but king of the French by the grace of God and the will of the people. . . . With Louis Philippe the reign of the upper-middle class began."[31] Georges Rudé notes that few reigns "have left so ignominious a mark on the historical record",[32] a view shared by most historians.[33] Louis Philippe's historical record includes a bloody suppression of working-class revolt, rigid obstinacy in resisting reform, usurpation of the Bourbon throne, betrayal of liberal hopes, and patronage of the *haute bourgeoisie.* Thus, his name was anathema to conservative, liberal, and socialist alike. Alfred Cobban, with devastating sarcasm, writes that the regime "has been so lacking in principles that it could only be known by the name of the month of its founding, the July Monarchy."[34]

The ascendancy of the middle-class radicals over democratic radicalism had put the forces of the Ultra-Conservatives and royalists on the defensive. Radical democracy, however, did not disappear as a force for social change. Jacksonian democracy represented this force in the United States and, in the central European state of Switzerland, democratic forces "slowly gained the upper hand and in 1848 transformed the loose confederacy into a federated modern state."[35] Kohn draws an instructive comparison:

> Whereas in Germany liberalism and democracy were defeated under the leadership of Prussia, the Swiss Germans who formed the large majority of the Swiss nation established in their country democracy on firm foundations and devised a federal constitution under which the French and Italian minorities lived in complete freedom and equality with the German majority.[36]

European middle-class liberals were not ready to accept a system of government advocated, in the main, by left-wing revolutionaries. Ironically, it would in time become the characteristic political framework of capitalism, "defended as such against the onslaughts of the very people who were in the 1840s advocating it."[37]

The most eloquent and telling recorded insight that Ryerson had into these European social and political affairs is revealed in a long letter he wrote to Metcalfe's secretary, Higginson. He clearly and unequivocally states, once again, his concerns and objectives. He reaffirms his belief that in a country such as Canada,

> . . . where conservative elements are comparatively few and feeble the fundamental principles of the System of Public education are of the gravest importance.
>
> My leading idea has been—as I have more than once explained it to His Excellency Sir Charles Metcalfe and yourself —not only to impart to the public mind the greatest amount of useful knowledge based upon, and interwoven throughout with sound Christian principles, but to render the Educational

system, in its various ramifications and applications, the indirect but powerful instrument of British Constitutional Government.[38]

His conversations with numerous educators and public officials, and observations of several educational and political systems encouraged Ryerson to think that these objectives were possible. For instance, he can scarcely hide his enthusiasm when he discovered that the French example had particular relevance for Canada. Their compulsive drive to "go ahead of every other Nation" prompted him to designate them "the Yankees of Europe".[39] But the most instructive aspect of development in France was of a political nature. He informed Higginson that although the July Revolution of 1830 was based on "Republican principles", the country was subsequently ruled by a monarchy under Louis Philippe in more absolute terms than England. This "extraordinary anomaly", he reported, was only possible with the total support of the French system of education, from the university down to the primary school. The implication for his "leading idea" was not lost on Ryerson: "The problem which Louis Philippe is solving, of governing a restless people upon even popular principles and yet strengthening the Throne, suggests much of great importance in respect to Canada."[40] The reference to the Canadian scene aside, Ryerson's attitude towards the notorious Orleanist regime is quite revealing, especially viewed in the light of recent interpretations of Louis Philippe's reign.[41]

In this same communication with Higginson an analysis of the political mood of Europe throws more light on Ryerson's concept of education as a medium to influence and control the political thinking and conduct of citizens. He describes, with obvious approval, the manner in which European monarchs responded to "the spread of popular, and even democratic principles" which were widely espoused by their peoples following the American and French revolutions. Those monarchs, according to Ryerson, instinctively saw the eventual loss of their thrones unless they were able to propose and institute some compromise form of monarchial government with greater appeal to the people than that offered by outright republicanism. In his view, the monarchy responded with alacrity and practically met with universal success.

He was happy to report that democracy, popular opinion to the contrary, was on the wane in Europe and constitutional monarchy was in the ascendancy. Even a casual perusal of the countries of central and western Europe, he claimed, would support his contention. Prussia, Bavaria, Austria, Holland, Belgium, and France provided supportive examples. Switzerland, on the other hand, amply illustrated the folly of republicanism: "Republican Switzerland—enlightened and intellectual as it is—is at present practically the worst government, and the most distracted Country in Europe."[42] Again, this is a particularly instructive remark when viewed in the context of recent interpretations of European history.[43] Swiss democracy at this time enjoyed high prestige among liberals. It was not until after Ryerson's visit that the radical liberals began their move to strengthen the central government and suppress the reactionary forces in the federated Catholic cantons.[44] From the perspective of a Canadian in 1845, one would think that the Swiss model where the Germans, French, and Italians were attempting, with some success, to work out a *modus vivendi*, would have had greater appeal.

Another reason for the success of the European monarchs, reported Ryerson, was the personal interest and command they assumed for those various aspects of government that particularly advanced the interests of their subjects. He noted how they had "placed themselves at the head of the Commerce, the Agricultural, the Manufactures, and the Education of their respective Kingdoms".[45] In this way they have "increased the security and strength of their own power" without "relying upon arms".[46] It is interesting, too, to observe that he was referring particularly, in this instance, to Prussia, France, and Russia.

The attention European monarchs gave to the broader demands and needs of society led Ryerson to observe that England, under the masterful hand of Sir Robert Peel, was also moving in that direction, although the country had not undergone a violent revolution. It was true that the movement was hindered by vested interests and "long acknowledged rights", but, "Not a question of commerce, or finance, or law, or social or intellectual advancement, or association, or foreign, or domestic policy, that can be mooted by the sharpest man in Parliament but Sir Robert gives evidence that it has not escaped his attention. . . ."[47] Ryerson's point, of course, is that a country need not turn to democracy or become a republic to achieve social, political, or economic advancement. Indeed, such advancement was more likely to come under an enlightened constitutional monarchy. This conviction, reinforced by his European experience, prompted him to stress again his particular bias and position within the context of Canadian politics. He claimed that he early perceived that the moderate William Draper would eventually emerge in the same position as Peel in England. "It was the conviction that such was the substratum of his [Draper's] views of policy which had induced me, in past years, to show him more respect and consideration than I have any other Canadian politician . . . ."[48] Ryerson saw that Draper, despite his "Compact" contacts, was not cast in the mould of the old-line Tory with whom he had done battle for so many years in Upper Canada.

With the examples of the European constitutional monarchies, and of Peel and Draper, before him, Ryerson pledged that in his position within the provincial governmental structure he, too, would strive "to be in advance of my adversaries in every thing that may minister to the improvement, and gratification, and occupation of the popular mind."[49] In other words, he would accept, as a personal challenge, the task of making a moderate view appear more attractive than radical political change or reform, towards either the extreme right or left. With this in mind, he noted that his personal observations with respect to the mere external features of the various school systems became, in reality, of peripheral importance. The most vital aim of his tour, therefore, was to evaluate, critically, the various systems vis-à-vis their effect on society. Through intensive reading, observation, and personal conversations it was essential that he learn "the peculiar connection of the whole system with, and its influence upon, the thinking and feelings of the public mind, and the various parts of its Governmental machinery, combining to produce the general results, and the connection of these with other branches of public policy. . . ."[50] The immense appeal that the European systems had for Ryerson in this context is undeniable as is so strongly suggested by even a casual reading of his correspondence and report. He saw in those systems the means to inculcate the political ideas he considered necessary, not only to preserve a distinctly British and Canadian presence in North America, but also a powerful instrument to guarantee an orderly and stable society capable of containing any widespread acceptance of radical democratic ideas. An unusual combination of delight and distress in making this discovery is illustrated by his scathing reaction to the obvious plagiarism of American educators who had so freely adopted European ideas. He charged that the Americans were flagrantly dishonest in failing to credit fully the foundation of their system to the Europeans from whom they borrowed whatever is "most attractive and valuable" in their schools. The same criticism applies to their writings in this field: "The American writers present their works to the public as original, except acknowledging in the preface, that several useful thoughts have been suggested by such and such, or by some German Authors; when the only thing properly American is the translation and the omission of European local, and the substition of American local, applications."[51] Canadians, too, could make this adjustment. According to Ryerson, it was only necessary to select the favoured attributes from European systems and adapt them to Canadian circumstances. In this way it would be possible to confer "some of the same advantages upon the Canadian public, without having such works modified and poisoned by the incorporation of American republicanism."[52]

It was with delight, too, that Ryerson discovered as simply untrue the American claim to have developed original pedagogical methods and materials through experimentation under republican institutions. Those "original" ideas, he charged, were copied intact from European countries "of which the Americans considered themselves much in advance".[53] He concluded, on the other hand, that Canada under a constitutional monarchial type of government could more easily select from the European experiences and "thus have them Canadian and not American".[54]

On one other essential point he noted implications for Canada. In their adaptation from the European system in his view, the Americans had not seen fit to adopt a most important element. They had "wholly severed" the educational system "from the supreme, and, to a great extent, from the state Executive Government".[55] The system, in large measure, was left to the people to control. In Europe, however, every link of the educational system, "is connected with the Executive Government, and is its most potent agent of influence and power over the popular mind."[56] The implications of the European approach for Canada West were enormous, in Ryerson's opinion, because an educational system under government control and guidance could compensate for the small numbers and weak principles of the "conservative elements" in the province.[57]

These observations notwithstanding, Ryerson undoubtedly

recognized the inevitability of change in the old political order; in fact he welcomed and encouraged the change brought about by the Union Act. However, the rebellions of 1837 and 1838 and the subsequent political instability, as evidenced daily in the political life of the united province, were as unsettling as they were potentially explosive. As noted above, for example, he feared that the crisis of 1844 would lead to the excesses of the previous decade. It was inevitable too, that in the new order the masses were destined to play an important role in shaping it. With this in mind he defined his role as chief educator, and it was from this perspective that he examined the European system of education.

With respect to the education appointment, it is important to observe that Ryerson accepted it "upon the understanding that the administration of the school system should constitute a distinct non-political department."[58] There were two principal but interrelated reasons for making this condition a *sine qua non* of his acceptance. First, there was Ryerson's profound antipathy towards party politics which he considered at the root of Canadian political, social, and economic problems. "Party spirit," he claimed, "has been the bane and curse of this country for many years past. It has neither eyes, nor ears, nor principles, nor reason."[59] Claiming "the public good" as the "one chief end of civil government"[60] he believed this end transcended the politics of party with which "no good man should be identified".[61] Indeed, since civil government was of divine origin, the true Christian has an obligation to see that it is not "perverted to party or sectional purposes".[62] The passion of the party only served to obscure and embitter rather than enlighten and unify. Politics, therefore, should operate at the level of principle rather than party. Second, his well-known efforts to prevent the triumph of either extreme party were hardly calculated to win their favour, rather he effectively alienated himself from a position of strength except with the then flaccid moderate Tories led by his friend, William Draper. His brother John warned, for example, that should Baldwin return to power "the *stool* would be kicked" from under him.[63] Later events would prove there were grounds for this view, although the attempts were not successful as Baldwin, himself a moderate, eventually came to support Ryerson. Thus, he realized fully that if the office was not removed beyond the reach of party politics, not only would it be subject to the caprice of party and his term of office as the "Governor's man" short-lived, but even if he did survive, his ambition to use the appointment as a vehicle to reduce the level of disruptive partisan politics would be aborted from the outset. He could accept it on other conditions but it was clearly at the risk of reducing his control, a risk to which he was implacably opposed. Indeed, for this reason he refused outright a seat on the Executive Council.[64]

Ryerson's designs, however, to mould the youth of the country according to a specific pattern did not go undetected or unchallenged by the "ultra" parties. As Gidney[65] has recently argued, one of the main concerns of the anti-Ryerson forces was the potential they saw in a highly centralized school system for control over people's minds. The Reformers, particularly, were concerned that without local control over such matters as textbooks and teacher certification there was little guarantee that a person of Ryerson's known political leanings would resist the temptation to use this power for political purposes. Given his abandonment of the reform movement in 1835, and subsequent political support of those whom Reformers considered the chief stumbling blocks to responsible government, the governors and their executives, there was little willingness to accept the superintendent's recommendations without subjecting them to close scrutiny. The issue was well expressed by Thomas MacQueen, editor of the Reform *Huron Signal*, who wrote: "when we consider the influence which education exerts on the opinion and character of mankind and consider the influence which the Chief Superintendent is to exercise over the education of the youth of Canada, we feel bound to declare such a power should not be entrusted to Egerton Ryerson nor to any other man. The truth is, that the office of Chief Superintendent should be abolished."[66] The supporters of local control, therefore, argued that the acceptance of their position was a powerful guarantee against the inevitable risk that central control could grant an individual power to influence "opinion and character" in a particular direction. Indeed, the cries of "Prussianism", "despotism", and "czarism" that were hurled at Ryerson from his first days as superintendent had their roots in this concern for the political implications of his centralized system of education for the future of the country. Ryerson's insistence on uniformity was quickly equated to political conformity. In the endless struggle waged for political advantage among the sharply divided political groups of Canada West in the mid-1840s, the mere suggestion that a person as politically tainted as Egerton Ryerson should be given absolute control over such a powerfully perceived instrument for shaping the attitudes of future citizens, was sufficient to arouse sustained widespread opposition. It is no surprise that this opposition reacted most strongly to the suggestion that uniformity prevail throughout the system. To most opponents, the definition of the "public good" to come from the new superintendent would not likely accommodate their diverse interests.

As indicated above, the weight of evidence demonstrating Ryerson's belief in the power of the school to mould character and shape attitudes is overwhelming; indeed, in his view, society had a "duty" to establish schools for these purposes. Society could no more leave to mere chance the behavioural outcomes of the educational experience than the academic. "The training of the moral part of man cannot . . . be neglected without inflicting the greatest possible injury both upon the individual and upon society. It is our duty to augment the intellectual power of society to the utmost; but it is equally our duty to give that power a right direction."[67] Implicit in this statement was his solid conviction that all behaviour was learned. Acting on this conviction, therefore, he attempted to articulate for the schools a set of political attitudes that complemented desirable social attitudes and values supportive of a stable political system. Taken in the context of Ryerson's numerous public addresses and writings concerning individual liberty and the self-directing value of education, it is perhaps surprising to find frequent references to the need to control and directly influence individual behaviour, but in his view, this stance was perfectly consistent with his general philosophy. The lack of perceived inconsistency in this matter is exemplified in his attitude towards social class.

According to Ryerson, next to legislation and government, social progress depended on the harmonious and sympathetic relations existing among the various classes. Indeed, he characterized it as a "law" that "the interests of the whole society are binding upon each member of it."[68] By this he meant that each member of society, no matter what their occupation or class, must contribute to "the one great end of individual and public happiness".[69] The various classes should not be "rivals, but fellow-helpers, not aliens, but members of the same household, and parts of the same body".[70] He declared, "All arbitrary class distinctions, professional exclusiveness, and hostile factions are, then, so many impediments to the social advancement of the country; and as they prevail to a less or greater extent, will the energies of society for the common welfare be crippled and paralyzed."[71]

It was not an argument for the elimination of a class structure, which he considered divinely ordained, but for the elimination or reduction of class conflict. In a society where the visibility of class distinctions and separation were clear and absolute there always loomed the danger of open conflict with ominous potential for serious social strife. Ryerson intended that the common school should play an important part in reducing these traditional class tensions. His solution would leave intact the hierarchical structure or ordering of society, but concentrate on values of the "lower orders".

Ryerson asked the people of property in Upper Canada to "place the poor man on a level with the rich man in the divinely ordained means of such instruction for his children as will *qualify* and dispose them for their duties in the social system."[72] Thus, it was planned to involve all classes in education by implementing that "great Principle of Universal Education", the property tax.[73] In this way "you open the School House door to every child in the land,"[74] thus making public education "free". The poor, the chief objects of this system, would neither be purposely excluded nor able to offer an excuse for exclusion. His approach was intended to encourage class harmony and lessen isolation in that children from all classes would attend the same school, as well as implant and nourish "the spirit of true patriotism by making each now feel that the welfare of the whole society is his welfare—that collective interests are first in order of importance and duty, and separate interests are second."[75] In return for their largesse the propertied classes were promised a stable and loyal citizenry, making the community a safer place in which to live and conduct business. Again, it must be emphasized, Ryerson was not concerned with altering the "divinely ordained" social order, but in the interests of "social progress" was concerned that the "lower orders" adopt the more acceptable and trustworthy values of the middle class. In effect, it was an attempt to convince the working classes that their interests were also those of the middle and upper classes, and that, as a collectivity, there was a "common" or "public good" towards which all must work. Divisiveness was destructive to this common goal. In practice, it was an attempt to impose a set of values on the working-class youth that were not particularly helpful for interpreting the social reality with which he was in contact. Indeed, it sought to gloss over the fact that the interests of this class were in conflict with those of the classes above them. As a result it was more likely that the working class would *accommodate* to the values of the higher classes. Since these values were imposed and not relevant to their experience, it was too much to expect that they actually *adopt* those values. Their acceptance of the social order was designed to give legitimacy to the dominant ideology, and not to increase feelings of political competence.

This strategy is common and recognized by political scientists. For example, David Easton has noted that when a political system is under stress and facing a decline in support, there are at least three important forms of response. Among them the less radical measure is to attempt "to instill in its members a high level of diffuse support in order that regardless of what happens the members will continue to be bound to it by strong ties of loyalty and affection."[76] To generate this support the means may entail "the positive encouragement of sentiments of legitimacy and compliance, the acceptance of a notion of the existence of a common good transcending the particular good of any particular individuals or groups, or the kindling of deep feelings of community."[77] In Ryerson's view a truly, "common" school would provide the means to generate support for the social and political system in the manner described by Easton. Further indication of his thinking in this regard is also evident in references to the provision of specialized training for an élite.

If youth is to be prepared "to fulfill aright the relations and duties in society assigned them in the order of Providence", Ryerson wrote, they will not contribute to the progress of society unless society assures that not only classical education or "high culture" is received by the few, but that an "appropriate culture" is received by all.[78] He recognized, however, that those in the former group, especially those who pursue their studies at university level, must be encouraged and supported because society needs those who have had their "mental faculties early disciplined", "tastes refined", and "views enlarged".[79] After all, this tried route had traditionally supplied Europe and America with its "ablest statesmen" and could only be neglected in Upper Canada with punity to the body polity. He was at pains to stress that he did not want to destroy, or even disturb, this proven route to the training of a solid, reliable cadre of leaders. His real interest was to provide the means and opportunity for the less fortunate to at least be exposed to and made to recognize the importance of the values of the more enlightened, even if the full appreciation and implication of this recognition is not wholly grasped. Without this "understanding" government of the masses remained at best a most difficult task. After all, Ryerson argued, "It is principles that make men; and it is virtue, not merely knowledge that gives strength to government and law, and security to freedom. The intellectual culture of the country, in all its degrees, varieties, and forms, should be conducted in harmony with this essential law of man's moral constitution, and this cardinal want of his social state."[80]

The great task of the school, then, was not only to direct intellectual behaviour, but also moral and social behaviour. The safety of the state depended on the "safe" citizen. The ideal state was one in which there was order, stability, and loyalty.[81] Order implied an hierarchical concept of authority as well as the absence of political and social chaos. Citizens knew their "places" in this state where issues were decided on a cold, rational basis by a ruling élite, rather than in the heated, emotional political arena of party divisiveness. Once political and social stability had been achieved, the passive but enlightened citizen, whose intellectual, moral, and physical faculties have been "educated" to recognize and to accept legitimate authority, could be relied on to give the social and political order a permanent measure of stability. Moreover, those same citizens could also be depended upon to be loyal to the state, especially in time of crisis. The school, of course, was ideally designed to contribute to this particular state of political and social equilibrium. Through the school, the public mind could be manipulated "in the right direction".[82]

A close examination of Ryerson's views, therefore, reveals significant implications for the intended orientation of political education in Upper Canada. From the outset, it was intended that schools support a political system about which there was to be no serious examination or questioning. As indicated earlier, the superintendent was "opposed to the introduction of new and untried theories of government".[83] The student was presented with a model of government and the task of the educator was to ensure its uncritical acceptance. Moreover, in spite of the rhetoric with respect to change, the emphasis in this approach to political education was on *passivity* rather than on the actual involvement of the citizen in political activities. Although Ryerson believed that, in the present state of Canadian party politics, a citizen did not need education, because "to be a mere passive tool in the machinery of party he will require to know no more than to do as his leaders or masters may dictate,"[84] paradoxically, the alternative he proposed also assigned the citizen a passive role in the political process.

He believed that change could only be effected if politics as practiced in Upper Canada could be purified. The school would become an antidote to counter the divisiveness and partisanship inflicted on the country by party rivalry. Indeed, it was this argument that became such a familiar theme in Ryerson's appeals to the public for support of public schools. "Every man of wealth and intelligence who stands aloof from the noble and patriotic work of promoting the education of the masses of his fellow-countryman, is so far their enemy and the enemy of his country."[85] By the "education of the masses" was meant their "intellectual and moral elevation" to a condition of virtue and refinement in order to render them less vulnerable to the unthinking, demagogic appeals of self-seeking politicians. By the same token, however, the masses (read labouring classes) would become more manageable for another group of masters, namely the educated élite. In this context Ryerson quoted approvingly the "enlightened" Anglican Archbishop of Dublin: "If the lower orders are to be the property, the slaves of their Governors . . . the more they are degraded toward the condition of brutes, the more likely they are to submit to tyranny. But if they are to be governed as rational beings, the more rational they are made the better subjects they will be of such a government."[86] The point being made is not that education will guarantee the "lower orders" some degree of input into government, but rather that education will make them better *subjects*.

In short, education for Ryerson, was a protective influence for society, that is, a form of social control. The economic and professional élites who refused to support these objectives were viewed as little less than traitors. After all, they were told that it was to their distinct advantage to help fashion a truly peaceful and united society. Those elements of society presently cast outside the pale due to their "ignorance and apathy" could easily be added to the human resources of the community. Surely, when the argument was reduced to these terms, all right thinking members of "the professional, the better educated and the wealthier classes"[87] were forced to acknowledge its validity.

The whole thrust was a corrective one as it was based on the assumption that contemporary developments in Canadian politics were straying far from the traditional direction appropriate to a British colony. The educator's deliberate task was to indoctrinate the student into the norms, values, and attitudes which complemented a "proper" view of government. Later, the schools were to serve as a guarantee or safeguard that the turmoil and confusion of the earlier period would not return. Schools were simply to serve the functions of the state. They were to assist in establishing a stable and loyal citizenry, and then aid the maintenance of the status quo.

For the summation and conclusion to the first part of his 1846 report, Ryerson quoted from the "appropriate and nervous language" of the *Westminster Review*. The quotation read in part: "The education required for the people is that which will give them the full command of every faculty of mind and body; . . . which in the social relations of life, and as connected with objects of legislation, will teach them the identity of the individual with the general interest. . . ."[88] He wished to generate diffuse support for the political system, defined in his own terms. As one of the means necessary to achieve this support he considered it essential, first, to encourage acceptance of the existence of a common good transcending the particular good of any individual or interest group. With the recognition that there was a public good to be preserved, the next step was to convince the populace that the preservation of a monarchial system of representative government was the citizens guarantee that the public good would be protected. Thus, it now becomes incumbent on all to encourage sentiments of legitimacy and compliance towards this view of government. To achieve this objective, of course, the role of education was essential to the political socialization of the province's youth.

Another obvious implication in this approach to political education is that the stability of the political system and the loyalty of its adherents depended in large part on the indifference and, indeed, deference of the citizenry. If the citizen was expected to show support for the political system it was in a passive fashion. The vote was certainly viewed as the most active form of participation in the political process. The emphasis, then, was on authority rather than on reason. The citizen was expected to accept rather than learn the means to change the system or to participate actively in it. Since Ryerson was strongly opposed to party politics, it was expected that he should discourage discussion of the practice of politics. The realities of conflict and disagreement in politics were to be avoided. He advanced a non-conflict view of politics where decisions were made on the basis of principle rather than self-interest or vested interest. In Ryerson's view of society, individual interests should be sacrificed if there was conflict with the public good.[89]

In many respects it was a naive, perhaps utopian, view to argue that politics would be purified by the simple act of mass education. Representative governments, Ryerson declared, should exist for the people, not vice versa, and if the people were "pure, intelligent, and enlightened"[90] might not politics also be in a similar state? The unscrupulous politician would not easily advance to power on the mere basis of partisan issues, sectional interests, or party labels. The "pure, intelligent, and enlightened" voting citizen, whether farmer, manufacturer, professional, tender, or mechanic, would make a more responsible decision based on reason rather than passion. Thus, governments could really be made responsive to the collective needs of its citizens:

> One chief design of a Monarchial system of Responsible Government is to stamp the sentiment and spirit of the public mind upon the administration, as well as legislation of the country, and to sever the collective acts of the country against the antagonistic or selfish acts of individuals or isolated sections. It makes the Executive Government not only the representative of the whole community in its actual composition, but also in the execution of every part of the law for the benefit of the community.[91]

The implication from this view would suggest that Ryerson believed government should receive its initial impulse from the grass roots. The ultimate source of authority for governmental decision-making should be firmly rooted in an educated citizenry. "It is one of our dearest and justly cherished tenets," he wrote, "that the people of Canada make their own laws."[92] However, when this pyramidal paradigm of the polity is compared to the working model that Ryerson presented to the public, both in the operations of his own department and the organization and structure of the school system, there is little resemblance to the ideal outlined above. In practice the pyramid was inverted. Ryerson believed in a hierarchical view of society in which input for political decisions came from the top. Authority was vested in government office by law, and the officeholder was entitled to seek advice and/or help in whichever direction he would decide, but there was no real obligation to seek such advice or help. The Council of Public Instruction of which Ryerson was an appointed chairman was a prime example. Members of the council, also appointed, were among the most highly educated in the formal sense in Upper Canada, yet there is little evidence that their advice was sought on a regular basis or that they had any influence in the decision-making process. The same applied to the schools. The teacher, student, and parent at the bottom were controlled by the superintendent, inspectors, boards (trustees), and principals, who enforced government and council regulations prescribing required training, the curriculum in great detail, working conditions, holidays, professional development, and, in the earlier years, personal conduct as well as teaching methods. The school system, in effect, reflected Ryerson's model of the political system—authority and acceptance. On the announcement of Ryerson's impending resignation, for example, the editor of *The Nation* was not untypical in making the case for a change to a minister of education. He wrote that, under Ryerson "there has been unity of administration with a vengeance, but there has not been responsibility. There has been practically an unchecked despotism, the evil effects of which, in more than one direction, have already begun to appear . . . . That [the Council] has had to contend with difficulties is plain from the outrageous violence of the Chief Superintendent's personal attacks on the colleagues who had differed from him on a public question."[93]

Although the public verdict of Ryerson's three decades of hegemony over Ontario's educational affairs was generally favourable, there were strong feelings that it had been achieved at the expense of public consultation, co-operation, and participation.[94] This would suggest that either the public educational system had failed to produce those "pure, enlightened, and intelligent" citizens from whom true representative government

was to seek direction, or Ryerson had indeed achieved his objectives in that direction was accepted from the top down. The
high-sounding rhetoric that earlier told of the manifest results
to flow from a publicly supported educational system was a
mere tool in his arsenal to get the system firmly established.

At a more personal level, too, Ryerson's office and activities
underlined his negative view of political life in Upper Canada.
The superintendency by personal preference, was an appointed
office, and remained so until his resignation. In this way he
removed education beyond direct party influence, but he also
obtained practically absolute control and authority over all
matters affecting public education. This open gesture of distrust towards politicians and parliamentary procedure was not
calculated to inspire confidence in the political system. Moreover, his rigid, authoritarian public manner and often bitter
public confrontations with those who challenged his decisions
or questioned his activities further heightened the public image
of the "despot", "dictator", and "Czar". Although the choice to
keep his office outside the political mainstream was consistent
with his view of party and practical politics in Upper Canada,
it was not a model for change *within* the political system. His
position was based on power and authority that was given
legitimacy by parliament, but his activities did not have to
undergo the public scrutiny to which other departments of
government were subjected. The distinct impression projected
by this arrangement is that the parliamentary process as represented by party was not the most desirable, effective, or indeed,
necessary, means to effect change in matters affecting public
policy. Parties or associations he argued, served useful legislative purposes only when they were motivated by a vital
"principle" such as free trade, the abolition of slavery, or
responsible government. The next most useful purpose was
that they self-destruct. "Free and independent men in the
Legislature, as in the country, are the best counterpoise to
faction, and the mainspring of a nation's progress and greatness."[95] It is not suggesting an anachronism by faulting Ryerson
for resisting the party system when it was barely emerging as
an organizing principle of parliamentary government, but, in
the context of this paper, there are several grounds for criticiz-
ing his stand. First, there is his arrogance. By adopting this
position he was effectively saying that criticism was destructive
of political activity. There were certain ideas, principles, and
policies that debate, delay, and compromise served as mere

obstructions in the way of "a nation's progress and greatness". Second, this concept was too utopian and idealistic. Given the human condition, there are very few issues indeed where goodness and truth are so self-evident that they command immediate and universal assent; clearly, public schooling was not one of them, notwithstanding Ryerson's rhetoric. Moreover, it represented a political state where lobbies, vested interests, conflicting opinions, and divided loyalties did not play a significant role in human affairs. Third, this view was more appropriate to a closed, hierarchical society than an open, democratic one. It was designed for a society in which a citizen was trained to know his proper "place", and to recognize and accept what is "right and good". It was not a society, again in spite of the rhetoric, in which the citizen was taught how to effect change or how to participate actively in the political process. Although he vigorously opposed the organization of government along party lines because it would mean the whole machinery of legislation would become "an engine to party",[96] he did not find it repugnant or contradictory to declare that his "leading idea" had been "to render the educational system, in its various ramifications and applications, the indirect but powerful instrument of British Constitutional Government."[97] By this double standard of application, it was considered a noble principle to manipulate the system, provided it was done for the right "principle", and the intention of the manipulator was to advance the "public good".

NOTES

1. Herbert Hyman, *Political Socialization: A Study in the Psychology of Political Behavior* (London, 1959).
2. Jack Dennis, *Socialization to Politics: A Reader* (Toronto, 1973), p. 13.
3. David Easton and Robert D. Hess, "Youth and the Political System", in Seymour M. Lipset and Leo Lowenthal, eds., *Culture and Social Character* (New York, 1961), p. 228.
4. Richard E. Dawson and Kenneth Prewitt, *Political Socialization* (Boston, 1969), p. 100.
5. Ibid., p. 101.
6. *Christian Guardian*, 11 July 1838.
7. Ibid.
8. Ibid.
9. Ibid.
10. Ibid.
11. Egerton Ryerson to John Ryerson, 3 April 1844, quoted in Egerton Ryerson, *The Story of My Life*, ed. J. George Hodgins (Toronto, 1883), p. 324.
12. Ryerson to Metcalfe, 7 March 1844, ibid., p. 320.
13. *Christian Guardian*, 21 November 1829.
14. Egerton Ryerson, "The Importance of Education to a Manufacturing and a Free People", *Journal of Education for Upper*

Canada I, No. 10 (October 1848), 291.

15. Egerton Ryerson, *Sir Charles Metcalfe Defended Against the Attacks of His Late Councillors* (Toronto, 1844), p. 7.

16. Ryerson to Sydenham, 4 April 1840, in C. B. Sissons, ed., *Egerton Ryerson: His Life and Letters* (2 vols.; Toronto, 1937–47), I: 537.

17. Ibid.

18. John Carroll, "Egerton Ryerson", *Canadian Methodist Magazine*, February 1874, p. 103.

19. Ryerson to T. W. Mulloch, 14 January 1842, quoted in Ryerson, *The Story of My Life*, p. 342.

20. Ibid., Sydenham's approval of Ryerson's plans is indicated by his desire to have Ryerson accept the post on passage of the bill. His untimely death, however, precluded any such appointment.

21. Ryerson to Sydenham, 4 April 1840, quoted in C. B. Sissons, *Egerton Ryerson* I: 539–41.

22. Egerton Ryerson to John Ryerson, 3 April 1844, quoted in Ryerson, *The Story of My Life*, p. 324.

23. Ryerson to Higginson, 12 April 1844, ibid., p. 326.

24. Ibid., p. 345.

25. E. J. Hobsbawn, *The Age of Revolution: Europe, 1789–1848* (London, 1962), p. xv. The analysis which follows leans heavily on this work.

26. Ibid., p. 299.

27. Ibid., Chapter 16, *passim*.

28. Ibid., p. 301.

29. Ibid., p. 302.

30. Hans Kohn, *Absolution and Democracy: Europe 1814–1852* (Toronto, 1965), p. 63.

31. Ibid.

32. Georges Rudé, *Debate on Europe, 1815–1852* (New York, 1972), p. 143.

33. Ibid.

34. Alfred Cobban, *A History of Modern France* (London, 1968), II: 129.

35. Kohn, *Absolution and Democracy*, p. 77.

36. Ibid.

37. Hobsbawn, *The Age of Revolution*, p. 302.

38. Ryerson to Higginson, 30 April 1845, in J. G. Hodgins, ed., *Documentary History of Education in Upper Canada, 1791–1876* (28 vols., Toronto, 1894–1910), V: 240.

39. Ibid., p. 239.

40. Ibid.

41. *Supra* notes 30 to 36.

42. Ryerson to Higginson, 30 April 1845, in Hodgins, *Documentary History* V: 239.

43. *Supra* notes 25 to 29.

44. Hajo Holborn, *The History of Modern Germany, 1840–1945* (New York, 1969), p. 47.

45. Ryerson to Higginson, 30 April 1845, in Hodgins, *Documentary History* V: 240.

46. Ibid.

47. Ibid.

48. Ibid. The comparison with Peel is not original. Draper had indeed often described himself as the Peel of The Canadas, a claim that gave some of his contemporaries more than a little amusement. On close examination, however, there is some basis for a comparison: their common dislike and distrust of parties; the attempt to travel the difficult middle path between Tory and Radical; and their unique positions within their respective administrations in that there were no obvious successors. See George Metcalfe, "Draper, Conservatism and Responsible Government in Canada, 1836–1847", *Canadian Historical Review* XLII, No. 4 (December 1961), 308–09.

49. Ibid.

50. Ibid., p. 241.
51. Ibid.
52. Ibid.
53. Ibid.
54. Ibid.
55. Ibid., p. 239.
56. Ibid.
57. Ibid.
58. J. G. Hodgins, "Sketch of the System of Public Elementary Instruction in Upper Canada", *Journal of Education* IV, No. 7 (July 1851), 104.
59. *Christian Guardian*, July 1838.
60. Ryerson, *Sir Charles Metcalfe Defended*, p. 7.
61. Ibid.
62. Ibid.
63. John Ryerson to Egerton Ryerson, 6 March 1844, quoted in Sissons, *Egerton Ryerson* I: 56.
64. Egerton Ryerson to John Ryerson, 3 April 1844, quoted in Ryerson, *The Story of My Life*, p. 324.
65. R. D. Gidney, "Centralization and Education: The Origins of an Ontario Tradition", *Journal of Canadian Studies* VII, No. 4, (November 1972), 33–48.
66. *Huron Signal*, 27 June 1850, quoted in ibid.
67. Egerton Ryerson, "A Lecture on the Social Advancement of Canada", *Journal of Education* II, No. 12 (December 1849), 184.
68. Ibid., p. 181.
69. Ibid.
70. Ibid.
71. Ibid.
72. Ibid. I, No. 1 (January 1848), 14.
73. Ibid. I, No. 2 (February 1848), 33.
74. Ibid. I, No. 1 (January 1848), 14.
75. Egerton Ryerson, "Address to the Inhabitants of Upper Canada", *Annual Report of 1848*, p. 37.
76. David Easton, *A Framework for Political Analysis* (Englewood

Cliffs, 1965) pp. 124–25.
77. Ibid., p. 125.
78. Ryerson, "A Lecture on the Social Advancement of Canada", p. 184.
79. Ibid., p. 183.
80. Ibid., p. 184.
81. Egerton Ryerson, "Report on a System of Public Elementary Instruction for Upper Canada", Hodgins, *Documentary History* VI: 200.
82. Ibid., p. 181.
83. *Christian Guardian*, 11 July 1838.
84. Ryerson, "The Importance of Education", p. 294.
85. Egerton Ryerson, "Duty of Public Men of all Classes in References to Common Schools", *Journal of Education* II, No. 5 (May 1849), 72.
86. Egerton Ryerson, "*Report on a System*", p. 146.
87. *Journal of Education* II, No. 10 (September 1849), 137.
88. Ibid., p. 195.
89. *Journal of Education* I, No. 1 (January 1848), 14; and I, No. 12 (February 1848), 38.
90. Ryerson, "The Importance of Education", p. 290.
91. *Journal of Education* I, No. 2 (February 1848), 38.
92. Ryerson, "The Importance of Education", p. 291.
93. *The Nation*, 27 August 1875, p. 402.
94. Ibid., 1 October 1875, p. 462.
95. Egerton Ryerson, "The New Canadian Dominion: Dangers and Duties of the People in Regard to their Government", (Toronto, 1867), pp. 14, 18.
96. Ibid., p. 14.
97. Ryerson to Higginson, 30 April 1845, Hodgins, *Documentary History* V: 240.

III Developing the System

The Professionalization of Teachers in the Mid-Nineteenth Century Upper Canada

JAMES LOVE

The Rebellion of 1837 provided a traumatic experience for conservative Upper Canadians, illustrating as it did not only the rifts present in their society, but the resulting potential for a political revolution based on American-style republicanism or even outright American intervention. From the obvious conclusion that a significant element in the population was disloyal, or, at best, neutral, an inference was drawn that social institutions, including the school, had failed to either assimilate American immigrants or produce a solid pro-British loyalty among non-Americans. Education reform for the next decade was focused around this lesson of 1837, and the centralizing trend which culminated in Egerton Ryerson's program of 1846 and 1847 was a direct result.

Most immediately, attention was given to the question of alien teachers in Upper Canadian schools. Newspaper editorials and reports to the government led Sir George Arthur to conclude that the disaffection revealed by the rebellion could be traced to a general lack of central direction and surveillance which had resulted in "the madness of allowing Americans to be the instructors of the Youth of the Country".[1]

Governmental response in the form of legisation resulted in the passage of an education Act in 1841 which included the provision that only British subjects could be certified as teachers,[2] a provision widely ignored.

In 1843, another Act was passed which placed teacher certification in the hands, not of trustees, as had previously been the case, but of provincially approved district and township superintendents of education.[3]

The creation of superintendents of education provided a mechanism by which detailed information on the quality of teaching could be provided the Education Office, and several of the superintendents became influential regarding policy-making, both through the conditions they reported and the recommendations they made for government action. During the period of Ryerson's administration as assistant superintendent (1846–50), particularly, this advice was used in policy-formation to a significant degree.

Certification was to be done using a standard form, but there was a delay in sending these to the districts, and Robert Murray, Ryerson's predecessor, recommended that the local superintendents grant interim certificates "in what form they think best", making certain however, that these specify the branches which the person receiving the certificate was qualified to teach.[4] The emphasis on the teacher's possession of a specialized body of knowledge is clear. Certificates from either township or district superintendents were equally binding and valid, but if an appeal was made by a teacher against a township superintendent's decision, the district superintendent could overrule it. The certification power was clarified by an Education Department statement entitled, *Alien Teachers and the 1843 Act:*

> Under the *present Act* a certificate from the Old Commissioners cannot be considered valid, the County or Township Superintendents being the only person authorized to grant certificates of qualifications to Teachers. From among the individuals so qualified, the Trustees are at liberty to select a Teacher for their district, to whom, and to no other person can they legally order the payment of the School Fund.[5]

The weak element in this apparently strong position was that the school grant was so low that trustees could, and often did, hire teachers who were willing to teach without it, and thus avoid the certification regulations. This became a special problem in relation to alien teachers.

A general feeling continued to exist that such teachers, particularly Americans, were a "real and present" danger from their potentially seditious influence on children. Even if neutral in outlook, they were certainly not likely to foster a respect for British institutions or encourage Canadian loyalty. Legislation was vague enough to be open to different interpretations, and this resulted in a controversy between 1843 and 1846.

It may be argued that the Education Department generated the debate over the legality of employing aliens. Murray replied to a request for clarification from Hamilton Hunter, the district superintendent of education in Toronto, that, "There is considerable difficulty in the case of aliens, but from the provisions of the new School Act, and from the arguments used in the House of Assembly during the progress of the Bill. . . , I am inclined to think that they should not on that account be excluded."[6] Shortly thereafter he wrote to another superintendent that since the Act of 1843 stated that the school fund was to be payable "in accordance with the intention and Spirit of the School Act of 1841, but that Act expressly excluded Aliens as Teachers, I am therefore of opinion that they are not strictly entitled to a Share of the fund for 1843." Despite this opinion, he advised that the matter be left largely to the discretion of the township superintendents.[7]

Several local superintendents apparently took the position that, given any option, they would certify Americans. Whether this was a matter of availability or sympathy is difficult to detect. In the Niagara District, for example, where there was a large American-born element in the population, as well as proximity to the border, the district superintendent, Jacob Keefer, made a deliberate policy of certifying aliens. The Act of 1843 stated that no alien could be licensed after January 1, 1846, so Keefer issued a public "Notice" that any such who desired a certificate should apply to his office before that date. Once granted, a certificate was valid until revoked, so Keefer was able to create a "pool" of legally qualified Americans in his district. Keefer's successor in office, Dexter D'Everardo, affirmed the policy by issuing a public statement to the effect that all general certificates of qualification granted by his predecessor would be valid unless "annulled or otherwise revoked".[8] Despite complaints to Murray, this procedure was upheld by an opinion of the Attorney General. Murray, however, expressed his opinion on the decision in a letter to Rev. H. Bosworth, superintendent of the Brock District:

> The impolicy of continuing the practice of employing Aliens to instruct the Youth of our Country was as apparent, I have reason to believe, to the Legislature, on the occasion of getting up the School Bill, as it has long been to a majority of the people of the Province. Persons of this description have often been engaged to teach school by Trustees for the sole reason that they could be hired at the lower rate than others, and thus the best interests of the rising generation in a thousand instances have been sacrificed, for the sake of saving some few dollars in the course of a year.[9]

Murray added that this policy had also excluded qualified British subjects from teaching, and recommended that the prohibition be acted upon, as, he claimed, there were enough properly qualified teachers to fill the positions required.

THE CAMPAIGN FOR NORMAL SCHOOLS

The normal school became advocated as an integral part of a new general education program. If consistent political and social values and attitudes, as well as "useful" knowledge, were to be taught to children, this must be done by competent teachers. Such teachers must, therefore, be trained in methodology by a state institution. The aim was to produce a standardized curriculum to be taught by trained professional pedagogues, using graded textbooks and uniform methods. By the same means, teaching would become a respected profession, so gaining public acceptance of a state-controlled education system. Earlier attempts to encourage teachers to adopt professional qualifications and ethics on their own initiative were seen to have failed.

The major frustration facing those who, like Murray, had wished to improve teachers' status had been not only the attitude of trustees but also of the teachers themselves. This is revealed in a letter written by Murray to a teacher in Vaughan Township[10] who had complained that the local trustees refused to set the amount of salary they would pay. "I can see no good ground of complaint against the Trustees or Commissioners for refusing to guarantee a Stipulated Salary. . ." he said. "True the law authorized them to do so, but there were and still are, many difficulties in the way, and if they can find Teachers who will engage to teach without bringing them under personal responsibility it is natural that they should do so." Murray felt that this was not the real problem, and went on to make the following case:

> The fault is not in the people, nor in the Trustees, but in the Teachers themselves. Every Teacher acts as if he were the only Teacher in the Province, and while this is the case, each and every one of them must indeed be Slaves. It cannot possibly be otherwise. But if Teachers were to unite as a body, to protect each other, and to bear each other's burdens, as they have long done in Scotland, they would very soon occupy their

proper place, and exercise their proper influence in Society. But without this they must be degraded still.

Murray's plea for self-help as the answer to teacher-status improvement reflects his Scottish background and may explain why little state assistance had been given to teacher ̃ining during his administration.

The policy and philosophy of his successor, Egerton Ryerson, was quite different, as is shown in his letter acknowledging receipt of his appointment as assistant superintendent for Canada West in October of 1844. In discussing his proposed trip to Europe, Ryerson noted that, "In Prussia School Teaching is a profession, much as Law or Medicine. School Teachers are professionally educated, and supported like other public servants. . . ."[11] Once the idea of the teacher as a trained public servant became the standard, it justified a strong positive state role in providing the training for teachers.

Sir Charles Metcalfe's instructions to Ryerson, on the occasion of the latter's taking office in 1844, summarized the intent of the government with regard to education, and revealed the influence of earlier recommendations made by Dr. Charles Duncombe, Robert Baldwin Sullivan, the McCaul Commission, and Rev. Robert Murray. The new assistant of education was charged with the responsibility of "devising such measures as may be necessary to provide suitable schoolbooks; to establish the most efficient system of instruction; to elevate the characters of both Teachers and of Schools; and to encourage every plan and effort to educate the youthful mind of the country."[12]

Professional training for teachers was still non-existent in Canada West, and this lack was, therefore, an immediate problem to be overcome. An early indication of this realization is given in an "Address on the Subject of Grammar Schools" presented to the Johnstown District Council in 1842. This outlined the difficulties of carrying out the Act of 1841 where no qualified teachers were available and there was no uniform system of teaching. The institution of a provincial normal school was urged as an answer to these problems.

An attempt had been made to introduce normal schools and model schools in the 1843 bill, but without success, although the latter could have been instituted if a locality had so desired, on a purely voluntary basis. Murray noted in a letter of January 31, 1844, that "Model Schools are contemplated in several Districts but I am not aware that any definite steps have yet been taken towards their formation. . . ."[13] In November of that year he wrote to the provincial secretary enclosing a notice from the Dalhousie District clerk giving information regarding the establishment of a county model school "some months since" in the town of Bytown.[14] Such efforts, however, were not regarded as being very effective, nor were other voluntary measures which were apparently tried.

Alexander McNab, while acting as assistant superintendent during Ryerson's absence in Europe, agreed that "The intellectual improvement of the Teachers is certainly a matter of the greatest moment and should be promoted by every means within our power . . ." but noted that the Act only allowed this to be done through normal schools, for which no money had been allotted, and there was no way of providing substitute financing out of the common-school fund.[15] He conceded that the main difficulty in setting up model schools lay in providing them with competent, qualified teachers, in the absence of a normal school to produce such.[16] That the time might be ripe for the introduction of such training and the subsequent employment of graduates seemed indicated by the increased prosperity of the province and particularly the greater amount of cash in circulation in the mid-1840s.

As in previous instances, the district superintendents' reports were a valuable aid in assessing local readiness to finance better teaching, as well as in identifying local concerns for its quality.[17] Ryerson received support for the idea of establishing a normal school from many correspondents throughout Canada West, notable among them being Rev. William Hamilton of Picton. Hamilton, a former headmaster of the Royal Academical Institution at Belfast, advised that county model schools be abolished in favour of one teachers' college under state financing, and that the department should carefully select the best teachers to be trained in it, in order to attract public support.[18] Ryerson, in thanking Hamilton for his support and the benefit of his experience, noted that he hoped to see such an institution established in a few months.[19]

William Hutton, superintendent of common schools for the Victoria District, was another advocate of teacher training on the Irish model. In his report of 1845 he had noted the shortage of good teachers in the province, and suggested that this might be remedied by larger salaries, fewer and larger school sections, and the establishment of a good normal school like that at Dublin.[20] He urged the last recommendation again in December of 1845,[21] and received the reply from Ryerson that "I quite agree with you that a Provincial Normal School must be the precursor of *good* model schools."[22] In a letter home to Ireland, Hutton mentioned that in his report to the government he had urged the necessity of "*teaching* the *teachers* in Normal Schools" and that the chief superintendent had taken up the matter warmly, and that he had hopes that something would be done.[23]

The Common School Act of 1846 included provision for the establishment of a normal school, although delays in obtaining a headmaster from Dublin prevented the opening until 1847.

The decision to employ Mr. Rintoul of the Dublin Model School staff was due to Ryerson's stated determination to introduce the Irish National Common School system in Canada West, including organization, textbooks, and normal schools.[24] In correspondence with Irish authorities he had cited as his reason, his admiration for the "benevolent patriotism" of the system administered by the commissioners of national education.[25]

In a "Circular to Municipal Councils" dated August 4, 1846, Ryerson requested the councils to select and support candidates for the normal school in order to obtain a supply of the "best class of native Teachers" and expressed the hope that their "early, as well as patriotic and benevolent" attention would be paid to this end. Ultimately, he said, all schools in the province would be provided with teachers trained in the country and in the same system of instruction, as "It is the purpose of the Board to educate young men for Canada, as well as in it. . . ."[26] The system, however, was to be Irish.

When Rintoul could not come to Canada, due to family problems, another Dublin master was hired in his place, and when the Toronto model school was established the next year, the senior post went to a former Dublin master.[27]

RYERSON'S ADMINISTRATION AND THE PROFESSIONALIZATION OF TEACHING: 1845–50

One of the first steps of the Ryerson administration was directed towards the final elimination of American teachers. The Act of 1846 expressly forbade the certification of aliens, a clause which created some consternation in Waterloo Township, where it was interpreted as preventing the employment of German teachers. Some areas had French-born teachers as well, and Ryerson was compelled to define the term more closely, stating somewhat delicately that the Act was never intended to apply to "Aliens from the Foreign Countries of Europe".[28] Similarly, he was willing to accept American teachers who had received certificates before January 1, 1846, and American female teachers.[29] When one overly zealous township superintendent refused to certify an American who had been resident in Canada from the age of seven, Ryerson sharply reminded him to keep in mind the spirit, rather than the letter of the law.[30]

That the clause allowing local option in hiring American teachers might be inconsistent with attempts to increase the professional status of teachers was recognized. A petition from the Niagara District advised Ryerson that the new Common School Act, by allowing aliens, would produce competition for normal-school graduates that would drive both pay and status to a level lower than that of "ditchers and wood-choppers". The warning was also given that removal of protection would cause dismay and resentment on the part of teachers, who would not go through the years of study required to be a common-school teacher only to earn less than a labourer. "It is a well known fact," the petitioners claimed, "that, previous to the late School Act, American Teachers flocked into this District, and many of them taught school for prices ranging from 8 to 12 dollars a month; and it is morally certain that such will be the case again under the operations of the new School Act."[31]

Possibly in order to sidestep the issue, Ryerson publicly evinced more concern for the threat from American textbooks than that from American teachers, and proposed to correct the latter problem by introducing a standard set of books for use in the schools. This measure would, in fact, allow the employment of American teachers as their bias would presumably be rendered ineffective by the use of the new textbooks. The books alone would not ensure that correct attitudes were promoted, but would add to the professionalization of teachers by providing the basis of a graded system with a standard curriculum. Even pedagogical technique could be, and usually was, included in the format of the texts, so that to some extent, the problem of lack of teacher training was overcome. Ryerson preferred the Irish National Series because they were pro-British, classified by grade level, and non-sectarian. Moreover, they were inexpensive, and Ryerson obtained permission to republish them in Canada at a price that would be less than most other books.

A study of the official circulars issued by the Education Office in 1846 illustrates the ideas related to improving the quality of teaching which Ryerson was promoting. "A Letter to the Municipal Councils of the Several Districts and Cities in Upper Canada" informed the members of the appointment of the Board of Education which would be responsible for books and teacher training. It requested the councils to co-operate with the normal-school plan by each supporting two or more candidates, prospective teachers who were "entirely destitute of means", and promised that the municipal schools would soon be "supplied with the best class of native Teachers, and ultimately, through the Normal and Model Schools all the Schools of the Province will be provided with Teachers trained in the Country, and in the same system of instruction."[32] The "Circular to Wardens of Districts" emphasized the advantages of direct assessment on the property of all ratepayers to support education, as it would result in better teachers, their punctual payment, and the end of conflicts over the collection of fees and payments of salaries.[33] In a "Circular to District Superintendents", stress was placed on the advantages of adopting standard texts in terms of doubling the value of the teacher's time and replacing "the most repulsive part of a Schoolmaster's toils" by a "comparatively measurable and successful labour". It also encouraged a high standard of certification. "The more elevated the standard (provided it is practical) of a Teacher's character and qualifications, the more respectable and desirable does the Profession become, and the better will it be remunerated." Superintendents were encouraged to conduct frequent and detailed "visitations" of their schools, and conduct regular public examinations of the students. They were reminded that teachers were deserving of their sympathy and that complaints against, and interference with, teachers should be prevented.

> It should be understood that the Teacher—humble though his circumstances may be—is nevertheless legally authorized for his office—has his duties prescribed by law, and even the principles and methods of teaching—as recommended in the prefaces to the National School Books. . . . The Teacher should therefore be maintained in the rights of his office, as well as its obligations. . . . Indeed it is essential to the improvements

and success of school instruction, that the influence of Managers and Teachers of Schools should be strengthened and sustained. . . .[34]

Increase in teachers' pay, extension of the education bureaucracy, detailed training, high entry standards, and separation from outside authority were all elements of the developing concept of teaching professionalism of the time.

The reality of the teacher's lot in 1846 was scarcely in accord with such idealism. There were still instances of "boarding around" although Ryerson deplored this, saying that "the very idea of it indicates all absence, among the people, of any notion of improvement of preparation of his duties on the part of the Teacher; who, if there were any just conception of his office and of the interests of those entrusted to his care, would be expected to have his study and therefore his place of abode."[35]

Ryerson responded to the previously cited Johnstown District report by congratulating the district on the establishment of their model school. He agreed that the uniformity of education throughout the province was indeed the intention of the Act. The problem lay in the lack of trained teachers. As he explained, "Model Schools must therefore be comparatively inefficient until Teachers can be procured according to the 62nd and 65th Sections of the Act; which of course cannot be done until after the establishment of a Provincial Normal School."[36]

A letter from a Mr. John Kingdom, a teacher from Grantham in the Niagara District, is illustrative of the complaints voiced by teachers regarding payment of salaries. Kingdom wished to call public attention to the mismanagement of both District Council and Legislature grants in the district. As he explained it, the district collector collected the tax (rate-bill levy) from the rateable inhabitants, and was supposed to hand this over directly to the district treasurer or district superintendent who would then apportion it to the trustees of the respective school sections. These in turn issued the teacher an order on the superintendent for the amount of their salary (from the provincial grant) that was covered by local rates. Under this system, the teacher complained, he had to wait for three to six months for his pay, and travel fifteen to twenty miles to the district superintendent's office to obtain it. If lucky enough to find him at home, the superintendent was likely to say that he had no money, since the collector had not yet paid into the district office moneys collected from the rate bills (the payment of the provincial grant to a district was contingent on the district raising at least half the value of the grant). The superintendent might advance a little. "He then offers him about one-fourth of the order, saying he would send the rest as soon as collected, at the same time presenting a receipt in full for the Teacher's signature, saying it was the usual way, as all public vouchers must be receipted in full." The teacher agreed to this offer in order to get anything, and received as well a memorandum to the effect that he would be paid in full after all had been handed over by the collector. Kingdom said that he knew of one case where a grant had been due almost two years and was still unpaid. Either, he said, the collector had not done his duty in collecting the tax, or had not paid it over, or the superintendent had not appropriated it to its legitimate purpose. Wherever the fault may lie, he concluded, "The poor, hard worked, patience-tried Teacher is the sufferer."[37]

Despite such complaints, there is evidence to indicate that teachers' salaries increased rather markedly in the period 1845 to 1850, whether due to increasing general prosperity, price and wage inflation, or to a real relative increase is somewhat difficult to establish. The average salary for 1845 was £29 for twelve months, and £26 for the average period of tuition.[38] While Ryerson noted that this showed a "manifest improvement" in salaries,[39] it would seem to represent little change from the 1830s. P. C. Campbell, in his "Memorandum on Common Schools" of 1839, had noted that, in the Eastern District, the maximum salary had been £36.[40] By 1850, however, the average salary for male teachers was £52 4s. and for females £31 1s.[41] Ryerson observed, in a letter dated April 24, 1850, that one of the normal-school graduates had, "the other day", declined an offer of £70 saying that he could get £80 in another section. The chief superintendent offered the opinion, in the same letter, that a good teacher for junior pupils could be obtained for £60 with effort and delay and a first-rate one for £75, "where the Trustees pay his salary quarterly, and cause him no trouble or anxiety as to the collection of it."[42] That this was likely an increase in real income is suggested by evidence that inflation did not become a major influence until a few years later.[43] Whether other incomes rose proportionally to those of teachers is a more complex question. In some areas, for example the Home District, wage scales for agricultural labourers seem to have been declining, to a level of perhaps £35 per year.[44] In

Cobourg, in 1845, labourers received 2s. per day (with board).[45] However, in comparison with artisans, the teacher fared less well; they averaged £75 per annum in 1839,[46] while carpenters and masons averaged over £100 on an annual basis in Cobourg in 1845.[47] Such calculations are complicated by other factors, however, since many artisans were employed only seasonally, and teachers could often supplement their salaries by taking other jobs when the schools were closed.

Certification changes were, like salary levels, significant in the period after 1845. In 1846, the Act removed certification power from township superintendents and concentrated it in the hands of the district superintendents. One of these, Dexter D'Everardo, superintendent of the Niagara District, outlined the advantages of the new system in a letter to William Hamilton Merritt. Under the former Act, he said, each township superintendent had a system (or no system, perhaps) and a standard of qualification for teachers which might differ entirely from all others, so that there was no means of judging the comparative abilities of teachers or their progress. "The above points", he added, "are of much consequence if teaching is to become a distinct profession, and our schools can never be efficient until the Teachers regard themselves and are regarded as Teachers or professionals."[48]

In 1848, Ryerson proposed the establishment of a uniform system of certification and examination by the district superintendents, to set up a threefold program of classification so that "first rate Teachers will occupy their proper place of distinction" and the "profession would be gradually sifted of incompetent members, and be elevated in character, respectability and efficiency—becoming both a means and indication of the advancement of society."[49] The tendency towards centralized and more expert control of certification led, in 1853, to the Council of Public Instruction setting minimum requirements for classification of certificates, and issuing, in addition, first- and second-class provincial certificates for normal-school graduates. Teachers were thus raised above the level of mere civic or county employees, and became, in essence, representatives of the provincial government.

This change was objected to in some areas, and the protest was taken up by Ryerson's old enemy, George Brown, editor of *The Globe*. Brown published a letter from "Grapple" of Streetsville entitled, "Why Does the School Bill Cause Such Universal Discontent?" In reference to the proposed Common School

Bill of 1849, the writer protested control over the designation of school sections and teachers' qualifications being exercised by the government through the chief and district superintendents, especially when the government did not pay the full amount for these. Trustees, it was argued, should decide on who should teach. There were, Grapple added, too many visitors to schools who were not qualified to do anything but obstruct teaching.[50] Such protests, however, were too late to effect a change in a policy which had resulted from local demands earlier. Once effected by the central administration, no chance for further local control of policy existed, this now becoming the prerogative of the Education Office and the provincial government.

Changes in supervision served to enhance the professional aspects of teaching by 1850. Earlier complaints of trustee interference through "visitorial" powers were assuaged to some degree, by the encouraging of district superintendents to carry out this function after 1846. The expansion of the office of superintendent provided a sort of bureaucratic "buffer" between teacher and trustees, and the Education Department encouraged district superintendents to become expert in educational matters, and to see their role as one of assisting the teacher.[51] In 1850, the new Act set the salary for superintendents at £1 per school visited. Admittedly, this was only the beginning of anything that might be termed professional supervision, and the role of county councillors and local clergy remained strong.[52]

By 1850, the normal school was well established and seemed to promise to raise the quality of teaching to a professional level. Although in practice its curriculum was still largely concerned with remedying students' weaknesses in the basic skills, it was aimed at the German model of teaching things, rather than words alone, unfolding and illustrating the principles of rules, rather than assuming and resting on their verbal authority, and "developing all mental faculties instead of only cultivating and loading the memory".[53] If this sounds rather grandiose and jargonistic (not to say optimistic) today, still it indicates a move towards a formal pedagogy. The idea of the teacher as a specially prepared practitioner, set apart from the non-professional by academic qualifications for even the lowest certificate, was fostered by the increasing number of normal school graduates. If one of the commonly accepted characteristics of a genuine profession then, as now, was the need of extensive and specific preparation for it,[54] then a beginning, at least, had been made by 1850.

The introduction of the normal and model schools received almost unanimous support. Even *The Globe* expressed approval of the results of the first examinations when these were announced in October 1848.[55] In discussing the need for better qualified teachers, the editor stated that there should be more normal schools, or more students enrolled at a time. He hoped to see teachers (who needed higher pay) soon taking their proper place in society, which should be "a most respectable and influential one". In this instance, at least, George Brown's usual animosity towards the assistant superintendent was overcome by his support for the measure which Ryerson had promoted.

The *Journal of Education for Upper Canada,* begun by Ryerson in 1848, provided a means of disseminating ideas and information, and tended to unite educators by so doing. It aimed initially at explaining the system to trustees and superintendents by interpreting laws and discussing policies in detail, but it also advocated certain educational measures and sought to inspire teachers and encourage them to improve. Circulation increased rapidly—the Niagara District alone ordered 184 copies (one for each school section) for 1849,[56]—and the movement towards such things as free schools and the acceptance of the normal school was undoubtedly promoted by its efforts. The journal suggested to teachers the need to use techniques such as mass association and the press in order to influence public attitudes, and it occasionally encouraged their self-esteem by placing the blame for educational failure and discipline problems on parents rather than the school. It worked hard to bar transients and drunkards or the immoral from teaching, and to advocate a high standard of entrance qualifications for the profession, in addition to its primary purpose of achieving a professional level of supervision and certification. To some extent, it may have served to encourage a particular attitude on the part of teachers, that his was a calling above materialistic concerns, above money, that he stood with the clergyman in counteracting the sordid influences of the age, promoting morality and social cohesion. By such means, Ryerson may have hoped to instill in teachers a concept of their role as providing an almost exalted public service, a concept which might allow them to sublimate the frustrations otherwise resulting from an occupation characterized by low salaries and difficult working conditions.

Another means of promoting the professional standards of teaching which had been adopted by 1850, was the Teachers' Institute. Ryerson had proposed the establishment of these in 1848, to provide, at a local level, lectures, explanations of instruction techniques, and methods of improving discipline and school efficiency.[57] In 1850 such institutes were held for the first time. They were conducted by normal-school masters and consisted of sessions lasting from two to five days, when lectures were delivered and model lessons taught. The institutes, however, were discontinued after a year's trial, not being supported by teachers generally. Ryerson blamed the superintendents for this, but the real reason was likely that the teachers had little share in the conducting of the meetings, and this did little to foster professional pride.[58]

More successful, and more closely related to the interests of the teachers themselves, were teachers' associations. Information on these is sparse, the earliest reference in the Education Department correspondence being a letter from a Joseph Fenton of Hamilton to Ryerson in 1846. As vice-president of the Gore District Teachers' Society he offered some advice on textbooks, recommending the Irish National Series, "As many of the teachers in this county were trained in the Model School, Dublin. . . ."[59] This suggests that the society idea itself may have been an import from Ireland. At any rate, Fenton was glad to find in Ryerson's Special Report on Education of 1846 that he recommended meetings or conferences of teachers, and said that, in Hamilton, "A few of the Teachers of this town have met once every two weeks for mutual improvement and I know that they have made considerable advance in their knowledge of Arithmetic, E. grammar, Geometry, Mensuration, Trigonometry and Algebra."[60] The teachers' associations which became formalized after 1850 held local meetings which tended to exclude trustees and superintendents, and concerned themselves more with controlling entry and setting standards than with the sort of "self-help" described above. By 1860 such associations were common, although no provincial organization had developed and no Education Department grants were made to them.[61] The development of these societies and associations may be interpreted as evidence of the growth of professional pride among teachers, organization for mutual benefit being an aspect of class consciousness.[62]

There is some evidence that not only were teachers becoming more conscious of their group identity, but that the public was as well. As early as 1848, George Brown, the editor of *The Globe*, had observed that, with regard to salaries, "Teachers have generally been the most neglected and worst used members of the community. . . ." and he offered the hope that "they will soon take their proper place in society which should be a most respectable and influential one."[63] The next year, the superintendent of the Niagara District included some observations on the subject of teacher status in his report to Council: "A decidedly more healthy state of public feeling with regard to that important class, their attainments, standing, general bearing, and usefulness in community, not only as Teachers but as men, is beginning to exist. . . ." D'Everardo recommended the repeal of the prohibition of aliens, but thought that there was another source of a "permanent cure" for the "evil" of inadequately qualified teachers. "I am of the opinion that the true remedy will be to make teaching a distinct profession, to allow it to rank with the learned professions. . . ."[64]

Ryerson was sufficiently in agreement with the conclusion that teaching had reached professional status, that in 1850, he addressed a circular for the first time to common-school teachers, as he explained, "believing that their position and prospects are now sufficiently encouraging to justify me in holding up the profession of a Teacher as a comfortable, as well as a respectable and useful employment for life."[65] He pointed out in this circular that the Act of 1850 provided for the punctual payment of salaries, the independence of the teacher in the teaching and classification of his school, and the proper differentiation of teachers by certification.[66] He then went on to indicate the means by which teachers could elevate themselves in the eyes of the public. They must value their profession, he said, or others would not do so. This could not be done by "assuming lofty airs, or making lofty pretensions", but by becoming a master of it, by devoting energy to it, "by becoming imbued with its spirit". A teacher could not become respectable by Act of Parliament, but by acting in such a way as to win respect. Ryerson argued that teachers, to achieve this, must show themselves the "possessors of noble principles". Remuneration, he admitted, was a problem, but persons with "narrow and mean views" had the same attitude towards the pay of all "Public Officers". The profession of a teacher, he said, existed not for the sake of the teacher himself, but for the interests of society. "It is work indispensable to the progress and well-being of society" and Ryerson defined that work as the moulding of future citizens. The teacher was to preach the values of education as an "Educational Missionary as well as Educational Pastor".[] Teachers were not to be discouraged by long hours and low pay, but to remember that they were members of a "public profession" and the image of service to society "will sweeten his toil, and add fresh attractions to every successive year of his increasingly useful and efficient labours."[67]

This statement of Ryerson's sums up his aims of the previous five years. He had visualized the educational system as serving to counter forces threatening society. Representative of an innately conservative intellectual leadership in Upper Canada, he was attempting to design a system which would promote and preserve the values which the ruling group held. A threat to these derived from two principal sources in the 1840s, the presence of American influences in and on the province, and this complicated by the influx of Irish immigrants in large numbers. To deal with both of these elements, Ryerson developed the objective of creating a universal school system in which trained teachers would impart, by standardized curricula, a socialization process which would assimilate the immigrant and instill the values of a British North American culture. The professional teacher was a key element in this plan.[68]

The extent to which the plan was successful may be seen by 1850. By that time, or shortly after, the main attributes of professionalism had been established in contracts, certification, a body of methodology, even superannuation. Teaching was defined as a profession in the terms of the time, that is, it required training, was a long-term or lifetime vocation, and had career opportunities (advancement to grammar, model, or normal school). Moreover, an educational bureaucracy had been established, with central control over curriculum, and, although only partially, entry to the ranks of the group.

What is most important to note is that the idea of professionalism was imposed on teachers from above. Rather than being a product of group self-consciousness, it was seen by Ryerson as a means of carrying out his objectives of instilling loyalty and morality in the young. In this, he was only supporting the interests of the political establishment of the day, both Conservatives and Reformers supported education as a socializing agency. Because of its purpose and the method by which it was introduced, the professionalism of teachers was limited to a civil servant status, rather than becoming independent as in the cases of law, medicine, and religion. The provincial control of training, certification, and financing, all made certain of that. What distinguished teachers from other civil servants, however, was the almost mystical attitude which was encouraged, of their serving a "higher" goal in the transfer of culture which would produce future prosperity and security for the society. They were told that this was the case, and they came to believe it, less perhaps from any perception of the truth and the myth, but because it allowed them to rise above the penury and hardship of their lives.

NOTES

1. Arthur to Bishop Mountain, 18 December 1838, in C. R. Sanderson, ed., *The Arthur Papers* (Toronto, 1943) I: 465.
2. J. George Hodgins, ed., *Documentary History of Education in Upper Canada, 1791–1876* (28 vols.; Toronto, 1894–1910) III: 241.
3. Donald Wilson, Robert Stamp, and Louis-Philippe Audet, *Canadian Education: A History* (Scarborough, 1970), p. 211.
4. Murray to N. Bosworth, 30 July 1844, ibid.
5. McNab to D. Walker, 6 February 1845, ibid.
6. Murray to Hunter, 26 April 1844, ibid.
7. Murray to W. Sharts, 18 May 1844, ibid.
8. Dexter D'Everardo, "To Trustees and Teachers", *The Niagara Mail*, 13 January 1847.
9. Murray to Bosworth, 14 November 1845, O.A.R.G. -2, C-1, Letterbook A, Public Archives of Ontario (PAO).
10. Murray to D. MacLeod, 2 April 1884, ibid.
11. Ryerson to Daly, 2 October 1884, ibid.
12. Daly to Ryerson, 28 September 1844, Incoming General Correspondence, PAO.
13. Murray to J. Howell, 31 January 1844, R.G. -2, C-1, Letterbook A, PAO.
14. Murray to Daly, 14 November 1844, R.G. -2, C-1, Letterbook B, PAO.
15. McNab to A. Mann, 24 April 1845, ibid.
16. McNab to W. Elliott, 17 November 1845, ibid.
17. Hutton to his mother, 12 January 1845, in W. E. Boyce, *Hutton of Hastings* (Belleville, 1973), p. 125.
18. Hodgins, *Documentary History* VI: 293–94.
19. Ryerson to Hamilton, 26 January 1846, R.G. -2, C-1, Letterbook C, PAO.
20. William Hutton, District Superintendent's *Report*, 1845, in Boyce, *Hutton of Hastings*, p. 133.
21. Hutton to Ryerson, 25 December 1845, ibid., p. 134.
22. Ryerson to Hutton, 3 January 1846, R.G. -2, C-1, Letterbook C, PAO.
23. Hutton to Mrs. Hutton, 22 March 1846, in Boyce, *Hutton of Hastings*, p. 135.
24. Ryerson to the secretaries, Education Office, Dublin, 24 July 1846, R.G. -2, B, Letterbook A, PAO.
25. Ibid.
26. Ryerson, "Circular to Municipal Councils", 4 August 1846, ibid.

27. Ryerson to T. Donnelly, 21 January 1848, ibid.
28. Ryerson to J. Ferrall, 29 January 1846, ibid.
29. S. E. Houston, "Politics, Schools and Social Change in Upper Canada Between 1836 and 1846" (MA thesis, University of Toronto, 1967), p. 55.
30. Ryerson to R. Home, 14 September 1846, R.G. -2, B, Letterbook A, PAO.
31. McAlpen (and others) to Ryerson, 23 January 1850, Education Department Records, Incoming General Correspondence, PAO.
32. Ryerson, "Letter to The Municipal Councils", 10 November 1846, R.G. -2, B, Letterbook A, PAO.
33. Ryerson, "Circular to Wardens of Districts", October 1846, ibid.
34. Ryerson, "Circular to District Superintendents", ibid.
35. Ryerson to G. Hendry, 7 November, 1846, ibid.
36. Ryerson to J. Wiltse, 13 January 1846, R.G. -2, C-1, Letterbook C, PAO.
37. St. Catharines Journal, 21 June 1849.
38. Ryerson, Annual Report of the Common Schools of Upper Canada, 28 January 1847, R.G. -2, C-1, Letterbook C, PAO.
39. Ibid.
40. P. C. Campbell, "Memorandum on Common Schools", ed. J. D. Wilson, The Journal of Education of the Faculty of Education, Vancouver, No. 15 (April 1969), p. 65.
41. N. Burwash, "The Social Status of the Teacher", Proceedings of the O.E.A. (Toronto, 1905), p. 75.
42. Ryerson to J. S. Hughes, 24 April 1850, R.G. -2, C-1, Letterbook E, PAO.
43. W. T. Easterbrook and H. J. Aitken, Canadian Economic History (Toronto, 1963), p. 311.
44. L. A. Johnson, "Land Policy, Population Growth: A Social Structure in the Home District, 1793–1851", Ontario History LXII, No. 1 (March 1971), p. 60.
45. J. G. Althouse, The Ontario Teacher 1800–1910 (Toronto, 1967), p. 27.
46. Campbell, "Memorandum on Common Schools", p. 65.
47. Althouse, The Ontario Teacher, p. 28.
48. D'Everardo to Merritt, 1 July 1847, Merritt Papers, Pkg. 28, PAO.
49. Ryerson to Leslie, 16 November 1848, R.G. -2, C-1, Letterbook D, PAO.
50. The Globe, 13 September 1848.
51. "Circular to District Superintendents", R.G. -2, B, Letterbook A, PAO.
52. Althouse, The Ontario Teacher, p. 40.
53. Hodgins, Documentary History X: 2.
54. Althouse, The Ontario Teacher, p. 40.
55. The Globe, 14 October 1848.
56. Ryerson to Brown, 20 December 1848, R.G. -2, PAO.
57. Ryerson to Leslie, 16 November 1848, R.G. -2, C-1, Letterbook D, PAO.
58. Althouse, The Ontario Teacher, p. 33.
59. Fenton to Ryerson, 21 September 1846, R.G. -2, C-6-C, Incoming General Correspondence for 1848, PAO.
60. Ibid.
61. Althouse, The Ontario Teacher, p. 33.
62. Ibid., p. 31.
63. St. Catharines Journal, 19 October 1848, reprinted in The Globe, n.d.
64. "Report of the Superintendent of Education", Minutes of the Niagara Council, February Session, 1849. Appendix, p. 32.
65. Ryerson, "Circular to the Teacher of Each Common School in Upper Canada on His Duty Under the New Common School

Act of 1850", in Hodgins, *Documentary History* x: 215.

66. Ibid., x: 215–16.

67. Ibid., x: 216–17.

68. The degree of concern over the presence of American teachers seems to have declined after 1846, as tensions between the two countries decreased following the final western boundary settlements, and as the normal school produced more and more Canadian teachers. As early as 1847 Ryerson advocated removal of the ban against aliens (Ryerson to G. Hendry, 21 April 1847, Letterbook C, Education Department Correspondence, PAO; and Ryerson to Daly, 23 June 1847, Letterbook D, ibid.), and this was carried into law by the Education Act of 1849. From this time, the hiring of teachers was left to the discretion of local authorities, and the legal right of Americans to teach in Upper Canada was thereby, in effect, conceded.

The Public Instructor: Ryerson and the Role of Public School Administrator

ALISON PRENTICE

Eight years before Egerton Ryerson's retirement as chief superintendent of the Ontario school system, the Education Department published a pamphlet entitled *Acts of the Chief Superintendent Explained and Vindicated*. The title suggests much about the flavour of the Ryerson regime in Ontario education and Ryerson's own concern to have his role understood and appreciated. A quotation from Pericles's Funeral Oration on the title page also reveals something of the underlying motive. According to the quotation, it is not "wealth that delights in the latter stage of life . . . so much as honour."[1]

This was not the first time that Ryerson had entered the public forum to defend his reputation. On many occasions during the thirty years that he was chief superintendent of schools, Ryerson felt that he was misunderstood and unjustly attacked. His response was to expend enormous amounts of energy justifying his role in the creation and administration of the Upper Canadian school system. One of the major reasons, therefore, for an analysis of Ryerson's views on the role of the public-school administrator is the wealth of material that exists on the subject, resulting from Ryerson's anxiety to defend both the office of chief superintendent and his own use of it. A second reason is the absence, in contemporary North American educational history, of studies focusing on the administration of provincial or state school systems. The tendency has been, rather, to concentrate on the development of educational bureaucracies in cities, or on national organizations and movements.[2] Yet the development of bureaucracy at the state or provincial level is clearly an important theme. At the same time, students of provincial administrative history have tended to neglect the school systems. The otherwise thorough history of Canadian administration during the union period by J. E.

Hodgetts, for example, touches only briefly on the development of educational bureaucracies in Canada East and West between 1841 and 1867.[3]

A third reason for looking at Ryerson's approach to the role of the public-school administrator is his typicality. Ryerson came to the superintendency just at the stage when new administrative careers in education were being carved out in many North American jurisdictions. His career thus has much in common with the careers of Paul Mattingly's "first generation" of American schoolmen, the educators who were born in the last decade of the eighteenth century and came to prominence in the middle decades of the nineteenth.[4] Ryerson was born in 1803. The third son of a Loyalist family which evenutally settled in Upper Canada, he was converted to Methodism in adolescence and ultimately abandoned the life of the farm for a career in the ministry. As was the case with many of the first generation of schoolmen, his appointment to the Upper Canadian superintendency followed an extensive apprenticeship in other fields of endeavour. At one time or another, Ryerson had been assistant to a grammar-school master, itinerant preacher, missionary to the Indians, newspaper editor, resident clergyman of a parish in Toronto, and principal of a Methodist college. He was forty-one when he was made assistant superintendent of education for the province in 1844, and forty-three when he took on the elevated title of Chief Superintendent of Schools.

There are several issues traditionally associated with Ryerson's tenure of the superintendency that relate to his views on administration. The first concerns the Methodist preacher's need for and success in achieving personal power. Accused by his contemporaries of mounting a dictatorial campaign to control the province's schools from Toronto for his own sectarian purposes, Ryerson continues to appear in most Canadian educational history as, at the very least, a person of immense authority who, it is implied, wielded great power during his time in office. How accurate is this picture? Ryerson has been credited, furthermore, with the creation of the "Ontario school system" virtually in its entirety. To what extent is such an impression correct? Certainly the answer to neither question is simple. Ryerson was responsible for much that was said and done in the name of education in the mid-nineteenth century, but as Robert Gidney and Douglas Lawr have shown, some of the most crucial legislation creating the Ontario system predated his appointment. It is also clear that J. George Hodgins and George Paxton Young, to mention only two of Ryerson's closest associates in the Education Department, as well as some of his bitterest critics outside of it, played important roles in the articulation of the laws and administrative practices that became the Ontario system. Finally, the extent to which power was actually centralized in Ryerson's hands or in the Education Department considered as a whole remains problematic. We need a detailed administrative history of the early development of the Ontario school system before either of these questions can be answered adequately.[5]

What follows, therefore, does not address itself to either question directly. It focuses, rather, largely on matters of opinion and belief, on the ideology[6] of educational administration as espoused by a typical schoolman of the mid-nineteenth century. It does so in the belief that the ideas expressed by Ryerson about administration, and the ways in which he put some of those ideas into practice, shed light not only on the subsequent behaviour of school officials in Ontario or elsewhere, but illuminate some of the processes of institutional development that were at work during this transitional period in educational history. We will see that an underlying theme of institutional growth in the mid-nineteenth century was the attempt to adapt and reconcile a number of different and sometimes conflicting behaviours within new or changing roles. Where, contemporaries asked, did Ryerson the Methodist preacher leave off and Ryerson the superintendent of schools begin? Well might they ask, for the answer was by no means obvious. To what extent should or could an officer of the government separate his personal and private business from that which was public or official? In sum, what were the rights, prerogatives and duties of the chief superintendent of education in mid-nineteenth-century Upper Canada? What were the attributes and functions of the office? As he stated his views on such questions, Ryerson was not only defending his own career, but defining the parameters of a new role in education: that of the public-school administrator. [8]

Among Egerton Ryerson's most fundamental beliefs was a belief in government. In a lecture on "The Social Advancement of Canada" which he published in the *Journal of Education for Upper Canada* in 1849, the power of government for good was a central theme, and Ryerson made it clear that a great part of the government's power was to be found in its influence on the thought as well as the behaviour of the people. "Government operates on mind," he told his audience. It was or ought to be "a minister of God for good" to its subjects and should therefore "exert a potent influence upon their social condition".[7]

In a private letter of the mid-forties, Ryerson expressed admiration for those European governments that had expanded their functions beyond the military and the legal, to become "Educators, Merchants, Tradesmen and Farmers". As the power of these governments had advanced so had the happiness of their subjects.[8] In the field of education, Ryerson had a vision of government as an almost miraculous, life-giving force, which, like the sun, could bestow endless energy on the people. If the schools were placed under "a vigorous and active government," he declared to local educational authorities, "the spirit of that government will be communicated to every part of the machine, and will impart to it life and motion." The energy flowed in a downward direction. "From the office of the Chief Superintendent, down to the desk of the humblest Teachers", a force would descend that was capable of transforming the schools and the people.[9]

Equally significant was Ryerson's belief in administration in government. Educational legislation was not enough. He argued from the first that the education of the people was in fact more dependent on the "administration, than on the provision of laws relating to Public Instruction".[10] This, in turn, was related to his view that administration was in itself a valuable form of education. Over and over again, Ryerson reiterated the idea that the school system was "a training school of local self-government". It taught the people how to transact public affairs in a "business-like manner". Habits of punctuality, accuracy, and method learned in carrying out the business of the schools would be transferred to other spheres, even to domestic and private life, to the ultimate benefit of the Upper Canadian populace.[11] The creation of a system for the province's schools was more, then, than simply a solution to an administrative problem. By creating a system and the rules and regulations that went along with it, the administrator could gradually move people, Ryerson believed, into whole new patterns of thought and behaviour.

In the light of these beliefs, it is easy to understand the two basic functions that Ryerson saw as central to his position as chief superintendent of schools. The first was to act as a kind of moral force on behalf of educational improvement in the province. Thoroughly convinced that he knew what ought to be done, Ryerson brought to the superintendency a moral fervour that was typical of the first generation of schoolmen.[12] The Education Department in his scheme of things was to be a potent source not only of energy, but of enlightened views and correct information on the subject of schooling. Educational reform was conceived of in much the same terms as religious renewal and the superintendent's role as that of a guide and mentor much like that of the revivalist preacher. Secondly, the chief superintendent was responsible for the machinery of the school system, for all the regulations, forms, and administrative measures that would make the system work. *Acts of the Chief Superintendent Explained and Vindicated* pointed out that there had been one founder of the Ontario public school system and that founder had been Egerton Ryerson.[13] What was meant, essentially, was that Ryerson had made the system operational. Towards the end of his career, Ryerson defended himself as having had a "mission" to establish and work out the "practical details" of the school system. The people of the province had contributed too, but it had been "imposed" on the chief superintendent of schools to "construct the machinery".[14] The role of the administrator, then, was a dual one: on the one hand he constituted a moral and inspirational force; and on the other, he was a maker of administrative machinery, a man who organized things and people and made the organization work. In both roles, his ultimate goal was the growth and improvement of the school system.

If these were the general characteristics of the superintendent's role, Ryerson also had a great deal to say in detail about its attributes and functions. He believed and acted on the belief that an administrator should provide stability in government; that he should represent both the responsibility and the authority of the government; and that he should be non-partisan and stand for the government's essential benevolence and good intentions towards all of its subjects. Finally, he believed that one of the chief functions of the administrator was to gather information and to communicate it, perhaps even preach it, to the people.

It was from these attributes and functions that Ryerson derived his arguments on behalf of the career administrator, arguments that became more articulate as his experience of the superintendency lengthened. The developing sense of commitment to the administrator's role is certainly in considerable contrast to the amount of time and energy that Ryerson apparently associated with the job when he first accepted it. The sense of mission was no less great perhaps, but letters written in the spring of 1844 and 1846 suggest that in the beginning, Ryerson intended to combine the superintendency with the principalship of Victoria College, albeit conceiving of the latter as the more nominal of the two responsibilities. The 1846 letter was a complaint, one of many to follow, about the expenses involved in Ryerson's position as superintendent of schools and the relatively poor salary that he commanded for the job. Ryerson argued that, had he been able to stay in Cobourg (where Victoria was then located), he would have had his "House furnished with heavy furniture, and fuel, free of expense" for presiding over the college, whereas the move to Toronto, made necessary by the increasing responsibilities of the superintendency, had involved him not only in the costs of moving, but in all kinds of additional expenditure, including "House rent, Fuel, and living generally".[15] Clearly Ryerson had no idea at first of the way in which the superintendency was gradually to develop—or be made by him—into a full-time career, and of the costs of commitment that such a career would entail.

Equally interesting is the absence at first of any real sense of separation between Ryerson's private life and his position as superintendent. Before the construction of the Normal School and Education Office building, completed in 1852, Ryerson's home and the Education Office were at the same address, on Bay Street one door south of Wellington.[16] And, as John Langton and William Lyon Mackenzie discovered when they began the work of establishing parliamentary control over departmental budgets in the 1850s, Ryerson also made no absolute distinction between the Education Department's bank account and his own. A parliamentary inquiry into the fact that Ryerson had pocketed the interest on school fund moneys deposited in his name by the government revealed that until the mid- or late-1850s the line between what belonged to Ryerson and what belonged to the public was somewhat blurred. For one thing, Ryerson, like Dr. Jean-Baptiste Meilleur, who was his counterpart in Lower Canada from 1842 to 1855,[17] spent considerable sums of his own money on projects connected with his position. The first official tour of Europe in 1845, the early upkeep of the Education Office rooms and the first issues of the *Journal of*

Education were, Ryerson later claimed, all paid for out of his own pocket.[18] He also had difficulty getting the government to defray expenses connected with the normal school on time, and for a period in 1848 was advancing sums to meet weekly bills, on his own credit.[19] To the parliamentary committee which finally investigated Education Department finances in 1858, Ryerson maintained his belief that the retention of interest on government money by those who administered it was "customary under the old system". He argued further that it was unprecedented and unjust that "a public officer should, in addition to his duties prescribed in law, act as Treasurer and Paymaster for the sum of more than £200,000 without any compensation for such extra official responsibility and labour." John Langton, for his part, felt that Ryerson's approach to the matter was outrageous and could lead to the investment of government funds whenever and wherever administrators wished, to their own profit. John A. Macdonald's evidence before the committee took the form of an attempt to stress the pitiable situation that Ryerson found himself in, in contrast to the elevated status his position warranted. If Ryerson had to repay the interest, Macdonald revealed, he would have to sell his house, "the only property he had been able to acquire". Friends had offered to help, but it seemed that this was not enough. In Macdonald's view, the situation was shameful. "I think that the Chief Superintendent of Education should have as high a Salary as any Public Functionary in Canada, except the Governor-General. I think it is the most important office in Canada," he concluded grandly.[20]

Macdonald's statement suggests the importance with which Ryerson had been able to invest his office in the fourteen years between his first appointment as assistant superintendent in 1844 and the parliamentary inquiry in 1858. The superintendency of a provincial school system was no part-time job, as he frequently attempted to show by outlining for the public his growing responsibilities in the department. The practice of describing the department and its various branches and functions began with the annual report of the chief superintendent to the Legislature in 1852 and was repeated from time to time in subsequent reports and issues of the *Journal of Education for Upper Canada*.[21]

It is apparent from these accounts that by the mid-1850s the Education Department was well into what J. E. Hodgetts has labelled the "adolescent" phase of bureaucratic development.[22]

Differentiation of function was clearly in evidence. By 1852, there were three distinct branches, Ryerson noting that each branch was "separate and complete in itself" and had its own letterbooks, ledger, and current accounts.[23] In 1855, four branches were listed: the Council of Public Instruction (which included under its jurisdiction the provincial normal and model schools); the Map and School Apparatus Depository; the Public Library Depository; and the Education Office. The latter, Ryerson pointed out, was "the chief branch of the whole department" and had by mid-century acquired, or taken upon itself, a multitude of new responsibilities, not the least of which was the auditing of local school accounts. This, "though a serious task and involving much and sometimes painful correspondence, secures considerable sums to the School Fund, and introduced into each Municipality and School Corporation the practice of faithfully accounting for the receipt and expenditure of public moneys." This was an ironic touch, considering the difficulty that would face Ryerson over his own use of public funds. Interestingly, Ryerson stressed the educational aspect of this branch of administration: it not only returned money to the government, but was "an important element of public instruction". The department would teach the people how to keep accounts.

In addition to the growing work load, which was also illustrated by showing that between 1850 and 1854 departmental correspondence had almost quadrupled, the 1855 annual report also emphasized the efficiency and order with which the department was conducted. "It is only by this strict attention to details, and this separate and methodical arrangement of each branch of the Department," Ryerson explained, "that it has been practicable to avoid confusion and embarrassment, to get through with the work undertaken, and to render the department an approved and efficient agency for advancing the educational and social interests of the country."[24]

The annual report for 1858 took a slightly different tack. An appendix on the workings of the department listed and described not only its various branches, but all of the employees with the dates of their appointments. The total came to thirty, counting those who worked in the normal and model schools, and twenty-five of the thirty had been appointed after 1850.[25] The appendix also gave a breakdown of the "documents furnished annually" by the department to school officers in various parts of the province. Listed and described were the *Journal of Education*, the school registers, trustees' half yearly and annual reports, local superintendents' annual reports, auditors' and treasurers' returns, and various other forms, the chief superintendent's annual report, circulars from the department to local authorities, and "letters & c., sent and received", some 11,717 in all. The grand total, it was estimated, came to a staggering 38,867 items per year.[26]

Clearly, the same principle was being applied to the Education Department that mid-nineteenth-century schoolmen thought should be applied to schools, the principle of "division of labour". And the chief reasons cited for adhering to the principle had to do with simple growth: an increase in work load and the need to avoid confusion. But the increase in the work load was itself no accident. To understand why the Education Department expanded so rapidly under Ryerson, it is necessary to examine in more detail the many roles and functions that Ryerson and his supporters increasingly felt the chief superintendent and his department should perform.

One of the most important aspects of his work, in Ryerson's view, was the assurance of continuity and permanency in the province's educational affairs. Despite the fact that he was himself partially responsible for many of the mid-nineteenth-century innovations in Upper Canadian education, it was Ryerson's constant complaint that the school law was forever changing and one of his most frequently articulated goals to see "the system" stabilized. "Permanence and stability," he explained in an address to the people of the province in 1851, "are essential conditions of growth, whether in an oak of the forest, or in a system of national instruction." Every "practical man and friend of education", would wish that the system he was attempting to render efficient should endure.[27] Although there was no rule to the effect that he should do so, Ryerson in fact prepared a great deal of the school legislation after his appointment, and was certainly consulted on most if not all of the school laws that were devised. Moreover, on the one occasion when a new law might have weakened his position and altered the direction of educational reform, Ryerson threatened to resign and won the day for his own approach to the administration of the schools.[28] He frequently referred in the 1860s to his belief that the school law was settled and should remain so, deploring Roman Catholic efforts to improve the position of the separate schools, through laws proposed and prepared by themselves, as unwarranted and dishonourable attempts to undermine the stability of the system.[29] It followed from such arguments that amateurs and even elected officials were not altogether competent to undertake legislative or administrative reform. Only the permanent educational administrator, the appointed superintendent who held office from one election to the next, Ryerson argued, could provide the necessary continuity, the "careful preparation, varied study and observation, and independent and uniform action" so important to the development of a system of public instruction. The person placed at the head of such a system needed time to bring its branches into effective operation, and Ryerson stressed the unfortunate lack of permanency that resulted when superintendents were elected, as was sometimes the case in the United States.[30] True to his beliefs, Ryerson himself held office for thirty-two years; his clerks and assistants in the Education Department were also remarkable for their longevity, with J. George Hodgins winning the prize with over sixty years in the department's service.

If the superintendency brought stability and continuity to the school system, it also represented the provincial government's authority in educational matters. In Ryerson's view, the school laws of the early 1840s were defective because the government had no power to interfere in local educational activities, and the school acts of 1846 and 1850 were clearly designed to rectify this situation. If there was to be a provincial or "national" system of schools, he argued, "it must be *one* throughout the Province". It was essential to the proper working of responsible government that "the sentiment and spirit of the public mind" be stamped upon "the administration as well as the legislation of the Country", so that they could ultimately be stamped on the schools.[31] For this reason, the authority of the government had to be vested in a single individual. Administration by boards or committees was not only unworkable, but irresponsible, in Ryerson's opinion, because only an individual head of a department could be called upon to account for what he did. He could be called before the government or the Legislature to answer for his actions and, if necessary, dismissed for neglecting or failing in his duty to correctly carry out the will of the government. "Acting under a responsibility in which his character and prospects in life are involved," Ryerson explained, "an individual will not only seek the best information from men and books, but act with corresponding caution and energy."[32] To combine caution with energy was clearly no mean feat; the position was obviously a delicate one, all the more so when its encumbent saw both his character and prospects dependent on how he performed.

Yet Ryerson's own performance was not all that was involved. His reputation—and authority—depended to some extent on the willingness of local officers to comply with the law, and the power of the government was exercised by disbursing or withholding school funds on the basis of local performance. All of this, especially after 1850 when the Education Department began to audit school accounts, meant mountains of paperwork to explain the law to local school officers, to find out if they had obeyed it, and to give out or refuse to give out the appropriate financial rewards.

But the authority was not necessarily stern and unbending. More paperwork still was involved in the attempt to exercise power without harshness. If Ryerson saw himself as the responsible representative of the provincial government's authority in educational matters, he also believed that he should represent its benevolence. New laws, especially, presented difficulties to local school authorities and he attempted to soften the blow by allowing delays. The outgoing correspondence of the Education Department thus contains letters by Ryerson to local superintendents of schools instructing them to be less rigid in their interpretation of the law. In June of 1847, for example, M. McLean of Kingston was advised that "no advantage should be taken of technical omissions to deprive school sections, in which schools have been kept open according to law, of any part of the School Fund apportioned to them." Ryerson's assistant, John George Hodgins, wrote to the clerks of municipal councils in May of 1851 to tell them that county councils wishing to distribute the school fund on the basis of population figures rather than annual attendance figures could continue to do so, despite provisions requiring the latter method of distribution in the school law of 1850.[33] Ryerson was also reluctant to enforce too rapidly the laws governing the selection of school books, arguing in 1847 that the discontinued use of foreign or other unsuitable materials in the schools would have to be "the work of time, and not of sudden measures", whatever the laws or regulations might say.[34] As he put it in 1846 to a township superintendent who, he felt, was insisting too much on the letter of the law respecting the return of school section reports, its "benevolent intentions" would be better accomplished by indulgence than by strict enforcement.[35]

Whatever the merits of such lenience in some circumstances, it is not clear that it always worked towards justice or was uniformly applied. Ryerson apologized in 1847 for the fact that black children were discriminated against in the common schools in some localities, and lamely attributed the resulting evil to "prejudice of caste, [which] however unchristian and absurd, is stronger than the law itself."[36] Yet he found it regrettably necessary to enforce the law in other situations. A notorious case concerned a new Roman Catholic school section in the early 1850s which was deprived of any share of the provincial school fund because the appropriate letters and forms had not been sent by the right persons to the right people at the right time.[37] Although a more detailed analysis of Ryerson's administrative style might reveal some inner consistency not apparent on the surface, it was surely such cases as these that gave him the reputation, among some critics at least, of exercising power in an arbitrary rather than a just manner.

Charges of favouritism usually provoked an impassioned response in the chief superintendent of schools, who was at pains to demonstrate that one of the essential characteristics of educational administration was impartiality. From the time in the late 1830s when he had himself appealed on an educational question to the representative of the Crown in order to avoid "local collisions and embarrassments",[38] it remained a fundamental belief of Ryerson's that distant authority almost by its very nature represented justice. From the beginning of his tenure of the superintendency, he argued that the administration of the school system ought to be "a distinct non-political department" and many of the letters that he directed to the press in connection with the free school and local control debates of the late 1840s stressed his own claim to neutrality, always in contrast to the political partyism of which his opponents were guilty.[39] The claim to neutrality was never abandoned; the school system was above politics and the school law, therefore, by definition non-political. All agreed, according to Ryerson, that the influence of the chief superintendent's office should "like the genial light and warmth of the Sun . . . be employed for the equal benefit of all without regard to party, sect or colour."[40] In 1868, American educational systems were criticized on this point. Although it was wrong that school legislation should be constantly unsettled, as was often the case in the United States, the making of laws was clearly a function of the representative side of the government, whose power to exercise this right was properly "based on popular election". But, Ryerson went on, the Americans seemed to forget that "the *administration* of the law should be free from the influences of popular passion." Administration, in contrast to legislation, had to be non-political; it was almost by definition based on "immutable maxims of justice and patriotism".[41]

Enormous importance was attached by Ryerson to his function as an advisor to local authorities on matters connected with the education law, a function which expaned to the role of arbitrator when local disputes were referred to his judgment. In December of 1846, the chief superintendent stated that the law authorized him to decide on cases that had been referred to him "as a cheap and expeditious mode of settling differences, and in order to prevent litigation", although apparently quarrelling parties also had the right to take their cases before the courts.[42] This applied to certain kinds of cases only, however, for in 1847 Ryerson pointed out that magistrates had no authority to intervene in disputes arising over the election of trustees, this matter lying entirely within the jurisdiction of either the district or provincial superintendent of schools.[43] By October of 1848, Ryerson was able to report that the Education Office had become "a kind of equity tribunal of appeal" which had settled several hundred disputes in a period of three years.[44] It may be that he found the power of arbitrator onerous, however, or that the proponents of greater local control in education were able to convince the government and Ryerson that his power was too great. In any case, the school law of 1850 contained clauses apparently designed to relieve the province's chief school administrator of at least some responsibilities in this area. A circular to the reeves of townships, dated the 12th of August 1850, announced that in future, local disputes would be settled by "a simple inexpensive system of local arbitration", and that there would be no appeal to the chief superintendent or any tribunal.[45] The hope that Ryerson's role in this area would be reduced seems to have been in vain, however, and disputing parties continued to appeal to him, if not for a final decision, at least for the advice which many clearly believed would settle matters on the local scene whatever his actual authority to do so. As one local superintendent put it when he was about to be sued in connection with the school law, Ryerson's advice (which he hoped would be given in consultation with the Attorney General) might deliver him from a difficulty out of which he saw "no other way of escape".[46]

The complicated question of what kinds of disputes Ryerson was entitled to settle, which could go to law courts and which had to be settled by local arbitration was apparently as confusing to school authorities in the 1850s and 1860s as it is to the historian trying to unravel it in retrospect. Ryerson's attemps to enlighten his contemporaries are helpful only up to a point. He explained to one inquirer, in 1859, that on questions having to do with his own instructions and regulations issued by the department, his authority was not only final but that he felt it his duty to launch appeals in the Court of Queen's Bench to have certain contrary decisions of county judges set aside. Arbitrations between teachers and trustees were also outside the jurisdiction of the courts, but these were to be settled by local authorities, under the general supervision of the local superintendents. From the settlements reached there was no appeal.[47] To a schoolmaster who requested his assistance on a complicated question of school discipline, Ryerson responded as follows:

> I have the honour to state in reply to your letter of the 26th ultimo that, I have no positive authority in cases such as you have submitted. By the Fifth clause of the Thirty-fifth Section of the School Act of 1850, I have authority to decide questions affecting the expenditure of the School Fund; and by the Seventh clause of the Thirty-first Section of the same Act, I am authorized to decide upon questions referred to me by Local Superintedents, also appeals from dissatisfied parties; but there is no provision in the Law, by which to enforce my decision in regard to such appeals. *The Law, therefore, seems to have intended that I should express my opinion, or offer advice, when applied to; but leaving it optional with parties to acquiese in my opinion, or advice, or not, except in questions relating to the expenditure of School Moneys apportioned by me.*[48]

Since, as Ryerson pointed out, he himself had written the school law of 1850,[49] one can only presume that except in matters related to the school fund, which were of course in every way crucial, the chief superintendent preferred to advise than decide.

Nevertheless, Ryerson was still describing the Education Department as "a court of equity" in 1855[50] and in 1856 so many legal questions had arisen in connection with his role—and that of the various local officers connected with the schools—that John George Hodgins entered the Faculty of Law at the University of Toronto, so that the Education Office might eventually have its own resident expert.[51] By 1860, Ryerson was calling for new legislation to deal with the growing problem of litigation, for court cases involving the schools had apparently trebled in a space of three or four years. The chief superintendent claimed to be satisfied that, in the final analysis, there was no legal means of forcing school trustees to account for funds that had been misapplied, or of giving "legal effect" to the awards of arbitrators. In addition, there were difficulties that had emerged as a result of changes in the municipal law.[52] It is clear that confusion about the law and Ryerson's role as advisor-arbitrator, as well as the role of local authorities in this area, continued to give difficulties throughout the 1860s.[53]

If Ryerson's actual role in the administration of the school law cannot be completely defined by the present discussion, his opinion of what his role should be does begin to emerge. For one thing, he clearly thought that the chief superintendent should be the final authority in all matters to do with the school fund, or any instructions or regulations tied to its disbursement. On other matters he saw his office as a sort of informal court of appeal, whose decisions were advisory in nature, rather than legally binding. Last, but not least, he preferred that school matters be kept out of the law courts, and in the hands of those appointed to administer the school system.

Ryerson believed that his position especially qualified him for the role of advisor-arbitrator. With respect to the 1850 school law, he argued a unique competence based on having written the law and, after some years had passed, on having administered it over a long period of time.[54] Then, as an administrator he claimed to have no axe to grind; an administrator could have nothing to gain one way or the other and was, almost by definition, not an interested party.[55] Finally, and this is perhaps the most telling argument of all, although he seems to have used it only once, the distant administrator was perhaps the person most able to defuse conflict on the local level. In an elaborate defense of the new regulations for public school libraries emanating from the department in 1853, Ryerson pointed out that the advantage of rules dictated by a central authority was that local authorities were "relieved from the responsibility and the odium" that came with their imposition. All that they had to do was to seek out the delinquents and apply the penalties; the "odium" it was implied, would all be attached to the chief superintendent or the Education Department.[56] Ryerson seems to have understood that one of the basic attractions of bureaucracy was the possibility of assigning the blame to someone else—ideally someone not actually on the local scene. If the blame was actually placed on the "department" rather than on any individual, there was the further advantage of depersonalizing conflict altogether: no one, essentially, was to blame. The ideal administrator, in this glimpse of things to come, was not only impartial but impersonal, by virtue of his distance from the nitty-gritty of face-to-face conflict between the people concerned with everyday issues.

If preparing and administering the school law and acting as the neutral representative of the government's authority in educational affairs were basic functions of the superintendency, a further side of Ryerson's work as he saw it might be subsumed under the general heading of communication. The written word was seen as the vital means to the end of efficient government and was also increasingly viewed as almost an end in itself. Ryerson wrote copiously in response to requests for advice. Frequently the correspondence with aggrieved parties went on for months and months, until finally an irritated chief superintendent stated that this was his last communication on the subject. That Ryerson sought and welcomed the voluminous correspondence is evident both from the length and the tone of his letters, and from his own testimony. He defended the growth of the Education Department's correspondence with local school officers by explaining that its purpose was "not to deal in dry technicalities, but to give every possible information; to impart correct views, and inspire proper feelings in regard to the great objects and interests of the School System."[57] Nor were the recipients of his letters the only ones to receive their benefit, for Ryerson, like many of his contemporaries, was addicted to publishing his correspondence. In addition to the countless letters he wrote directly to editors of Upper Canada's newspapers, the reading public was treated to samplings of Ryerson's correspondence in a variety of sources. The *Journal of Education* printed his letters under the caption "Official Replies of the Chief Superintendent of Schools to Local School Authorities in Upper Canada"; many were printed and reprinted in Ryerson's annual reports to the Legislature; entire files of correspondence on particularly vexing issues came out in pamphlet form.

If Ryerson wrote a great deal, he also expected that others would write. It was the duty of local school officers to put their transactions in writing, Ryerson told them, "for what is stated verbally is not considered official."[58] Certainly, it did not take a great deal of encouragement to get at least some of the people to write. As one gentleman put it to the chief superintendent early in Ryerson's career, he had originally planned to appeal to the Governor General in Council, but decided to go to Ryerson first, as the latter was the "middle man between us and the Government".[59] Many wrote often and at great length, and some demanded instant replies to their inquiries. In such cases, Ryerson used his office to lecture those whose letters seemed to him obtuse. "Had every Secretary-Treasurer of a Trustee Corporation as little judgment as yourself in this matter," he wrote to one of them, "I should have had upwards of *three thousand letters* to reply to; and had each of them been like yourself, I should have been assailed for neglecting them, if I had not answered their 3,000 letters in *three* days." Ryerson went on to answer the original inquiry anyway, but could not resist the final comment, that he had made it a rule, "to go much beyond the strict duties of his office", to answer questions that ought to have been directed to others, and to give every possible information "even to the least reasonable, and the most querulous persons" that wrote to him.[60]

It must have taken great energy to keep up with the Education Office correspondence. Ryerson's draft letters (which occasionally turn up as inserts in the departmental letter-books) became almost illegible and it is also apparent that Hodgins took on a substantial share of the letter writing. By 1861, the department had come to the conclusion that it was necessary to issue rules governing future incoming correspondence. The size and weight of the paper to be used was specified; correspondents were required to list all previous communications both to the department or others on the subject; and questions on different topics were to go on separate sheets of paper.[61] Ryerson continued to write lengthy letters to local school officers and to hear from them on all sorts of subjects, but it is also clear that the personal touch that he had tried to maintain was beginning to be sacrificed to the desire for order.

Already a great deal of spontaneity in the conduct of the system had been sacrificed to the ubiquitous form letter. It would appear that the first blank forms for local reports to the

Education Office date from 1842,[62] but it was with the school act of 1846 that they began to be used in a major way. Ryerson noted in a letter to the Governor General in Council accompanying the draft of the bill, that when the new law came out, blank forms for the trustees' and district superintendents' reports ought to accompany it, "so that all parties may commence properly, and that there may be an uniformity forthwith in the administration of the law throughout the Country."[63] In a circular subsequently addressed to the district superintendents, it was pointed out that the blank printed forms were intended to relieve local officers "as far as possible . . . from inconvenience".[64] He later noted to an official of the government that they were designed to prevent disputes[65] and to keep local officers from turning in sloppy, incomplete reports.[66] As the years passed, the blank forms increased in number and in length. By the late 1860s and early 1870s, the forms that school trustees had to fill out contained over one hundred and forty questions.[67]

In addition to the forms that Ryerson developed for reports to himself there were also the many forms and documents that the department printed and circulated for the use of local authorities exclusively. Such were the printed forms for trustees' notices of meetings, which were designed to help local school officers avoid mistakes,[68] the standardized school attendance registers, which Ryerson claimed at one point were an Upper Canadian invention,[69] and report cards which were an innovation of the early 1870s.[70] Were all the forms and printed materials helpful? Ryerson claimed that they were. In 1859, he made one of his many comparisons of the Upper Canadian school system with systems in the United States, focusing on that of the state of New York. In Upper Canada the returns were fuller and more reliable. Fascinatingly, in view of complaints about the increase of litigation in the 1850s, the other point of contrast was supposedly "the inviolability of the school law" in Upper Canada compared to what went on in New York.[71] No doubt many of the local school officers appreciated having the forms for their records and reports ready made. One local superintendent who sent in a request for printed attendance rolls for teachers and record books for himself in 1850 pointed out that these would be "aids to order" and, as he put it, "nothing can be done comfortably and advantageously without order."[72] But not all were pleased. According to A. Dingwall Fordyce, who was one of the more perceptive county superintendents of the late 1860s, the forms provided for reporting on annual school meetings to the local superintendents contained space for notice of no more than "one or two matters of routine". It was thus impossible for the superintendents to get a real idea of what trustees thought, in this case, about proposed changes in the school law. Fordyce clearly implied that what the forms left out was room for criticism of Education Department policy, which, as he noted, was roundly and unanimously condemned in the one report which managed to squeeze in any comments at all.[73]

Whatever the amount of space provided on the printed forms for criticism, Ryerson would have denied any intention on his part to prevent the flow of information. If one of the chief functions of his office was to "impart correct views" and information to local school people, another and almost equally vital one was the collection of information from them. Dry facts and figures, furthermore, were not enough. In a circular to the district superintendents in 1846, the chief superintendent urged them to make their school visits more than routine occasions. Their reports, he told them, should penetrate beneath the surface to "the whole moral and social character" of the schools. They should seek to know "the interior regime of the Schools, —the aptitude, the zeal, the deportment of the Teachers—their relations with the Pupils, the Trustees and the neighbourhood,— the progress and attainments of the pupils, and, in a word, the whole moral and social character and results of the instruction given, as far as can be ascertained."[74]

Despite this or any other pleas for qualitative materials, it was the statistical information that Ryerson craved the most. "Statistics are sober facts," he explained in an article written in 1853 on the progress of education in Upper Canada. They were frequently eloquent, but had "none of the illusion of romance". Although they recorded decay as well as progress, according to Ryerson, it is noteworthy that he rarely mentioned them except in the context of educational improvement. From numbers, one could form an idea of the "educational progress of a country". Knowledge of the statistical facts were the best answers, furthermore, to objections to the public-school system as well as the best means towards "strengthening and extending its operations".[75]

Ryerson did not take responsibility for the absolute accuracy of his statistics. At least once, he made a disclaimer to the effect that the figures giving the number of children between five and fourteen (in the superintendent's annual report for 1848) were taken from "a special document" furnished to him from another (presumably governmental) source; likewise the aggregate number of children registered as attending school depended for their accuracy on the correctness of the returns of local school officers.[76] Clearly there was much criticism of the statistics gathering, both as to its purpose and its usefulness. At least one critic in 1850 saw the attempt to gather statistical information as an insidious form of control; another noted that mere statistics were hardly a good indication of the quality of education, while a third pointed out that the elaborate nature of the forms encouraged the people filling them out to guess the answers, resulting in gross inaccuracy.[77] But the statistics gathering went on despite these reservations, for it was the mania of the age. When requests came from local politicians for figures to back up Ryerson's claims, or from as far away as Australia for materials descriptive of the educational scene in Upper Canada, where would the chief superintendent have been without his numbers?[78]

Tables on aspects of the school system also made up, along with excerpts from local superintendents' reports and reprints of Education Department circulars and correspondence, the largest part of the appendices to Ryerson's annual reports to the Legislature. And the latter were an essential part of Ryerson's growing information machine, the writing and dissemination of which he saw as a vital part of his role from the beginning.

Introduced by a ten- or twenty-page analysis and summary of their contents by the chief superintendent, the reports, according to Ryerson, were intended as "a simple statement and practical exposition of the operations of the . . . school law", rather than controversial discussions of educational policy.[79] He wanted them disseminated far beyond the members of the government for whom they were in theory written, and very early on requested that they be printed in large numbers.[80] The hope was that they would "create an interest in the public mind in behalf of elementary education", encourage the towns and townships of the province to look at and compare each other's educational doings, and furnish material for "earnest and useful discussions at school meetings".[81] The reports, and the statistics they contained, were also seen as guides to the future educational legislator, not to mention the future historian, of Upper Canada's "educational state and progress".[82]

If the annual reports were intended to sum up the year's

proceedings in education for the information of the public, the *Journal of Education for Upper Canada* which Ryerson began to publish in 1848 was meant to do a similar job on a monthly basis. Ryerson had conceived of the idea for a journal as early as 1840. In a letter to the Governor General, he explained his view that such a publication could not "fail to prove an engine of immense and even irresistible moral power in the country."[83] Within eight years, he had his chance to start one. It would, he explained to a correspondent, confine itself exclusively to educational matters "to the exclusion of all political and religious party questions". Designed chiefly for teachers and local school officials to read, it was intended to promote in the former a "knowledge of their civil, social and professional relations", and in both a better understanding of their proper relations with each other. Indeed, according to J. George Hodgins, it was chiefly with a view to removing the ignorance that teachers and trustees had of each other's rights and roles that the periodical had first been established.[84] If this was the intention, the *Journal* certainly did not confine itself to discussions of these topics. Like the annual reports and the correspondence of the Education Office it devoted itself to the dissemination of "correct views" and information of all kinds having to do with schools and school systems. Designs of the newest and best in school furniture appeared along with plans for school buildings and illustrated programs for school gymnastics and callisthenics. Speeches that Ryerson had given on his tours of the province were printed for the benefit of those who had missed them, as well as articles and speeches by other well-known educators from home and abroad. Materials and books available from the department were advertised and school news from various parts of the province reprinted from a local newspapers. But there was supposed to be nothing controversial: the object of the *Journal* was to encourage educational improvement, not educational debate.

The *Journal*'s path was not a smooth one, however. Ryerson's way of founding it was simply to finance it himself and to hope that subscriptions would help him to make ends meet eventually, but they did not. In 1850 he requested and was granted permission to make the *Journal* the official Education Department medium for notices and instructions to local school officers, arguing that this tactic would save the province all kinds of expense on postage, as well as the department a great deal of trouble. Since the 1850 school law required every corporation of trustees to procure annually "some periodical" devoted to education, it might have seemed that the *Journal* would finally sell.[85] Local superintendents were requested to act as agents, and may have been offered a free subscription if they sold a certain number; certainly one of them claimed "one copy free for my own use" in return for his labours.[86] But even these tactics failed, and finally in 1853 the chief superintendent urged the government to bail him out. The result was a subsidy of £450 a year so that the *Journal of Education* could be distributed gratuitously "to all local School Authorities".[87] By 1855, some five thousand free copies were mailed monthly across the province.[88]

Clearly there were recipients of the *Journal* who appreciated it. One subscriber wrote from India to complain that he had not received his copies recently and to renew his subscription; another less distant subscriber testified to its usefulness, even though he disagreed with many of the views of its editor.[89] In response to public criticism of the *Journal* in 1869, at least one local superintendent wrote to say that he for one found it inspiring.[90]

But from the beginning there were also serious doubts cast on its value. One critic wrote in 1850 that it was a "legal fiction" to suppose that local school officers were "cognizant of every-thing contained in the *Journal of Education*"; the government should not expect to use it as an official medium of communication, when some did not receive it and those who did, did not necessarily read it.[91] But the more serious criticism concerned not just its usefulness, but the propriety of allowing Ryerson to produce it at the taxpayers' expense. The critic was a Toronto merchant named Angus Dallas, and his concern extended beyond the question of the *Journal* itself, which he saw as merely one part of "a powerful machinery" designed to stifle the expression of free opinion on the subject of the school system. Ryerson's publications, Dallas claimed, constituted "a gigantic apparatus", the purpose of which was "to curb and control public opinion, on the merits of an experiment of which, at its commencement, every one, even the government itself, was profoundly ignorant." The annual reports and the *Journal of Education* were not used solely to furnish necessary information to the public and local school officers, but were also "directed . . . to the propagation of educational doctrines which are hostile to our form of government, as well as to our domestic relations, on the grounds of religion and the general circumstances of a mixed and heterogeneous community."[92] Dallas shared with other critics the view that Ryerson was using public documents as vehicles for a special brand of state and sectarian propaganda. If one kind of critic simply found the annual reports a bore,[93] those of Angus Dallas's persuasion were outraged to think that the province was put "to the expense of printing the sectarian religious lectures of one of its officers!"[94]

Certainly, if there was one absorbing and major role to which Ryerson was wholly dedicated in his occupation of the superintendency, it was the role of educational propagandist, although he would not perhaps have liked this term. As Toronto's *Daily Recorder* put it in 1874, Ryerson's strong point was the written word, and the "old Militant Methodist" was less effective on the platform than he was at his desk: "But writing, i.e. enforcement of great controlling ideas with the pen . . . is his principal forte."[95] Not that the chief superintendent avoided speaking. If his writing was the major theme, talking up the school system was a minor one and every three or four years saw Ryerson touring around the province to speak to school "conventions" that the Education Department and local authorities organized for him. Once again, his function was to argue and persuade, as well as to absorb local opinion, although it's fairly clear that the former was the stronger of the two motives for the tours.

For all the emphasis on Ryerson's thoughts and words, whether written or delivered orally, they of course were not the only content of the Education Department's growing information machine. For it was also under Ryerson's superintendency that the department became what amounted to a huge mail-order house for educational goods of all kinds. The principal product was, of course, books—school textbooks, prize books, and library books, and of these no doubt the most important items were the texts. From the situation before 1846, when control of schoolbooks was vested in the boards of school trustees, subject to approval of the township or county superintendent, Upper Canada passed under Ryerson's leadership to a time when he could proudly boast that the province was ahead of any country or state in Europe or the United States when it came to uniformity of school texts.[96] The authorization of and preparation of Canadian textbooks, along with the selection of library and prize books became a major preoccupation of the Education Department, and a major reason for dividing it into branches. The tendency to monopoly in the educational depository (as the branch dealing with books came to be known), and Ryerson's efforts to control what was read in the schools, became major sources of hostility to the department during his tenure of office.[97] Less controversial perhaps, but equally significant for their subtle power of persuasion, were the many items of school furniture and apparatus manufactured under the department's auspices and distributed by the depository for the use of schools. From the globes, slates, and maps that educational reformers increasingly thought essential to every well-conducted school, to the latest in school desks and "philosophical apparatus", all could be obtained through the Education Department in Toronto. And in case local school authorities did not read the advertisements in the *Journal of Education*, samples of what could be bought were displayed at agricultural fairs. In a circular to local superintendents and trustees informing them of one such display at the provincial fair in Brantford, Hodgins expressed his satisfaction that all would agree with him "as to the importance and value of thus adding an Educational feature to these great yearly exhibitions of industry and skill in various parts of the Province, so as to afford to all parties connected with our public schools an opportunity of seeing what are the facilities and means provided by the Department for their improvement and elevation."[98] For Ryerson, there was another purpose. The possibility of obtaining these materials meant not only the potential enlightenment of the people, but a boost to the province's prosperity, for one of his chief aims was to see that, if possible, they were all the products of "home industry".[99] Thus economic growth was tied in the most concrete way possible to the educational advancement of the province, as defined and promoted by the Department of Education.

If Ryerson's chief preoccupation was the promotion of his grand design—an Upper Canadian school system to elevate the moral, social, and economic condition of the province—his days were also filled with the minutiae of running an office and exercising supervisory powers over the normal school and its affiliated model schools. It was the chief superintendent who had to decide if the cost of gas lighting for the normal school was reasonable and enter into contract for the same.[100] It was equally the chief superintendent to whom the public complained if normal-school students were seen at the theatre, or if the normal-school janitor rudely ejected a casual evening stroller from the grounds.[101] It was, finally, Ryerson who had to engage the various officers of the Education Department, supervise their activities, and fight the government to get better salaries for them.[102] Yet it should be added that it was also Ryerson who went on a grand tour of the United States and Europe, spent vast sums on art objects for the new provincial museum in the normal school, and had an audience with the Pope.

What can we conclude about Ryerson's career as an educational administrator in mid-nineteenth-century Upper Canada? Clearly, he was a person who combined two controversial roles and made them one. The former Methodist missionary transformed himself gradually into a missionary for education in his role of superintendent of schools for the province. While the administration of the school system under Ryerson involved him in the writing of the law and in the enforcement of its provisions, as well as in a great deal of day-to-day administrative activity, he also made of it an immense propagandistic enterprise. For Ryerson, administration was inseparable from education. If some Upper Canadians saw the chief superintendent as the ideal middle man between themselves and the government and were prepared to seek his opinion and listen to his advice, there were others who deeply resented his highly personal style of missionary endeavour on behalf of the burgeoning Upper Canadian educational establishment. To them, Ryerson was a dictator. But Ryerson refused to see himself in this light. So convinced was he of the correctness of his approach to the superintendency, that critics of his personal style were accused of failing to distinguish between his person and his office. Their attacks were condemned as irrelevant abuse directed only against his private character, and therefore not requiring any official reply from the chief superintendent of schools.

A slightly different treatment was meted out to these critics who attacked Ryerson's policies directly or the school system itself. His official title was "Superintendent", a title which had roots in Methodist as well as American educational history. But Ryerson, also described himself as a "public instructor", and as such he was prepared to defend his vision of the school system against all opposition whatsoever. Critics of the system were condemned as the ignorant enemies of true educational reform. "I was, of course, much assailed by the parties [so] rebuked," he wrote in 1867. "But no consideration of that kind should prevent the public instructor—whether educator or preacher—from rebuking what he believes to be wrong in itself and injurious to the progress and interests of society, or from teaching what he believes to be true and essential to the advancement of society, please or offend whom it may, or however it may affect him personally."[103]

The cloak of neutrality with which Ryerson clothed himself as an administrator was thus abandoned when, as "public instructor", he summarily dismissed the opposition to Upper Canada's newly established system of schools. When it came to the system, one could not be neutral; one could only be for it or against it.

NOTES

1. Department of Public Instruction, *Acts of the Chief Superintendent Explained and Vindicated* (Toronto, 1868), title page. Ryerson was assistant superintendent of schools for Canada West from 1844 to 1846 and chief superintendent from then until his retirement in 1876, when his department became a full-fledged ministry.

2. See Michael B. Katz, *Class, Bureaucracy and Schools* (New York, 1971); David Tyack, "Bureaucracy and the Common School: The Example of Portland, Oregon, 1851–1913," *American Quarterly* XIX, No. 3 (Fall 1967); Carl F. Kaestle, *The Evolution of an Urban School System: New York City, 1750–1850* (Cambridge, Mass., 1973); Robert M. Stamp, "The Response to Urban Growth: The Bureaucratization of Public Education in Calgary, 1884–1914", in Anthony W. Rasporich and Henry C. Klassen, eds., *Frontier Calgary: Town, City and Region, 1875–1914* (Calgary, 1975); Paul H. Mattingly, *The Classless Profession: American Schoolmen in the Nineteenth Century* (New York, 1975).

3. J. E. Hodgetts, *Pioneer Public Service: An Administrative History of the United Canadas, 1841–1867* (Toronto, 1955).

4. For a description of the first generation of American schoolmen, see Mattingly, *The Classless Profession*, especially Chapter 3.

5. A thorough study of these questions will raise another: How powerful was the Upper Canadian central bureaucracy compared to similar bureaucracies elsewhere? Was Ryerson right or wrong when he claimed in 1847 that the chief administrator of the New York State school system had far more power than he did? Ryerson, *Special Report on the Measures which have been Adopted for the Establishment of a Normal School* (Montreal, 1847), p. 13.

6. I concur, in general, with Mattingly's use of the word "ideology" (*The Classless Profession*, p. 187), and intend it to mean a changing construct of ideals and beliefs governing action, rather than a closed or entirely rigid doctrinal system that impedes or is divorced from action.

7. *Journal of Education for Upper*

Canada II, No. 12 (December 1849), 179–80.

8. Ryerson to J. M. Higginson, 30 April 1845, Egerton Ryerson Papers, United Church Archives (UCA), Toronto.

9. *The Common School Acts of Upper Canada; and the Forms, Instruction, and Regulations for Executing their Provisions . . . by the Chief Superintendent of Schools* (Toronto, 1853), pp. 67, 84.

10. Ryerson, "Report on a System of Public Elementary Instruction for Upper Canada", in J. George Hodgins, *Documentary History of Education in Upper Canada, 1791–1876* (28 vols.; Toronto, 1894–1910) III: 205.

11. *Annual Report of the Normal, Model, and Common Schools, in Upper Canada, for the Year 1851 . . . by the Chief Superintendent of Schools* (Quebec, 1852), pp. 155, 160; *Annual Report* for 1857, p. 38. (The titles of the chief superintendent's annual reports changed from year to year; hereafter cited as *Annual Report* for the given year.)

12. Mattingly, *The Classless Profession*, chapters 1–3.

13. *Acts of the Chief Superintendent*, p. 33.

14. C. B. Sissons, ed., *Egerton Ryerson: His Life and Letters* (Toronto, 1937–47) II: 570; J. George Hodgins, ed., *Ryerson Memorial Volume: Prepared on the Occasion of the Unveiling of the Ryerson Statue* (Toronto, 1889), p. 125.

15. Ryerson to John Ryerson, 13 April 1844, and A. Green to Ryerson, 10 April 1844, Egerton Ryerson Papers, UCA; Ryerson to Hopkirk, 12 November 1846, R.G.-2 (Education Papers), C-1, Letterbook C, Public Archives of Ontario (PAO), p. 168.

16. Ryerson to Hopkirk, ibid., p. 110.

17. Louis-Philippe Audet, "Création du Conseil de l'Instruction publique dans le Bas-Canada, 1856–60", *Mémoires de la Société Royale du Canada* XIV, 3ᵐᵉ Serie (June 1960), 4.

18. Hodgins, *Documentary History* X: 188, and VII: 133. See also Ryerson to Shuttleworth, 7 March 1849, R.G.-2, C-1, Letterbook D, PAO, p. 409.

19. Ryerson to Sullivan, 25 March 1848, R.G.-2, B, Letterbook A, PAO, p. 49.

20. Hodgins, *Documentary History* XII: 186, 200, 201, 204. The situation was resolved when the government decided to reimburse Ryerson for expenses dating back to 1845. The two debts, it was apparently decided, would cancel each other out. Ibid., pp. 214–21.

21. *Annual Report* for 1858, Appendix K, and *Journal of Education* VIII, No. 3 (March 1855), 40–42.

22. Hodgetts, *Pioneer Public Service*, pp. 276–77, 280. Michael Katz has used the term "incipient bureaucracy" to describe the same phenomenon. "From Voluntarism to Bureaucracy in American Education", in M. B. Katz, ed., *Education in American History: Readings in the Social Issues* (New York, 1973), pp. 38–50.

23. *Annual Report* for 1852, Appendix G, p. 273.

24. *Journal of Education* VIII, No. 3 (March 1855), 41.

25. *Annual Report* for 1858, Appendix K, pp. 180–81. The figures given by Hodgetts for the "headquarters" and "field" staffs of the combined Education Offices of Upper and Lower Canada suggest that the Edu-

cation Office headquarters grew more rapidly in Lower Canada than Upper, probably because, as Hodgetts points out, local municipal institutions were less fully developed in the eastern part of the province. See *Pioneer Public Service*, pp. 36 and 40, and compare Hodgett's table with the list of employees in Appendix K, cited above.

26. *Annual Report* for 1858, Appendix K, pp. 188–90.

27. *Journal of Education* IV, No. 1 (January 1851), 1.

28. The bill in question was the "Cameron Bill" of 1849, which was actually passed in the Legislature. Ryerson's offer to resign was not accepted and the school law of 1850 was passed in its place. For excerpts from the debate on the Cameron Bill, see Alison L. Prentice and Susan E. Houston, eds., *Family, School and Society in Nineteenth-Century Canada* (Toronto, 1975), pp. 78–87.

29. See for example, Ryerson, *Remarks on the New Separate School Agitation, by the Chief Superintendent of Schools* (Toronto, 1865), p. 13. Dr. Daniel Wilson was also accused of disloyalty to the system when he mounted an attack on the department's book depository. Ryerson to Wilson, 29 May 1875, in *Dr. Ryerson's Defence: Educational Department Fifth and Last Paper* (Broadside, n.p., n.d.).

30. Ryerson, *A Special Report on the Systems of and State of Popular Education on the Continent of Europe, in the British Isles, and the United States of America, with Practical Suggestions for the Improvement of Public Instruction in the Province of Ontario* (Toronto, 1868), p. 177.

31. Ryerson to the Secretary of the Province, 3 March 1846, cited in Hodgins, *Documentary History* VI: 72; *Journal of Education* I, No. 2 (February 1848), 37–38.

32. *Journal of Education* I, No. 2 (February 1848), 55.

33. Ryerson to R. McLean, 7 June 1847, R.G.-2, C-1, Letterbook C, PAO, p. 388. (See also the correspondence with H. Hunter, Letterbook C, pp. 237, 242, and Letterbook D, p. 80.) Hodgins to Clerk of the Municipal Council, 1 May 1851, R.G.-2, C-1, Letterbook E, PAO, p. 517.

34. Ryerson to G. Hendry, 1 February 1847, R.G.-2, C-1, Letterbook C, PAO, p. 229.

35. Ryerson to J. Hartman, 23 February 1846, R.G.-2, C-1, Letterbook C, PAO, pp. 46–47.

36. Hodgins, *Documentary History* VII: 211.

37. The lengthy and acrimonious correspondence between Ryerson and Rev. Tht. Kirwan on this case was printed in *Copies of Correspondence between the Chief Superintendent of Schools for Upper Canada and Other Persons, on the Subject of Separate Schools* (Toronto, 1855), pp. 209–26. Excerpts are reproduced in Prentice and Houston, *Family, School and Society*, pp. 144–58.

38. Hodgins, *Documentary History* III: 117.

39. *Annual Report* for 1850, Appendix XVIII, p. 342; Ryerson to Rev. Dr. Burns, 14 January 1847, and Ryerson to the *Examiner*, 31 December 1849, R.G.-2, C-1, Letterbook C, p. 209 and Letterbook E, PAO, p. 97. Also Ryerson to the *British Colonist* (30 June and 7 July 1848), ms. inserted in R.G.-2, C-1, Letterbook D, PAO.

40. *Journal of Education* IX, No. 1 (January 1856), 10.

41. Ryerson, *Special Report on*

THE PUBLIC INSTRUCTOR 157

Popular Education, p. 178.

42. Ryerson to D. Hefferman, 24 December 1846, R.G.-2, C-1, Letterbook C, PAO, p. 190.

43. Ryerson to W. Clark, C. Jones *et al.*, 11 March 1847, R.G.-2, C-1, Letterbook C, PAO, p. 270.

44. Hodgins, *Documentary History* VIII: 84.

45. Circular to Reeves of Townships, 12 August 1850, R.G.-2, C-1, Letterbook E, PAO.

46. John Flood to Ryerson, 4 November 1850, R.G.-2, C-6-C, PAO.

47. Hodgins, *Documentary History* XIV: 319.

48. Ibid., p. 321, my italics.

49. Ibid., p. 319.

50. *Journal of Education* VIII, No. 3 (March 1855), 42.

51. Hodgins, *Documentary History* VII: 203.

52. Ibid. XVI: 96.

53. *Annual Report* for 1865, Appendix E, pp. 106–08.

54. Hodgins, *Documentary History* XIV: 319.

55. Ryerson to John Dwyer, 5 March 1846, R.G.-2, C-1, Letterbook C, PAO, p. 71. See also a letter dated 24 February 1846, ibid., p. 49.

56. *Annual Report* for 1853, Appendix F, pp. 144–45. A similar argument was used by a Port Hope school officer in 1865 who, in connection with the regulations on compulsory grammar school subjects, found it "a great relief to be able to tell unwilling pupils and parents, that I can allow them no option, for the law allows me none." *Annual Report* for 1865, Appendix A, p. 67.

57. *Annual Report* for 1850, Appendix X, p. 315.

58. Ryerson to C. Gregor, 5 May 1847, R.G.-2, C-1, Letterbook C, PAO, p. 355.

59. P. Shirley to Ryerson, 22 July 1846, R.G.-2, C-6-C, PAO.

60. Ryerson to O. Hammond, 22 August 1850, R.G.-2, C-1, Letterbook E, PAO.

61. *Annual Report* for 1861, Appendix F, pp. 228–29.

62. Hodgins, *Documentary History* IV: 263.

63. Ryerson to J. Hopkins, 3 March 1846, R.G.-2, C-1, Letterbook C, PAO, p. 60.

64. Hodgins, *Documentary History* VI: 266.

65. Ryerson to Daly, 10 March 1847, R.G.-2, C-1, Letterbook C, PAO, p. 265.

66. Ryerson to F. Hincks, 26 July 1848, R.G.-2, C-1, Letterbook D, PAO, pp. 264–65.

67. See forms for annual reports dating from these decades in R.G.-2, Q, PAO.

68. Hodgins, *Documentary History* VII: 108.

69. *Annual Report* for 1859, pp. 16–17.

70. *Journal of Education* XXVI, No. 10 (October 1873), 160.

71. *Annual Report* for 1859, p. 18.

72. J. W. Baird to Ryerson, 26 September 1850, R.G.-2, C-6-C, PAO.

73. *Annual Report* for 1868, Appendix A, p. 29.

74. Hodgins, *Documentary History* VI: 268.

75. Ibid. XI: 94; *Annual Report* for 1862, p. 5; *Annual Report* for 1866, p. 20.

76. J. G. Hodgins to the editor of *The Globe*, 2 January 1851, R.G.-2, C-1, Letterbook E, PAO, p. 429.

77. Ryerson to the editor of *The Church*, 17 August 1850, R.G.-2, C-1, Letterbook E, PAO, pp. 273–74; Hodgins, *Documentary History* VIII: 267–68; *Annual Report* for 1864, Appendix A, pp. 26, 28.

78. See secretary of the Education Office, Melbourne to Ryerson, 9 November 1868, and Committee on Common School Education, New York City, to

Ryerson, 29 January 1851, R.G.-2, C-6-C, PAO.

79. Ryerson to the Provincial Secretary, 8 September 1848, R.G.-2, C-1, Letterbook D, PAO, p. 232.

80. Ryerson to the Provincial Secretary, 16 September 1848, R.G.-2, C-1, Letterbook D, PAO, p. 282.

81. *Annual Report* for 1858, p. iii.

82. *Journal of Education* IX, No. 3 (March 1856), 34.

83. Sissons, *Egerton Ryerson* I: 539.

84. Ryerson to H. Pinhey, 20 February 1847, R.G.-2, C-1, Letterbook C, PAO, p. 253; J. G. Hodgins to the Council of Public Instruction, 18 January 1851, R.G.-2, C-1, Letterbook E, PAO, pp. 427–28.

85. Ryerson to the Provincial Secretary, 16 July 1850, R.G.-2, C-1, Letterbook E, PAO, p. 217; Provincial Secretary to Ryerson, 30 July 1850, R.G.-2, C-6-C, PAO.

86. Hodgins, *Documentary History* X: 201; D. P. McDonald to Hodgins, 2 October 1850, R.G.-2, C-6-C, PAO.

87. *Annual Report* for 1851, Appendix B, p. 149; Hodgins, *Documentary History* XV: 241.

88. Hodgins, *Documentary History* XI: 289.

89. R. Maclagan to Ryerson, 25 June 1859, and J. Jarron to Ryerson, 19 March 1850, R.G.-2, C-6-C, PAO.

90. *Annual Report* for 1869, Appendix D, p. 78.

91. H. Craigie to Hodgins, 9 November 1850, R.G.-2, C-6-C, PAO.

92. Angus Dallas, *Statistics of the Common Schools: Bring a Digest of the Evidence Furnished by the Local Superintendents and the Chief Superintendent of Schools in their Reports for 1855, by a Protestant* (Toronto, 1857), p. iii.

93. *Remarks on the State of Education in the Province of Canada, by "L"* (Montreal, 1849).

94. Adam Townley, *Seven Letters on the Non-Religious Common School System of Canada and the United States* (Toronto, 1853), pp. 3–4.

95. *Daily Recorder* III, No. 3, 18 September 1874.

96. *Forms, Regulations and Instructions for Making Reports, and Conducting all the Necessary Proceedings under the Act 7th Victoria, Cap.* XXIX *and for the Better Organization and Government of Common Schools in Upper Canada* (Cobourg, 1845), pp. 30–31; *Annual Report* for 1856, p. 13; *Annual Report* for 1866, p. 7.

97. See *The School Book Question: Letters in Reply to the Brown-Campbell Crusade against the Education Department* (Montreal, 1866).

98. "Circular to Local Superintendents, Trustees and School Officers in the Counties west of Toronto", n.d., R.G.-2, Q, PAO.

99. *Annual Report* for 1858, Appendix K, p. 185. See also Hodgins, *Documentary History* VI: 287 and XVI: 83.

100. "Minutes of the Council of Public Instruction", 22 March 1852, R.G.-2, B, Vol. 2, PAO, p. 225.

101. See anonymous to Ryerson, 21 February 1849, and A. W. Otter to Ryerson, 25 July 1859, R.G.-2, C-6-C, PAO.

102. On the type of employee Ryerson wanted in the Education Department, see Hodgins, *Documentary History* IX: 186. The salary question is discussed in ibid. XI: 239–44; XII: 161; XV: 241–42; and XXI: 3, 219–22. The relationship of the chief superintendent to his Education Department staff and the issue of their salaries is also discussed in *Acts of the Chief Superintendent*, pp. 17–19, 23. Ryerson played a patriarchal

role in the department, believing that his employees were "faithful sons" to him, rather than "hirelings" or "servants". One applicant for a clerk's position seemed to think that the relationship resembled rather that of courtier to king, explaining in his reply to the department's ad (which he offered in verse) that he was the right age, of fine manners, and altogether fit "to be a page" to tend on Ryerson's "Majesty", as well as a legible and speedy writer. YN to Ryerson, 30 November 1865, R.G.-2, C-6-C (No. 6723), PAO.

103. Ryerson, *The New Canadian Dominion: Dangers and Duties of the People in Regard to their Government* (Toronto, 1867), p. 4.

The Development of an Administrative System for the Public Schools: The First Stage, 1841-50*

R. D. GIDNEY and D. A. LAWR

In the eyes of Canadian historians, administrative history has been one of the least attractive of Clio's progeny. Though we know a good deal about the course of government expansion—it is the very bone and marrow of our national history—we know considerably less about the structures set up to administer new branches of government, and even less about how or why those structures worked. The fledgling administrative historian has little published Canadian historiography, beyond the pioneering work of Professor Hodgetts, to help clarify relevant issues or even raise salient questions.[1] Recent studies by British historians, however, have demonstrated that administrative history need not be bloodless or uninteresting, indeed that it has important things to say about the origins, rise, and nature of the modern state.[2] To what extent was there a "revolution in government" in the nineteenth century? In what ways did individuals, ideas, or particular circumstances shape the course of administrative change?[3] Does a bureaucracy, set up in response to a social need or demand, evolve according to its own inherent processes, independent of outside influence; is it, in essence, "creating and self-generating ... ''

*Early drafts of this paper were read and criticized by Dr. G. P. de T. Glazebrook, Dr. A. K. McDougall, Department of Political Science, and Dr. J. D. Purdy, Althouse College, University of Western Ontario. Dr. Henry Roper of Huron College, University of Western Ontario, and Dr. V. Seymour Wilson of Carleton University gave us astute criticism and helped us refine the final drafts. Our thanks to them for their help; our errors are our own. Grants from Althouse College and the Canada Council have helped finance the research for this paper.

[gathering] its own momentum . . . [turning] unexpectedly in new directions . . . [reaching] beyond the control of anyone in particular"?[4] Must a bureaucracy inevitably become ossified and responsive only to external pressures?[5] And what are the ideological implications for the historian who finds the administrative solution inherent in the social problem itself?[6] // These issues, far from being bloodless, reach to the heart of the historian's craft.

The Ontario Education Department in the nineteenth century provides both opportunity and challenge for the Canadian administrative historian. It represents one of the earliest ventures of the state into the daily lives of its citizens. By the century's end it was a highly centralized branch of government, with a well-developed administrative structure controlling almost every aspect of elementary and secondary education, and employing every device of bureaucracy known to man. Moreover, it left copious records—by the 1870s the volume of the Education Office's correspondence surpassed that of any department in Canada and equalled that of the Colonial Office.[7] Here is ample material for interpretation and analysis, and eventually an illuminating history of the Education Department: Who shaped that system? What was the relative influence of bureaucrats and politicians? To what extent was innovation internally generated or forced upon the department, and who did the forcing? What influence did the burgeoning urban school administrations have on the rest of the province, and on the Education Department itself? What was the effect of professionalization upon the bureaucracy? How did relations with the Cabinet and various departmental officers evolve? Is it correct to assume that local people preferred local control, or did they welcome government administrative rationalization? Why did government control increase at the very time the proportion of government financial assistance was declining?

Before any of these questions can be answered, however, historians will have to begin with a much more elementary task of sketching the outlines of the department's development, for not even this first step has yet been taken. We propose in this paper to examine that development between 1841 and the early 1850s, and more specifically, to answer three questions: How effectively did the successive school laws of the 1840s transform into reality the aims of the school reformers of the 1830s? What administrative mechanisms were necessary to do this? What was accomplished before Ryerson, and what did he add to the emerging administrative structure?

During the 1830s and early 1840s there was a growing consensus among Upper Canadian public men that the schools were not doing their job. Teachers, they claimed, were ill-educated, incompetent, and perhaps even disloyal; the variety of textbooks used within any given school made good teaching difficult; local trustees were too ignorant, too indifferent, or too busy with their own affairs to supervise the schools properly; and too many children were escaping education altogether. To remedy these defects, Upper Canadians looked to government. The state, they agreed, must take a more positive role to ensure that the schools were better financed and that government money was spent more effectively. It must, through some system of supervision and inspection, see that the minimum conditions of good schooling were met; that competence, not cheapness, determined which teacher was hired; that suitable and uniform texts were used; and that enough schools were provided to meet the needs of a growing population.[8]

Though throughout the 1840s there were differences of opinion about the degree to which government intervention in education was desirable, the principle itself was not at issue.[9] The real problem of the decade was how to construct machinery that could impose a *system* upon the existing schools—how to devise an administrative structure that would promote necessary reform. This is always a major problem in implementing new social policy, but, as Professor Hodgetts has shown, it posed special difficulties at a time when Upper Canadians were only beginning to learn the techniques of effective public administration.

Many of the administrative problems in education were no different than those faced by other government departments in the 1840s.[10] How was political responsibility to be established and financial accountability ensured? How was a clear hierarchy of authority with adequate lines of communication to be created? In addition to these common problems, however, the systematization of schooling posed some particular difficulties. In public education, administrative power was not created, but transferred. All the powers required to administer individual schools were already vested in locally elected trustees. If a system was to be imposed, many of these powers would have to be removed to, or at least shared by, other administrative authorities. At the same time, it was essential that community interest in schools be fostered and local financial participation encouraged. This required a very careful balancing of powers and responsibilities. Effective school administration, moreover, meant the involvement of a very large number of local people, many of them relatively uneducated and unfamiliar with the most elementary administrative procedures. And all legislation had to be framed and drafted to take account of the disparate social and economic circumstances of town and village, the mature settlement, and the edge of the frontier. Some of these problems were to prove remarkably resistant to solution, not only in the 1840s but throughout the century. The broad outlines of an effective administrative structure, however, would be established between 1841 and 1850.

The first of several attempts to improve the effectiveness of elementary schooling during the 1840s was made in 1841. The Common School Act of that year introduced compulsory property taxation for the support of elementary schools, and doubled the size of the government grant. These two measures substantially reduced the rate of tuition fees and put school finance on a more stable basis. The Act also created a new administrative structure involving the co-operation of three levels of government, and at the same time left the internal control of the schools in local hands. A new central educational authority was established consisting of a provincial superintendent of schools, appointed by the Governor. His duties were to administer the Act, collect statistics, and diffuse information on methods of improving the schools. He had, however, no control over "in-school" affairs beyond his power to cut off the grant if local authorities failed to levy the school tax or report on the state of the schools. The new district councils were responsible for dividing each township into school sections, for apportioning to each township the district's share of the government grant, and for raising an equivalent amount through a property tax. The immediate responsibility for the schools was placed in the hands of an elected township board of school commissioners which replaced the traditional school section trustees. The school commissioners were responsible not only for maintaining the schools in a township, but for certifying and hiring teachers, selecting textbooks, drafting regulations, and visiting or inspecting each school to see that their rules were enforced. The Act came into force in January 1842.[11]

It had an inauspicious beginning. With so many new provisions, the Act desperately needed intelligent implementation.

But the appointment of the superintendent, whose chief responsibility was the administration of the Act, was delayed for months, first by Lord Sydenham's death, then by growing doubts about the wisdom of a single appointment for both the Canadas, and finally by the difficulties of selecting a suitable candidate from among the large number of applicants. The Ministry finally settled on Robert Murray, a Presbyterian clergyman from Oakville, as the assistant superintendent of Canada West. Thus it was the middle of April 1842 before anyone representing the government assumed responsibility for administering the Act—seven months after it had been passed and more than three months after it came into force.[12]

In the meantime, local authorities, new at their jobs, were left without any form of systematic information about the Act. Local newspapers did their best, printing it (often inaccurately) and discussing it in editorial columns, but many councillors arrived at the first session of their District Council without even the most elementary knowledge of its terms.[13] As the editor of the *Kingston Herald* complained, "great confusion prevails throughout the country regarding the Common School Laws. The old system is overthrown and no one knows what is established in its place."[14]

These early difficulties might have been overcome had the Act been a sound piece of legislation. It was, however, anything but sound: instead of improving schooling it brought government-imposed chaos. During the two years it was in force, three major defects emerged: it failed to provide for the exercise of administrative leadership, it established no mechanisms for supervision or accountability, and it did not take adequate account of local conditions.

The lack of administrative leadership crippled the Act from beginning to end. Murray had no discretionary power to resolve disputes, clarify obscurities, or interpret doubtful points of law. Faced with a problem he couldn't resolve, his only recourse was to refer the matter to the Executive Council through the provincial secretary. That official, however, had no special responsibility for the schools and did no more than lay the matter before the Council. No other member of the Ministry was answerable for the working of the Act. Without someone to ensure that the business of the schools received its fair share of attention from the Ministry, decisions were too often postponed or put off entirely.

The serious consequences of such indecision were evident in a wide variety of matters which affected the day-to-day operation of the schools.[15] But one particularly damaging example may serve to indicate the nature of the problem. By the summer of 1842 it was clear that some districts would refuse to levy the school property tax for that year and might therefore be liable to forfeit the government grant. Because of the "novelty of the provisions of the Act", the government decided to apportion the grant to all districts, including those that had not raised the school tax in order "to avoid the evils from which the country would suffer if the appropriation were withheld".[16] But it took the government more than nine months—till April 1843—to reach this decision. And while the government fiddled, the localities burned. Some district councils had already introduced the tax and would inherit the wrath of their constituents when it proved unnecessary. Some councils vacillated, passing an assessment by-law and then repealing it. Other councils hedged their bets: the Brock District Council refused to levy the school tax as such, but, in case the government did decide to enforce the law, raised an equivalent amount in the general assessment and thereby vaulted from illegality to illegality.[17] Township commissioners, moreover, discovered that if the district councils failed to raise an assessment, they might become personally liable for their teachers' salaries. Hence many commissioners simply refused to sign contracts. Meanwhile the Ministry ignored both local pleas and Murray's protests. Consequently, schools began to close their doors and many teachers suffered real hardship.[18] Because no one within the Ministry was responsible for the administration of the law, matters which were crucial to the operation of the schools went unattended.

Handicapped by ministerial indifference, Murray found it difficult to assert his own leadership even in the most routine matters. On assuming office, for example, he discovered that the Act made no provision for the financial support of the Education Office: no funds had been allotted for rent, a clerk, firewood, or even stamps. Indeed there were no funds provided in the Act for printing the forms required to meet its own provisions. Nor was the Ministry eager to find funds from other sources. It took Murray weeks to wheedle from the government the money he needed just to begin his work.[19] Then he discovered that, in any case, he often did not know whom to write.

Until well into 1843 he frequently had no idea who the local officials were, either because district clerks did not know themselves or failed to report the information.[20]

The communications gap between central and local authorities, moreover, worked both ways. Because of certain financial clauses of the Act, the Ministry had found it could not do away altogether with a single superintendent for both of The Canadas. Thus Robert Jameson, Vice-Chancellor of Upper Canada, was appointed as a figurehead superintendent. His salary and his duties, however, had been divided between the two sectional assistant superintendents. But the Act made no reference to the latter posts and no attempt was made to explain the change to either Parliament or the people. Thus local people, with no clear idea who Murray was or what he was supposed to do, were left to guess whom they should consult. District clerks, treasurers, or wardens, accustomed to dealing with ministers on other issues, frequently wrote them about minor school problems and their requests had to be passed on to Murray, though he could never be sure that would in fact happen.[21] Well-known politicians like Robert Baldwin were plagued by such letters; and these were not, it must be emphasized, requests for special privilege or esoteric information, but for information of the kind that would later be routinely handled by the superintendent or his clerks.[22] The public was simply not aware of any standard communications procedure and the government made no attempt to establish one. The lack of administrative leadership proved to be a serious weakness in the Act.

A second major weakness was its inadequate provision for supervision and accountability. Murray had no field officers to examine the work of the township boards, and indeed, no means even to ensure that the provisions of the Act were actually carried out or that government money was not misappropriated. The Act left the township commissioners their own inspectors, auditors, and arbiters. As Murray discovered, the commissioners, like the trustees before them, found it easiest to hire the cheapest teachers and to allow parents to send their children to school with the textbooks at hand.[23] And the power given them to settle local disputes proved positively dangerous. The many pleas for redress that found their way to Murray, the Ministry, or the Governor tell a sorry tale of petty tyranny and occasionally of gross injustice.[24] Without greater powers, and especially powers of inspection and audit, the central authority was impotent.

↳Finally, the <u>Act failed to take account of local practices and conditions</u>. A few clauses, probably due to nothing more than careless drafting, caused particular consternation at the local level. The Act appeared to prohibit the attendance of children under five and over sixteen years of age.[25] It excluded female teachers and thus threatened to upset the growing custom of hiring a girl to teach the summer term in the rural areas, or of paying the grant to female schools in the towns.[26] The Act forbade the establishment of school sections formed from parts of two townships, imposing, in the words of the *St. Catharines Journal*, "a very severe hardship upon a large portion of the inhabitants, who, from necessity, have formed 'union' sections, many of which are among the oldest sections in the country . . . ."[27] The Act, in other words, <u>trampled on a variety of long-established and in some cases essential local practices</u> and left in its wake mounting confusion and frustration.

↳The most important flaw at the local level, however, proved to be <u>the new township-wide boards</u> established in the Act of <u>1841</u>. The replacement of school section trustees by a township board had been a favourite proposal of the 1830s: it would reduce the number of local officials, attract more men of standing to local school administration, and encourage greater uniformity within each township.[28] But <u>by 1843 the boards were an admitted failure</u>. The main reason appears to have been the <u>onerous workload imposed on</u> them. The commissioners were busy men—millers, doctors, clergymen, or farmers—already carrying a full load of business and family responsibilities. They received no remuneration for their new obligations, not even travelling expenses, yet their duties were heavy and exacting: maintaining the schools, inspecting them, certifying teachers, drafting regulations, and keeping financial accounts for the dozen or more schools in the township. The plea of the Charlottenburgh commissioners, who resigned *en masse*, was probably shared by many of their colleagues:

> some of us had not read the Act and were therefore ignorant of the nature and extent of the duties required. These duties are so numerous and so various that an attempt to discharge them in a manner that would be satisfactory . . . would occupy so much of our time as to leave us no other alternative than to give up for a twelve month our present professional duties

and employments and devote our whole energies to the carrying into effect of the provisions . . . of said Act.[29]

Hyperbole perhaps; but the same point was made over and over in Murray's correspondence and in petitions and protests about the Act. The amount of clerical and administrative work was overwhelming, and the duties of supervision and visitation were "intolerable".[30] Whatever the merits of the original idea, the township boards failed to meet the hopes held for them in the 1830s.

Tory or Reformer, teacher or parent, all alike dismissed the practical operation of the Act of 1841 in what one local politician described as "unmeasured terms of disapprobation".[31] A revised bill could not be drafted soon enough to be introduced in 1842, but in the session of 1843, a new Act, guided through the Assembly by Francis Hincks, was passed with what was, apparently, a unanimous sigh of relief.[32]

The Common School Act of 1843 introduced important changes in three areas.[33] It paved the way for more effective central administration, it re-established the school section trustee boards as the unit of local administration, and it created a corps of local field officers to assist in administrative work and to supervise local educational activities.

Though the Act did not actually use the phraseology, it created what was in effect a minister of education for Upper Canada by naming the provincial secretary as chief superintendent of schools, *ex officio*. The superintendent's powers remained, as in 1841, to apportion the government grant, administer the Act, and report annually to Parliament. Within this limited role, Dominick Daly, the "perpetual minister" and now chief superintendent, gave firm leadership. He dealt efficiently with those matters forwarded by Murray and ensured that policy decisions received due attention from the Ministry.[34] By establishing political responsibility for the schools, the new Act marked a significant advance over 1841 in the administrative capability of the central educational authority.

At the same time, Daly made sure that his assistant superintendent could operate more effectively. Murray was re-appointed immediately upon passage of the Act and though only three weeks elapsed between that time and the beginning of 1844 when the Act came into force, he managed to get copies of the Act printed and distributed to local officials and newspapers by the end of December.[35] He was there as well to answer the multitude of questions that arose during the first months under the new legislation. By April or May 1844, the Act was more or less in operation throughout Upper Canada—a remarkable contrast to the chaos that had followed the introduction of the Act of 1841.

Murray's administrative role was clarified as well. Shortly after assuming office, Daly issued the first formal directive on administrative procedure Murray had ever received. Murray was to act "as you think the circumstances of the case render proper, and when you think it necessary to submit drafts for approval . . . where you are doubtful as to the proper course, you can consult me, but in all cases let the drafts or steps to be taken, be suggested by you, in the same manner as the business connected with other Departments is done by the Assistant Secretaries."[36]

Finally, with the approval of Daly, a circular went out to all school officials requesting them to address all relevant correspondence to the Education Office.[37] The effect of this directive is obvious more than a century later. From 1816 until the mid-1840s, routine school correspondence is scattered through a variety of private and public archival sources, with the bulk of it buried in the immense and undifferentiated files of the civil and provincial secretaries. From early 1845, most of this correspondence can be found in the Education Office files.[38] For the first time, all the routine business of the schools began to flow through one set of hands.

At the local level, the Act of 1843 dispensed with the township boards of commissioners and returned the immediate responsibility for running each school to three elected school section trustees. Their responsibilities were much the same as they had been under the Act of 1816—to build and maintain the schools, to hire the teachers, to draft and impose school rules, and generally to see to the day-to-day affairs of their school. We know very little about the reasons why the Ministry chose to decentralize local school administration from the township to the section, outside of the animus aroused by the township boards of 1841 to which the section boards were an obvious alternative. But certainly the decision was an important one. For good or ill, it saddled Upper Canada with thousands, rather than a few hundred, local educational authorities. And it re-affirmed a pattern of local administration that would prove remarkably resistant to modification for over a century.

The third area of change introduced by the Act of 1843 was

perhaps the most important: the creation of a corps of local superintendents. The Act itself proposed two levels of superintendents: township and district. The township superintendents however, never did play a significant role under the Act, for they were shorn of many of their responsibilities when the municipal bill of 1843 failed to become law, and in 1846 the office was formally abolished. The district superintendents, on the other hand, were crucial to the operation of both the Acts of 1843 and 1846. Though their powers varied somewhat in the two acts (a point that will be discussed later), it is useful to consider their role between 1844 and 1849 here.

The district superintendents were important in three respects: as administrative agents of the central authority, as supervisory officers or inspectors, and as local leaders in education. First, the district superintendents provided the central authority with a corps of regional field officers by which the assistant superintendent could pass on instructions and advice on matters of general concern. They gave local people a local officer to turn to for information.[39] They audited accounts and codified reports and forwarded them to the Education Office. In the process they began the standardization of record-keeping and reporting in hundreds of school sections across the province. And they got out and visited the schools. Jacob Keefer's rough notes of a tour of part of the Niagara District in 1845 have survived to show a short notation on the citizenship of each teacher, the books used, the physical state of the school house, the number and progress of the pupils.[40] It was this kind of work that, in 1845 and 1846, provided the first useful school statistics the province ever had.[41]

The local superintendents, moreover, were given powers by the Act of 1843 which, for the first time, limited the autonomy of the local educational authorities. School section trustees now had to hire a teacher certified as competent by the local superintendent, and their school rules and textbooks were subject to his approval. The superintendents were required to verify that government money had been spent as the Act directed, and could, if necessary, withhold the grant for misappropriation. Thus with the Act of 1843, the process of subordinating locally elected officers to appointed administrative functionaries had begun.[42]

By modern standards, it must be emphasized, these field officers would not fit well into any but the very loosest model of a well-organized bureaucracy. They had no special training.

They were part-time officials only, and until 1846 unpaid. They were appointed not by the central government but by the District Council. They were responsible to the central authority for certain administrative and financial affairs, but under the 1843 Act at least, completely independent of it in setting standards for teacher certification, textbooks, school rules, and the like. Thus, the effectiveness of the local superintendent depended largely on the men appointed to the post. In some cases they were nonentities or worse: in at least one case, the local superintendent actually absconded with the year's school funds.[41] Geography, moreover, tended to overwhelm them all. The districts were large, and as their reports make clear, schools often went unvisited and teachers unexamined.[42] None the less, many of the district superintendents were remarkably effective. Men like William Hutton for Victoria, Jacob Keefer and then Dexter D'Everardo for Niagara, John Steele for Newcastle, Elias Burnham for Colborne, or Hamnet Pinhey for Dalhousie, not only performed their administrative and supervisory functions to the best of their ability, but, in part because of their personal prestige in their localities, provided local leadership in education. To teachers and trustees they addressed missives on everything from the minutiae of bureaucratic procedure to larger issues such as the proper organization of the school day or the construction of healthy school houses.[43] To the general public they gave speeches and made reports, frequently printed in the local newspapers, which familiarized people with the state of the schools and argued the case for improvement.[44] This kind of local leadership was of particular importance during the formative years of the school system.

The Act of 1843, then, began the process of establishing political responsibility for the schools, routine departmental procedure, effective lines of communication, and the supervision of the schools by officials independent of the local educational authorities. It also removed many of the irritants of 1841; for example, it included women within the definition of common-school teacher, and provided for the formation of union school sections. But one major technical flaw made revision essential from the day it came into force. The Act had been drafted in tandem with Baldwin's municipal bill and many of its clauses relating to local appointments, finance, and legal responsibilities, were dependent upon the establishment of the new county and township councils Baldwin envisaged. When the municipal bill died in the Legislature, the school act was left with a multitude of loose ends, obscurities, and conflicting clauses which caused administrative difficulties at all levels of authority.

The responsibility for drafting suitable amendments fell to Egerton Ryerson, the assistant superintendent since September 1844. Much to the chagrin, however, of those Reformers who had drafted and passed the legislation of 1843, Ryerson had in mind much more than merely technical emendations of the Act. With the help of a sympathetic conservative Ministry he would use the necessity of minor revision as an opportunity to introduce a significantly altered structure for elementary schooling.[45]

Ryerson did not make Ontario's system of public instruction. He inherited an operating system. The school trustees, the Education Office, and an experienced body of regional officers were already functioning when Ryerson became chief superintendent in 1846. Indeed, the Act of 1843 has as much claim to the title of founding legislation as Ryerson's school acts of 1846 and 1850.[46] None the less, Ryerson's contribution to the development of the administrative system is undeniable. His most significant achievement was the establishment of a more powerful and more effective central authority. What powers did he add that had not existed before? How did he strengthen the links between the central authority and the local superintendents and trustees? What mechanisms did he establish to promote financial accountability? How did the new central authority actually work? And, to what extent was political responsibility and control maintained?

In the Act of 1843, the central authority had no power to regulate "in-school" affairs. Only the local superintendents could certify teachers, and approve rules, textbooks, and the like. In the Act of 1846, Ryerson added to the administrative powers of the central authority the crucial regulatory element—the power to make regulations concerning "the organization, government and discipline of common schools", the classification of teachers and schools, and the textbooks to be used. Local trustees were explicitly directed to hire only teachers who were "qualified according to the provisions of the Act", to select only approved textbooks, and to see that their schools were conducted according to the regulations. The law gave the central authority the power to withhold the grant if its regulations were flouted. For the first time, the Education Department had

a voice in determining what actually happened in the schools.
The effectiveness of the expanded powers of the central educational authority were, in Ryerson's mind, largely dependent
on an effective inspectorate. In 1846, fresh from his tour of
Britain and the continent, he envisaged a set of full-time field
officers, appointed and paid by the government, who would have
the power to visit the schools, advise, inspect, and enforce the
will of the central authority.[47] On this point, however, the
politicians balked. He was forced to compromise in his draft
bill of 1846 and even his compromise was partially defeated in
Parliament.[48] In the final version of the Act, the arrangements
of 1843 were continued: the district superintendents were to
be appointed by the district councils alone. On the other hand,
Draper did manage to preserve one key clause which brought a
marked change from the Act of 1843. The local superintendents
were now *required* to follow the instructions of the chief superintendent. It was this clause that would provide the crucial
supervisory link between the central authority and the local
trustees.

Ryerson's statutory power over local superintendents was
continued in the Act of 1850. But one clause in the new act
materially weakened their effectiveness as agents of the central
government. With the passing of the Municipal Act of 1849, the
question arose as to the most appropriate level of operation
for the superintendents—the county or the township. From
experience, Ryerson probably preferred the county superintendents. Like the district superintendents he had worked with
between 1844 and 1849, they would constitute a relatively small
group, would be drawn from influential men in their communities, and Ryerson would know many of them personally. Yet
he had to admit that geography and time made it nearly impossible for part-time officials to inspect the schools of a whole
district or county regularly. Township superintendents, on the
other hand, would be closer to the scene, and would be responsible for fewer schools. Yet there would be more of them and
their quality might vary greatly. Ryerson struggled with the
problem in 1849 without reaching a solution that satisfied him.[49]
Hincks took the matter up early in 1850, sending circulars to
a wide variety of local people throughout the province for their
opinion.[50] But there was no consensus. In the end, Ryerson
and Hincks left the matter open. The Act of 1850 gave the
county councils the right to appoint a single county superintendent or a number of township superintendents. Generally the

councils opted for the latter. The result was that for the next twenty years, Ryerson's impact would be filtered through the work of more than three hundred part-time local superintendents, of varying ability and degrees of commitment, and often with strong local loyalties that would qualify their effectiveness as agents of the central government. Nevertheless, in 1850 a chain of command existed which brought the central authority in touch with the thousands of trustee boards in the province. The links were stronger than in 1843, but they were still much weaker than Ryerson had originally envisaged.

Ryerson also extended the influence of the central authority when he created the *Journal of Education for Upper Canada*. Like Murray before him, Ryerson was beseiged by demands from all quarters for advice and information, much of it of the most basic kind. Even in the late 1840s, for example, there were still many local authorities operating without those most essential tools, the Act and regulations.[51] As well, there were numerous issues of school law and practice which needed clarification and emphasis. The school acts, as Ryerson himself said, were necessarily complex and "no man can administer a school law . . . which he does not understand; the proper understanding of it involves considerable information . . . ."[52] The *Journal* was Ryerson's answer to this problem. The propaganda value of the *Journal* has often been noted: it was the springboard for most of Ryerson's educational campaigns. But its administrative function was no less important. It carried in issue after issue the official regulations, forms, and instructions, as well as column upon column of advice and explanation. For over twenty years it would be the standard guide to school law and procedures for trustees, teachers, and local superintendents. Indeed, it was superseded only when its function could be entrusted to those trained and certified servants of the department, the county inspectors.

In 1850, moreover, Ryerson brought a new degree of financial accountability to the system. Prior to that year, government money was distributed to school sections either in proportion to the total number of children of school age, or between 1843 and 1846, in ratio to the total population, regardless of the number of children actually in school. In the Act of 1850, however, Ryerson stipulated that the grant be apportioned to schools on the basis of average attendance. The change introduced a more relevant standard for the spending of public money and one that could be easily verified. Teachers were now required to keep a daily register showing enrolment and attendance. Local superintendents were required to examine it on their quarterly visits and ascertain its accuracy. The new grants system thus gave the central authority some clear test of the relationship between money spent and educational results achieved.

The increase in the power of the central authority was accompanied by a change in the nature of the central authority itself. In 1846 and again in 1850, Ryerson attempted to enhance the Education Department's moral authority and ensure its political autonomy by ensconcing its policy-making function in a semi-independent board. In addition to the chief superintendent, the General Board of Education (1846), later the Council of Public Instruction (1850), consisted of prominent clergy and laymen appointed on the pleasure of the Governor General. They were responsible for making policy decisions regarding the general regulations, selection of texts, and classification of teachers. In theory, the Council made policy and the Education Office, under the chief superintendent, administered it. In fact, however, the situation was rather different. The records of the Council are incomplete, but from the minutes and the surviving internal correspondence there is no evidence, for the 1850s at least, to suggest that it ever initiated any policies except those recommended by Ryerson.[53] It might, of course, have been different had the Ministry appointed men representing a variety of educational viewpoints. But Ryerson's close relations with William Henry Draper in 1846 and Francis Hincks in 1850 assured him of a sympathetic Council.[54] Its most significant role in the 1840s and 1850s seems to have been that of a buffer: when under fire, Ryerson could always point to the disinterested, intelligent, and experienced clergy and laity who had already approved and sustained his own views. The real work of policy formation was always done by Ryerson with the growing assistance of John George Hodgins, his chief clerk and future deputy superintendent.

One of the most frequent criticisms of the Act of 1846 was that both the chief superintendent and the General Board were independent of Legislature and Ministry alike—a notable change from the Act of 1843 and, Reformers asserted, an intolerable political affront.[55] If judged by modern standards of political responsibility, the charge had some truth in it. Though Ryerson was responsible to the Governor, he was, in theory at least, independent of the politicians. Too much should not be made of this, however, since Ryerson normally submitted policy decisions and such things as draft regulations to the Ministry for approval.[56] In any case, with the Reformers back in power at the end of the decade, political responsibility was re-asserted, though in a somewhat unconventional way. From 1850, the chief superintendent was, in the words of the Act of that year, "responsible to, and subject to the direction of, the Governor General, communicated to him through such Department of Her Majesty's Provincial Government, as by the Governor, may be directed in that behalf. . . ."

This arrangement represented a compromise between the Ministry's determination to impose political control and Ryerson's determination to head a department "above politics". It meant that while he was not formally subordinate to any particular politician, he was not independent of the Ministry. And at first the arrangement seems to have worked well. Certainly, government control was exercised. Policy recommendations, amended regulations, and the like were routinely forwarded to the Ministry for approval, usually through the provincial secretary's office. Nor did the Ministry act as a rubber stamp, as the occasional rejection of departmental policy indicates.[57] Moreover, Ryerson maintained close links with Draper, Hincks, and initially at least, with Macdonald, and was generally successful in getting them to carry his projects within the Ministry and through the Legislature, whether these projects involved amended legislation, expanded grants, pensions for teachers, or the creation of school libraries. In the early 1850s, at least, there was little ministerial indifference to public education. None the less, Ryerson's success was ultimately based on his personal relationships with individual ministers. And when the good relationships of the 1840s and early 1850s began to cool ten years later, Ryerson paid the price for shaping a department "above politics". Increasingly, he found that far from being above politics he was merely outside it, unable to influence cabinet deliberations or even to command ministers' attention should they choose to ignore him. At that point, Ryerson began to think the unthinkable. His growing advocacy of a ministerial department for education, however, is another story.[58]

Ryerson, then, increased the autonomy and the powers of the central authority, created a chain of command between it, the local superintendents, and the boards of trustees, improved communications with local officials and the public, and introduced a new measure of financial accountability to the system.

Ryerson's second major contribution to the development of the school system was his relentless concern for administrative detail—a concern that enabled him to impose a remarkable degree of coherence and consistency upon the system even by 1850. "As the 'care of shillings and pence' is necessary in the accumulation of pounds," he wrote in 1846, "so attention to details is essential to the success and efficiency of a System of Public Instruction. Vague generalities will be of little practical use. It is the fitting of the minute and less conspicuous parts, which constitutes the real strength of a structure."[59] Ryerson turned out to be a master at getting the "minute and less conspicuous parts" of the system to work effectively and smoothly.

In short time, for example, he managed to reduce the reporting and communications system to a set of rigorous bureaucratic procedures. A plethora of standardized blank forms were drawn up to avoid the inconsistency and variation that occurred when local officials were allowed to draft their own.[60] Ryerson, moreover, was insistent that they be filled out properly and would repeatedly return them for correction if necessary.[61] The appropriate locus for giving advice or resolving disputes was publicized in the *Journal of Education*, and, indeed, printed on every letterjacket mailed out from the Education Office. That done, he expected procedures to be followed: much of his official correspondence consisted of letters referring local authorities to their local superintendent, and reminding them that that official's decision was final.

Ryerson provided institutionalized procedures for settling many local problems as well. Prior to 1846 there was no administrative or legal continuity at the local level. In both the Acts of 1841 and 1843, the local boards were elected annually. But after 1846 only one trustee retired each year, and the remaining board members provided the desirable continuity of experience. At the same time, the boards of trustees became corporations, which both reduced the degree of personal liability of individual trustees and ensured long-term responsibility for debts. In 1847 Ryerson turned his attention to a bill to meet the needs of towns and cities.[62] Earlier acts had imposed the pattern of the school sections upon them—a pattern which did not suit the circumstances of urban areas. The school bill of 1847 provided for boards of education and a variety of other educational institutions that would not have been possible under the 1846 Act. In quick time, then, Ryerson was able to provide different kinds of administrative structures for different kinds of communities.

In 1846 Ryerson was too inexperienced to anticipate all the many difficulties which beset local people in operating a school system. But his correspondence revealed them soon enough: the endless conflicts over school sites, the intricacies of organizing and holding the annual school board elections, the problems in keeping and auditing accounts, and a wide variety of issues relating to trustee-teacher and trustee-ratepayer relations. Some of these problems proved insoluble.[63] But in 1850 Ryerson was able to draft a bill that delineated the rights and duties of local officials in a much sharper way than ever before.[64] The process of building an administrative structure to contain local difficulties was under way.

Ryerson, then, not only created a strong, regulatory central authority, but imposed a degree of order, uniformity, and effectiveness in administration unknown before. Yet to put too much emphasis on the coercive power of the central authority is to misunderstand its administrative style. True, Ryerson was occasionally willing to use coercion, or at least the threat of it, when local authorities failed to meet their basic obligations under the Act or attempted to abuse teachers or local minorities,[65] but in the vast majority of cases, Ryerson used his powers cautiously, and this caution extended even to basic departmental policy such as uniform texts, minimum qualifications for teachers, and the test of average attendance. Even a cursory reading of his correspondence reveals Ryerson's preference for persuasion rather than coercion.[66] Indeed, compulsion was seldom necessary because for the most part the central authority was moving no faster and often more slowly than public opinion. Many school boards raised taxes well beyond the minimum, established school libraries and graded classes, hired teachers qualified above the minimum standard, and provided improved accommodation. The central authority created an administrative and legal framework for such progress. The administrative style that emerged (and persisted) had Ryerson's stamp upon it: methodism in administration, and an unending flow of exhortation—praise for the virtuous, homilies for the laggard, a scourge for the unrepentant, uplift for all.

It would be wrong to suggest that in 1850 the administrative system was complete. At mid-century the powers of the central authority were relatively limited compared to what they would eventually become. Control over the local superintendents was still weak. The grammar schools were still outside the system. Communications between parts of the system were often uncertain. Financial accountability throughout the system was not firmly established, especially the accountability of the Education Office to the Legislature.[67] Nevertheless, the outlines of an administrative system had taken shape. The state now had the administrative machinery to impose minimum standards and see that public money was spent for the purpose for which it was appropriated. Political control and responsibility were established, though in a somewhat roundabout and irregular way. Departmental officers existed to formulate policy and administer the law. Local field officers, responsible to the central authority, supervised the schools. Uniform business and reporting procedures were being established among the three thousand local authorities who actually operated the schools. None of this had existed ten years before. In a word, an effective public bureaucracy had begun to take shape.

NOTES

1. J. E. Hodgetts, *Pioneer Public Service; An Administrative History of the United Canadas, 1841–1867* (Toronto, 1955); and id., *The Canadian Public Service; A Physiology of Government, 1867–1970* (Toronto, 1973).

2. See for example Valerie Cromwell, "Interpretations of Nineteenth-Century Administration: An Analysis", *Victorian Studies* IX (March 1966), 245–55.

3. See for example Richard Johnson, "Administrators in education before 1870: patronage, social position and role", pp. 110–38, and S. E. Finer, "The transmission of Benthamite ideas, 1820–50", pp. 11–32, in Gillian Sutherland, ed., *Studies in the Growth of Nineteenth-Century Government* (London, 1972); Steven J. Novak, "Professionalism and Bureaucracy: English Doctors and the Victorian Public Health Administration", *Journal of Social History* VI (Summer 1973), 440–62.

4. Oliver MacDonagh, *A Pattern of Government Growth 1800–60; The Passenger Acts and their Enforcement* (London, 1961), pp. 15–21, 320–36. Professor MacDonagh's qualifications of his self-generating principle should be carefully noted. See also id., "The Nineteenth-Century Revolution in Government: A Reappraisal", *Historical Journal* I (1958), 53. This was Professor MacDonagh's opening broadside in a long and productive controversy.

5. Sutherland, *Nineteenth-Century Government*, p. 10.

6. Jenifer Hart, "Nineteenth-Century Social Reform: A Tory Interpretation of History", *Past and Present* XXXI (1965), 39–61.

7. W. Atkinson to Hodgins, 15 February 1878, R.G.-2, E-1, Box 3, Public Archives of Ontario (PAO). In the early 1870s the Education Department's incoming and outgoing correspondence was approaching 30,000 items, while the

Colonial Office was handling a mere 25,000! Colonial Office figures quoted in Henry Parris, *Constitutional Bureaucracy; The Development of British Central Administration since the Eighteenth Century* (London, 1969), p. 112.

8. See R. D. Gidney, "Upper Canadian Public Opinion and Common School Improvement in the 1830s", *Social History* v, No. 9 (April 1972), 48–60; Susan E. Houston, "Politics, Schools and Social Change in Upper Canada", *Canadian Historical Review* LIII, No. 3 (September 1972), 249–71; J. D. Wilson, "The Teacher in Early Ontario", in F. H. Armstrong, H. A. Stevenson, and J. D. Wilson, eds., *Aspects of Nineteenth-Century Ontario* (Toronto, 1974), pp. 218–36.

9. See R. D. Gidney, "Centralization and Education: the Origins of an Ontario Tradition", *Journal of Canadian Studies* VII, No. 4 (November 1972), 33–48. It is important to note that many of the arguments for and against administrative devices used to improve the schools had already been anticipated by John Strachan, though for a variety of reasons they were never effectively implemented.

10. See Hodgetts, *Pioneer Public Service*, chapters 2 and 3.

11. The Act is printed in J. G. Hodgins, ed., *Documentary History of Education in Upper Canada, 1791–1876* (28 vols.; Toronto, 1894–1910), IV: 48–55. On the politics of the Act of 1841 see Danielle Garcia, "L'Elaboration du Système Scolaire Bi-Confessionnel au Canada-Est, 1840–1867" (M.Phil. thesis, University of London, 1973), pp. 82 *ff*.

12. The background to Murray's appointment is discussed in R. D. Gidney, "The Rev. Robert Murray: Ontario's First Superintendent of Schools", *Ontario History* LXIII, No. 4 (December 1971), 191–204.

13. See the *Examiner*, 29 September 1841; *British Colonist*, 20 October 1841; *Christian Guardian*, 24 November 1841; *Bathurst Courier*, 21 December 1841. The *Upper Canada Gazette* published it on November 4 with a major error in one of the financial clauses. The error was not corrected until the *Kingston Herald* noted it, 5 January 1842.

14. *Kingston Herald*, 18 January 1842. Similarly see the *British Colonist*, 9 February 1842.

15. For instance there was the question of whether a female teacher could be hired when the Act used only the masculine pronoun. See "Opinion of the Law Officers of the Crown on the Petition of Mr. A. H. Blake", 17 February 1840, R.G. -5, A-1, Vol. 240, Public Archives of Canada (PAC); *Kingston Herald*, 5 July 1842; *St. Catharines Journal*, 1 December 1842; Hopkirk to the President, Board of Police, Belleville, 30 January 1843, R.G. -5, C-1, Vol. 103, No. 5200, PAC.

16. See "Documents relating to the Common School Act. . . . Report of a Committee of the Executive Council. . . . April 1, 1843", Journals of the Legislative Assembly, 1843, Appendix Z.

17. Murray to Hopkirk, 11 October 1842, R.G. -5, C-1, Vol. 96, No. 4550, PAC; W. Lapenotière to Murray, 19 December 1842, R.G.-2, C-6-C, PAO; *British Colonist*, 21 May 1843.

18. *Examiner*, 11 May 1842; David Johnson to Murray, 22 July 1842, and S. B. Coate to Murray, 18 July 1842, R.G. -2, C-6-C, PAO; *Christian Guardian*, 10 August 1842 and 22 February 1843; Robert McNair to Murray, 5 March 1843, R.G. -2, C-6-C, PAO.

19. Murray to Hopkirk, 14 December 1842, R.G.-5, C-1, Vol. 100, No. 4908, PAC; Murray to J. W. Powell, 24 March 1843, R.G. -5, C-1, PAC.

20. Murray (and the government) had no exact idea of even the number of boundaries of the school sections until mid-1843, when all the returns were finally in. See "Boundaries of the School Districts, 1842", R.G. -2, F-1, PAO.

21. See for example, Treasurer, Victoria District, to Hincks, 31 November 1842, R.G. -5, C-1, Vol. 97, No. 4699, PAC; D. O'Connor to W. H. Dunn, 3 December 1842, Vol. 99, No. 4849, PAC; President, Board of Police, Belleville, to Hopkirk, 30 January 1843, Vol. 103, No. 5200, PAC.

22. For example, see William Hutton to Baldwin, 19 July 1842, T. A. Hughes to Baldwin, 24 November 1842, and Johnston Neilson to Baldwin, 25 February 1842, Robert Baldwin Papers, Metropolitan Toronto Central Library (MTCL).

23. "Report of the Deputy Superintendent . . . Canada West for 1842", Journals of the Legislative Assembly, 1843, Appendix Z.

24. For two typical examples see Murray to Hopkirk, 31 March 1843, Vol. 106, No. 5514, and Petition of James Cunningham and related documents, Vol. 108, No. 5750 and Vol. 110, No. 5956, R.G. -5, C-1, PAC.

25. *Kingston Herald*, 14 December 1841. Also, the *Examiner*, 13 September 1843.

26. *Kingston Herald*, 5 July 1841.

27. *St. Catharines Journal*, 3 March 1842.

28. For example, see Burwell's common school bill printed in Hodgins, *Documentary History* III: 280–83, and Duncombe's bill in id., *Report on Education* (Toronto, 1836).

29. School Commissioners, Charlottenburgh, to James Pringle, 15 August 1842, R.G. -2, C-6-C, PAO.

30. Murray to James Strong, 17 September 1842, R.G. -2, C-1, PAO; R. F. Budd to Murray, 25 February 1843, R.G. -2, C-6-C, PAO.

31. William Merrill to Cartwright, 23 September 1842, J. S. Cartwright Papers, PAO; John Carey to Baldwin, 20 January 1843, Baldwin Papers, MTCL.

32. See a comment of Murray's in Murray to Craigie, 5 December 1843, R.G. -2, C-1, PAO.

33. The Act is printed in Hodgins, *Documentary History* IV: 251–62.

34. See for example, Murray to Provincial Secretary, 23 August 1844, R.G. -5, C-1, Vol. 134, No. 8252, PAC; Minutes of the Executive Council, 10 March 1845, and Daly to McNab, 6 December 1845, R.G. -2, C-6-C, PAO.

35. Murray to Hopkirk, 13 December 1843, R.G. -5, C-1, Vol. 120, No. 6842, PAC. It was in the hands of the editor of the *Brockville Recorder*, 29 December 1843. For some of the problems in implementing the Act see the *St. Catharines Journal*, 12 January 1844.

36. Daly to Murray, 17 April 1844, R.G. -2, C-6-C, PAO.

37. McNab to the township superintendents of common schools, 25 March 1845 (and in the following days to all other officials), R.G. -2, C-1, PAO.

38. Most of the routine elementary school correspondence from 1816 to 1845 is in the Upper Canadian Sundries and the Provincial Secretary's records in the PAC, though from 1842 the assistant superintendent's correspondence in the PAO should also be consulted. Important papers can be found as well in a number of private collections. After 1845,

however, nearly all the significant correspondence is in the PAO, R.G. -2, C-1, and C-6-C, the incoming and outgoing files of the Education Office.

39. For example see Memorial of Gideon Gibson, 16 May 1845, John Steele Papers, PAO—a typical case which in 1842 or 1843 would have gone to Murray and the government but which, in 1845, was dealt with by the district superintendent.

40. Keefer Papers, PAC.

41. Charles Fletcher to Ryerson, 1 April 1850, R.G.-2, C-6-C, PAO.

42. See for example, their summary reports for 1845 in Journals of the Legislative Assembly, 1846, Appendix P.

43. See for example W. Wilson to Higginson, 17 June 1844, and Circular to Township Superintendents, Trustees and Teachers, by W. Wilson, District Superintendent, London, April 1844 (encl.), R.G. -5, C-1, Vol. 130, No. 7860, PAC; Circular from D'Everardo to School Trustees, 1 December 1848, Gonder Papers, Niagara Historical Society Museum.

44. See for example the *Kingston Herald*, 10 December 1844, 25 November 1845, and 10 November 1846; *Examiner*, 21 May 1845 and 24 June 1846; *Brockville Recorder*, 23 January 1845; Elias Burnham, *An Address to the Inhabitants of the Colborne District* (Peterborough, 1846).

45. The administrative and political history of the Education Department cannot and should not be separated. The fact that this key administrator was appointed is best explained by political circumstances. Moreover, Ryerson's ideas are crucial to the administrative structure he created. We have eliminated them here only because of the

exigencies of space and any full account of this period in the administrative history of the department would require detailed discussion of them. For the nonce, on Ryerson's appointment see Gidney, "Murray", pp. 202–04; on the ideological and political background, see Gidney, "Centralization and Education", pp. 38–41; and Houston, "Politics, Schools and Social Change", pp. 249–71; on why Ryerson and his Act survived the return of the Reformers to power, see Gidney, "Centralization and Education", pp. 41–47.

46. The Act of 1846 is printed in Hodgins, *Documentary History* VI: 59–70. Similar provisions existed in Ryerson's second major school law, the Act of 1850. See ibid. IX: 31–49.

47. Ryerson to Hopkirk, 3 March 1846, R.G. -2, C-1, PAO.

48. Ibid.

49. Ryerson to Executive Council, 23 February 1849, R.G. -2, C-1, PAO.

50. The mix of opinion can be seen in Hodgins, *Documentary History* IX: 54–70. Replies not printed there can be found in January–May 1850, R.G. -2, C-6-C, PAO.

51. Ryerson to William Hutton, 4 February 1847, and Ryerson to the Provincial Secretary, 26 October 1848, R.G. -2, C-1, PAO.

52. Hodgins, *Documentary History* IX: 184–85.

53. Some of the board and Council records are in R.G. -2, B, PAO. There are also internal correspondence and memoranda scattered through R.G. -2, C-1 and C-6-C, PAO. We can find only one rather minor exception to our generalization—see R.G. -2, B, Vol. II, p. 130, PAO. It should also be noted that the greatest burden of work for the Council of Public Instruction was the establishment and administration of the

normal school. Here they seem to have exercised greater authority, or at least influence.

54. See for example Ryerson to Draper, 14 and 30 May 1846, Hodgins Papers, PAO.

55. See almost any issue of either *The Globe* or the *Examiner* during December 1846–January 1847 when the "great prussianism debate" was at its height. Hincks took quite a different view— see the *Pilot*, 19 May 1846.

56. See for example, Draper to Ryerson, 1 January 1847, Hodgins Papers, PAO.

57. See for example, R.G. -2, B, Vol. II, No. 333, PAO.

58. See for the first clear indication of the problem, C. B. Sissons, ed., *Egerton Ryerson; His Life and Letters* (Toronto, 1937–47), II: 386–87.

59. Hodgins, *Documentary History* VI: 266.

60. Ryerson to Hincks, 26 July 1848, R.G. -2, C-1, PAO.

61. Ryerson to Rev. William Clarke, 26 February 1849, ibid.

62. Ryerson to Provincial Secretary, 24 March 1847, ibid.

63. For example, a variety of problems related to union school sections would haunt the Education Office throughout the century. The school sites issue was not resolved until trustees acquired the power of expropriation.

64. For more detail see *Annual Report* for 1850, pp. 307–10.

65. Ryerson to Jas. Shaver, 23 December 1847, R.G. -2, C-1, PAO.

66. Ryerson to George Hendry, 12 January 1847, and to Hamilton Hunter, 19 August 1847, ibid.

67. This was also true for most government departments and would not begin to be remedied until the reforms initiated by Auditor General Langton in the late 1850s. See Hodgetts, *Pioneer Public Service*, Chapter 7.

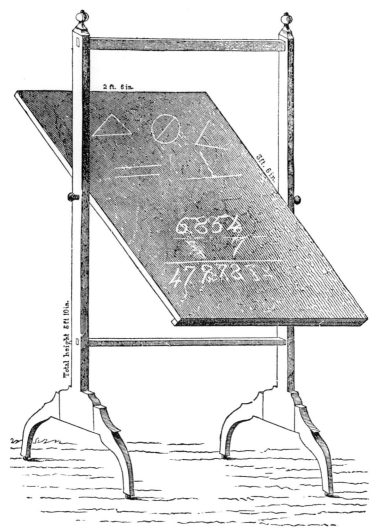

IV Evaluating the System

The Reality Behind the Rhetoric: The Social and Economic Meanings of Literacy in the Mid-Nineteenth Century: The Example of Literacy and Criminality*

HARVEY J. GRAFF

"First, such a system of general education amongst the people is the most effectual prevention of pauperism, and its natural companions, misery and vice."[1] With this statement, made early in his career as chief superintendent of education for Upper Canada, Egerton Ryerson embraced a central tenet of the mid-nineteenth-century school promoter. That education could prevent criminality, if not cure it, was integral to school promoters' programs. They marshalled reams of evidence, rhetorical and statistical, to prove the perceived relationship between ignorance or lack of education and criminality. In their formulations, ignorance and crime were associated not only with each other, but also with illiteracy, a visible and measurable sign of a lack of schooling.

The prominence accorded formal schooling and instruction in literacy for the masses, as social insurance against criminality and disorder, forms one significant example of the broad new consensus about education which emerged throughout Anglo-America by mid-century. In a period of massive social change, of urban-industrial modernization, education was increasingly seen as the dominant tool for social stability in societies where stratification by social class had replaced traditional paternalistic control by rank and deference. The changing scale and bases of society demanded the creation of new institutions, like the school, to aid in the inculcation of restraint, order, discipline, and integration: the correct rules for social and economic behaviour in a changing and modernizing context. No longer could proper social morality and values be successfully trans-

---

*This essay draws heavily upon my "Literacy and Social Structure in the Nineteenth-Century City" (PHD thesis, University of Toronto, 1975), especially Chapter 6.

mitted by informal and traditional means; the forces of change necessitated formal institutions to provide morally grounded instruction aided, eased, and speeded by a carefully structured provision of literacy. Literacy became the vehicle for the efficient training of the population. Morality without literacy was more than ever seen as impossible, and literacy alone was potentially dangerous. The nineteenth-century educational consensus was therefore founded upon a "moral economy" of literacy. Agencies created to prepare men and women for their future places in society seized upon the controlled transmission of literacy. The potential of print to achieve the desired and expected ends in the inculcation of a morally ordered and religiously rooted behavioural code: the guarantee of conservative and orderly social and economic progress.[2]

Despite the existence of this unified attitude to the place of the school in society and the goals of education, the connections advanced between the provision of proper education, literacy, and the reductions of disorder and criminality, or conversely, illiteracy and criminality, were often less than satisfactory or conclusive. Egerton Ryerson's statements, consequently, were not always clear and unambiguous, especially with regard to the role of illiteracy. To a significant extent, of course, the moral importance of schooling represented the critical factor, but in their use of the statistics of illiteracy school promoters in Canada and elsewhere confused their arguments. They were uncertain at times about what form of schooling would best serve their purposes. Their focus on schooling, moreover, obscured the role of other factors which contributed to criminality and made their notions of causality less than convincing. In spite of their explanations, criminality, or more properly arrest and conviction, related to much more than illiteracy. Illiteracy, to be sure, was often symptomatic of poverty and lower-class status, which were also associated with arrest and punishment, but it was only one element in a complex of factors. Ethnic affiliation, class, sex, and the crime of apprehension, rather than illiteracy alone determined conviction, since those with the fewest resources were most often convicted. Apparently, systematic patterns of punishment might relate to factors other than guilt.

Importantly, the structure of social inequality as well as the distribution of literacy often centred upon ethnic affiliation and sex. Ascribed characteristics thus determined social stratification, access to economic opportunity, social discrimination, and apparently judicial treatment as well, contradicting much of the school promoter's rhetoric about the advantages of educational achievement in countering factors of birth (one key premise of modern society). Literacy, the evidence suggests, in spite of the schoolmen's arguments, did not relate directly to individual advancement or to social progress as exemplified here by the majority of criminals. Similarly, illiteracy, in isolation from ethnicity, or sex, did not relate solely or unambiguously to criminality, or to poverty or immobility. The centrality of literacy in educational rhetoric and the promise of schooling itself, past as well as present, demand revision.[3] The case of criminality, significantly, supports the emerging outlines of a new historical sociology of education.

This essay focuses upon the relationship between criminality and illiteracy perceived and discussed by school promoters. First, their causal notions and their evidence will be examined, and then tested through an analysis of a nineteenth-century gaol register which included literacy among its data.

The extent of criminality was among the most pressing of social concerns for Upper Canadians in the mid-nineteenth century.[4] With other Anglo-Americans, they asked: What had caused the apparent increase in crime and violence? What produced criminality in the populace? The complex answers given to these questions included immigration, poverty, urbanism, immorality, ignorance, and of course illiteracy. These forces, all at work in Upper Canada as elsewhere, were woven into a causal explanation of criminality. In these explanations, the connections between ignorance, illiteracy, and criminality, always crucial, formed the central assumptions of men who attempted to build and expand systems of mass schooling. To them, education was fundamental to the prevention of crime and disorder.

Crime in Upper Canada, it was thought, was intimately connected to "an influx of criminal elements from outside the country, and particularly from Ireland".[5] To Ryerson, immigrants were as "notoriously destitute of intelligence and industry as they are of means of subsistence".[6] Lack of schooling, idleness, and poverty were the causes of this social problem, and foreigners were the greatest offenders. Cities, moreover, were the scene of the greatest difficulty; they represented the seedbed of crime and were of course the centres of reform attention. Crime, according to Ryerson, "may be said in some

sort to be hereditary, as well as infectious . . . to multiply
wretchedness and vice . . . [as] the gangrene of pauperism in
either cities or states is almost incurable."[7] The city, especially
Toronto, provided his common examples, and throughout his
tenure in office he regularly provided evidence from gaols and
prisons to show that most inmates came from the most popu-
lous places. Summarizing this widely held belief, Michael Katz
has concluded, "in the lexicon of reformers the first fact about
crime was its urban nature."[8] Agreement was complete on this
point throughout Anglo-America and in much of the west.[9]

These factors were associated with causes of criminality;
ignorance, however, was the source. Consequently, Ryerson and
many of his contemporaries urged that their systems of popular
education were the most effective preventatives of ignorance,
pauperism, misery, and vice.[10] How schooling was to accom-
plish this, and conversely, how lack of schooling resulted in
criminality were crucial points on which the school promoters
were less than clear. At least this was where their statements
became vague. To document an apparent relationship and to
urge prevention was one thing, to explain it was quite another.

Egerton Ryerson enunciated the commonly perceived connection in its starkest and most direct form in his first report.

> Now the Statistical Reports of Pauperism and crime in dif-
> ferent counties, furnish indubitable proof that ignorance is the
> fruitful source of idleness, intemperance and improvidence,
> and these the fosterparents of pauperism and crime. The his-
> tory of every country in Europe may be appealed to in proof
> and illustration of the fact . . . that pauperism and crime pre-
> vail in proportion to the absence of education amongst the
> labouring classes, and that in proportion to the existence and
> prevalence of education amongst these classes, is the absence
> of pauperism and its legitimate offspring.[11]

To this he would soon add the history of Upper Canada. Here,
however, Ryerson succinctly stated that ignorance—the lack of
schooling—was the first factor in a life of crime. Simply, "the
condition of the people and the extent of crime and violence
among them follow in like order" from the state of education.
Among other evidence, he cited English Poor Law Commissioners ("a principal cause of [Northumberland's lack of crime]
arises from the education they receive"), and the example of
Prussia's school system.[12] Others in Upper Canada concurred.

The Globe, which disagreed with Ryerson on many issues, declared: "educate your people and your gaols will be abandoned and your police will be disbanded; all the offenses which man commits against his own peace will be comparatively unknown. . . ."[13] Thus, education was not only effective, it was the cheapest agency of prevention: "The education of the people forms part of the machinery of the State for the prevention of crime."[14] Costs and public expenses were important as well, and often central to the school promoter's arguments. To them, schools were both cheaper than gaols and prisons and a better investment. Naturally, they felt "it is much better to prevent crime by drying up its sources than by punishing its acts."[15]

Ignorance and illiteracy, as Ryerson argued, were the first causes of poverty and crime, which in turn were inextricably linked. Each was seen to cause the other, particularly among immigrants and in cities.[16] The result was a simple causal explanation or model of criminality: ignorance caused idleness, intemperance, and improvidence, which resulted in crime and poverty.[17] Ryerson and other promoters saw crime not only as the "legitimate" child of this chain of factors, they also labelled each factor a crime itself. For example, idleness and ignorance were more than causes, they also were offenses: "If ignorance is an evil to society, voluntary ignorance is a crime against society . . . if idle mendicacy is a crime in a man thirty years of age, why is not idle vagrancy a crime in a boy ten years of age? The latter is the parent of the former."[18]

Ignorance also led to poverty, and education, conversely, led to success. Again *The Globe* agreed: "If we make our people intelligent, they cannot fail to be prosperous."[19] The poor, therefore, were ignorant, often living lives of crime and withholding their children from school—preparing the future class of criminals.[20] In fact, families and parents were blamed for the prevalence of ignorance, non-attendance, and the resulting illiteracy, and neglectful parents were as guilty as their children. Indeed, they were "bringing up and sending abroad into the community [children] who are prepared by ignorance, by lawlessness, by vice, to be pests to society—to violate the laws, to steal, to rob, and murder. . . ."[21] The crime was not only against the victim for "Training up children in ignorance and vagrancy, is a flagrant crime against Society," depriving it of "examples, labours, and talents . . . and inflicting upon it serious disorders and expenditures."[22]

The eradication of ignorance through education was the solution, a characteristically Victorian one. Schooling was the right of each child and the preparation of each citizen, as well as the security of the rich.[23] Consequently, neglect of education was itself a crime, and social order would be "better conserved by having [Toronto's] thousands of idle boys industriously and appropriately receiving instruction in her hitherto empty schoolhouses than in contracting vicious habits in the streets and on the sidewalks of the city."[24] Nevertheless, crime persisted, especially among the young, after the founding of mass public-school systems. Rather than re-examining his premises, Ryerson maintained that further provision for schooling was needed and that the schools were not full, thus not reaching all the children.[25] Arguments explaining criminality, therefore, continued to be stated negatively, stressing the results of no schooling and not the specific ways in which education would prevent crime.

In their explanations, moreover, reformers seldom considered other factors, or that their factors might be re-ordered. Disregarding the social and economic realities which determined school attendance, poverty, for example, was not considered a cause of ignorance or illiteracy. Chief Justice Robinson made this clear in addressing a Grand Jury: "I am satisfied that no proper excuse can be given for the Children of the poor not being sent to the Schools ready to receive them in Towns and Cities."[26] It is difficult to censure schoolmen for ignoring problems of immigration, poverty, and neglect, which were all too real to their immediate vision. Their notions of causality, however, may be questioned, for they were unable to recognize poverty as a structural feature of society or capitalism. To them pauperism and idleness emanated from ignorance; economic failure derived from moral weakness, and many were considered paupers by choice, not by chance or structural inequality.[27] Ignorance, idleness, and intemperance, then, remained the result of individual behaviour, and the reformer's answer was education to prevent illiteracy, ignorance, and criminality. This was the role of the state.

Schoolmen were certain that ignorance and illiteracy lay at the heart of criminality. Statistical evidence was gathered as proof: data which described the educational condition of prisoners who were assumed guilty of criminal offenses. Ignorance of course meant more than illiteracy; nevertheless, illiteracy was taken to be its measurable sign. From these statistics,

educational promoters derived their arguments, and recipro-
cally, in them they found continuing support. As a result,
illiteracy itself was raised to a casual factor in their explanations, along with ignorance. Indeed, wherever in the west
promoters inquired, the same results were found: the periodic
examination of the literacy of the arrested and convicted served
to bolster the cause of education. As direct evidence of ignorance and the lack of schooling, these tabulations became the
statistical foundation upon which the rhetorical house explaining criminality was built.

Indeed, it is significant that goals and prisons, as well as
reformatories, regularly inquired into the educational condition
of their inmates, and that literacy was the universal measure
chosen. Since illiteracy was accepted as the sign of ignorance,
the knowledge of the prisoners' achievements or status was an
essential concern. Moreover, efforts were made in Upper Canadian prisons to provide instruction in reading and writing, and
J. George Hodgins, Ryerson's lieutenant, pressed for the establishment of prison libraries. Not only did annual prison reports
detail the literacy of all inmates, chaplains and schoolmasters
told of their repeated efforts to instruct and tabulated the
numbers and progress of their pupils.[28] They too linked criminality with ignorance and sought to replace it with literacy:
"such being the almost barbarous ignorance in which the great
majority of convicts have been raised, it would seem an unnecessary cruelty to deprive them of the means of the 'limited
education' which the humanity of Christian legislation has
provided for them in this institution."[29] R. V. Rogers, a chaplain
who failed to secure funds for either library, schoolroom, or
schoolmaster, summed up their goal in instruction: "a Professed School of Reform, without the needed Machinery for
Reformation—a Penitentiary in Name—A Jail in Fact!!"[30]

Egerton Ryerson referred to English and European statistics
in his first report, and often included them in his *Journal of
Education*. A decade after that report, he presented the evidence
for Upper Canada itself. "How intimate and general is the connexion between the training up of children in igorance and
vagrancy and the expenses and varied evils of public crime may
be gathered from the statistics of the Toronto Gaol during the
year 1856, as compiled by the Governor of the Gaol from the
Gaol Register." As on other occasions, he reproduced the statistics on literacy for the inmate population. For 1967 prisoners,
the registers presented this distribution:

	Male	Female
neither read nor write	401	246
read only	253	200
read and write imperfectly	570	198
read and write well	68	—
superior education	1	—

Just what literary abilities these categories may have described will be considered below, but regardless, Ryerson's conclusions from them rang familiarly in support of his stated assumptions. To him, they revealed that more than 95 per cent of the incarcerated "had grown up without the advantages of a good common school education; and that less than five per cent of the crimes committed, were committed by persons who could even read and write well."

Here then was the evidence for his causal model and for the centrality of illiteracy; but what was to be done? Ryerson continued, arguing prescriptively, that these were "facts which show that had a legal provision been made, such as would have secured to *all* these 1967 prisoners a good common school education, the number of prisoners committed to the Toronto Gaol would scarcely have exceeded one hundred . . . their crimes would have been prevented, and the time, trouble, and expenses attending their detection and punishment would have been saved."[31] Of course there was a certain circularity in these common arguments, for it was assumed that in keeping the potential youthful offenders off the streets and in the schoolrooms the prisons would be emptied of the great bulk of their numbers (95 per cent to Ryerson). Funds saved on one would then become freed for the other.

Ryerson was far from alone in recognizing the importance of literacy in the educational prevention of crime or in the use of illiteracy statistics in support of his argument. Either summary statistics or the more common practice of presenting raw numbers of prisoners at each level of education was a standard feature, significantly, of both the educational and the penitentiary report of the last century. Massachusetts reports, for example, frequently cited them, whether the discussion related to prisons, juvenile reformatories, or schools, which all were seen as weapons attacking the same social problems.[32] Standard also was the reproduction of foreign statistics to illustrate the universality of the problem, or to demonstrate that progress could occasionally be made, either to censure or to applaud the situation at home.

Others in fact went further than Ryerson in their investigations of the relation between illiteracy and crime, continuing of course to equate ignorance in criminals with illiteracy. Reformers in the United States, in particular, scoured the records to produce statistical summaries which rang with the truth of arithmetic exactness. One summary was a report by James P. Wickersham to the National Educational Association, which investigated the charge, "that a very high proportion—60 per cent, I think—of the convicts then confined in the prisons of Philadelphia, were high school graduates."[33] His report, "Education and Crime", concluded to the contrary, in 1881,

1. that about one-sixth of all the crime in the country is commited by persons wholly illiterate.
2. that about one-third of it is committed by persons practically illiterate.
3. that the proportion of criminals among the illiterate is about ten times as great as among those who have been instructed in the elements of a common-school education or beyond.[34]

These facts led Wickersham to conclude that the amount of crime is about as uniform from year to year as the amount of ignorance or illiteracy. Ten years earlier, another commentator established an even stronger relationship between illiteracy and criminality. E. D. Mansfield surveyed Europe as well as the United States, finding a strong connection between illiteracy and criminality wherever he looked. His mathematical relationships led him to conclude,

First. That one-third of all criminals are totally uneducated, and that four-fifths are practically uneducated.
Second. That the proportion of criminals from the illiterate classes is at least tenfold as great as the proportion from these having some education.[35]

Despite the certainty with which education was advanced as the best preventative of criminality and the evidence which repeatedly revealed that the criminals were largely ignorant, the eradication of illiteracy did not always seem to reduce crime. Of course, schools, as Ryerson argued, are "not responsible for defects in criminal laws, or police or municipal regulations".[36] Nevertheless, as attendance increased, Ryerson continued to reprint the gaol statistics, and importantly, he never reported a diminution in crime. The happy result of expanding educational provisions reducing offenses was not often to be found. In Massachusetts, for example, Frank Sanborn, the first secretary of the State Board of Charities, discovered that the number of illiterates in the prison population fell by 50 per cent, from 74 per cent in 1854 to 38 per cent in 1864. In spite of such apparent progress, he was startled. First, he discovered that in England and Wales, without a system of common schools, only 33 per cent of prisoners could neither read nor write, and in Ireland only 50 per cent.[37] More importantly, while Massachusetts figures led him to believe that the proportion of illiterates among the prison population was far greater than among the entire population, the decadal decrease in criminal illiteracy had not been accompanied by a corresponding decrease in crime.[38]

Sanborn and Ryerson were not alone in making unsettling discoveries, which ran counter to their models and expectations. Some resorted to explanations of continuing high rates of crime by referring to improved enforcement and enlightened judicial systems. Commonly, however, the situation led to a confused, sometimes contradictory, posture by school reformers and public officials who used the illiteracy statistics to demonstrate that ignorance was a primary cause of criminality. Witness the efforts of Wickersham on this quandary, as he discussed the hypothetical possibility that Prussia possessed more criminals than France in spite of better schooling and higher rates of literacy. "It will be found that the cause is not in her schools but in spite of her schools, for in Prussia, as in all other countries, an illiterate man is many times more likely to commit crime than one who is educated." This alone was not a sufficient reason for continuing criminality; the cause could also be "a crime-producing factor in his nature or in the circumstances that surround him which his education has not been able to eliminate." Education could then fail to achieve its goal. With this information in mind, however, Wickersham could conclude securely and optimistically, "were it not for the restraining effects of intellectual, moral, and religious factors, our opinion is that [crime] would completely disrupt society and resolve its broken fragments into chaos."[39] Ryerson, of course, argued the same point.

In fact, school promoters covered themselves nicely. If education failed to decrease criminality as they predicted, they retreated to explanations which stressed a poor environment, immigration, poverty, heredity, the wrong sort of education, or non-attendance. However, if ignorance, as discovered by statistics of illiteracy, were the cause, educational provision would protect order, with training in literacy the essential aim. Some spokesmen attempted to use both arguments and to have their claims accepted both ways, seemingly unaware of the potential for circularity or contradiction. The way around problems of argument and evidence often centred upon their definitions of ignorance, and as a result the applicability of literacy statistics varied according to the chosen meaning. Illiteracy, then, represented either *the fact* of ignorance or merely *one possible* symptom of the lack of a proper education. To the former, statistics of prisoners' literacy were relevant and germane evidence. To the latter, however, measures of literacy—or of intellectual education—were insufficient and inappropriate proof to connect illiteracy with ignorance and criminality. Literacy, if unrestrained by morality, could be very dangerous, and an individual's literacy alone was hardly a guarantee of his or her orderliness.[40] In spite of the clear differences in the role of literacy in their discussions, schoolmen turned to both models, revealing their confusion and the contradictions inherent in their uses of literacy.

By mid-century, the school was more than ever before seen as the vehicle required to replace the family and church in giving moral instruction. Its success, moreover, was sometimes determined by the proportion of literate men and women produced for the society. Literacy, then, indicated that the expected training had occurred; illiteracy, conversely, meant a lack of schooling or the presence of a deeper ignorance rooted in personal deviance which schooling could not eradicate. The provision of schools to properly teach literacy was sufficient for *The Globe*: "give the child the simple rudiments of education and to him all else is opened . . . if we make our people intelligent, they cannot fail to be prosperous: intelligence makes morality, morality industry, industry prosperity as surely as the sun shines."[41] The process was automatic; intelligence, prosperity, and morality followed from literacy. Prison chaplains and masters agreed. J. T. Gardiner claimed, "reading and studying of books is a powerful means of leading men to consider and abandon the evil practices by which their youth may have been contaminated. . . ."[42] Or, as a Kingston Penitentiary schoolmaster exclaimed, "to be a reading man, is to be a

powerful man . . . a moral man and a useful member of society."[43] Here, illiteracy was equated with ignorance, and statistics of prisoner illiteracy were relevant and necessary to the
arguments.

Simultaneously, though, arguments were advanced which
stressed the insufficiency of literacy as a preventative of crime.
Ryerson, for one, remarked that schooling did not always end
in moral training, as "much of this moral degradation and social
danger must be charged on the neglected or perverted, culture
of the Schools." False education, "which severs knowledge from
its relations to duty", could be found in many schools, and as
a result, "a reading and writing community may be a very
vicious community, if morality be not as much a portion of
education as reading and writing."[44] Henry Mayhew, in England, was even more vehement in his critique of "ragged
schools". These institutions, he concluded, "may be, they are,
and must be, from the mere fact of bringing so many boys of
vicious propensities together, productive of far more injury
than benefit to the community. If some boys are rescued many
are lost through them."[45] Some schools could stimulate rather
than prevent crime, and if schooling prevailed without morality
at its core, illiteracy could decrease while crime did not, much
as Frank Sanborn had discovered. The result then of educational expansion can be no more than more clever and skilful
criminals.

This issue was directly confronted by the *Christian Guardian*,
which under Ryerson's editorship addressed earlier fears about
the dangers of over-education. Responding to the question,
"Does Mere Intellectual Education Banish Crime?" the *Christian Guardian* noted that "the only ascertained effect of intellectual education on crime is to substitute fraud for force, the
cunning of civilized for the violence of savage life." To increase
intellectual power without inculcating moral principles made
men restless and dissatisfied, "hating those that are above him,
and desireous of reducing all to his own level". To convince
their audience of the truly conservative nature of proper
schooling, as Ryerson continued to do, the *Christian Guardian*
explained that intellectual and secular education alone were
insufficient. The formation of the Christian character was the
only proper end, and literacy itself did not erase the crucial
ignorance. The fault of the age, they concluded, was that "men
have hitherto been prone to take for granted, that it was only

necessary to teach the Art of reading, and before this new power all vice and error would flee away." Though education such as this might not cause crime, surely it did not prevent it.[46] This was the argument which Ryerson made central to his discussions and promotions of the succeeding decades. Schooling, he often urged, included the moral as well as the intellectual; literacy, the tool of training, was to be provided in carefully structured institutions. The pace of social change demanded no less a solution; the maintenance of the social order mandated it. Prison chaplains and instructors agreed too, contradicting their other statements. Reading and writing, while important, were not education; further instruction in morality was necessary and the moral faculties must be directly trained.[47] The role of literacy was to provide the vehicle for the efficient transmission and reinforcement of morality and restraint.

These were the principal lines of argument, then, in the relationship joining ignorance and criminality. Forming two poles in the elaboration of the perceived connection they were not seen as exclusive or contradictory. Each was used as it fit the situation, and definitions and processes differed with the argument chosen, both functioning towards the same end. School promoters vacillated between the two, and importantly, they continued in many cases to employ the statistics of literacy regardless of their line of argument. If the first formulation were expounded, that learning to read led naturally to the inculcation of restraint and morality, the use of literacy and the prisoners' statistics was both necessary and appropriate as proof. If, however, the second argument were advanced, stressing morality as independent of literacy or intellectual training, the use of literacy as a measure of proper education was highly problematic, for, "the moral must advance contemporaneously with the intellectual man, else we see no increased education, but an increased capacity for evil doing."[48] In this formulation, literacy was hardly the crucial element; its role was unclear, and individuals could be ignorant whether literate or illiterate. Its importance instead lay in its usefulness for efficient mass schooling in a growing and changing society. Nevertheless, those who argued in this way continued to draw upon the statistics of criminal literacy, while their words denied the relevance of this evidence. Thus, Egerton Ryerson, within the span of several pages, could recognize the potential immorality and viciousness of the literate *and* employ the gaol registers as proof for his explanations, contradicting himself with his own data, as did Wickersham and Mansfield. Apparently, they never realized that the literacy statistics simply could not be used to prove both arguments. In attempting to do so, school promoters confused their efforts, reducing their credibility, and forcing a re-examination of both their assumptions and their explanations. The questions about which they were so certain, in fact, bear reopening.

Some contemporaries realized the contradictory employment of literacy tabulations and not all accepted the use of their evidence. From Great Britain came a scathing attack on their application to demonstrate the relationship between education and crime. W. B. Hodgson, addressing the Social Science Association in 1867, declared that although there may be "fallacies more palpable than that ignorance of reading and writing is productive of, or accompanied by, a greater amount of crime there can be few more gross or serious." While granting that the inability to read or write may represent the ignorance of all that lies beyond, he concluded that "the ability . . . (not to cavil about the degree of ability), by no means as gives the knowledge of aught beyond. Negatively, the ignorance implies much, positively the knowledge implies little."[49] Twenty years later another English commentator, Rev. J. W. Horsey, continued the attack on the role of literacy and education in the equation which accounted for criminality. "One can get no clear evidence or trustworthy statistics," he discovered, "to prove that the greater attention to educational matters has largely diminished even juvenile crime. There are fewer boys and girls sent to prison happily, but this arises from various causes, and *not entirely from their increased virtue and intelligence.*"[50] The statistics did not prove the case; the explanation was faulty. The expansion of educational provision, it would seem, did not prevent crime. If the convicted were and continued to be illiterate or if more were literate, there must be other causes, or the factors must be differently ordered. Illiteracy simply could not represent the first cause of criminality; their relationship, it would appear, must be mediated by other factors.

Other problems, moreover, result from the use of literacy statistics. First, and most superficially, school promoters simply found what they were looking for; the statistics became part of a self-fulfilling prophecy. And they could be manipulated. For example, if one-third of prisoners were illiterate, it was then claimed that one-third of all crimes were committed by the illiterate (a questionable deduction in itself), of course disproportionate for their share of the population. This does not negate, however, the fact that the criminals may have had a lower rate of literacy than the population at large. But the degree of difference could vary radically from place to place and from year to year. Levels of comparison between prisoners and other groups beyond those who could "neither read nor write" are very difficult, and entire populations, enumerated only by censuses, were never questioned about their *levels* of education or literacy, only about literacy or illiteracy. The very ambiguity of the classifications for the different levels obscures their meaning as well as their comparability, for nowhere were they defined.

Several difficulties are apparent here. First, we are never told how prisoners compared with the population on levels of education above that of simple illiteracy. Nor are we told how they compared with the arrested but not convicted or with the unapprehended criminal. The reinforcing role the statistics played obscured attention from these questions. Moreover, there is no *a priori* reason for contemporaries' ceaseless combination of the illiterate with those of imperfect education in applying this evidence to their explanations. This too was done without regard to the wider distribution of educational skills in the society.

Problems with the employment of criminal statistics are exacerbated by the irregularity of the statistical relationships found for the past century. Stability in rates of crime could be accompanied by increases or decreases in rates of inmate literacy. Similarly, rises or falls in rates of crime need not correspond with changes in criminal literacy rates which seem to have been remarkably stable in the face of movement in rates of other relevant factors.[51] As the century passed, more children enrolled in and attended school, and rates of adult literacy increased. Yet there was little discussion of crime's reduction as a result; at best, reformers claimed that more offenses would have been committed or that the situation was worse elsewhere. In sum, too many paradoxes and contradictions exist among the relationships in the simply causal models of Ryerson and other reformers. Consequently, they failed to prove that illiteracy caused criminality, that the association was either direct or causal, unmediated by other factors of potentially greater significance.

The data used by the reformers, the extraordinarily detailed nineteenth-century gaol registers, have survived for places in Upper Canada, allowing us to move beyond the rhetoric and to directly re-examine the relationships claimed by educational promoters. In discussions of the relationship between education and crime, the low level of literacy of the inmate population represented the most commonly cited characteristic of the annual tabulations, to the neglect of other regularly collected information about the prisoners. The registers, in fact, on an annual and individual basis, inquired about birthplace, religion, age, sex, occupation, moral habits, crime or offense, and judgment by the authorities, all in addition to the educational condition of each arrested person.

With this information, patterns of arrest and conviction may be recreated. As we will see, conviction in fact was associated with illiteracy, but the clearest patterns of successful prosecution relate directly to ethnic affiliation, occupational class, and sex, when the effects of illiteracy are controlled. These important factors, largely ignored in nineteenth-century explanations of criminality, blur a direct connection between illiteracy and conviction, for they intervened to form patterns of a systematic discrimination and prosecution by the judicial system. Illiteracy, of course, was often symptomatic of factors which made for high rates of punishment, as both were rooted in social inequality;[52] however, the most illiterate groups did not always fare the worst in judgments. Illiteracy's role was in many ways, then, a superficial one, acting through its associations with poverty and social structural inequality, and not necessarily with guilt. The crime for which one was apprehended was an important determinant as well, and the interaction of variables was more complex than the causal explanations of men like Ryerson would allow, forcing us to develop a new, more subtle understanding of crime and punishment in the past and a re-evaluation of the role played by literacy. School promoters' use of aggregate tabulations obscured the complex interrelationship of variables; to them the literacy statistics served as blinders.

The manuscript gaol registers of Middlesex County, Ontario, for the year 1867–68, were selected for this analysis. The earliest registers located, they provide complete information on all persons arrested, permitting us to distinguish between the convicted and acquitted, and to analyze their characteristics.[53] Urban crime and prosecution form the core of this discussion, as Middlesex County was dominated by the fledgling metropolis of London, a source of the majority of the county's criminals, although its population represented less than one-fourth of the county's 48,000 in 1861. The city and the county were growing prosperous centres of trade and transportation in western Ontario.

In the thirteen months the register spans, 535 men and women were arrested, and their profiles and characteristics recorded. Overwhelmingly urban residents, 64 per cent claimed London as their home with an additional 3 per cent reporting other Ontario cities. They were arrested for a broad range of crimes (over sixty in all) and two-thirds of them were convicted. Arrest and conviction, however, were far from random, as certain groups (Irish and English) were disproportionately arrested and the Irish were most often convicted. Similarly, those holding lower-class occupations, the officially unoccupied, and women were dealt with severely, as were those arrested for crimes related to drink and vagrancy.[54] Illiteracy related to these patterns in both reinforcing and contradictory ways.

Differences in educational background existed among the convicted, the acquitted, and the arrested. (See Table 1.) Among the arrested, though, the number who read well and very well exceeded the number of illiterates, as more educated than uneducated persons were apprehended as suspects. Reformers, of course, would not accept this statement, for as we have seen, they readily combined the numbers with an imperfect grounding in literacy with the illiterates. For Middlesex, therefore, they would have observed instead, that 80 per cent of the arrested and 86 per cent of the convicted lacked a good common-school education. If their combination were justified, it remains interesting that 68 per cent of those acquitted had not been well educated and that over 60 per cent of those released as innocent were imperfectly educated; many supposedly ignorant individuals, then, had not been found guilty. More important, however, was the slight difference in educational achievement between those suspected and those convicted; the proportion largely uneducated diverged marginally from one group to the other, though somewhat more from those released. Ignorance, as defined by those who assumed it to be the first cause of crime, apparently did not significantly differentiate suspects from convicts, and was only slightly better in distinguishing the acquitted from the accused. Illiteracy, then, was not an accurate predictor of criminal conviction.

TABLE 9:1

LITERACY OF MIDDLESEX CRIMINALS (PERCENTAGES)

	all arrested	convicted	acquitted
neither read nor write	17.8	22.7	7.2
read and write imperfectly	62.6	63.5	60.8
read and write well	16.3	11.9	25.9
read and write very well	3.2	1.7	6.0
N	535	362	173

Source: Manuscript Gaol Registers, County of Middlesex, Ontario, 1867–1868.

It is far from clear, however, that the reformers' combination of the lowest educational classes was a justifiable action. The representativeness of the imperfectly educated, in comparison with the larger population, is the key to an answer, and, in fact, there is little reason to consider them disproportionately represented among suspects or criminals. They were arrested, convicted, and acquitted with the same frequency, and, indeed, the published tabulations of prisoners' illiteracy in the province's Sessional Papers did not even include them in their statistical tables, presenting *only* county totals of those who could not read or write. Moreover, it is possible that the imperfectly educated were broadly representative of popular levels of education. As other research suggests, the high statistical level of literacy in Upper Canada may belie a lower qualitative level of achievement.[55]

Direct evidence on this question comes from research in progress in extraordinary Swedish sources, conducted by Egil Johanssen of Umea University. The parish catechetical examination registers include, for some years and on an individual basis, measures of both oral reading ability and comprehension. For Bygdea parish in 1862, Johanssen discovered that of those who achieved the highest grade in oral ability, 77.6 per cent only comprehended partially at best. Of those who read orally with less proficiency, 28 per cent had poor comprehension, while less than 4 per cent read with "passible" understanding. The ability to read well did not correlate with an ability to understand or to use one's literacy, and regardless of literacy, few comprehended even passably and only a tiny proportion totally understood what they read.[56]

The implications of these findings for a country with a long heritage of high levels of literacy cannot be minimized. Not only do they effectively contradict the efforts of Ryerson and others to combine the imperfect with the illiterate as without education, they suggest that the imperfect range was a broad one which encompassed a large proportion of the population. In this way the close correspondence of distribution of the imperfectly skilled among the arrested, convicted, and acquitted is significant, and should be expected. In all probability, they were individuals generally representative of the city's and county's educational condition. They cannot simply be combined with the illiterate in the effort to prove that paucity of education or ignorance contributed directly to criminality: apprehension and conviction. Rejection of the school promoters' categorization radically revises the statistical relationship that supposedly joined ignorance with crime. No longer might they claim that more than five-sixths of the convicted were exceptional persons without education; only 23 per cent remain fairly within those ranks.

That fewer than one-fourth of the convicted criminals were illiterate, and that fewer than one-fifth of the arrested were uneducated, severely modifies the contentions of the reformers. The weight of numbers shifts to individuals who were at least partially educated, who may now be seen as the great majority of the supposed offenders. Among the arrested, as noted, the well educated, in fact, equalled the illiterates. Among those convicted, the illiterates outnumbered those with a good education, but the margin is not large (10 per cent). As well, the illiterates convicted only slightly overrepresented their distribution among all arrested. Nevertheless, the balance shifts when the convicted are compared with the acquitted: the illiterates form a small proportion of those released, representing only one-third of their strength among the convicted. This difference, however, must be qualified too; the illiterates, significantly, were not underrepresented among the acquitted, for their proportion corresponded closely to the 1861 rate of adult illiteracy in London, home of the majority of arrested.[57] Although they were somewhat overrepresented among all arrested, a direct causal relationship linking illiteracy with criminality should have led to a far greater underrepresentation of illiterates among those found innocent and released rather than only a proportionate representation.

Illiterates, then, in Middlesex and London, were not the most frequent offenders; nevertheless, they were punished with greater regularity than others.[58] While their place in the criminal population was far from the extraordinary one reformers claimed, their rate of conviction was high, for five-sixths of them were convicted, and frequency of conviction related directly to level of education. Does this imply some measure of truth in reformers' arguments, that although the convicted were not overwhelmingly illiterate, the uneducated suspects were almost certainly guilty? This, however, is not the only interpretation of the statistics. Their incredible rate of conviction was related first of all, to patterns of discrimination and social prejudice against the Irish, the lower class, and women—these individuals were convicted most often regardless of their level of literacy. Punishment was of course more frequent for the least educated members of these groups, and illiteracy related more directly, perhaps, to arrest and successful prosecution than it did to guilt or criminality. Social inequality was the root of both illiteracy and conviction, and the actions of the courts were based in the social hierarchy.

Moreover, we cannot doubt the agencies of law enforcement and justice, the constabulary and the courts, accepted the dominant explanations of criminality, naturally accusing the ignorant and the illiterate, who were very often poor, and expecting them to be guilty. The ideology of criminality and its causes, and the mechanisms of inequality, were thus operational, as illiterates, with their supposedly unrestrained ignorance and immorality, were perceived as a threat to social order. Their other characteristics, of class, sex, and ethnicity, only reinforced their social marginality and the severity with which respectable society would react to them. As a result, their vulnerability was increased. No doubt they were visible, not hidden in ghettos like the poor today, working outdoors when employed, living near the rich, or perhaps begging in the streets. As well, they would have few resources to employ for their defense, whether for legal aid or for a bribe. They also lacked the formal training and experience to deal with the procedures and the language of a courtroom. Prepared by life in the streets or work place, rather than the school, illiterates could perhaps be intimidated, unable to respond properly, or to make themselves understood in a situation where their guilt might be presumed. Some of them, too, might welcome the gaol as a refuge, a warm shelter with food regularly provided. Consequently, patterns of conviction involved much more than simple illiteracy or ignorance, contrary to the school promoters' explanations. Expectations, ideology, inequality, and physical circumstances were combined in conviction.

Ethnicity was one factor upon which the wheels of justice turned, as the courts meted out judgments of varying severity to arrested members of different groups. With extraordinary frequency, the Irish (Catholic and Protestant) were arrested and convicted well above the mean rate of conviction, and more often than any other ethnic group. (See Table 2.) Significantly, however, the Irish were not marked by the highest levels of illiteracy. Among the arrested, five ethnic groups had greater proportions unable to read or write than the Irish Catholics, and three counted more than the Protestants, yet these groups were not convicted as regularly. (See Table 3.) Conversely, native-born Canadians (Protestant and Catholic) were most often illiterate, and they were acquitted most frequently. Clearly conviction was determined by more than measurable ignorance.

Among all the ethnic groups, rate of conviction corresponded to level of education, as illiterates were most often convicted. Nevertheless, Irish Catholics, and Protestants to a lesser extent, were convicted most frequently regardless of their educational attainments. Moreover, Catholics who read and wrote well were successfully prosecuted with greater frequency than those who were imperfectly skilled. These patterns point directly to systematic conviction of Irish men and women in mid-nineteenth-century London and Middlesex, and discrimination against them regardless of their literacy. Illiterates of course were isolated for severe prosecution, and Irish illiterates, especially Catholics, were certain to be convicted. Thus, ethnicity figured prominently in criminal conviction, as it did in the economic and occupational stratification of mid-nineteenth-century urban society. As social inequality often derived from the facts of ethnic ascription, successful prosecution apparently did as well. Irish men and women, especially the Catholics, faced inequality in the courtroom as in the marketplace. Concommitant poverty and illiteracy could only reinforce their precarious position; illiteracy was hardly a prior or first cause in itself. Their acquisition of literacy, moreover, neither guaranteed their economic success nor their security from criminal conviction.[59]

TABLE 9:2

MIDDLESEX CRIMINALS: RATE OF CONVICTION FOR EACH ETHNIC GROUP, CONTROLLING FOR LEVEL OF LITERACY

literacy level		Irish Catholic	Irish Protestant	Scottish Presbyterian	English Protestant	Canadian Protestant	Canadian Catholic	others	total
neither read nor write	N	5	7	3	3	24	16	24	82
	%	100.0	87.5	100.0	75.0	75.0	94.1	92.3	86.3
read and write imperfectly	N	35	29	13	38	39	23	53	230
	%	85.4	86.0	72.2	63.3	54.9	51.1	82.8	68.7
read and write well	N	10	4	1	7	15	0	6	43
	%	90.9	66.7	16.7	50.0	46.9	0.0	37.5	49.4
read and write very well	N	1	0	2	2	0	1	—	6
	%	50.0	0.0	100.0	40.0	0.0	33.3	—	35.3
total arrested total convicted	N	59	53	29	83	137	64	110	535
	%	86.4	75.5	65.5	60.2	56.9	60.9	77.3	67.7

TABLE 9:3

MIDDLESEX CRIMINALS: ETHNIC AFFILIATION BY LITERACY

literary level		Irish Catholics	Irish Protestant	Scottish Presbyterian	English Protestant	Canadian Protestant	Canadian Catholic	others	total	% convicted
neither read nor write	N	5	8	3	4	32	17	26		
	%	8.5	15.1	10.3	4.8	23.4	26.6	23.6	17.8	86.3
read and write imperfectly	N	41	36	18	60	71	45	64		
	%	69.5	67.9	62.1	72.3	51.8	70.3	58.2	62.6	68.7
read and write well	N	11	6	6	14	32	2	16		
	%	18.6	11.3	20.7	16.9	23.4	3.1	14.5	16.3	49.4
read and write very well	N	2	3	2	5	1	—	3		
	%	3.4	5.7	6.9	6.0	1.5	—	2.7	3.2	—
total arrested	N	59	53	29	83	137	64	110	535	
	%	11.0	9.9	5.4	15.5	25.6	12.0	20.6		35.3
total convicted	%	86.4	75.5	65.5	60.2	56.9	60.9	77.3	100.0	67.7

Class, status, and wealth, as signified by occupational rank, represented a second factor which determined the course of justice.[60] Lower-class workers, the unskilled, and the officially unoccupied, predominantly women, were both arrested and convicted far more often than those more highly ranked. (See Table 4.) Here there was a direct relationship with illiteracy, for literacy corresponded with occupational class as it did in the larger society, and, within each occupational rank, the uneducated were punished most frequently. Nevertheless, the class convicted most often, the semi-skilled, was not the most illiterate (10.3 per cent illiterate). The unskilled, moreover, with slightly higher illiteracy (13.3 per cent), were punished far less often, and those with no occupation, and much greater illiteracy (30.5 per cent), were convicted no more often.

As with the Irish, lower-class workers were selected for severe judgments; the poor and unemployed with least re-sources for defense were disproportionately arrested and con-victed. Their numbers included many Irish and women as well as illiterates, and these factors combined to produce swift pronouncements of guilt. Indeed, they were by and large pre-cisely those expected to be offenders by theories of criminality. Lower-class status and poverty could be synonymous conditions, and they could cause illiteracy as well as the need to resort to crime. Idleness was equally an offense. From this it does not follow, however, that illiteracy or ignorance alone resulted in crime. By contrast, in the formulations of the reformers, poverty or structural features of society or economy did not cause illit-eracy or ignorance. Inequalities of social stratification, with their basis often in ethnicity, were an important source of convictions, whether reinforced by illiteracy or not.

The courts' decisions to convict also pivoted upon the sex of the suspect, as women were convicted in 80 per cent of their cases compared to 60 per cent of men. (See Table 5.) Regardless of literacy, ethnicity, or crime, women received harsh judg-ments, and this was related to both their lack of occupation or idleness and their rate of illiteracy (27 per cent). Falling into categories which were severely adjudged (10 per cent were semi-skilled, as well), they no doubt were seen as failing in society's expected standards of feminine behaviour.[61] They were not at home, nurturing a family or properly domesticated, and their perceived deviance endangered the maintenance and propagation of the moral order, the family, and the training of children. While Irish and illiterate women were convicted

TABLE 9:4

MIDDLESEX CRIMINALS: RATE OF CONVICTION FOR EACH OCCUPATIONAL CATEGORY, CONTROLLING FOR LEVEL OF LITERACY

literacy level		professional, proprietor	white collar, small proprietor, farmer	skilled, artisanal	semi-skilled	unskilled	none	total
neither read nor write	N	—	0.0	2	6	15	59	82
	%	—	0	66.7	100.0	83.3	88.1	86.3
read and write imperfectly	N	—	8	27	37	59	99	230
	%	—	44.4	65.9	86.0	59.6	73.9	68.7
read and write well	N	1	4	17	2	8	11	43
	%	100.0	30.8	51.5	28.6	57.1	57.9	49.4
read and write very well	N	0	5	1	0	—	—	6
	%	0.0	62.5	20.0	0.0	—	—	35.3
total arrested	N	4	40	82	58	131	220	535
	%	0.8	7.5	15.4	10.7	24.5	41.2	
total convicted	%	25.0	42.5	57.3	79.3	62.5	76.8	67.7

most often, sexual discrimination saw women punished more often than men within each ethnic group and for virtually all crimes. Pervasive inequality had deep roots in sexual stratification.

TABLE 9:5

MIDDLESEX CRIMINALS: RATE OF CONVICTION FOR EACH SEX
CONTROLLING FOR LEVEL OF LITERACY

literacy level		male	female	total
neither read	N	33	49	82
nor write	%	76.7	94.2	86.3
read and write	N	132	98	230
imperfectly	%	62.6	79.0	68.7
read and	N	37	6	43
write well	%	50.0	46.2	49.4
read and write	N	6	—	6
very well	%	35.3	—	35.3
total arrested	N	345	190	535
total convicted	%	60.3	81.1	67.7

The crimes for which individuals were most often arrested and found guilty, not surprisingly, were moral offenses, and most striking was vagrancy, an offense marked by high rates of conviction and of illiteracy. (See Tables 6 and 7.) This was of course the crime of idleness, to which ignorance and illiteracy were presumed to lead. Perceived as dangerous, rather than as the poor in need of aid, vagrants were largely women (77 per cent, while only 35 per cent of all arrested) who were visible and seen as moral and social failures. Indeed, vagrancy would be a charge quite easy to prove, and it is unlikely that poor, homeless women, unaware of legal subtleties, could plead other than guilty. Moreover, the shelter of the gaol might often be welcome, for there were few other institutions to care for them.

Crimes related to drink, the offense of intemperance, which could also be easily proved, illustrate the discrimination against the Irish. Perhaps a realization of the myth of the drunken

TABLE 9:6

MIDDLESEX CRIMINALS: RATE OF CONVICTION FOR EACH CATEGORY OF CRIME, CONTROLLING FOR LEVEL OF LITERACY

literacy level		against property	against persons	crime related to drink	related to prostitution	vagrancy	against by-laws	others	total
neither read nor write	N	16	7	5	7	39	7	1	82
	%	72.7	77.8	100.0	70.0	100.0	77.8	100.0	86.3
read and write imperfectly	N	41	42	22	22	82	10	11	230
	%	43.6	70.0	81.5	61.1	95.3	76.9	61.1	68.7
read and write well	N	10	11	7	1	6	2	6	43
	%	33.3	57.9	77.8	12.5	85.7	66.7	54.5	49.4
read and write very well	N	1	0	2	—	—	—	3	6
	%	16.7	0.0	66.7	—	—	—	42.9	35.3
total arrested	N	152	89	44	54	133	25	38	535
total convicted	%	44.7	67.4	81.8	55.6	96.2	76.0	51.5	67.7

TABLE 9:7

MIDDLESEX CRIMINALS: CRIME BY LITERACY

literacy level		against property	against persons	drink related	prosti-tution	vagrancy	against by-laws	others	total	% convicted
neither read nor write	N	22	9	5	10	39	9	1	82	
	%	14.5	10.1	11.4	18.5	29.3	36.0	2.6	17.8	86.3
read and write imperfectly	N	94	60	27	36	86	13	19	230	
	%	61.8	67.4	61.4	66.7	64.7	52.0	50.0	63.5	68.7
read and write well	N	30	19	9	8	7	3	11	43	
	%	19.7	21.3	20.5	14.8	5.3	12.0	28.9	16.3	49.4
read and write very well	N	6	1	3	—	—	—	7	6	
	%	3.9	1.1	6.8	—	—	—	18.5	3.2	35.3
total arrested	N	152	89	44	54	133	25	38	535	
total convicted	%	44.7	67.4	81.8	55.6	96.2	76.0	51.5		67.7

Irishman, these offenses were severely judged, and the Irish were arrested for drunkenness twice as often as they were for all other crimes combined (43 per cent to 20 per cent.) Nevertheless, those suspected of drunkenness were among the least illiterate of all arrested (11.4 per cent) yet they were among the most often punished (82 per cent). A severe moral offense, intemperance was convicted regardless of the literacy of the suspects; other causes were more direct.

Even the relationship between immorality, illiteracy, and criminality, so central to explanations of deviance, was ambiguous. Moral offenses were certainly harshly judged, but contrary to Ryerson's formula, immorality was *not* always related to illiteracy. Significantly, when the moral habits of those arrested are examined, the intemperate included fewer illiterates (14 per cent) than the temperate (22 per cent).[62] Moreover, prostitution, clearly a moral offense, was marked by neither high illiteracy nor a high rate of conviction. Perhaps this was a crime more difficult to prove, but nevertheless, it represented another example of discrimination against women, as they were convicted more often than their male clients. Prostitutes, moreover, were among the most literate of arrested women, and they were convicted less often than virtually all other female offenders.

Other crimes further illustrate the lack of congruity between rates of conviction and the rates of literacy of the social groups suspected. High rates of illiteracy joined with high rates of conviction in cases involving vagrants and by-laws, while lower rates of conviction and illiteracy are found for prosecutions of property violations and miscellaneous crimes. This was what the reformers would expect. However, in cases involving drink low levels of illiteracy met frequent conviction; in offenses against persons low illiteracy resulted in average rates of conviction; and finally, prostitution saw average illiteracy and less frequent conviction. Overall, the relationship between illiteracy and conviction was less than direct.

The fact that for any crime illiterates were most often convicted obscured the ambiguities behind this first and most obvious relationship; this superficial connection no doubt only reinforced the popular views. Blurred from school promoters' vision, or perhaps ignored as contrary to expectations or even incomprehensible, were the literacy of the suspected and acquitted as well as the literacy of the convicted, patterns of discrimination, and varying rates of conviction for different offenses. Indeed, the crime for which most arrests were made, property offenses, was least often convicted, marked by the literacy and not illiteracy, of the suspects. Most attention of the courts, it would seem, was focused on crimes of idleness, intemperance, and disorder (by-law violations), crimes which were expected to follow directly from ignorance, even though they did not even constitute a majority of supposed offenses. Both educational promoters and the judiciary presumed the illiterate, or ignorant, the Irish, and the idle to be guilty of social offenses; it is not surprising that they were found guilty so often. Expectations, then as now, influenced justice, even though the perceived connection between illiteracy and criminality was neither the only nor the most important relationship.

Criminal prosecution, and probably apprehension as well, derived from the facts of inequality. Punishment, stratification, and illiteracy too were rooted in the social structure; pervasive structures of inequality which emanated from ethnic and sexual ascription ordered groups and individuals in mid-nineteenth-century urban areas. Achievement of literacy, or education, had little impact upon these structures, and in many cases only reinforced them. Despite the superficial relationship linking literacy and status and illiteracy and criminality, social inequality represented the primary determinant of criminality. Stratification by ethnic or sexual factors influenced the hierarchy of class, status, and wealth; in similar fashion, they turned the wheels of justice. Rather than illiteracy or ignorance leading directly to a life of crime, ethnic affiliation, class, and sex lay behind and strongly mediated the relationships most commonly drawn.

NOTES

1. Ryerson, "Report on a System of Public Elementary Instruction for Upper Canada", in J. G. Hodgins, ed., *Documentary History of Education in Upper Canada, 1791–1876* (28 vols.; Toronto; 1894–1910) vi: 143.

2. For an evaluation of the educational consensus and an extended discussion of the "moral economy" of literacy, see Harvey J. Graff, "Literacy and Social Structure in the Nineteenth-Century City", (PH D thesis, University of Toronto, 1975), especially Chapter 1, and the documentation provided therein.

3. Ibid., especially Chapter 2 for the analysis of literacy and social structure. The data presented there demonstrate broadly that as the allocation of literacy followed the structure of ethnic stratification, the achievement or acquisition of literacy did remarkably little to alter the struc-

ture of inequality or the ranking of individuals and groups. Success in occupation and wealth derived from factors of ethnicity, age, and sex; ascription dominated over achievement. Literacy, moreover, tended to reinforce rather than counter the effects of stratification, with some few exceptions. See also, Michael B. Katz, *The People of Hamilton, Canada West: Family and Class in a Mid-Nineteenth Century City* (Cambridge, Mass., 1975), especially Chapter 2.

4. J. J. Bellomo, "Upper Canadian Attitudes Towards Crime and Punishment", *Ontario History* LXIV (1972), 12, 13.

5. Ibid., p. 12.

6. *Journal of Education for Upper Canada* I, No. 10 (October 1848), 300.

7. Ryerson, "Public Elementary Instruction", p. 143.

8. Michael B. Katz, *The Irony of Early School Reform* (Cambridge, Mass., 1968), pp. 170–71.

9. Bellomo, "Attitudes"; J. H. Tobias, *Crime and Industrial Society in the Nineteenth Century* (Harmondsworth, 1972); Susan Houston, "The Victorian Origins of Juvenile Delinquency", *History of Education Quarterly* XII (1972), 254–80.

10. Alison Prentice, "The Social Thought of Egerton Ryerson", (paper for the Department of History, University of Toronto, 1970), and id., "The School Promoters: Education and Social Class in Nineteenth Century Upper Canada", (PH D thesis, University of Toronto, 1974). See also Walter Houghton, *The Victorian Frame of Mind* (New Haven, 1957); and Susan Houston, "The Impetus to Reform: Urban Crime, Poverty, and Ignorance in Ontario, 1850–1875" (PH D thesis, University of Toronto, 1974).

11. Ryerson, "Public Elementary Instruction" p. 143.

12. Ibid., pp. 143–44.

13. *The Globe*, 11 December 1851.

14. *The Globe*, 11 December 1862; Ryerson, *Annual Report of the Chief Superintendent of Education* for 1857, p. 17 (The titles of the chief superintendents' annual reports change from year to year, hereafter cited as *Annual Report* for the given year.); on their disagreements, J. M. S. Careless, *Brown of the Globe* (2 vols.; Toronto, 1959–63); C. B. Sissons, ed., *Egerton Ryerson: His Life and Letters* (2 vols.; Toronto, 1937–47).

15. *The Globe*, 11 December 1851; "Truancy and Juvenile Crime in Cities, 1859–1860", in Hodgins, *Documentary History* XV: 1–5.

16. Katz, *The Irony*, p. 180. The same was found in Massachusetts.

17. The stark simplicity of the causal model is striking:

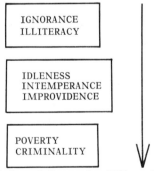

18. *Annual Report* for 1857, p. 47; and Prentice, "The School Promoters", p. 66.

19. *The Globe*, 11 December 1851; "Address of Dr. Daniel Wilson to the Teachers' Association, 1865", in Hodgins, *Documentary History* XIX: 48.

20. "Truancy and Juvenile Crime", p. 4.

21. Ibid.; *The Globe*, 11 December 1851.
22. *Journal of Education* X, No. 1 (January 1857), 9.
23. Ibid., I, No. 4 (April 1848), 151.
24. Ibid., II, No. 6 (June 1849), 96; on these points see also "Truancy and Juvenile Crime" and "Address of Dr. Daniel Wilson".
25. Truancy and Juvenile Crime", p. 2.
26. Ibid., pp. 1–5.
27. "Address of Dr. Daniel Wilson".
28. "Report of the Board of Inspectors of Asylums, Prisons, & etc.", Penitentiary Reports, Canada, *Sessional Papers*, especially 1841, 1846–49, 1852–58, 1862.
29. Ibid., 1852–53.
30. Ibid., 1847.
31. *Journal of Education* X, No. 1 (January 1867), 64; and "Truancy and Juvenile Crime".
32. See Katz, *The Irony*; and David Rothman, *The Discovery of the Asylum* (Boston, 1971).
33. James P. Wickersham, "Education and Crime", *The Journals and Proceedings and Addresses of the National Education Association of the United States*, Session of the Year 1881 (Boston, 1881), pp. 45–55, especially p. 45.
34. Ibid., p. 50.
35. E. D. Mansfield, "The Relation Between Crime and Education", *Report of the U.S. Commissioner of Education* (Washington, D.C., 1872), pp. 586–95; see id., "The Relation Between Education and Pauperism", ibid., pp. 596–602 on the role of poverty. Mansfield states, "Pauperism and crime are so closely allied that the same individuals belong to both fraternities . . . steals when he cannot beg, and begs when he cannot steal," p. 602.
36. *Journal of Education* X, No. 1 (January 1857), 9; see also "Truancy and Juvenile Crime".
37. These statistics must not be confused with national rates of literacy for the British Isles determined by the percentages of signatures on marriage registers. There is no necessary relationship.
38. Board of State Charities, Massachusetts, "Secretary's Report", 1865 (Public Document Supplementary, No. 19), quoted in Katz, *The Irony*, p. 184.
39. Wickersham, "Education and Crime", p. 50.
40. On the meaning and relationship of literacy to education and the inculcation of morality and restraints, see again, Graff, "Literacy and Social Structure", especially Chapter 1.
41. *The Globe*, 11 December 1851.
42. "Report of the Board of Inspectors of Asylums, Prisons, & etc.", 1857.
43. Ibid., 1860.
44. Ryerson, "Public Elementary Instruction", p. 150, and Thomas Wyse, "School Reform", from the same volume, p. 151.
45. *Morning Chronicle*, 29 March 1850, quoted in Tobias, *Crime*, p. 207. See also, M. Hill and C. F. Cornwalles, *Two Prize Essays on Juvenile Delinquency* (London, 1853), p. 220, quoted in Tobias, *Crime*, p. 207. See also G. Stedman Jones, *Outcast London* (Oxford, 1971).
46. *Christian Guardian*, 2 July 1834; see also *The Church*, 12 October 1839, and 15 May 1851. See also Graff, "Literacy and Social Structure", Chapter 1.
47. "Report of the Board of Inspectors of Asylums, Prisons, & etc.", 1862, 1852–53.
48. *Christian Guardian*, 2 July 1834; see also Ryerson, "Public Elementary Instruction", *passim*.
49. W. B. Hodgson, *Exaggerated Estimates of Reading and Writing as a Means of Education*

(London, 1867), pp. 6–7.

50. J. W. Horsey, *Jottings from Jail* (London, 1887), p. 57, quoted in Tobias, *Crime*, p. 206 (emphasis mine).

51. See V. A. C. Gattell and T. B. Hadden, "Criminal Statistics and their Interpretation", in E. A. Wrigley, ed., *Nineteenth-Century Society* (Cambridge, 1972), pp. 363–96, statistical tables and *passim*.

52. See again, Graff, "Literacy and Social Structure", especially Chapter 2, for the data and argument linking illiteracy to inequality and stratification to ascription.

53. I must acknowledge my gratitude to Edward Phelps from the Regional History Library at the University of Western Ontario, who not only saved these records from destruction, but drew my attention to them and made them available to me. I have discussed the general patterns found in an analysis of the registers in "Crime and Punishment in the Nineteenth Century: The Experience of Middlesex County, Ontario", Canadian Social History Project, *Report*, v (1973–74), 124–63, and I have described the registers in "Crime and Punishment in the Nineteenth Century: A Note on the Criminal", *Journal of Interdisciplinary History* VII (1976-77), 477–91. This paper includes, as well, a complete listing of all crimes of apprehension and their categorization.

The historical study of criminality remains in a primitive condition. Most attention to date has centred on either attitudes towards crime or criminality or on the establishment of permanent police forces in the nineteenth century. While some recent work has now been completed on the irrascable problem of estimating rates of crime for the past (only now appearing in print), precious little energy has been focused on the criminals themselves. See, however, the important study by Eric Monkkonen, *The Dangerous Class* (Cambridge, Mass., 1975), and the special issue of the *Journal of Social History* VIII (Summer 1975), among a newly blossoming literature.

54. Graff, "Crime and Punishment".

55. See Graff, "Literacy and Social Structure", especially Chapter 7, for argument and evidence; see also the important and fascinating study of Daniel Calhoun, *The Intelligence of a People* (Princeton, 1973).

56. Egil Johanssen, "Literacy Studies in Sweden: Some Examples", in *Literacy and Society in a Historical Perspective: A conference report*, ed. Johanssen (Umea, 1973), p. 56. The incomparable Swedish parish registers provide data on annual examinations on the quality of literacy as determined by either oral ability or comprehension. Sponsored by the state church, the examinations record individual and community progress over the years as well as demographic and socio-economic data. Available from the seventeenth to the nineteenth centuries, they allow more detailed analysis of literacy's transmission, dimensions, and correlates, as well as distinguishing levels of literacy, than any other Western source. Johanssen has begun a large-scale project, but unfortunately little work has focused on the relationship of reading to comprehension.

57. On illiteracy in London, see Graff, "Literacy and Social Structure", Part One.

58. Conviction rates for each group are as follows: Neither read nor write, 86.3 per cent; read and write imperfectly, 68.7 per cent; read and write well, 49.4 per cent; read and write very well, 35.3 per cent.

59. See again, on ethnic stratification, Graff, "Literacy and Social Structure", and Katz, *Hamilton*.

60. The classification of occupations is based on the International Association of Social History Project rankings, as developed by Michael Katz, Theodore Hershberg, ·Laurence Glasco, Clyde Griffen, and Stuart Blumin, for comparative urban social structural analysis. See their discussion in "Occupation and Ethnicity in Five Nineteenth-Century Cities", *Historical Methods Newsletter* VII (1974), 174–216. Of course, we know that occupation is an imperfect proxy or approximation of social class, status, or wealth. On this prob-lem, see, Katz, "Occupational Classification in History", *Journal of Interdisciplinary History* III (1972), 63–88, and Griffen, "Occupational Mobility in Nine-teenth-Century America", *Journal of Social History* V (1972), 310–30.

61. See for example Barbara Welter, "The Cult of True Womanhood", *American Quarterly* XVIII (1966), 151–74, among a growing litera-ture. See Carroll Smith-Rosen-berg and Charles E. Rosenberg, "The Female Animal: Medical and Biological Views of Woman and her Role in Nineteenth-Century America", *Journal of American History* LX (1973), 332–56; Charles E. Rosenberg, "Sexuality, Class and Role in 19th-Century America", *American Quarterly* XXV (1973), 131–53.

62. All arrested men and women were classified by "moral habits", defined by temperate or intem-perate.

The Rhythm of Work and the Rhythm of School

IAN E. DAVEY

These returns present us with the painful and startling fact, of nearly one hundred thousand children of school age in Upper Canada, not attending any school. This awful fact furnishes a hundred thousand arguments to urge each friend of Canada, each friend of virtue, of knowledge and of civilization, to exert himself to his utmost until the number of children attending our schools shall equal the number of children of school age.

The average attendance of pupils, compared with the whole number, is little more than half . . . I doubt not but the provision of the present Act to distribute the school fund to the several school sections according to the average attendance of pupils in each school, (and not according to the school population as heretofore), the mean attendance of summer and winter being taken, will contribute very much to increase the regular attendance at the schools and to prolong their duration.[1]

Egerton Ryerson, writing in the chief superintendent's *Annual Report* for 1850, presented the challenge to the friends of educational reform in the province. The School Act of 1850 gave legislative recognition to property assessment for school purposes, making it possible for the individual school boards to introduce free schools. If the schools were free, then there was no reason why every child of school-age should not attend them. The task was to bring the children into the schools and, just as importantly, to ensure that they attended with sufficient regularity to gain the benefits of education. The goal was regular school attendance throughout the year for all school-age children, a remote possibility in 1850 when enrolments were low and average attendance even lower.

TABLE 10:1

NUMBER OF CHILDREN, 5 TO 16, ATTENDING COMMON SCHOOLS, 1851–71*

	in Ontario			in the counties			in the cities**		
	children	students	%	children	students	%	children	students	%
1851	258,607	158,159	61.2	227,052	141,400	62.3	13,841	5,228	37.8
1852	267,755	167,278	62.5	228,745	148,502	64.9	14,326	6,097	42.6
1853	268,957	175,422	65.2	228,776	154,185	67.4	17,272	6,812	39.4
1854	277,912	193,337	69.6	232,742	167,749	72.1	16,886	8,317	49.3
1855	297,623	211,629	71.1	257,411	184,742	71.8	26,000	11,739	45.2
1856	—	227,992	—	—	197,368	—	—	13,098	—
1857	324,888	247,434	76.2	273,836	209,754	76.6	23,524	17,136	72.4
1858	360,578	267,383	74.2	296,273	223,297	75.4	30,511	18,143	59.5
1859	362,085	279,490	77.2	298,973	233,124	78.0	26,021	18,773	72.1
1860	373,589	295,680	79.1	308,781	244,848	79.3	26,316	19,599	74.5
1861	384,980	309,895	80.5	318,499	257,994	81.0	25,811	19,526	75.6
1862	403,302	324,818	80.5	331,304	270,815	81.7	27,684	20,222	73.0
1863	412,367	339,817	82.4	340,767	280,826	82.4	25,086	21,721	86.6
1864	424,565	350,925	82.7	353,165	289,516	82.0	24,938	21,899	87.8
1865	426,757	361,617	84.7	352,166	297,335	84.4	26,955	22,823	84.7

TABLE 10:1—continued

	in Ontario			in the counties			in the cities**		
	children	students	%	children	students	%	children	students	%
1866	431,812	369,768	85.6	353,221	303,535	85.9	27,533	22,606	82.1
1867	447,726	380,511	85.0	365,096	311,066	85.2	27,663	22,603	81.8
1868	464,315	397,792	85.7	377,325	323,695	85.8	28,605	24,190	84.6
1869	470,400	409,184	87.0	386,190	331,917	85.9	28,780	25,581	88.9
1870	483,966	420,488	86.9	391,261	339,423	86.8	31,893	26,516	83.1
1871	489,615	423,033	86.4	392,559	337,033	85.9	32,953	28,068	85.2

*It should be noted that the percentages are not particularly accurate as the estimated number of children in the province was often based on guesswork by the local superintendents.

**The reason that there is a sharp increase in the number of children in the cities in 1855 is that the figures for London and Ottawa were included from then along with those of Toronto, Hamilton, and Kingston.

Source: Annual reports from 1851 to 1871.

In the succeeding years Ryerson's chronicle of the progress of the free-school movement was based largely on the increasing proportion of the province's school-age (five to sixteen) children enrolled in the schools. Every year in his annual report he compared the number of children five to sixteen years old with the number of children enrolled in the schools, commented on the narrowing gap between the two figures and deplored, as a "public blot and disgrace", the ever diminishing residual group of unschooled children. According to this criterion, the success of the free-school movement was easily demonstrated. In the two decades prior to 1871 virtually all cities, towns, and school sections abandoned the old rate-bill system in favour of property assessment and free schools, and at the same time, registered substantial increases in the number and proportion of children who enrolled in school.

The number of five to sixteen year-old children reported by the local superintendents as enrolled in the common schools rose from 158,159 in 1851 to 423,033 in 1871, an increase in the proportion of the growing school-age population attending school from 61.2 per cent in 1851 to 86.4 per cent in 1871. (See Table 10:1.) Moreover, the increase in the common school enrolment accounted for most of the increase in attendance as the enrolment in the various private schools and academies only increased from 6,753 in 1850 to 8,562 in 1871. The increase in enrolment was more spectacular in the cities but this was only because much lower proportions of urban school-age children attended the common schools in the earlier years. In 1851 over 62 per cent of the five to sixteen year-old children in the rural areas were enrolled in the common schools, compared to less than 38 per cent in the cities. (Of course, many city children attended private schools.) In 1871 over 85 per cent of the school-age children in both the cities and the rural areas were enrolled in the public schools of the province. Within two decades the free schools had become an accepted fact of life in Ontario and part of the experience of growing up for most children.[2]

However, the total yearly enrolment is a somewhat misleading measure of school attendance as it grossly exaggerated the number of children attending school at any one time. The figure was derived from all of those who registered in the public schools at any stage of the year. In consequence, the total enrolment included those children who were in a particular school for a week, a month, or six months, but who subsequently left.

Thus, children who were working or had moved to another neighbourhood, city, town, or farming area were still counted as enrolled by the local superintendents in their annual reports to the chief superintendent.

At the same time that the total enrolment figure implied a much greater rate of attendance than actually existed, the success of the free schools was severely limited by the continuing irregularity of attendance of those enrolled. For the majority of children, schooling remained a part-time activity throughout the period. In 1856 fully 57 per cent of those who were enrolled in the common schools of the province attended for one hundred days or fewer. In 1871 the equivalent proportion was 56.5 per cent and in no intervening year did it drop below 54 per cent. (See Table 10:2.) The proportion of children who attended for one hundred days or less was much higher in the rural areas than in the cities. In 1856 the proportion of rural students in this group was 59 per cent and in 1871, 58.4 per cent; and in the intervening years their proportion never fell below 56 per cent. The proportion who attended for a similarly short time in the cities was much less although it fluctuated considerably. In 1856 it was 42.9 per cent and in 1871, 46.2 per cent. In the intervening years the proportion attending for one hundred days or less rose as high as 50.3 per cent in 1857 and dropped as low as 39.1 per cent in 1868.

It is paradoxical that at the same time the free-school system was being adopted throughout almost all of Ontario and the proportion of children enrolled was increasing rapidly, the actual number of days most children attended remained relatively low. It became increasingly clear in the local superintendents' reports of the 1860s that the real issue was not so much non-attendance but irregularity. The structure of a permanent school system had been erected remarkably quickly; by the end of the 1860s most areas were served by schools which were free and which were open throughout the year.[3] Furthermore, as Ryerson continually pointed out, the idea of schooling had been generally accepted as the increasing enrolments demonstrated. By 1871 the actual number of children reported as not attending any school had declined to 38,535 and less than one-third of those, 12,018, were between the ages of seven and twelve, during which years attendance was made compulsory by the 1871 Act. Even though the number of non-attenders was probably larger, given the fact that the enrolment figures exaggerated the number in school, only a small group of children

TABLE 10:2

PROPORTION OF COMMON-SCHOOL STUDENTS BY NUMBER OF DAYS ATTENDED, 1856–71

year	under 50 days			50 to 100 days			100 to 150 days			150 to 200 days			200 days and over		
	Ontario	counties	cities	Ontario	counties	cities	Ontario	counties	cities	Ontario	counties	cities	Ontario	counties	cities
1856	31.7	33.0	24.3	25.3	26.0	18.6	19.9	20.2	15.4	13.2	12.8	16.0	9.9	8.1	25.9*
1857	31.9	33.2	26.1	25.0	25.5	24.2	19.7	19.7	19.5	13.8	13.1	17.2	9.6	8.5	13.0
1858	30.2	31.3	25.0	24.5	24.9	20.8	19.6	19.8	18.9	14.9	14.4	18.6	10.8	9.6	16.6
1859	29.7	31.0	23.4	24.9	25.4	22.2	19.9	19.9	18.4	14.6	13.9	18.0	10.9	9.7	18.0
1860	30.2	31.7	22.7	25.0	25.4	23.5	19.9	19.9	20.3	14.9	14.2	17.7	10.0	8.8	15.8
1861	30.2	31.5	23.5	25.3	25.8	22.4	20.3	20.2	19.2	15.3	14.5	18.3	8.9	7.9	17.4
1862	30.7	32.1	23.9	25.8	26.2	22.8	20.1	20.1	19.3	14.8	14.0	18.6	8.6	7.5	15.9
1863	30.7	32.0	23.4	25.3	25.9	23.1	20.3	20.3	19.0	15.1	14.2	18.9	8.7	7.6	15.1
1864	31.0	32.3	22.6	25.3	25.7	22.4	20.0	20.0	19.5	15.2	14.4	19.0	8.5	7.7	15.7
1865	30.9	32.3	24.0	25.2	25.7	22.0	20.2	20.2	17.9	15.2	14.4	17.8	8.5	7.4	19.7
1866	30.7	32.3	20.8	25.9	26.3	22.2	20.5	20.3	18.4	15.0	14.1	18.3	7.9	7.1	17.1
1867	29.8	31.3	19.5	25.7	26.2	20.5	20.7	20.7	18.8	15.6	14.6	18.7	8.3	7.2	21.2
1868	29.4	31.0	21.5	25.0	25.5	19.6	20.9	20.9	19.5	15.9	14.9	21.0	8.7	7.8	20.4
1869	30.2	31.7	22.4	26.1	26.8	21.0	20.3	20.2	19.4	15.5	14.3	22.2	7.9	7.0	15.9
1870	29.9	31.6	23.0	26.1	26.5	22.7	20.5	20.4	18.7	15.6	14.5	21.1	7.8	7.0	15.0
1871	30.1	31.6	23.0	26.4	26.8	23.2	21.4	21.3	20.7	16.2	15.1	21.7	5.9	5.2	11.3

*This figure appears unrealistically high in view of the subsequent figures. It is high because 1,584 of the 3,197 students in Hamilton were recorded as attending for 200 days or more. I have found no other evidence to verify this high rate of attendance.

Source: Annual reports from 1856 to 1871.

were not exposed to any form of schooling and most of these resided in the rural areas. In the cities, where the fear of juvenile crime was greatest, the educators had come to recognize the existence of a permanent class of poor who were beyond the reach of the public schools and for whom special institutions, such as industrial schools, were needed.[4] Once most children had been gathered into the public schools, more and more attention was focused on the ways and means of keeping them there with sufficient regularity and for a long enough time for each child to learn the lessons the schools were designed to instil.

"Irregularity of attendance," one local superintendent declared in 1871, "is the bane and curse of the public schools; it is a log and chain upon the progress of instruction for it blasts and withers the noblest purposes of the best of teachers." Irregular attendance not only deprived the individual student of adequate schooling but disrupted the whole school. It made the school system inefficient as it meant that the teachers were "unduly occupied in uncalled for repetition" thus retarding the progress of the class.[5] It also confounded attempts to grade the students by age as those who attended irregularly remained in the lower grades much longer.[6] From 1860 when Ryerson asked each local superintendent to report the reasons for non-attendance, much of each report was devoted to the causes and effects of irregular attendance. By the late 1860s, the local superintendents, following Ryerson's lead, called for a measure of compulsion because it was inconsistent to have compulsory property assessment and voluntary attendance.

Opponents of the free-school system argued that the system increased irregularity of attendance because the parents did not value what they did not pay for directly. "Where a rate-bill is charged," one superintendent declared, "the pupil, if present at all during the month, is sure to attend as often as possible, for the parents feel that non-attendance causes them a pecuniary loss; whereas under the free-school system any trifle is too often deemed sufficient to excuse the absence of the child."[7] The free-school supporters, including most of the superintendents, were also inclined to lay the blame for continued irregular attendance on the "criminal apathy and negligence of parents" who did not appreciate the value of an education to their children.[8] Yet, clearly, the extent of irregularity of attendance was such that parental indifference could hardly be the complete explanation. Besides, it was contradicted by the rapid

increase in enrolments throughout the province which, plaus-
ibly, could be considered more an expression of parental concern. As one superintendent put it while rebuking his colleagues
in 1861, the term "parental indifference" was used to explain
poor attendance by some because it was "a convenient way of
filling up the column" in the annual report. "Not indifference,"
he continued, "but the pressing care of providing for their
bodily wants, is . . . the more general cause of non-attendance."[9]
Those other superintendents who went beyond "convenient
ways of filling up columns" agreed that material circumstance
rather than criminal negligence was the root cause of low and
irregular attendance.

> Compulsory attendance and the poverty of families, will
> scarcely ever harmonize. Indeed to carry out the provisions
> of the Free School System, we would require to furnish, either
> by the Legislature or the trustees, or by both combined, all
> the necessary books, and other things required for the school,
> together, with, in some, cases, even the clothes in which the
> children are to attend the school, or a proportion of the
> children, in the rural districts, as well as in the towns and
> cities, will be deprived of the benefits of a common school
> education.[10]

> When workers lost their employment—which they might do at
> the end of the job, of the week, of the day or even of the hour—
> they had nothing to fall back upon except their savings, their
> friendly society or trade union, their credit with local shop-
> keepers, their neighbours and their friends, the pawnbroker. . . .
> When they grew old or infirm, they were lost, unless helped
> by their children, for effective insurance or private pension
> schemes covered only a few of them. Nothing is more char-
> acteristic of Victorian working-class life, and harder for us to
> imagine today, than this virtually total absence of social
> security.[11]

The most potent determinants of attendance patterns in both
urban and rural areas were the same conditions which shaped
the economic and social realities of nineteenth-century Canadian
life. Attendance was naturally influenced by such ubiquitous
features as harsh climatic conditions, bad roads, and sickness.
However, those factors which contributed to poverty and economic insecurity—trade depressions, crop failure, transient
work patterns, and seasonal employment—largely determined

the regularity of school attendance throughout the province.

"Two successive years of failure in the productions of husbandry, attended by a large decrease in the public revenue, and an unprecedented stagnation in every branch of business, could not fail to be seriously felt in the operation of our school system."[12] In these words Ryerson summed up the impact of of the depression of the late 1850s on Ontario. Its effect was more devastating in the larger cities which were brought to a standstill, making it difficult for them to bear the cost of the school system at the same time that attendance was more irregular. In Toronto, in fact, the superintendent of schools in 1857 and a committee of the board in 1864 advocated a return to the rate-bill schools because the free-school system was financially burdensome and had not improved either the proportional enrolment or the regularity of attendance of children in the city.[13] Depressions increased the irregularity of attendance because they brought increased hardship for many people, particularly the poor who, lacking financial resources at the best of times, were often reduced to reliance on charity to survive. In Hamilton, for instance, the depression of the late 1850s brought widespread unemployment as many establishments were forced to close, and one observer reported that before 1857 "the common labourer could make almost as much in a day as he now can in a week."[14] The Ladies Benevolent Society and the City Council distributed bread, wood, and soup in the winter months of the depression, and the ladies expressed relief that many of "the lowest and unsatisfactory class of applicants" for aid had been forced to leave the city because it enabled them to assist "those whose necessities are as great, but who are more diffident in making known their wants."[15]

The effect of economic privation on school attendance during depression years was twofold. First, many children were withdrawn from school through dire necessity and scavenged for the means of keeping themselves and their families alive—stealing money, objects to sell, and coal or wood to keep them warm.[16] Second, many children were withdrawn from school when their parents were forced to leave the city in search of work. The population of Hamilton, for example, dropped rapidly during the depression of the 1850s and, as Superintendent Ormiston remarked in 1860, "a large number of those returned as attending school only a short time, are removed from the city".[17]

Depressed prices and bad crops had similar effects in the rural areas, reducing school expenditures and affecting the rates of attendance. As one superintendent in Haldimand County commented in 1861, "Inferior crops and low prices for produce have caused some undertakings to be stationary and others to retrograde; but as soon as farmers are blessed with better harvests and more remunerative markets, the children will be more regular in their attendance, they will be sent longer to school, and far more attention will be given to furnishing the school-houses."[18] Similarly, one inspector noted that the aggregate attendance was less in the first half of 1879 than in the corresponding period of 1878 while in the second half it was greater. "It seems fair," he concluded, "to infer that the hard times forced people to seek help from their children, till the good harvest justified them in sending them back to school."[19] In short, cyclical depressions and crop failures affected school attendance because in good times more parents sent more of their children to school and sent them more regularly. Yet, lower attendance during bad times resulted largely from a magnification of those factors which caused irregular attendance throughout the nineteenth century—transience and poverty.

Recent research has given us insights into the nature and extent of transience in the nineteenth century—large numbers of people in both urban and rural areas were on the move.[20] Labourers moved from farms to cities in winter and back to farms in the spring; farmers sought work in logging camps and elsewhere in the winter months; canal, railroad, and road construction workers worked their way through the countryside; skilled workers moved on when there was no more work to be found in a particular city or town; and people from all walks of life packed their bags when opportunities to better themselves seemed more probable in another neighbourhood, city, town, farming area, or county. The actual number of transients was immense. In Hamilton, for example, only about one-third of those recorded on the 1851 census were found on the 1861 census, and Katz has estimated that at least twice as many people lived in the city during a whole year as were there at any one time.[21] Those who left in the decade spanned the spectrum of Hamilton's occupational and ethnic structure, but they were less likely to be married and more likely to be young, poor, and to own no property in the city than those who stayed.[22]

The skilled workers who moved on may have drawn on past experience. Those artisans who came from England, for example, brought with them a tradition of "tramping" which was organized to the extent that card-carrying members of particular unions moved from place to place looking for work and calling on the local branches for welfare and support. It was, as Eric Hobsbawn has pointed out, a form of unemployment relief with the numbers on the tramp much greater in depression times although younger men were likely to spend a number of years on the move.[23] Such organized tramping was not widespread in Canada in the 1850s and 1860s because the union movement was in its infancy. However, it is likely that even then itinerant workers knew where to ask for work in the various towns and cities, and numerous public houses probably acted as receiving centres as they did in England. For example, the "Stonemason's Arms" and two or three other centrally located hotels in Hamilton were the residences of most of the city's unemployed at the time of the 1851 census. The tramping system points to a facet of artisan life also noted by Charlotte Erickson in her study of British immigrants to America.[24] Journeymen were much more likely to move around in search of work in their specific trade than to take alternative employment. Undoubtedly, many of those who left Ontario were on their way west to Detroit and beyond, but in the 1850s the lack of industry in the province may have encouraged many artisans to leave. As one contemporary observer bemoaning the lack of moneyed capital and manufacturing in Ontario put it: "It is not true that the establishment of manufactures amongst us would detach our population from agricultural pursuits; since the first settlement of the Province, tens of thousands of citizens have passed through because they could find no employment in their trades, and tens of thousands have been deterred from coming here for the same reason."[25]

At least the artisans had a portable skill to carry with them in their search for work. The position of the labourers was even more precarious for they had only their brute strength to sell. Much of their work such as farm and lumber work was seasonal, or else it was institutionally transient in nature like canal and railroad construction. Labourers were forced to move on when the source of work dried up, although Thernstrom concludes that those who worked in the cities only left "when the depressed state of the local labour market made it impossible to subsist where they were."[26] Economic conditions forced workers to move on and, in a sense, it was a vicious circle. Transience bred transience and those on the tramp were usually the last to be employed and the first to be laid off.[27] As one builder in Petrolia told the Royal Commission on Capital and Labour:

> If a tramp came along, or a man from a distance, and recommended himself to be a mechanic in want of work, and told me what he could do, and after I had given him work I found he could not perform what he had undertaken to accomplish, I would give him his money and let him go. But, if I had a man working who had been working for me for two or three months, perhaps for a year, and I knew well enough that he was not a perfect hand in certain classes of work, I would keep him on, because he would be a faithful hand.[28]

The implications for school attendance of this widespread geographic mobility were profound. On the one hand, children who enrolled in school and later left the area exaggerated the degree of irregularity in any one school by inflating the enrolment and lowering the average attendance figures. On the other, the number of children whose schooling was interrupted must have been immense. If the distance of migration was small—from neighbourhood to neighbourhood within a city or from farming community to farming community within a school district—it was possible that a child's name would appear on more than one school register in the area. One inspector of schools in the County of Middlesex, for example, pointed out that he had "found pupils reported from a school in Metcalfe as having attended less than 100 days also reported from a school in Lobo", as the family had moved from Metcalfe to Lobo during the year. It was possible, he suggested, that they might have attended for more than 100 days if their attendance at both schools was taken together.[29] For those who moved beyond the jurisdiction of a particular school board, it was impossible to gauge how many days each year they may have attended. Certainly, school superintendents remarked on the effect of transience on poor attendance rates in their schools. The fact that Collingwood's population was "a floating one—continually changing", was given as the reason that the average attendance was much lower than the number enrolled on the books.[30] Similarly, the failure to increase the number of students in Ottawa in 1865 was "caused by the number of mechanics and labourers who have migrated to the U.S., in consequence of the falling off of work at the public buildings here.[31]

Some superintendents reported that the continual movement of parents from place to place was unsettling because "many having recently come to the place, or expecting soon to go, feel . . . indisposed to go to the expense of a set of school books, and the trouble of sending their children for the short time they may remain."[32] The unsettled character of the population was seen to be detrimental to the progress of education. As one superintendent in the County of Prescott wrote of the French Canadian majority in his school section: "One great impediment is . . . they do not remain long enough in one locality for their children to be benefitted by the schools."[33] It was difficult to teach transient students whose movement in and out of the schools disrupted the efficient working of the system. How efficient and settled the school system would have been if its clientele was less mobile is a moot question because, particularly in the rural areas, the teachers themselves were not immune from the transient experience. In one county, for example, "out of one hundred and one employed on the First of January, 1868, seventy-nine were not found in the same position in January, 1870, and of this large number, fifty-seven had either given up teaching or had left the County."[34]

Although geographic mobility cut across all classes in the society, as a cause of irregular attendance it was usually associated with the working class and the poor. In England, for instance, in the 1850s the president of the Department of Education noted that "in the lower class schools the irregularity and shortness of attendance hinder the results . . . [t]heir habits are so migratory that only 34% are found in the same school for more than two years."[35] The migratory "habits" of the working class were perceived as part of their general want of discipline along with their unpunctuality, irregular work habits, affection for alcohol and inability to save money. And, in a sense it was true. Living in poverty or, at least, within easy reach of it, most working-class families, particularly below the skilled level, operated on a boom and bust economy. They spent their money when they had it (often in celebration of Saint Monday if they were paid weekly) and eked out an existence when they were penniless in accordance with the irregularity of their income. If, as Michael Katz has suggested, Gibbon Wakefield's evocative term "the uneasy class" applied to Canadian entrepreneurs at mid-century, it was no less apt for artisans and labourers as economic insecurity was a fact of working-class life.[36]

Their insecurity stemmed from the practices of employing labourers by the day and journeymen irregularly throughout the year. In fact, the irregularity of employment probably contributed more to the poor economic condition of the working class than did the low wages.[37] In 1864 the editor of *The Workingman's Journal*, which was published in Hamilton, declared that the city's workers were likely to be on short-time amounting to five days a week for eighteen weeks in the year. He was critical of the mayor's practice of declaring general holidays "whenever a few individuals take a fancy to have it done", and pointed out that each holiday cost the 3,000 workers in Hamilton a minimum of $3,500.[38] It was a matter of necessity for the working man to earn as much as possible in the good seasons to ward off periods of unemployment in winter and during depressions. As one moulder put it, they went on strike because "we felt we should have more wages when we were working in order to be able to live during those portions of the year when there was nothing to do."[39]

Moreover, it is likely that in the second half of the nineteenth century the rise of industrial capitalism brought increasing irregularity of employment for skilled workers and made their work experience much more similar to that of the unskilled labourers. As both Pentland and Langdon have demonstrated, the traditional job security of artisans was undermined by the emergence of a self-regulating capitalist labour market and "the driving mechanization of industry".[40] The personalized ties between master and journeymen which cushioned artisans against downturns in the economy disintegrated in the factory setting. Employers simply laid off excess workers in slack periods and rehired them when the economy rebounded.[41] At the same time, mechanization severely diluted the skills required in some trades such as tailoring, shoemaking, and printing.[42] Some artisans lost their jobs to children and "greenhorns" who were able to operate the machines and were cheaper to employ. Those who kept their jobs were often forced to accept lower wages because of the increased competition for their jobs. The result of these processes was the weakening of the artisans' position as their hold on their employment became less secure and cyclical unemployment increased.

The plight of working people was aggravated as well by the method of wage payment. Some were paid in truck and thus forced to buy at prices set by the company store, while others who were paid monthly found themselves continually in debt to the local shopkeeper. Many workmen had "to run monthly accounts and that puts them entirely at the mercy of the corner grocers . . . you have to take what he has got and you cannot go anywhere else . . . if a man could get his wages weekly he could run his business more on a cash basis and go where he pleased."[43] Even those who were paid weekly found it difficult to shop economically if they were paid on a Saturday night.

> The 'hewers of wood and drawers of water', of this thriving City [Hamilton] live . . . 'from hand to mouth', and each end of the week, and we fear, in many cases the beginning, finds the dependent family, reduced to a state not very far from actual want, with no means to provide for the necessities of the Sabbath, until the week's wages is paid late on Saturday evening . . . The poor unfortunate who has, from a combination of circumstances, antagonistic to virtue, found an appetite for the maddening bowl, finds himself exhausted with the week's labour, and weary waiting around the office door for his turn to be paid. After which they too often go straight to the Recess or Tavern . . . where they remain until part or all of their earnings are spent; and when it is too late for the prudent house-wife to expend her share of her husband's hard earned money profitably, but whose necessities afford the vulturous huxter an opportunity to practise his penchant for extortion . . . Were all employers to pay any other day of the week, the poor labourer's wife could do her marketing to the best advantage and curtail very materially the year's expenditure.[44]

Plainly, the experience of most working-class families militated against the formation in their children of the virtues of orderly, regular, punctual industry. The irregularity of their work patterns made it difficult for them to commit themselves (and their children) to regular activities for any length of time. The "lack of discipline" that middle-class observers considered to be the cause of working-class poverty was, rather, more of an accommodation to the insecurity of their economic reality. For, as Henry Mayhew shrewdly noted of the casual labourers in London:

> Regularity of habits are incompatible with irregularity of income; indeed, the very conditions necessary for the formation

of any habit whatsoever are, that the act or thing to which we are to be habituated should be repeated at frequent and regular intervals. It is a moral impossibility that the class of labourers who are only occasionally employed should be either generally industrious or temperate—both industry and temperance being habits produced by constancy of employment and uniformity of income.[45]

To the list of industry and temperance observed by Mayhew, we should add the regular attendance of their children at school.

An acquaintance with irregular income and periods of poverty was not confined to the urban working class and the agricultural labourers. Many of the province's small farmers, especially those who scratched out a living from the rocky soils of the shield in the eastern and northern areas of the province, experienced the same deprivations. In one sense, the problem of irregular attendance at school was rooted in the success of the free-school program itself. It had succeeded in enrolling most of the children of the province in the schools, including most of the poor in both rural and urban areas. To expect regular and punctual attendance from them without a concomitant improvement and regulation of their life style, was to expect the impossible.

"I can say that a man with a family of two children, a son and a daughter, will find his earnings, if an ordinary workman, readily absorbed in the education of these two children, if he is so disposed . . . the moment you have any children, if even an only child, it seems to me that the earnings of an ordinary mechanic would count for very little."[46] The ordinary workman and the small farmer had little room for manoeuvre, and if the former lost his job or the latter's crops failed, their families were often thrown into poverty until conditions improved. These not infrequent occurrences had considerable influence on school attendance patterns. The "hard struggles of the tillers of the soil" often meant that they either required "the actual assistance of their children, or they are unable to clothe them sufficiently well to appear in school."[47] Some indication of the extent of hardship is provided by this latter reason, for the lack of adequate clothing and shoes was frequently given as the reason for low attendance in both rural and urban areas.[48] Moreover, those parents unable to clothe their children properly were unlikely to be able to afford the necessary books that students required for their studies. As late as 1890, one working-class journal dismissed "free education" as "a piece of rhetorical bombast", and declared that "it is not to be wondered at that people, who are barely able to provide their families with bread and blankets and coal during the winter, should keep their children at home rather than incur the liability of having to find them textbooks."[49]

Much of the poverty was associated with the seasonal rhythm of work as the harsh winter swelled the ranks of the unemployed in the cities and brought work to a standstill on the farms. Not surprisingly, this had considerable impact on attendance patterns although its manifestations were quite different in the urban and the rural areas. In the cities and towns, the coming of winter meant increased misery for large numbers of people. Those who worked outside were likely to be laid off. Labourers, carpenters and joiners, painters and decorators, bricklayers and brickmakers, and seamen lost their jobs or competed among themselves (and with the large number of agricultural labourers who came to the cities in winter) for the small number of jobs available. Those who were skilled enough, or sufficiently lucky, to keep their jobs were often forced to work for reduced wages because of competition for work and the shorter working day. Even those who worked inside were often faced with winter unemployment: the moulders, for example, were likely to be thrown onto the over-crowded labour market because most of the foundries closed down for six to eight weeks for stocktaking and retooling.[50] Winter was also the slack period in the sweated clothing trades, making it difficult for wives and daughters to supplement the family income and throwing most of the widows into the arms of the various relief agencies.[51] The plight of the urban poor was further exacerbated because of the increased price of food and fuel in the winter months. As Judith Fingard has remarked: "winter deprived the poor of their employment at the same time as it made the necessaries of life prohibitively dear; and it endangered their health by aggravating the plight of the sick and infirm, by creating dietary problems for those at or below the subsistence level, and by causing disablement or death for others through exposure."[52]

The effect of the harsh winter was reflected in the monthly enrolment figures in the urban areas. Without adequate clothing and nourishment, children were much more susceptible to sickness and disease in winter. "[W]hooping cough," *The Spec-*

tator (Hamilton) remarked in a review of the causes of death in the city in 1857, "seems to have been exclusively fatal to the poor."[53] In the same city in the 1880s, the number of children absent from school because of sickness in January, February, and March averaged well over 800 compared to only 306 in September.[54] Still others were kept at home because of sickness in the family or because they were needed to mind the younger children in the absence of the parents. The diaries of W. C. Wilkinson, who was the truant officer in Toronto in the 1870s, provide some insight into the depths of human suffering endured during the urban winter. Investigating the absence from school of one ten year-old girl, he discovered that the father had recently died from typhoid and the mother was ill in bed. The widow told him "she could not provide books for the girl to go to school nor, in fact bread for the family." Another seven year-old boy was absent because his father was out of work and the mother was unable to get the child boots to wear.[55] Wilkinson's diaries reveal clearly that most cases of irregular attendance involved some personal catastrophe in the home, especially sickness. Few of the children were working except in exceptional circumstances such as the eight year-old boy who, when found attending his mother's shop while she was sick in bed, admitted that he was "guilty of truancy".[56]

Undoubtedly, more children were able to find jobs in the summer months and contribute to the family income, but before industrialization, the commercial city did not provide large numbers of jobs for children. Some found work as messengers in the large stores, or deliverers of newspapers, girls found jobs in the sweated trades and in domestic service, and boys helped their fathers in their craft shops. Moreover, industrialization in Canada did not involve large-scale employment of young children in the factories. Only tobacco manufacturing and cotton and woolen mills provided employment for a great number of young children. Certainly, from the 1860s there was an increasing number of children working in factories and this affected school attendance. The superintendent for the village of Hespeler, for instance, complained of "the ebb-and-flow" of attendance and suggested that: "The irregularity is caused by the boys and girls, of almost all sizes and ages, staying out of School or going to it, according as their assistance is required or not at the factories."[57] But the evidence suggests that most of those children who found work in industry were over the age of twelve.[58] It seems that irregular attendance in the cities

and towns was not so much the result of large-scale employment of young children as of the lack or loss of jobs for their
parents. In large part, irregular attendance patterns in the
urban areas were the cumulative result of many personal disasters stemming from the instability of the labour market and
the incidence of sickness—conditions which intersected most
acutely during the winter months.

This was certainly not the case in the rural areas. The most
important feature of school attendance patterns outside of the
cities and towns was the pronounced seasonal variation. As the
figures for 1850 to 1854 indicate, average attendance was higher
in winter. (See Table 10:3.) Moreover, while more boys than
girls attended in both summer and winter, the difference between the sexes was approximately twice as large in the winter
months. That is, many more boys and fewer girls attended the
rural schools in winter. This seasonal pattern is similar to that
noted by Joseph Kett in rural New England for a slightly
earlier period,[59] and is explained by the fact the "the parents
think the working of their farms of more importance than the
education of their children."[60] The shortage and high price of
agricultural labour meant that the older children, particularly
the boys, worked on the farm "during the three-fourths of the
year" and were only sent to school (or allowed to attend) in
"those months, when by the very nature of the season, the tiller
of the ground is dismissed from his toil."[61] The result, according to one of the local superintendents in York County, was
that "in summer seasons those children who are too young to
labour are sent to school, and those whose labour is valuable
are kept at home: in the winter this order is reversed, thus
making two distinct sets of pupils in the year."[62] The pattern
of attendance, then, was determined by the seasonal demands
of the farm; even the young children were called on to assist
in the busiest periods and the schools were virtually emptied
"at the times of hay, wheat, oat, apple and potato harvests".[63]

The superintendents' reports indicate that the farmers' reliance on their children's labour was almost universal, although
it is likely that the practice was more prevalent in the poorer
and newer farming areas. The distinctly seasonal pattern of
attendance prolonged the number of years during which rural
children were in school, albeit often briefly. This is clearly
borne out by the annual reports from 1871 to 1883 which included an age breakdown of those enrolled. (See Table 10:4.)
In 1871, in the counties, 45.3 per cent of those enrolled were

TABLE 10:3

AVERAGE ATTENDANCE AT COMMON SCHOOLS, 1850–54

year	Ontario			counties			city		
	total	boys	girls	total	boys	girls	total	boys	girls
1850—summer	76,824	41,784	35,040	70,844	37,940	32,704	2,248	1,495	753
—winter	81,469	48,308	33,161	75,215	44,385	30,830	2,163	1,375	788
1851—summer	83,390	44,647	38,743	74,438	39,541	34,897	2,581	1,423	1,158
—winter	84,981	49,060	35,921	76,389	44,076	32,313	2,376	1,377	999
1852—summer	85,161	45,409	39,752	75,762	40,253	35,509	2,730	1,482	1,248
—winter	86,756	49,867	36,889	77,656	44,620	33,036	2,580	1,448	1,132
1853—summer	90,096	48,668	41,428	78,046	41,955	36,088	4,391	2,337	2,054
—winter	90,659	52,252	37,407	78,830	45,380	33,450	3,919	2,259	1,660
1854—summer	91,880	49,475	42,405	78,682	41,359	35,823	4,368	2,615	1,753
—winter	92,925	52,696	40,229	79,306	44,694	34,612	4,441	2,670	1,771

Source: Annual reports from 1850 to 1854.

between five and ten years of age, 47.9 per cent between ten and sixteen, and over 6 per cent between sixteen and twenty-one. In contrast, in the cities, fully 58.5 per cent were in the younger age group of the school-age population and only 39.1 per cent were between ten and sixteen. Furthermore, the proportion of city students between sixteen and twenty-one was only 2.1 per cent. The much larger proportion of older students in the rural areas was a function of the older boys attending only for three or four months in the winter. As one superintendent remarked, "a number of lads, who have outgrown their school-boy days, return to peruse old studies, and to make still further advancement."[64] Fewer girls attended in winter. The younger children who attended in summer were often unable to go to school in winter because of the distance from the school and the severity of the weather. It would seem that many older girls were kept home in order to look after them.

The pattern of rural school attendance that emerges was one of age- and sex-specific seasonal absenteeism rather than irregular attendance throughout the year. This was not the case in the cities, for although the deprivations of winter resulted in some seasonal variation, the personal disasters at the heart of irregular attendance were likely to occur at any stage of the year.

The experience of all children throughout the province was also affected by the harshness of the physical conditions and the prevalence of disease. While distance from school, severe weather, and impassable roads were obvious inhibiting factors on the attendance of young children in the rural areas, they also affected children in the urban areas. The attendance of the five and six year-olds was so irregular in London (about 50 per cent of the time), that in 1879 the inspector of schools questioned the worth of educating them. He thought it better to concentrate on children between seven and fourteen who were "physically more able to attend".[65] Glazebrook has pointed out that even though the main streets in the larger centres were often paved, "no one had to search far to find plenty of mud", especially in spring and autumn.[66] Moreover, at the same time that winter travel by sled was easier, walking any distance through the snow in bitterly cold weather was both difficult and dangerous. In consequence, any child living more than a few hundred yards from school, be it in a large city or on a farm, was often housebound because of the conditions. Wilkinson, the Toronto truant officer, found a number of children

TABLE 10:4

PROPORTION OF PUBLIC-SCHOOL STUDENTS BY AGE GROUPS, 1871–83

	under 5		5 to 10		10 to 16		over 16	
	counties	cities	counties	cities	counties	cities	counties	cities
1871	—	1.2	45.3	58.5	47.9	39.1	6.2	2.1
1872	0.5	0.1	46.4	58.9	47.6	38.7	5.5	1.2
1873	0.4	0.1	46.4	61.1	47.7	38.1	5.5	0.8
1874	0.4	0.1	50.7	58.3	44.3	40.0	4.6	1.7
1875	0.4	0.1	50.9	59.3	43.8	39.5	4.9	1.1
1876	0.3	0.01	50.3	61.2	44.0	38.0	5.4	0.8

	under 5		5 to 16		over 16	
	counties	cities	counties	cities	counties	cities
1877	0.3	0.1	94.9	99.3	4.8	0.6
1878	0.3	0.1	94.9	99.2	4.8	0.7
1879	0.3	0.1	95.4	99.2	4.3	0.7
1880	0.3	0.1	95.4	99.6	4.3	0.3
1881	0.4	0.1	95.9	99.3	3.8	0.6
1882	0.3	0.1	96.4	99.3	3.3	0.6
1883	0.3	0.1	96.9	99.5	2.8	0.4

Source: Annual reports from 1871 to 1883.

were kept at home "owing to bad roads and want of sidewalks" and he, himself, commented that in some neighbourhoods the snow was so deep that "it was utterably [sic] unreasonable for any child to go through."[67]

I have already illustrated the upsurge in sickness which accompanied the arrival of winter, however, people in the mid-nineteenth century lived in constant fear of illness and disease, and the privations of inadequate clothing, want of fuel, and insufficient food that characterized the winter months only heightened the extent of misery. Unsanitary conditions, impure water, and infected foods were a fact of life, particularly in the urban areas, and causes of infectious disease that ravaged the the population.[68] Cholera, smallpox, scarlet fever, diphtheria, measles, and whooping cough were among the infectious diseases which reached epidemic proportions and disrupted schools throughout the province. The concentration of children in the school was, itself, one of the causes of the spread of disease, as infected children passed them on to their classmates. In Hamilton, for example, when the scarlet fever epidemic of 1870–71 was at its peak, some suggested that the city's schools should be closed, although a subsequent investigation by the board revealed that most of the eighty deaths had occurred among children below school age.[69] It was not until the mid-1880s that provincial regulations were enacted compelling parents and teachers to report cases of infectious diseases and forbidding the infected children from attending school.[70] On a less dramatic plane, debilitating illnesses like dysentry were endemic in a society where food was stored for long periods over winter, the water was often impure, and meat was likely to become tainted in the hot summer months. As William Callowhil, an English immigrant, wrote to his parents: "[I have had] a severe bilious attack which for three or four days I thought would finish me, tho' we do not hear of anyone dying of them yet, they are so severe in this country."[71] Epidemics could close down the schools and "severe bilious attacks", suffered either by the child or the parent, could keep children home for days or even weeks at a time. Whatever its form or its extent, illness was a potent cause of irregular attendance in nineteenth-century Ontario.

There were other factors, outside of those related to the economic and physical conditions in the province, which affected school attendance although it is difficult to gauge their relative importance. As in the present, there were always some children who did not want to go to school and played truant. Wilkinson, the truant officer, interviewed a number of parents who were surprised (or feigned surprise) when informed that their children were absent from school and roaming the streets. Similarly, *The Spectator*'s (Hamilton) warning to the aspiring horticulturists of the area must have been repeated many times throughout the province: "as the season has now arrived when boys play truant from School, and pilfer fruit from the gardens and orchards, we would advise those concerned to keep a bright look out after the urchins."[72] Not unnaturally, children also stayed away when local fairs or travelling shows were exhibiting in the area. As one superintendent pointed out in 1863, "when a circus exhibited in the town, only 257 were at school out of 444 on that month's register."[73] In fact, any break in the normal routine affected school attendance: "The gold excitement during the first half of 1867, was the cause of many pupils in the rear townships of the Riding being withdrawn from the schools, and continuing so, until the excitement in some measure subsided, and business resumed somewhat of its accustomed routine during the last autumn."[74] More commonly, some children were kept at home, or refused to go to school, because of dissatisfaction with the local teacher or classroom accommodation. Many rural superintendents, particularly in the poorer counties, complained of the poor quality of the teachers or the indifference of the local trustees as an important reason for irregular or non-attendance. As one put it, rather cryptically, "the trustees select the teacher—the teacher makes the school."[75]

The plethora of reasons that combined to cause continuing irregular attendance certainly went far beyond the original glib assertions of the local superintendents of "parental indifference and negligence". And yet, in one sense, the "lack of appreciation of education" that they observed was rooted in the cultural reality of mid-nineteenth-century Ontario life. On the one hand, the extravagant claims of the free-school promoters regarding the benefits of education were not immediately obvious in the society. Crime and vice had not been eradicated, militant trade union organization and strikes were unlikely indications of increasing social stability, and poverty was still an ever-present problem. On the other, although it was said that "the public is beginning to appreciate the idea that a person without education must remain during life a 'hewer of wood and drawer of water'," most people probably knew someone who was a living contradiction of that same idea.[76] As one superintendent complained in 1869:

> A large proportion of our population consists of emigrants from nearly every clime and region of the earth. The majority of these came here with nothing but their sturdy thews and sinews, and their indomitable energy and perseverance. With their axes upon their shoulders, they marched boldly into the wilderness; and out of it, by stringent frugality and unremitting toil, they have carved for themselves an easy competence —a rude plenty. They have seen educated men settle around them, and decrease in wealth, whilst THEY the uneducated, have flourished and increased in it. Many of them, owing to the unavoidable force of circumstances—from sheer necessity —have been elected by those around them to situations of trust as school trustees and councillors. . . . They have waxed haughty in their grandeur, they have become inflated with their official pomp, they utterly eschew alike, education, reason and common sense.[77]

Clearly, education was not a necessary component of success in farming, unlike "unremitting toil" in an age when mechanization was not very far advanced.

Moreover, as Harvey Graff has demonstrated, illiteracy was not a complete stumbling block to an individual's progress in the urban areas either, for though most illiterates were labourers, many held skilled jobs and some even worked in non-manual occupations.[78] In fact, in the initial stages of industrial capitalism, the new opportunities for less skilled and child labour in the mechanized factories must have made it difficult for working-class people to appreciate the benefits of schooling. This was the concern of the superintendent for Guelph when he complained in 1873 that there were fewer children in the higher grades of the public system. The children left school early because of

> the desire of parents to avail themselves at too early a period of the earnings which their children can make, and the opportunities which stores and manufactures afford for child labour, in the disposition of employers to engage children, because of the higher wages which must be paid for the labour of grown-up persons. Account ought, also, to be made, of the course of instruction that has been prescribed and rendered imperative in our Public Schools, embracing subjects which,

while valuable in themselves, are not thought necessary by parents for their children, and who, consequently, grudge the time devoted to them, and the expense that must be incurred in the purchase of text-books.[79]

If farmers and working people could not readily discern the immediate advantages of sending their children to school regularly and for sustained periods of time, the type of education offered in the common schools was not likely to improve the situation. As the superintendent for Guelph suggested, much of the curriculum seemed irrelevant or unnecessary to those engaged in the business of making a living. Although Ryerson had emphasized the importance of practical education in his 1846 report, the initial battles to get the principles of free and compulsory education accepted in the province absorbed most of his energy prior to 1871. In consequence, the curriculum of the common schools remained oriented towards the tiny minority who went on to the grammar schools and the university, and little attention was paid to more practical subjects. Thus, while the children learned how to read and write and cipher, they were unlikely to learn much of practical use to them in their working lives. Ryerson remarked in 1869 when it had become obvious that a free and compulsory education system was generally accepted: "the tendency of the youthful mind of our country is too much in the direction of what are called the learned professions, and too little in the direction of what are termed the industrial pursuits . . . it appears to be very important, as the fundamental principles and general machinery of our School System are settled, that the subjects and teaching of the schools should be adapted to develop the resources and skilful industry of the country."[80]

There was, then, a tension between the reality and the possibility of education as the school curriculum, grading up to the classical grammar school, bore little relation to the everyday world of most of the clientele. And this tension was exacerbated by the emergence of new industrial order in the 1860s as mechanized factory production increased economic insecurity at the same time that it devalued the importance of education. To keep children in school was to forgo the contribution of potential wage earners to the family income, a form of denial that many could not afford, particularly as much of the schooling seemed irrelevant. Adolescent labour in the factory or the sweatshop became like adolescent labour on the farm—a necessary factor in the family's struggle to make a living. For both the farmer and the working man, the family's welfare took precedence over the child's education. However, the impact on school attendance patterns was quite different. The seasonal pattern of farming meant that rural children attended school seasonally and stayed there well into their teens. In the cities, the years of attendance were more compressed, most children leaving school to go to work or help around the home after they were twelve. Thus, although from 1871 onwards the majority of children were in school, family circumstance, economic pressures, and physical conditions dictated the length of their stay and the seasonality and the regularity of their attendance.

In these circumstances it is not surprising that attendance remained irregular after 1871. The legislation for compulsory attendance, after all, had absolutely no effect upon the material conditions in which people lived. The inspector for the County of Renfrew made exactly that point in 1872:

> We must not expect to find our schools in a healthy and vigorous condition, or the claims of education properly respected, until pupils and parents learn to appreciate the importance of regular attendance . . . we cannot overlook the fact that there are, in many of our rural districts, obstacles which are simply insurmountable at present. When we take into consideration the difficulties in the way of many pupils getting to school at all; when we think of the requirements of the farm in the seasons of sowing and harvesting, in which the aid of children is indispensably necessary, we feel that these things must unavoidably interfere with School Attendance. When we take into careful consideration the claims of industry, of domestic service, and the necessary interference by sickness, we feel that considerable time must elapse before the attendance of pupils will come up to the required estimate. . . .[81]

It was not that parents did not want to send their children to school—the almost universal enrolments deny that—rather the rigour and the rhythm of work made it difficult to keep them there for sustained periods of time.

NOTES

1. Upper Canada, Department of Public Instruction, *Annual Report of the Normal, Model, Grammar and Common Schools*, 1850, p. 12. (The titles of the chief superintendents' annual reports change from year to year, hereafter cited as *Annual Report* for the given year.)

2. The increase in enrolments resulted particularly from an influx of girls into the public schools, see Ian E. Davey, "Trends in Female School Attendance Patterns", *Histoire Sociale/Social History*, Fall 1975, pp. 238–54; and id. "Educational Reform and the Working Class: School Attendance in Hamilton, Ontario, 1851–1891" (PHD thesis, University of Toronto, 1975) especially chapters 3 and 5. It should be noted that Ryerson's figures for those enrolled in the common schools was an aggregate of those in the public and separate schools, although in the *Annual Report*, the number attending the separate schools is also listed separately.

3. In all but the most remote and poor areas, the schools were open throughout the year. As early as 1865, Ryerson remarked that "the time during which schools are kept open in cities, towns and villages embraces, with scarcely an exception, the whole period required by law; and the average time . . . was 10 months and 2 days . . . about 2 months longer than the schools are kept open in any state of America." *Annual Report* for 1856, p. 12.

4. See Susan E. Houston, "The Impetus to Reform: Urban Crime, Poverty and Ignorance in Ontario, 1850–1875" (PHD thesis, University of Toronto, 1974), Sec. III.

5. This aspect was often referred to by the local superintendents and, after 1871, the inspectors. See, for example, *The Second Annual Report of the Inspectors of Public Schools for the City of Ottawa, 1872* (Ottawa, 1873), p. 14.

6. For a discussion of this point, see Davey, "Educational Reform", pp. 243–45.

7. The superintendent for the County of Durham in the *Annual Report* for 1864, Appendix A, p. 19.

8. "Parental indifference" or "criminal neglect" or "carelessness" were the phrases most frequently used to explain non-attendance or irregular attendance, especially in the earlier years. Perhaps an extreme example of its use (misuse?) was that of the superintendent for Bruce County in 1865 who stated regarding non-attendance: "The common cause given in almost every report is the indifference of parents. Extreme poverty, sickness and religious convictions I would excuse, but all put together does not make one case out of ten." Ibid. for 1865, Appendix A, p. 46.

9. Superintendent for Wolfe Island, County of Frontenac, ibid. for 1861, Appendix A, p. 168.

10. *Annual Report* for 1868, Appendix A, p. 38.

11. Eric J. Hobsbawn, *Industry and Empire* (Harmondsworth, 1968), p. 155.

12. *Annual Report* for 1858, p. 1.

13. Superintendent Barber's 1857 report surveyed the progress of the Toronto free schools in the 1850s. The board passed a no-confidence motion against him in 1858 and reaffirmed the commitment to the free-school system, as they did in 1864 despite the select committee's report.

During the depression years of the early 1860s and the late 1870s, the City Council tried to reduce the board's estimates because of the financial drain they represented on the city's resources. The point is that the expense of maintaining the school system was most burdensome in depression times while, at the same time, poor attendance was most obvious. For a discussion of these reports, see Haley P. Bamman and Ian E. Davey, "Ideology and Space in the Toronto Public School System" (paper presented to the Conference on Historical Urbanization in North America, York University, 1973).

14. See Thomas Hutchison, *City of Hamilton Directory, 1862–63* (Hamilton, 1862), p. 14. For the effect of the depression on the city see "The City of Hamilton Past, Present and Future", a letter to the editor in the *Hamilton Spectator and Journal of Commerce*, 1 January 1861.

15. From the Hamilton Orphan Asylum and Ladies Benevolent Society, *Minutes*, Vol. 3, January 1859, Hamilton Public Library.

16. On one day, 21 May 1859, in Hamilton two boys aged eight and thirteen were charged with stealing iron to sell, another eight year old was charged with stealing coal and a nine year old with stealing $5. The latter on conviction was fined $10 or one month's gaol. See *The Weekly Spectator*, 21 May 1859.

17. *Annual Report* for 1860, p. 189.

18. Ibid., p. 180.

19. Inspector for York County, North, ibid., 1879, Appendix D, p. 66.

20. Historians have only recently become aware of the extreme geographic mobility in the nineteenth century. See Stephan Thernstrom and Peter R. Knights,

"Men in Motion: Some Data and Speculations about Urban Population Mobility in Nineteenth Century America", *Journal of Interdisciplinary History* I (1970), 7–36. For Hamilton, see Michael B. Katz, "The People of a Canadian City, 1851–2", *Canadian Historical Review* L, No. 4 (1972), 402–26; and id., *The People of Hamilton, Canada West: Family and Class in a Mid-Nineteenth Century City* (Cambridge, Mass., 1975), especially the chapter on transiency and social mobility; for rural Ontario, see David P. Gagan and Herbert Mays, "Historical Demography and Canadian Social History: Families and Land in Peel County, Ontario", *Canadian Historical Review* LIV, No. 1 (1973), 27–47.

21. See Katz's chapter on transiency and social mobility in *Hamilton* for an analysis of the rates of persistence in Hamilton and an analysis of the characteristics of those who stayed and those who left. It is important to note that rates for females are difficult to assess because it is hard to link those who got married in the interim period.

22. Ibid.

23. Eric J. Hobsbawn, "The Tramping Artisan", in his *Labouring Men: Studies in the History of Labour* (London, 1964), pp. 34–63. As he notes (p. 40) the system was widespread in mid-nineteenth-century England among a variety of trades including compositors, lithographers, tailors, coachmakers, bookbinders, smiths, engineers, steam-engine makers, stonemasons, carpenters, ironfounders, coopers, shoemakers, boilermakers, plumbers, and bricklayers. Friendly societies also provided support for those on the move, see P. H. J. H. Gosden, *Self-Help: Voluntary Associations in Nineteenth*

Century Britain (London, 1973), pp. 47–48.

24. Charlotte Erickson, *Invisible Immigrants* (London, 1972), pp. 246–54.

25. From Hon. R. B. Sullivan's address to the Hamilton Mechanics Institute on "The Connection Between the Agriculture and Manufacture of Canada", *The Spectator*, 1 December 1847.

26. Stephan Thernstrom, *Poverty and Progress: Social Mobility in a Nineteenth Century City* (Cambridge, Mass., 1964), p. 87.

27. Erickson, *Invisible Immigrants*, pp. 249–50.

28. *Royal Commission on the Relations Between Capital and Labour*, Vol. 5, Ontario Evidence (Ottawa, 1889), p. 704.

29. *Annual Report* for 1890, Appendix I, p. 182. Although this example is drawn from a later period, there must have been numerous examples of double reporting. The 600 children reported as moving from school to school in Toronto in 1852 would also have inflated the overall enrolment and lowered the average attendance.

30. Ibid. for 1866, Appendix A, p. 60.

31. Ibid. for 1865, Appendix A, p. 65.

32. Superintendent for Petrolia village in ibid. for 1869, Appendix D, p. 116.

33. Ibid. for 1861, Appendix A, p. 159.

34. Superintendent for the County of Durham, ibid. for 1869, Appendix D, p. 69.

35. Ryerson, in a footnote, quoting the Right Honourable W. Cowper, MP, in ibid. for 1857, p. 33.

36. Michael B. Katz, "The Entrepreneurial Class in a Canadian City: The Mid-Nineteenth Century", *Journal of Social History*, Winter 1975, p. 1.

37. Erickson concludes that the main grievances for most of the immigrant artisans at first "were not low wages or long hours but irregular employment and the difficulty of securing wages in cash". *Invisible Immigrants*, p. 250.

38. *The Workingman's Journal*, 18 June 1864. This paper was published for a couple of years in the mid-1860s in Hamilton, although this is the only issue found. It is located in the Hamilton Public Library.

39. See the evidence of Fred Walters of Hamilton in the *Royal Commission on the Relations Between Capital and Labour*, p. 796.

40. H. C. Pentland, "The Development of a Capitalistic Labour Market in Canada", *Canadian Journal of Economics and Political Science* xxv, No. 4 (1959), 450–61; Steven Langdon, "The Emergence of the Canadian Working Class Movement, 1845–1875", *Journal of Canadian Studies* viii, No. 2 (1973), 3, 13, and No. 3 (1973), 8–26.

41. An illustration of the capitalist labour market in operation is the climax of the struggle between Wanzer & Co., the large sewing machine manufacturer in Hamilton, and its employees during the Nine-Hours Movement in 1872. The company had refused to accede to the employees demands for a nine-hour day and had locked them out. (It took the opportunity then to make repairs to its machinery). When the company re-opened its employees stayed out on the picket line. At first. the factory had only about 150 of its 400 workers on the job, but there were numerous applications for positions from other areas in Canada and the U.S. At least one worker was arrested for assaulting another who crossed the picket line, but, faced with losing their jobs, the employees

eventually went back. See, *The Spectator*, 28 May 1872.

42. For a discussion of the relationship between the state of the craft, skill dilution, and persistence, see Clyde Griffin, "Workers Divided: The Effects of Craft and Ethnic Differences in Poughkeepsie, New York, 1850–1880", in Stephan Thernstrom and Richard Sennett, eds., *Nineteenth Century Cities: Essays in the New Urban History* (New Haven, 1969), pp. 49–77.

43. Evidence of Thomas Towers, a carpenter for the Grand Trunk Railroad and Hamilton District Master of the Knights of Labor, *Royal Commission on the Relations Between Capital and Labour*, p. 875.

44. "Veritas, The People's Friend", letter to the editor, *The Spectator*, 27 December 1854.

45. Quoted in Eileen Yeo, "Mayhew as a Social Investigator" in Eileen Yeo and E. P. Thompson, *The Unknown Mayhew* (New York, 1971), p. 83. For a superb discussion of casual labour in London in the period, see Gareth Stedman Jones, *Outcast London* (Oxford, 1971), especially pp. 92–97; and Frederick Engels, *The Condition of the Working Class in England* (London, 1969), especially Chapter 5, "Results". Engels noted: "But far more demoralizing than his poverty in its influence upon the English working-man is the insecurity of his position, the necessity of living upon wages from hand to mouth...." ibid., p. 146. For an excellent discussion of the conflict between working-class culture and the demands of industry, see E. P. Thompson, "Time, Work-Discipline, and Industrial Capitalism", *Past and Present* XXXVIII (1967), 56–97; for the North American experience, see Herbert G. Gutman, "Work, Cul-

ture and Society in Industrializing America, 1819–1918", *American Historical Review* LXXVIII (1973), 531–88.

46. William Collins, a retired engineer and machinist from Burlington, in *Royal Commission on the Relations Between Capital and Labour*, pp. 825–26.

47. Superintendent for Dereham Township, County of Oxford, in *Annual Report* for 1861, Appendix A, p. 184.

48. In 1865, when bad crop yields affected many areas, many superintendents attributed low attendance to inadequate clothing because of the parents' poverty. Similarly, a breakdown of the reasons for non-attendance in Toronto in 1863 showed that 216 of the 1,632 not attending reported "want of clothes" as the reason, ibid. for 1863, Appendix A, p. 150.

49. *The Labour Advocate* I, No. 3 (19 December 1890).

50. The evidence in the *Royal Commission on the Relations Between Capital and Labour* is an excellent source of information on seasonal labour patterns. For the evidence of winter unemployment among moulders, see, for example, the testimony of Fred Walters of Hamilton, pp. 794–95.

51. The poverty of female-headed households is well illustrated in Michael B. Katz, "On the Condition of Women, 1851–1861", *Canadian Social History Project*, Report No. 4 (Toronto, 1972), pp. 16–25. For the selective benevolence of the charity workers, see Haley P. Bamman, "The Ladies Benevolent Society of Hamilton, Ontario: Form and Function in Mid-Nineteenth Century Philanthropy", in the same report, pp. 161–217.

52. Judith Fingard, "The Winter's Tale: Contours of Pre-Industrial

Poverty in British America, 1815–1860", Canadian Historical Association, *Historical Papers*, 1974, p. 67. It should be noted that seasonal poverty was not confined to "pre-industrial" Canada. *The Palladium of Labour*, 1 December 1883, commented on the injustice of paying carpenters less in winter because of the shorter working day: "Man's wants are greater in winter than at any season of the year. It costs more for fire, food and clothing and all the necessities of life, and more are consumed on account of the weather."

53. *The Weekly Spectator*, 21 January 1858.

54. These figures are calculated from the monthly reports of the Internal Management Committee, Hamilton Board of Education, *Minutes*, 1882–90.

55. Toronto Board of Education Historical Collection, W. C. Wilkinson Diaries, 1872–74, v, 23 January and 12 March 1874.

56. Ibid., iii, 7 May 1873.

57. *Annual Report* for 1874, Appendix B, p. 71.

58. Davey, "Educational Reform", Chapter 4.

59. Joseph Kett, "Growing Up in Rural New England", in Tamara K. Hareven, ed., *Anonymous Americans* (Englewood Cliffs, 1971), pp. 1–14.

60. Superintendent for South Riding, County of Hastings, in *Annual Report* for 1861, Appendix A, p. 170.

61. Superintendent for London Township, County of Middlesex, ibid. for 1863, Appendix A, p. 140.

62. In ibid. for 1859, p. 167.

63. Superintendent for Nelson Township, County of Halton, in ibid. for 1861, Appendix A, p. 176.

64. Superintendent for Huron County, in ibid. for 1863, Appendix A, p. 160. This facet of winter

attendance is well captured in Charles William Gordon's [Ralph Connor] memories of his school days, *Glengarry School-Days* (Toronto, 1902). It should be noted that the figures in Table 10:4 indicate that in the 1870s and 1880s the trend in the rural areas was towards younger attendance.

65. See *Annual Report* for 1879, Appendix D, p. 74.

66. G. P. de T. Glazebrook, *Life in Ontario: A Social History* (Toronto, 1968), p. 179.

67. Wilkinson Diaries ii, 16 and 22 January 1873.

68. For a good discussion of the governmental response to disease in Canada, see Neil Sutherland, "To Create a Strong and Healthy Race: School Children in the Public Health Movement, 1880–1914", *History of Education Quarterly* xii, No. 3 (1972), 304–33.

69. See the summary statement taken from the minutes of the board in *The History and Romance of Education*, compiled by L. T. Spalding (Hamilton, 1972), p. 16.

70. Sutherland, "To Create a Strong and Healthy Race", p. 307.

71. W. Callowhil Papers, Letter, 30 September 1860, Provincial Archives of Ontario.

72. *The Spectator*, 8 September 1847.

73. Superintendent for Woodstock, in *Annual Report* for 1863, Appendix A, p. 160.

74. Superintendent for North Riding, County of Hastings, in ibid. for 1867, Appendix A, p. 25.

75. Superintendent for South Riding, County of Hastings, in ibid. for 1868, Appendix A, p. 14.

76. Superintendent for Welland County, in ibid. for 1868, Appendix A, p. 25.

77. Superintendent for Moulton Township, County of Haldimand,

in ibid. for 1869, Appendix D, p. 86. The perception of the immigrants as ignorant was common in the reports, see the superintendent for Markham, County of York, in ibid. for 1862, Appendix A, p. 114, who remarked: "The few discontented parties being ignorant persons from the old countries.... Happily the number is few ... and in a few years I hope it will be esteemed as great a disgrace to be ignorant as it is now considered to be intemperate. The immigrant children are growing up in ignorance, a strong contrast to our native born Canadian children, not one of whom at the age of ten years and upwards but can read, write and cipher."

78. Harvey J. Graff, "Literacy and Social Structure in the Nineteenth Century", (PHD thesis, University of Toronto, 1975).

79. *Annual Report* for 1873, Appendix B, pp. 77–78.

80. Ibid. for 1869, p. 24.

81. Inspector for the County of Renfrew, in *Annual Report* for 1872, Appendix B, p. 30.

School Reform and Education: The Issue of Compulsory Schooling, Toronto, 1851-71

SUSAN E. HOUSTON

"Why should we degrade the schools by mixing up with the question of a national education this other and totally different one of preventing crime by educating the Arabs of the Street?" asked Toronto school trustee, Charles Brooke, in a letter to *The Globe* in August 1865; "treat both questions, if you will, but treat them separately, for by mixing them you spoil the schools for either one thing or the other."[1] At least some of Brooke's constituents in St. James' Ward agreed with him, but his defeat the following January in a rare instance of a hotly-contested school board election in the city seemed to repudiate his efforts to direct board policy into line with the ambitions of the respectable classes increasingly eager to patronize the city schools. He simply could not separate the street arabs from the school question. To isolate the issue of a publicly supported, non-sectarian, state-controlled educational system from the precarious circumstances of the urban poor was, in effect, to amputate the common-school movement from its ideological source. The socializing potential of the common school was one of the most powerful inducements to the acceptance of compulsory property taxation for its support and, at the same time, to the adoption of some measure of compulsory attendance to increase its effectiveness. In the 1860s, some Torontonians questioned the credibility of the school's ambitions. Their concerns, so intimately linked to experience of the city, were scarcely unique. More than others, however, they voiced the distrust and unease with which many Upper Canadians viewed their society and its social relations.

Much of the reform enthusiasm of Torontonians in the middle decades of the nineteenth century was fanned by their sense of being involved in a larger Anglo-American world—a world of large cities, manufactories, slums, and a myriad of reform activities. In addition, concrete experience of the limitations of penal reform and philanthropy helped focus attention on the practical realities of providing sufficient and effective schooling in a society alive with movement and moral as well as social confusion. While, through the middle decades, reform-minded Torontonians retained a lively trust in the power of moral suasion, none the less, the self-conscious antistatist and individualist colouring of their mid-Victorian liberal convictions survived more on inexperience than philosophical commitment. Regardless of prevailing economic axioms, social critics were being seduced by the prospect of large, specialized, flexible, and rationally ordered systems.

A commitment to compulsory education was both a symptom and an incentive to this seduction. Throughout the 1860s, support for some measure of compulsion in school attendance gained strength. Like the common-school crusade of a generation earlier, the appeal of compulsory education was often contradictory and delusive. In part, it legitimized the promise of the common-school system, its direction, and its achievement, and in that sense was, as Egerton Ryerson argued, the logical companion to compulsory property assessment. In the form of compulsory attendance, legal coercion represented a basic professional and bureaucratic objective, a practical gesture to economy and efficiency. In what was perhaps its most common context, compulsory education was related to the school's mission of social reform. Since it was generally agreed by the mid-1860s that impoverished and neglected urchins had no place in the city schools, compulsory education provided urban reformers with the necessary first step to forcing the children of the lowest classes to attend an institution especially suited to their delinquent condition. In moments of waning reform enthusiasm, of course, compulsory education could also provide a strategic avenue of retreat.

As the rhetoric of school promotion illustrates, free schooling in Upper Canada, as elsewhere in the nineteenth century, was essentially a missionary undertaking; the schoolroom, in its studied severity, seemed neutral to social and sectarian distinctions and the universality of childhood once transferred to schooling conjured up images of a mighty moral force. The very term "common" in the context of the school system seemed to gain in profundity from its elusive ambiguity.

From the outset, it was clear, however, that the very lowest elements in society, as well as the working classes, were included in the school's mandate, for the association of education with the reduction of crime provided a staple ingredient of common school rhetoric. Few school supporters needed the urging of the chief superintendent to link the promotion of education with "administration of justice, organized systems for the repression or prevention of crime and other important subjects".[2] The existence and promised redemption of ignorant, ill-mannered street children proved a stock argument of free-school advocates, as it effectively dramatised the ingredients of character formation and social mobility which contributed much to the movement's appeal. The image of school as police in disguise was frankly endorsed in certain quarters. The local public-school inspector, G. A. Barber, berated Torontonians in 1854 for the low attendance at the city's schools with an un-equivocal statement of the rationale of free schooling: "the principle upon which free schools stand is the philanthropic argument that it is easier to prevent the commission of crime than to punish the culprit—that it is wiser to educate than to coerce—that a staff of schoolmasters is cheaper than a body-guard of policemen, and that school houses form a better in-vestment than prisons and penitentiaries."[3]

By mid-century, then, not only had the common-school move-ment become linked with salvaging the lowest classes, but the school system (although optionally free) provided a definition of "neglect" and "vagrant"—as not being in school—which enlarged and clarified the impression of a critical social prob-lem in the cities and towns. The extent of ignorance among the poorer elements in society was no longer to be a matter of con-jecture it could be defined and legislated against. In Ryerson's view, ignorance was no longer merely a cause of crime—it was a crime. "If ignorance is an evil to society, *voluntary* ignorance is a *crime* against society," he thundered in his annual report in 1857. "And if society is invested with power to relieve all from the evil of ignorance by providing for the education of all, the safety and interests of society, no less than the mission of its existence, require that it should be able to suppress and prevent the crime of voluntary ignorance by punishing its authors. If idle mendicancy is a crime in a man thirty years of age, why is not idle vagrancy a crime in a boy ten years of age? The latter is the parent of the former."[4]

School promoters, as it turned out, paid a heavy price for the appeals they made to the social anxiety of the propertied classes. No sooner had compulsory taxation in support of common schools taken effect in urban centres than complaints were voiced about the hordes of supposedly delinquent children who roamed the streets during school hours. Impressionistic evidence mounted of an indeterminately large number of urban children who were neither at school nor at work.[5] The problem was primarily—but not exclusively—a Toronto issue; but should the municipalities remain powerless to cope with the problem, the chief superintendent could see that this questioning of the school's effectiveness as an agent of social reform might undermine support for the system throughout the province. Unable to surmount the government's reluctance to infringe upon parental liberties, by 1857 Ryerson and urban school officials were quite evidently smarting from the criticism stirred up by Mr. Justice Hagarty's charges that the money spent on schools had had a negligible impact on the increasing incidence of juvenile crime and delinquency.[6]

School attendance was at the centre of the controversy. If the street arabs and the neglected offspring of the urban poor did not go to the costly schools erected for their benefit, who did? And if vagrant children did not attend the common schools, where else might they be "schooled" in literacy and self-discipline? Such questions demanded answers for no sooner had urban school districts been consolidated into single boards supported by compulsory property assessment than the experience of school attendance diverged abruptly from the rhetorical blueprint of school reform. If the free schools in Toronto in the 1850s and 1860s were to any degree "common", for example, it was in the sense of *ordinary*, not *universal*. As school visitors and board personnel frankly acknowledged, the schools were patronized primarily by the working classes, the children of "the respectable mechanics, small traders, the honest labourers of the city".[7] Such a state of affairs was not in itself objectionable, but quite obviously not even that segment of the city's population sent their children with sufficient regularity or devotion to warrant the expenditure of public money entailed in the construction of schoolhouses and the annual operating expenses of the system. Thus under pressure to justify the public's investment in free schooling, school trustees and officials wrestled to define the proper constituency of the public schools. From the outset various classes of children had remained outside the reach of the free school. As a result, initial efforts to stabilize support for urban school systems involved revoking the school's responsibility for certain elements as well as broadening its appeal to others. The working poor—rather than the destitute—became the real target of the school's mission and the measure of its success. This common interest, which many taxpayers and ambitious schoolteachers had in aiming the public-school system at the broad middle of the social structure, challenged its characterization as an agent of social reform.

However, the class character of the Toronto public schools did not go unchallenged. As the school routine slowly insinuated itself into the pattern of working-class life in Toronto, the bitter early pessimism of anti-public-school forces was generally superceded by a less melodramatic but equally disturbing realization: the "beau ideal" of common schooling, as *The Globe* called it, was not merely temporarily stalled by the lingering pride of class among Torontonians, it was smothered by "an exclusive spirit of class and cast [existing] here, which is nearly unknown in the States." As *The Globe* frankly admitted in 1867: "among ourselves, the common schools, in cities, are indisputably confined to the children of the industrious mechanic and tradesman; exclusive, on the one hand, of the wealthier merchant and professional man, and, unfortunately, on the other hand, to some degree, of the children of the poor and vagrant classes, who stand most in need of the free education they supply."[8] The question was thus two pronged: should one be satisfied with what was in reality working- or middling-class patronage of the free schools? or, if efforts were made to extend the school's reach to those elements not initially included in its orbit, should one look upward, to the commercial and professional classes, or downward, to the poorer unschooled children of ignorant parents? While there were sufficient cases of school children with illiterate parents for the Toronto board to prepare tickets reading "absent half a day" for the children to bring to school, in the background of the discussion of the social problem of the city's poor lingered the suspicion that strenuous efforts to include the children of the lowest classes in the common schools by means of compulsion might result in the wholesale flight of the working classes.[9]

In a lengthy series of letters in *The Globe* and as chairman of a trustees' select committee on school attendance in 1865, Charles Brooke battled against the board's dogged but unimaginative commitment to free schooling for the working classes.[10] Compared to Hamilton, for example, policy decisions of school placement and organization had clearly accentuated the working-class character of the Toronto schools. In all-age ward schools the numbers of older pupils in the senior division appeared insignificant when compared to the milling throngs of youngsters in the gallery classes, and a limited amount of specialization was possible given the scattered pockets of senior pupils. Determined to counteract the weight of heavy enrolment in the earliest years, which depressed the whole character of the city schools, Brooke focused on issues of comparative costs and efficiency, and the fatal omission of not grading schools which had resulted in keeping out the children of professional and business men. The select committee which he chaired on the whole concurred in Brooke's views, but with restraint. Noting the increased irregularity in attendance under the free system and the shrinking proportion of more advanced pupils, the committee alluded to "prejudices which now (rightly or wrongly) exist against the schools as they are now indiscriminately assembled," and proposed to increase the attractiveness and efficiency of the system by centralizing the senior divisions into the nucleus of a central high school. Not only would this increase attendance among older pupils, who would now be able to do more senior work, but the proposed weekly fee of 12¢ per pupil in the high school would help defray the cost of more teachers for the overcrowded primary levels.

In his response to the proposals, the local inspector, James Porter, rejected out of hand what he regarded as the select committee's attempt to undermine the free system and to deflect the public schools from their modest course of instructing and socializing the working classes.[11] Porter regarded the ambitions for the senior divisions in a high school to be singularly misplaced. "Youth are earlier fitted now for several modes of active life than they were twenty years ago," he maintained, "and more methods of making a living are open to them now than were ever dreamt of then; many being compelled to leave for active life before they have made such advancement . . . the supposed higher education to be thus aimed at would prove a delusion and would end in disappointment." In his view—and the one which finally carried the board—the proper business of the common-school system lay at the opposite end of the social scale, with "the uncultivated hundreds of children in our city whom parental neglect, partly perhaps parental poverty and their own consequent habits, indispose for attendance at our City Schools."[12]

There can be no doubt about the seriousness with which school officials throughout the 1860s regarded public displays of interest in a revival of school fees or proposals for "streaming" the schools, in effect by social class.[13] Immobilized in a climate of retrenchment in public spending, officials and school supporters had little scope for an effective counterattack against charges of high costs and lack of service: conditions within the schools were deteriorating with overcrowding and the problem of unschooled children persisted. Despite the criticisms, however, two critical factors bolstered the current policy: comparative statistics, even within the history of the Toronto schools, provided unreliable evidence of the condition of the school system; and the past two decades had seen fundamental shifts in the pattern of family and work life.

The statistical problem was perhaps the more immediately apparent, and, superficially at least, placed school officials at a tactical disadvantage. Aggregate census data suggest to the historian that behind the sluggish growth of school attendance in Toronto in the 1850s and 1860s lay a critically irregular pattern of population growth: in the decade 1851–61, the city population as a whole increased 45 per cent, and the population enumerated as going to school increased 78 per cent; on the other hand, the age group from 5 to 10 years old increased only 12.2 per cent and the 10 to 15 year-old group 37.4 per cent, giving an average increase for the school-age years of 23.8 per cent. Contemporaries, however, looked only at the relative proportion of youngsters attending or not attending school, and that figure did not seem to have markedly improved with the advent of free schools. The city census of January 1861 was particularly discouraging. Approximately 2,500 of the 11,500 children from 5 to 16 years of age were found "not enjoying educational advantages". *The Globe* confessed to no great surprise, considering the widespread employment of children under 16; however, the local inspector, James Porter, estimated that while perhaps 1,000 worked, "a large proportion of the remainder" were street arabs.[14] The school trustees came under mounting pressure to produce a more accurate estimate of the incidence of non-attendance. The results of a special school census, taken in August 1863, greatly cheered school officials. "Perhaps," Porter confessed, "in common with not a few who earnestly desire the mental and moral culture of the obviously neglected portion of the children of our city, I have supposed that their number is larger than it actually is." The outcome seemed to

TABLE 11:1

	population 5 to 16 years	total registered attendance	number not attending	% not attending
Protestant	7,053	5,877	1,165	16.5
Roman Catholic	2,455	1,999	467	19.0
total	9,508	7,876	1,632	17.2

REASONS FOR NOT ATTENDING

	Protestant	Roman Catholic	total	%
employed	340	113	453	27.7
wanted at home	203	60	263	16.1
sick	91	37	128	7.8
too young/too far	149	68	217	13.3
want of clothes	127	89	216	13.2
lately come to city	38	1	39	2.4
no return	217	99	316	19.4

Source: Annual report for 1863, p. 43.

*The census was taken down in books, with the name of the street, number of the house, name of resident, number of children of school age (5 to 16), male and female, Protestant or Roman Catholic, "number attending school or taught at home on the day before the enquiry is made, or who have attended school at any time during past 6 months," the number not so attending, age, reason why. Fifteen enumerators were employed: three for St. John's, St. James' and St. David's wards; two for St. Patrick's and St. Andrew's; one for St. George's and St. Lawrence's. $350 was appropriated for taking the census (Report of the meeting of Board of School Trustees, *The Globe*, 19 March 1863). Regretably, this material has not survived.

him unequivocal. "Its results by no means confirm the gloomy and painful conclusions which have been entertained as to the number of that portion of our juvenile population, which, being neither under instruction nor usefully employed, is growing up in ignorance and idleness."[15]

There, indeed, was the nub of the problem. What Porter had feared and what the census denied, was a large population of school-age youngsters for whose conduct *no explanation* could be given. The numbers accounted for as employed, needed at home, too young, too poor, or too far from the school were noted, but the conclusion to be drawn was "that the evil of unmitigated juvenile ignorance does not prevail so widely in Toronto as was feared" precisely because the social problem of juvenile vagrants really involved only those children growing up without restraint, who were neither at school, accounted for at home, nor at work. Obviously, too, Porter regarded the fact that fewer than half of the 7,876 children of school age (2,971) reported under instruction during some portion of the six months ending June 30, 1863, were on the registers of the common school at any one time as being of little consequence. What was noteworthy was that attendance in 1863 showed modest gains and reached an all-time high. The most plausible explanation for such equanimity is that the monopoly instincts of the public system were as yet to be unleashed. The timing is significant. While in the early 1860s the local superintendent was still tolerant of the diversity of legitimate activity and "educational" opportunity which existed for youngsters in Toronto, by the end of the decade schoolmen and reformers both would have become more critical of the inadequacies and competition of informal and private alternatives to the public system.

The changing pattern of youthful employment in the city was clearly an important aspect of the public-school situation. Although opportunities and inducements to youthful labour seem, in fact, to have increased with the good times of the 1850s, they were also changing character.[16] Errand boys and odd-job helpers were always in demand, but the pressure to have a sound elementary education was already making itself felt in family advice to ambitious twelve year olds and in editorials to prospective employers in praise of the intellectual and moral values of school training. In the 1860s, boys still frequently starting training for mechanical pursuits at 12 to 14 years of age, but large-scale manufacturing sharpened the distinction between dead-end unskilled labour and skilled trades. By 1871, the percentage of hands employed in industrial establishments in Toronto who were under the age of 16 was 10.9 per cent (and 5 per cent of the total work force). To social critics in Toronto in the 1860s and 1870s, however, the distinctions within the working-class experience were already obvious and alarming. Whatever opportunities might exist for skilled labour, the children of the lowest classes could look forward to a precarious economic and social existence. Growing up without adequate nourishment or restraint, they faced probable unemployment or exploitation in conditions of ignorance in factories. There was little in the alien restraint of the common schools to attract those children for all that they were free; and even less once the virtues of cleanliness, punctuality, and self-discipline were written into board regulations governing the duties of teachers and pupils. As the range of the public schools' appeal inched higher into the middle social strata, pressure increased for the schools to maintain their respectability by excluding the ragged progeny of the urban poor. But their absence from the common school did not appear quite so critical as long as other disciplinary influences seemed to be reaching their mark, and of course, if responsibility for the street arabs could be laid at another door, both the Board of Common School Trustees and its Protestant supporters could feel smug, if not entirely relieved.

In some quarters, the separate schools provided an easy target. To those critics who assumed that the urban poor were Irish Catholics, it seemed obvious that the unruly urchins and youthful criminals were their offspring. Prior to the school census in 1863, religious prejudice was encouraged to a certain extent by the lack of adequate attendance figures for either the common or separate schools; thus some school board trustees favoured the census hoping it would expose Catholic delinquency. It did not, and although a few trustees obviously did not abandon their convictions, others envied the success with which the separate schools held on to their pupils. When it seemed probable that the separate schools were doing as well, if not better, than the public system the public-school board and its officials tended to attribute the Catholic success to a tactic they could not be expected to emulate—the "ecclesiastical character" of the schools and the moral suasion Catholic clergy could exercise over their flock. By and large, considering the temptation anti-Catholic sentiment might have felt to discredit the separate schools as failing in their responsibility for juvenile vagrants, a striking aspect of the school debate is the relative absence of expressions of Protestant superiority, and any significant polarization of reform sentiment along sectarian lines.

The parochial schools of the Church of England might also have gathered in the children of the urban poor.[17] At first, in anticipation of receiving the same privileges as the Roman Catholic Church in respect of denominational schools, and later out of stubbornness, Anglican parishioners in Toronto contributed generously in the 1850s towards the building of parish schoolhouses. Like their free-school counterparts, parochial school promoters were fond of the phrase "poorer children", but the adjective expressed little more than their sense of social distance from the working classes. What fragmentary evidence exists of the operation of Anglican parish schools confirms *The Globe*'s suspicions that the Church of England was as aware as anyone of the gradations of poverty and decency and that the parochial schools would only take "the children of the well-to-do poor who appear clean and wellclad",[18] the same class which went to the common school.

Sunday schools were the most informal of the institutional alternatives to the common-school system. With a tradition of missionary service to the urban poor, the Sunday-school movement provided a flexible, eclectic, and remarkably resilient formula for religious and social proselytism. While the philanthropic aspect of Sunday-school work remained a minor aspect of its role, the problem of reaching neglected and impoverished children was one which the Sabbath-school teachers took very seriously. Increasingly conscious of their collective self-interest, by the 1860s the volunteer teachers of the various denominations met annually in a provincial convention to renew their sense of mission and their "professional" expertise as Sunday-school teachers.[19] Here they debated tactics for gathering in otherwise neglected children: the pros and cons of first providing clothing, the formation of non-denominational or union schools to allay sectarian feelings, and the locating of mission schools in impoverished areas. There were both practical and moral problems involved in enticing reluctant ragamuffins to first come to schools where they might then be civilized. In 1866, a visiting clergyman from New York had seriously recommended always having flowers for poor children, as "they are very fond of flowers"; however, the problem of mingling "sugar with our tea" was one which continued to disturb the delegates.

Sunday schools flourished in Toronto in the 1860s. A survey in 1865 indicated that the number of eligible children in the city "not attending Sunday school" closely approximated the number found to be "not attending school": 6,645 pupils were registered in 87 Protestant Sunday schools and were instructed by 704 teachers.[20] However, for all the survey's detail, it is little help in determining whether the 1,500 or so youngsters found to be absent from both kinds of schools were, in fact, the same individuals. One is left, then, with the question of the extent to which Sunday schools played any appreciable role in disciplining the street arabs. Into the 1860s it seems, Sunday schools were regarded as a valuable source of training in basic literacy. As late as 1867 *The Globe* believed there were "a surprising number in Toronto alone" who, "if not instructed in the Sabbath school, *will not be instructed at all.*"[21] Mission Sunday schools particularly, such as the one opened on Dorset Street by St. Andrew's Church in 1869, often performed vital and complex services for their neighbouring populations.[22] Nevertheless, the very conception of the "wholesome restraint" and training required to ensure the adequate upbringing of youth was changing to fit the social realities of urban life. In an address on "Child Neglect" delivered to the teachers' association in 1867, James Porter "cheerfully" acknowledged the work of the city's many Sunday schools, but "reminded his hearers that during the other days of the week there were multitudes of children either not comprehended within the range of Sunday school influence, or who were without instruction and without restraint."[23] In another era or another place, where the children of the very poor were needed to work long hours in various kinds of agricultural and domestic employment, Sunday schools served a vital role in rescuing children from the ignorance (and, it was suspected, vice) of their parents. In the early decades of the century, the towns and rural settlements of Upper Canada had supported a variety of "educational" facilities; in effect an ad hoc hierarchy of schools emerged to serve the social and intellectual requirements of the various strata of society. In this, Sunday schools provided a humble but critical bottom rung so long as the organization of family and community life commanded the children's time. Conditions in the commercial cities of mid-century Upper Canada were obviously quite different; the children of the urban poor were neither needed in the work force nor adequately supervised at home. Measured against rising standards of restraint Sunday schools were no longer sufficient safeguards against juvenile ignorance and depravity. As Porter explained to the teachers' convention: "The evidences of it are before us every day in the multitudes of squalid little ones whom we meet with on our public streets, for whom no one seems to care; in the groups of idle and mischievous lads who haunt the lanes and vacant lots of our city, and, as a natural consequence, in that sad yet terrible succession of juvenile offenders, the majority of whom probably escape detection and punishment."

The continued variety of alternatives to the common school well into the era of urban free schools provides a critical dimension to the development of public education often ignored by historians. In the 1850s social critics and school promoters had a range of options with which to try to reduce the alarming proportion of ignorant and idle youth in cities and towns, and in Toronto particularly. By the early 1860s as it became evident that economic demands for a casual labour force ensured the existence of a class of chronically underemployed labouring poor whose children neither would nor could attend the common schools, it seemed quite appropriate for school supporters to entertain ways of supplementing the publicly supported city schools. Unfortunately, possible alternatives proved fewer and more tenuous than tradition implied. However much social class considerations might curtail the operation of the common schools, nevertheless, as Ryerson discovered in 1862 when he proposed public financial support for denominational "ragged" schools, compulsory property assessment was a powerful incentive to the recognition of the "public" status of the school system and its mandate for comprehensiveness. Moreover, as the complimentary pressures of economic development and social anxiety increased the minimal standards of moral and academic training required of the urban working classes, fewer substitutes for formal schooling or full-time employment remained.

As it became increasingly clear how inappropriate it would be to force dishevelled street arabs into the common schools, awareness grew of how these children would be made as uneasy in school as they were unwelcome. "Those who know the poor can testify how they too shrink in their filth and tattered clothing from Church and School," Mr. Justice Hagarty remarked to the Grand Jury in 1865; "it is idle to discuss the soundness of their reasoning on such a subject—it is enough that the feeling exists." The delinquency of the street children who, in Hagarty's view, represented "a most dangerous symptom in our social state", was defined most clearly by their poverty, with its accompaniment of rags and dirt. Few publicly doubted that the city's philanthropies could meet the challenge, but the practicalities were troublesome. Experience suggested that some element of legal compulsion was required to reinforce charitable efforts, otherwise they could make little headway. A truant law, similar to the one in Massachusetts, attracted editorial interest, but the practical usefulness of compulsory education remained uncertain. While by the mid-1860s the common school might be absolved of any failure to encompass the very poor, the issue of the responsibility of the school board and the school system in the matter remained clouded. Perhaps, as James Porter concluded in 1867, "the only way . . . is by asking for the enactment of some law which shall deal with their ignorant and disordered condition as itself as species of crime, less indeed their own than that of their parents and guardians."[24] The orphaned, semi-orphaned, or temporarily abandoned children of impoverished but honest parents were already the object of charity in Toronto. But the youth who wandered beyond the reach of the school and for whom such urgency was felt were not only poor, they were the offspring of the most dissolute and unsavoury segment of the population and required an environment especially suited to their state: an "industrial school", somewhere half way between a boys' home and a juvenile reformatory. In 1857, during the second reading of the bill to establish the prison for young offenders, J. A. Macdonald had spoken of the government's intention, next session, to introduce a bill to enable municipalities to establish reformatory schools.[25] Nothing further was done, but the city's still unused House of Refuge, built in 1860 on part of the Scadding property purchased for the gaol, offered an obvious location and the idea gained further support from the provisions of the 1866 municipal Act which required (until they were made optional in 1868) that the city provide an industrial home or house of refuge.[26]

In 1868, the efforts of socially prominent and reform-minded Torontonians to resolve the issue of responsibility for the street children reached a climax. The year started with an impressive declaration of concern in an appeal to the responsibility of the public-school system. In a petition to the Legislature favouring compulsory education, eight judges of the superior courts, four clergy, the mayor, eleven alderman, and other prominent citizens requested an inquiry into the school systems in cities and towns "with a view to increasing its powers of usefulness and extending, so far as may be found practicable, its advantages to that class of children which, under the present law, it has been found impossible to reach, and from which the community has the strongest reason to apprehend danger to its peace and well-being."[27] Although the petition was generally well received by the public and the press, a reliance on compulsory education measures to solve the problem of urban delinquency seemed to some critics totally ineffectual.

As Professor Daniel Wilson pointed out in a letter to *The Globe* in March, launching his own scheme, people had been talking about compulsory education for so long a whole generation had grown up in the meantime.[28] Wilson proposed a modification of the industrial day-school provisions available in Britain. In essence, it hinged on a combination of voluntary effort and the provincial school system; the school trustees would provide the food and clothing. School hours would be deliberately flexible so as not to interfere with the children's "honest industrial pursuits"; even without compulsory regulations a truant officer would exercise persuasion to ensure attendance, and on Sundays there would be a Sunday school with special provisions for Roman Catholics if possible. Wilson's proposal aroused sufficient attention that public meetings were held in April and May to canvass opinion and draft a detailed proposal to be submitted to the school board.[29] The final estimate for feeding 100 pupils two meals a day (and second-hand clothing if necessary), with a matron, extra teachers' pay and furnishings was $2,535 over and above the ordinary expenses of a common school.

The board's Standing Committee on School Management acted swiftly and decisively on Wilson's communication.[30] Within the month the committee rejected his proposal, anticipating "too many practical difficulties likely to grow out of the voluntary system". Having resisted on behalf of the taxpayers any further claim to the board's resources, the committee deferred to the responsibility of the provincial government for devising, authorizing, and financing any scheme to reclaim the juvenile vagrants.

Wilson was scathing in his reply to the committee's report, reiterating his conviction "that the Common School system and the Board of School Trustees of the city furnish the legitimate organization for dealing with the practical evil of hundreds of children spending the time which their more fortunate companions of the same age pass in school, in vagrancy, with all its inevitable demoralizing accompaniments of mendicancy, street-gambling, petty-pilfering and general incipient criminality."[31] In order to salvage something from their collective efforts, the various prominent supporters of the scheme resolved to petition the Legislature to authorize the co-operation of school authorities and voluntary agencies in establishing industrial schools (under new school legislation), and the enforcement of compulsory education by a truant officer. Action was virtually immediate. Within two weeks a bill to provide for industrial schools was introduced by Hon. E. B. Wood, provincial treasurer. The government proposed to inspect, but not financially assist, schools teaching three classes of children by order of a magistrate: the vagrant, delinquent, and incorrigible. It also provided for the assessment of parents for the cost of maintaining their child in the industrial school. The bill received second reading on January 21, 1869, but there the matter was dropped. In April the Standing Committee on School Management, having been asked to reconsider Wilson's proposal, recommended that the matter be placed before the Legislature, but when the board met to consider the committee report, the vote was tied and the motion was defeated.[32]

What went wrong? An obvious villain is the Board of School Trustees, whose rejection of the industrial school proposal forced Daniel Wilson and his friends to abandon their plan and follow the more conventional path of founding yet another charitable venture—the Newsboys' Lodging and Industrial Home. But the position of the board became understandable when instead of being matched against Wilson's innovative scheme it is set in the context of the city's school situation. After more than half a decade of retrenchment policies, the cumulative effect of modest population growth had created its own priorities. The board was faced with critical overcrowding, and it had no doubt where its mandate lay: the respectable taxpayers of the city who wished to send their children to the common schools had a stronger claim than the parents of unruly urchins who had no inclination to go to school. Added to that was the threat which Wilson's proposal for collaboration posed to the board's fragile image of its own public status. As the debate in 1862 over Ryerson's proposed bill relating to vagrant and neglected children signified, only recently had the dimensions of the public-school system been affirmed as encompassing—and in that sense as being somehow above—particularist interests. As one such interest, voluntaryism was a threat. Thus as resistance to state intervention and compulsion eroded in these years, intolerance of a collaboration of voluntary and public authority increased. To the school trustees in 1868, the confusion about the jurisdiction involved in the board being responsible for the school, and philanthropists being responsible for feeding and clothing the street arabs, appeared an unjustifiable loosening of their tenuous grasp of public authority.

What followed after 1868 was in a sense an anti-climax. Some Toronto school trustees, especially W. B. McMurrich, pursued the idea of an industrial school while at the same time seeking legislation to clarify the jurisdictional confusion and to secure provincial financial support for the proposed institution.[33] Until 1871, however, the fate of Ryerson's comprehensive grammar- and common-school legislation—the cap-stone of his career-dominated legislative concern with educational matters—was uncertain. By then, compulsory education, so long sought after and publicized, had been shorn of much of its bite.[34] Ironically, despite the context of juvenile vagrancy so assiduously provided for by Ryerson in the *Journal of Education*, annual reports, and presentations to county school conventions, urban reform was no longer the chief rationale for compulsory education. Indeed, the proposal which Ryerson made to the county convention in 1866 appeared to James Porter, the Toronto inspector, "to consider especially the wants of rural sections". The astuteness of Porter's remark was borne out by the swelling chorus of professional support throughout the province for compulsory education measures to reduce irregularity of attendance.[35] With growing confidence speakers at the teachers' association meetings articulated the interests of the profession which were refreshingly unsentimental, if highly bureaucratic. Their endorsement of residential industrial schools for juvenile vagrants was unequivocal. There must be no confusion about the purpose and result of compulsory education: it was to enforce the regular attendance of ordinary pupils. Industrial schools were required to receive the vagrant and incorrigible. Indeed, the teachers' association lobbied successfully to have a clause added to the compulsory provisions, permitting the school trustees to remove refractory and vicious pupils to an industrial school.[36]

The contention that compulsory education served only the

needs of cities and towns was thoroughly aired by Edward Blake and other Grit critics of the school bill in 1871, not particularly to their credit. Beyond question, larger urban communities exhibited greater social stress which enhanced the schools' classic role as a force for social stability. But by the 1870s, the values of regularity, uniformity, and systemization had hold of the teaching profession and school supporters throughout the province. Blake came closest to the truth with charges that compulsion would prove unenforceable.[37] For many years the legislative provisions remained considerably less significant than the regulations relating to attendance passed by the Council of Public Instruction in 1871.[38] These provided the disciplinary framework within which the moral authority of a truant officer could operate. In Toronto, for example, as long as there was not an industrial school to which truants could be banished, the board took no legal action against parents. The truant officer, however, quickly learned of the salutory effect of a reminder of parental duty under the law. It is obvious, both from the record which survives in the diaries of Toronto's first truant officer, W. C. Wilkinson, and the published statistics of his and his successor's annual reports, that the primary objective was to reduce lateness and absenteeism among the pupils already enrolled. There is little evidence, in the first years, at least, of any significant resistance on the part of the parents to the schools' imposition of orderly behaviour. On the contrary, Wilkinson's record catalogues the parents' amazement, defeat, regret, and remorse on being confronted with their child's escapades; but no defiance.[39]

In the early 1870s the problem of youngsters who remained outside the reach of the school survived as a minor theme of the school board's deliberations, while new school buildings, increased attendance, and reorganized programs occupied the new inspector, James L. Hughes. At the provincial level, the perfunctory clause in the 1871 legislation pertaining to industrial schools required further clarification. However, while the pattern of educational policy-making had been shifting for some time, the defeat of Sandfield Macdonald's government late in 1871 and the ascendancy of Edward Blake and the Liberals dramatically ended the Ryerson era of educational policy. Partly this change represented a coming of age of the provincial administration. The politicization of government policy was a creature of greater political sophistication and the firming of party lines. Its consequence was clear, however. The deputations from the Toronto School Board and the teachers' association now brought their requests for further legislative action on the subject of industrial schools to the premier; and it was Oliver Mowat who showed Ryerson the draft legislation for his opinion.

Although regarded as a government measure "of considerable importance", the Industrial School Act of 1874 was not acted upon until the late 1880s, by which time it had been amended twice.[40] The hopes of the Toronto trustees that the provincial government might fund an industrial school had been dashed by Oliver Mowat's cautious approach to social policy and his preference for trusting to charitable exertions, at least in the beginning. The major capital expenditures involved in the school board's building program, the backlog of students willing and impatient to attend, and even the modest dint which the mere appointment of a truant officer could make in the depressing rate of infrequent attendance—all these combined to monopolize the attention and emotional commitment of schoolmen and their supporters.

The weakness of available statistical evidence, and what we have glimpsed of the relentless shifting of populations characteristic of nineteenth-century cities, make it difficult to estimate the growth or quality of school support in these critical mid-century decades. Obviously it was neither immediate nor unreserved. The modest rise in school attendance in Toronto in the 1850s and 1860s, for example, follows the pattern of a gradual acceptance of school attendance among the working classes which has been noted by historians elsewhere. Compulsory education was largely irrelevant to this development. The number of cases of children whose exploitation by their parents would be deemed to require the intervention of the state obviously remained minimal. Compulsory attendance, on the other hand, was designed to capitalize on the momentum of both schooling among the working population and regulation and consolidation within the school system.

More importantly, compulsory education was equally ineffective as a solution to the problems posed by a class of urban poor, but for quite different reasons. The element of moral coercion implicit in the common-school movement seemed appropriate to this population, and it was owing to that ideology that legal sanctions were provided to ensure a modicum of education for every child. Enforcing the provisions was quite another matter, however. Moral disorder and material squalor were both the defining traits of this class and the grounds for its exclusion from established social institutions. Not surprisingly, therefore, a reluctance to contemplate including vagrant children in the common school accompanied a growing apprehension of the permanent existence of a dangerous and demoralized element in urban society. Indeed, the former might be taken as evidence of the latter. Beyond the difficulties stemming from the exodus of neat and decent youngsters, which it was predicted would ensue should the schools become universal, lay a virtually unthinkable implication: were these elements not to be excluded, their behaviour and condition might not be judged unacceptable. Their exclusion—from school and church—was as necessary as it was alarming, for by labelling and so defining certain moral and social qualities as unacceptable Victorian Canadians sought to stabilize the social order and assert the bounds of decency in their community.

NOTES

1. Charles Brooke, letter to the the editor, *The Globe*, 26 August 1865; letter to the editor, ibid., 14 November 1865; for various items relating to the election, see ibid., 10 January 1866, 9 and 10 January 1867.

2. Egerton Ryerson, "The Spirit in which the present educational movement should be directed", in J. G. Hodgins, ed., *Historical and Other Educational Papers and Documents* III (Toronto, 1852), 27.

3. Report of a lecture on school attendance delivered at the Western Market Schoolhouse, *The Globe*, 8 December 1854. See also, report of school board meeting, ibid., 13 December 1861.

4. Upper Canada, Department of Public Instruction, *Annual Report of the Normal, Model, Grammar and Common Schools* for 1857, pp. 26–27. The titles of the chief superintendents' annual reports change from year to year and hereafter are cited as *Annual Reports* for the given year.

5. Joseph Lesslie complained to Alderman Baxter, on 27 September 1864, that the boys who drove cattle into town were "the most profane, obscene and wicked class I had ever known in any civilized community", Toronto City Council Papers, 1834–1876. The profanity of idle children was also a theme which Mr. Justice Hagarty returned to in his charges to the Grand Jury, *The Globe*, 9 January 1857; 13 March 1862; also Grand Jury presentments 24 October 1860; 5 April and 10 October 1861.

6. For characteristic charges by Hagarty, see *The Globe*, 9 January 1857; 12 October 1858; 10 April 1860; 13 March and 15 August 1862; 21 December 1865; 1 January 1868.

7. Toronto Board of School Trustees, *Report of the Past History and Present Condition of the Common or Public Schools of the City of Toronto* (Toronto, 1859), p. 35.

8. *The Globe*, 6 July 1867.

9. Extracts from the report of the

local superintendent in Toronto, *Journal of Education* VI (March 1853), 46; G. A. Barber, Report No. 25, *Copies of Documents Relating to the Common Schools of the City Forwarded by the Board of School Trustees to the City Council* (Toronto, 1858), pp. 11–12; *Leader* editorial reprinted in *Journal of Education for Upper Canada* XIV (December 1861); Mr. Hennings remarks, meeting of the Board of School Trustees, *The Globe*, 13 December 1861; Hon. John McMurrich's remarks, *Annual Report of the Local Superintendent* for 1865, pp. 22–24; Mr. Justice Hagarty to the Grand Jury, *The Globe*, 21 December 1865.

10. C. R. Brooke to the editor of *The Globe*, 31 July, 3, 8, 12, 16, and 26 August, 11, 19, and 30 September, 6 and 14 October 1865; Report of the Select Committee, in *Annual Report of the Local Superintendent* for 1865, pp. 52–58.

11. *Annual Report of the Local Superintendent* for 1865, pp. 58–79.

12. Ibid., pp. 9–10.

13. See the remarks of Mayor Bowes at the Annual Public Meeting, 31 July 1863, *The Globe*, 1 August; and editorial rebuttal, 6 August; remarks of Hon. John McMurrich on a similar occasion, ibid., 29 July 1865. Porter quickly gave a public lecture and wrote to the editor in reply to Brooke's public discussion, ibid., 25 October, 9 and 14 November 1865. The danger that such ideas might spread was quite real, as the *Leader's* support of Brooke and the proposals presented by the Grand Jury in December illustrate. *Leader*, 15 December 1865; *The Globe*, 27 December 1865; and Brooke's response, ibid., 5 January 1866.

14. Compare *The Globe*, 8 August 1861 and *Annual Report of the Local Superintendent* for 1861, pp. 5–6.

15. Ibid. for 1863, p. 5.

16. In certain areas of the city by the middle of 1866, school masters reported "an unusual demand for juvenile labour". *Annual Report of the Local Superintendent* for 1866, p. 50; but late in the previous year a correspondent to *The Globe* had complained of a lack of work opportunities for young people and suggested boosting manufacturing. *The Globe*, 26 December 1865.

17. For details, see Church of England, Incorporated Church Society of the Diocese of Toronto, *Annual Reports* (1846–57); also J. L. H. Henderson, "John Strachan as Bishop, 1839–1867" (DD thesis, University of Toronto, 1955), pp. 610–18.

In 1858 Bishop Strachan reported that the two schools in operation had upward of 300 children "in daily attendance" and that when the two other schools were completed, there would be parochial school accommodation for "upwards of 1000 children". In J. George Hodgins, *Documentary History of Education in Upper Canada, 1791–1876* (28 vols.; Toronto, 1894–1910) XIII: 274.

18. *The Globe*, 19 June 1862.

19. The first Provincial Sabbath-School Teachers' Convention was held at Kingston in 1857, the second in Hamilton in 1865, and annually thereafter. See *Proceedings*. By 1872 the organization was styled the Sabbath School Association of Canada. For a clear statement of the teachers' emerging self-image, see *Sayings and Doings of the Toronto Sabbath School Workers* (Toronto, 1871).

20. *Journal of Education* XVIII, No. 2 (February 1865), 17–21.

21. *The Globe*, 7 October 1867.

22. J. F. McCurdy, ed., *Life and Work of D. J. McDonnell* (Toronto, 1897), pp. 287ff.

23. *Journal of Education* XX, No. 10 (October 1867), 164.

24. Ibid.

25. Report of the Legislative Assembly, *The Globe*, 6 May 1857.

26. Ibid., 4 January 1866, 31 August 1867, and 27 February 1868; report of a meeting to discuss the industrial home, 11 and 13 May 1867; Canada, Statutes, 29 and 30 Vict., Chapter LI, p. 413.

27. *Journal of Education* XXI, No. 4 (April 1868), 51.

28. *The Globe*, 28 March 1868.

29. Letter to the editor from Alexander Topp, ibid., 4 April 1868; report of a public meeting, 18 April and 22 May 1868. The relevant documents are also reprinted in the *Journal of Education* XXI, No. 4 (April 1868), 63, (June), 93–95; and Hodgins, *Documentary History* XX: 265–81.

30. Board of School Trustees, *Minutes*, Book III, 3 June 1868; *Annual Report of the Local Superintendent* for 1868, pp. 62–75.

31. *The Globe*, 26 November 1868; *Daily Telegraph*, 26 November 1868; *Journal of Education* XXI, No. 12 (December 1868), 185–87. The version of this report (taken from *The Globe*) which appears in Hodgins, *Documentary History* XX: 272–74, has been fairly substantially edited without any acknowledgment to that effect.

32. Report of the Legislative Assembly proceedings, Hodgins, *Documentary History* XX: 307; *The Globe*, 17 December 1868; Journals of the Legislative Assembly of Ontario (1868–69) II: 50, 125. Board of School Trustees, *Minutes*, Book III, 21 April 1869.

Annual Report of the Local Superintendent for 1869, p. 47.

33. The 1871 Common School Bill, and specifically Clause 42 which permitted school boards in cities, towns, and villages to establish industrial schools, gave reformers hope. A favourable report, based on a tour by a deputation of American institutions, was adopted by the Toronto board early in 1872, and a draft bill was prepared for the guidance of the government. Negotiations with Oliver Mowat continued through 1873, and the board established a Standing Committee on Industrial Schools in 1874. The committee's estimate of the cost of maintaining an industrial school for fifty children for one year was $7,580; the annual salary of the truant officer, on the other hand, was $600. For documentation on the course of the board's debate, see especially Board of School Trustees, *Minutes*, 1871–75; Standing Committee on Industrial Schools, *Minutes*, 1875–76, 1878; *Annual Report of the Local Superintendent* for 1871, pp. 58, 79–90; for 1872, pp. 84, 91–92; for 1873; pp. 56–57, 60; for 1874, pp. 58–59; for 1875, p. 58

34. The age-span involved proved curiously unstable over the years. The resolutions passed in late 1865 for consideration at the county conventions recommended compulsion for the age group of 7 to 15 years; in draft legislation prepared later in 1866, Ryerson specified 7 to 14 years. The Common School Amendment Bill brought before the House in 1868 specified 7 to 12 years to attend *6 months* each year, a figure which was reduced to *4 months* in the final bill. 34 Vict., Chapter XXXIII, p. 3.

35. *Annual Report* for 1866, Ap-

pendix A, p. 55; the excerpts from many of the school inspectors' reports included in the annual reports in the early 1870s repeat this point, seemingly without regard to the particularities of locale; see also, *Ontario Teacher* I (January 1873), 30; (August 1873), 231–33.

36. Ontario Teachers' Association, *Report of the Proceedings of the Annual Meeting* (Toronto, 1868), p. 7; "Report of a Committee of the Ontario Teachers' Association on the Grammar and Common School Acts", Hodgins, *Documentary History* XXII: 26.

37. Legislative Assembly of Ontario, *Proceedings*, 1870–71, in Hodgins, *Documentary History* XXII: 195–204; "Mr. Blake's Speech on the Grammar and Common School Improvement Bill", ibid., 226–36; *The Globe*, 7, 12, 18 January, 6, 13, 15 February 1871; Richard B. Splane, "The Upper Canada Reform Party, 1867–1878" (MA thesis, University of Toronto, 1948), pp. 138–39; C. B. Sissons, ed., *Egerton Ryerson: His Life and Letters* (2 vols.; Toronto, 1937–47) II, 582–86.

In an effort to strengthen the so-called "penal clauses" of the 1871 Act, the school legislation of 1874 (37 Vict., Chapter XXVIII) contained supplementary provisions requiring school trustees to take a school census, to distinguish between children in school, not in school, or under instruction; and to either take parents before the Magistrate or impose a rate-bill penalty.

38. General Regulations for the Organization, Government and Discipline of Public Schools", *Annual Report* for 1874, Appendix D, pp. 109–10.

39. Toronto Board of Education Historical Collection, Wilkinson Diaries, 1872–74; "Programme of Duties and Requirements Connected with the Office of Truant Officer", *Annual Report of the Local Superintendent* for 1872, pp. 93–95.

40. *The Nation*, I (2 April 1874), 12; also *Weekly Leader*, 6 March 1874. As commentators observed, the 1874 Act (37 Vict., Chapter XXIX) was substantially modelled after the 1866 Imperial statute (The Industrial School Act, 29 & 30 Vict., Chapter CXVIII) with the addition of the category of incorrigibility, one of the most popular grounds for committal to the reform schools of the eastern American states. The Act was revised in 1883 (46 Vict., Chapter XXIX) to permit school boards to delegate their power to philanthropic societies, and further amended and consolidated the following year (47 Vict. Chapter XLVI). As in England the weakness of the measure stemmed in part from its seemingly generous powers: "any person" might bring before the police magistrate any child found wanting; and in this case *anybody* was effectively *nobody*.

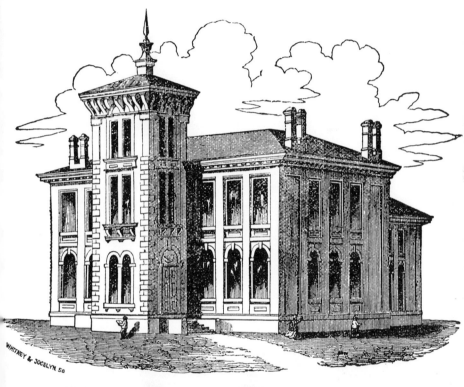

WHITNEY & JOCELYN SC

V Post-Ryerson

The Ryerson Tradition in Western Canada, 1871-1906

ALAN H. CHILD

INFLUENCES UPON THE DEVELOPMENT OF EDUCATION IN WESTERN CANADA

By 1871, what may be termed "the Ryerson tradition" had developed in Ontario: free, universal, Protestant education, designed to promote nationalism and social stability, controlled mainly by a central authority, and financed mainly at the local level. Between the Lake of the Woods and the Pacific Ocean, however, there was no firm commitment to a specific type of educational system. Yet by 1906, the Ryerson tradition was firmly established there. Ryerson's own influence was entirely indirect. The main factors determining the course of western education were the influences of Ontario and the desire to build a national school system.

Immigrants from Ontario, especially those who had attended normal school and taught in the province, had been strongly influenced by the Ryerson tradition. From Ontario came school officials such as John Jessop, John Somerset, and David Goggin; politicians such as Joseph Martin and Frederick Haultain; and visitors such as D'Alton McCarthy; all of whom brought Ryerson's ideas with them. Many teachers came to the west from Ontario. In 1875, Jessop, the superintendent of education in British Columbia, commissioned James Carlyle, second master of the Toronto normal school, to select suitable candidates for his schools.[1] As late as 1903, the Northwest Territories found it necessary to advertise for teachers in eastern Canada. In that year, 212 teachers came from outside of the Territories, a very high proportion of the total teaching force of 1,152.[2] Most immigrants to Manitoba and the Northwest Territories in the formative period between 1871 and 1895 came from Ontario.

British Columbia was also significantly affected by settlers from Ontario.

In view of all these influences, it is little wonder that the seminar school laws of 1871 in British Columbia, of 1890 in Manitoba, and of 1892 in the Northwest Territories were all copies, with minor changes, of contemporary Ontario legislation. But how is one to show that other aspects of the western school systems were imported from Ontario? At first glance, it might seem valid to identify similarities as importations, but this would require an assumption that the Ontario school system was unique. Such was not the case.

The common school in the western world was the product of the nation state, and designed to serve the interests of the nation state. All common-school systems tended to be basically similar whether they originated in France, Germany, the United States, Australia, or Ontario. So that all citizens would be trained to serve the nation, it was necessary that schooling be free, universal, and compulsory. National identity required cultural uniformity, which in turn required uniformity of teaching methods and curriculum. To ensure unity, schools had to be secular, or, at the very least, non-sectarian, and it was essential, furthermore, that the schools promote social stability. All this could be achieved only if the schools were centrally controlled. Finally, some method of financing the enterprise was necessary, and this suggested taxation. As national systems were basically similar, an independently developed system, which was the case to a degree in British Columbia, could well give the appearance of having been copied from the Ontario model.

Nationalism increased Ontario's influence. Western governments wanted a national school system, and yet the British North America Act had ruled that education was a provincial responsibility. The solution was obvious: make the various school systems as similar as possible.[3] And what was more logical than to use as a model the comparatively well-developed system of Canada's largest English province?

Although school officials spoke of the dangers of parochialism, their attitudes towards teachers from the east show that they were not able to avoid it completely. Encouraging teachers to migrate from Ontario to British Columbia was merely a temporary expedient. In 1877, Jessop wrote a letter to *The Globe* (Toronto) discouraging teachers from moving to British Columbia. "Hereafter," he said, "British Columbia, to a great extent at least, will be in a position to supply her own teachers,"[4] and the following year Jessop's successor, C. C. McKenzie, proudly announced that six of the province's fifty-eight teachers had received their entire education in British Columbia.[5] In spite of the lack of any normal-school training in the province, McKenzie believed firmly that locally educated teachers were more capable than "outsiders".[6]

That officials in the Northwest Territories were reluctant to hire outsiders is obvious from a statement of superintendent of education, David Goggin: "[The outsiders] do not understand our conditions . . . are ignorant of our school law, fail to appreciate our aims and neglect to read the Programme of Studies."[7]

The accuracy of statements about distinctive programs in the west may be doubted, especially as most authorized textbooks were published in Ontario, but perhaps what is more important is that officials perceived a difference. They were more specific concerning the living and teaching conditions which made their regions unique. Jessop said that in no other country were school districts so isolated and so far apart as in British Columbia.[8] Thirty years later, D. P. McColl, principal of the Regina normal school, claimed a similar distinction for the Northwest Territories. Sparcity of population and the newness of settlements, he reported, created difficulties greater than anywhere else in Canada, "except to a limited extent in Manitoba".[9] A sense of identity developed early in the west, based largely upon a recognition of distinctive difficulties.

In 1881, William Cyprian Pinkham, the first superintendent of Manitoba Protestant schools, said: "Even in Ontario, Manitoba is credited with being in some of the leading features of her educational system in advance of that most enlightened province."[10] Thomas Grover, a school inspector in the Northwest Territories, praised "the enterprising and intelligent spirit of the people who have made their homes in the 'Lone Land' in whose vocabulary there is no such word as 'failure'."[11] The influence of Ontario and the desire to build a national school system were reduced, to a degree at least, by a strong feeling of regional pride.

The remainder of this chapter will attempt to show that educational development in the west was, generally, in the Ryerson tradition.

FREE, UNIVERSAL, AND COMPULSORY EDUCATION

As Ryerson believed that all children should attend the common school, he also thought that common-school education should be free, universal, and compulsory.[12] Although elementary education was free in all of the western school systems, universality was an aspiration rather than an achievement. Accessibility to the high school was limited by the small number of schools and the barrier imposed by entrance examinations. The small size of most high schools together with élitist traditions caused the curriculum to be narrow, and thus discouraged many children from attending. In 1906, students in secondary grades comprised only 4 per cent of the total school enrolment in western Canada.[13]

For elementary education to be universal, the state had to provide schools wherever there were children, and children had to attend the schools. That central and local authorities were diligent in providing school facilities is strongly suggested by the fact that school enrolments more than kept pace with the rapidly increasing population. (See Table 12:1.) Encouraging children to attend the schools was a much more difficult problem. Table 12:2 reveals that, throughout the period being dealt with, the average attendance was between one-half and two-thirds of those enrolled. Figures for Manitoba for the years 1881 to 1905, showing "school population" (children aged seven to fourteen), and actual enrolments are given in Table 12:3. Possible reasons for the differences in the two categories are

TABLE 12:1

PERCENTAGE OF TOTAL POPULATION ENROLLED IN PUBLIC SCHOOLS*

	Manitoba	British Columbia	Northwest Territories
1871	3.2	1.5	—
1881	7.9	5.2	—
1891	15.7	9.2	—
1901	20.0	12.3	14.5

*Sources: *Census of Canada, 1871–1901*; Annual Reports of Schools: Manitoba, British Columbia, Northwest Territories.

the failure of children in established school districts to enrol, enrolments in private schools, and delays in establishing school districts in new areas of settlement. The extreme annual fluctuations suggest that the last of these was probably the main reason. At any rate, combining the pertinent information in Tables 12:2 and 12:3 show that in the years from 1900 to 1906, average attendance in Manitoba of school-aged children was only 46 per cent. Although detailed figures are not available for British Columbia and the Northwest Territories, it seems reasonable to assume from Tables 12:1 and 12:2 that the situation was probably no better in either region.[14]

British Columbia passed a law in 1873 authorizing local authorities to pass compulsory attendance by-laws. Jessop reported that "trustee boards manifest great unwillingness to come in [sic] collision with their neighbours."[15] It seems that no by-laws were passed.[16] In 1876, the Legislature made attendance compulsory throughout the province, but with no apparent effect.

In 1888, the Northwest Territories passed compulsory attendance legislation, and in 1892 made a part of the government grant to school districts dependent upon average daily attendance. However, the law was seldom enforced.

In 1875, Manitoba permitted cities and towns to pass compulsory attendance by-laws.[17] After the change to a non-sectarian system in 1890, the government believed that it could not constitutionally force Catholic children to attend public schools.[18] In Manitoba, as in the Northwest Territories, absenteeism was especially high in the autumn, children being kept home to help with the harvest, and trustees often had to close schools throughout September and October because no children attended.[19] Manitoba inspectors continually deplored non-attendance and irregular attendance, and advocated compulsion. Inspector T. A. McGuire, however, concluded as J. S. Putman did later,[20] that the effectiveness of compulsory attendance laws was debatable.[21]

One consolation for worried officials was that even the well-established Ontario school system suffered from non-attendance and poor attendance. In that province in 1901, the average attendance was only 57 per cent.[22] Probably, the realization of Ryerson's dream of universality had to wait for a change in public opinion.

TABLE 12:2

AVERAGE ACTUAL ATTENDANCE OF STUDENTS
ENROLLED IN WESTERN CANADIAN SCHOOLS*
(in percentages)

	Manitoba**	Northwest Territories†	British Columbia
1872	55		
1873	—		56
1874	—		62
1875	51		62
1876	50		58
1877	63		63
1878	—		63
1879	—		57
1880	—		53
1881	41		53
1882	47		51
1883	47		51
1884	56		52
1885	60		52
1886	54		56
1887	56		54
1888	60		49
1889	61		54
1890	50		54
1891	52		55
1892	55		58
1893	48		62
1894	49		62
1895	55		64
1896	61		64
1897	54		63
1898	56		63
1899	54		64
1900	55	46	62
1901	53	50	64
1902	52	50	65
1903	53	50	67
1904	53	51	66
1905	53	51	69
1906	48	51	68

*Sources: Annual Reports of Schools: Northwest Territories,
British Columbia, Alberta, Saskatchewan, Manitoba.
**Percentages for 1872–89 are for Protestant schools only; per-
centages are not available for the years where none appear.
†Percentages are not available for the years where none
appear.

UNIFORM EDUCATION

One of Ryerson's principles was that education should be
"uniform throughout".[23] That western educators agreed is
shown by their emphasis on authorized textbooks, common
programs of studies, and external examinations. By 1876, Jessop
was able to report that authorized textbooks were used exclusively throughout British Columbia.[24] "The Programme of
Studies . . ." said Manitoba inspector S. E. Lang, "is so well
adapted to the merits of our schools that teachers will do well
to consider most carefully any proposed departure from it."[25]
Examinations for entrance to high school and for graduation
were composed by the central authority. Haultain, chief executive officer of the Northwest Territories, favoured "uniform
instruction, uniform examinations, and uniform attainments of
teachers".[26]

The chief means of ensuring uniformity were normal-school
training and school inspection. Goggin said that, as the school
was the "moulder of the youth", the normal school should be
the "moulder of all the teachers".[27] In 1882, the Protestant
section of the Manitoba Board of Education established the
Manitoba normal school after Pinkham had visited normal
schools in Ontario, accompanied by his "good friend", John
Somerset,[28] who was working in Ontario at the time. The
Catholic section opened a normal school at St. Boniface in
1883, and one in Winnipeg in 1888. In its first year, only eight
students attended the Manitoba normal school. Under Goggin's
principalship the enrolment increased, reaching 63 in 1893,
when Goggin left for the Northwest Territories. In 1906, 148
students attended.[29] In addition, there were several "local
normal schools", operated for only part of the year. As previously noted, provisions were inadequate to meet the demand
for trained teachers. A normal school was established at Regina
in 1893, which by 1906 had trained over a thousand teachers.
Because the average teacher taught for only three years,[30] the

TABLE 12:3

SCHOOL POPULATION AND ENROLMENT IN MANITOBA, 1881–1906*

	school population (age 7 to 14)	enrolment	% of population enrolled**
1881†	7,000	4,919	70
1882†	9,641	6,972	72
1883†	12,346	10,831	88
1884†	41,129	11,708	83
1885†	15,850	13,074	81
1886†	16,834	15,926	96
1887†	17,600	16,940	96
1888†	18,850	18,000	95
1889†	21,471	18,358	86
1890	25,077	23,256	93
1891	28,678	23,871	83
1892	29,564	23,244	79
1893	34,417	28,706	83
1894	36,459	32,680	89
1895	44,932	35,371	79
1896	50,093	37,987	76
1897	51,178	39,841	77
1898	57,431	44,070	77
1899	59,811	48,660	81
1900	62,664	50,460	85
1901	63,881	51,888	81
1902	64,629	54,056	84
1903	66,603	57,409	86
1904	68,157	58,287	87
1905	73,512	63,287	86
1906	77,044	64,123	83

*Sources: Annual Reports of Schools: Manitoba.
**Percentages given are high, as some students enrolled were either younger than seven or older than fourteen.
†Figures indicate Protestant population and Protestant enrolments only.

Territories had to continue to rely upon teachers trained elsewhere. Not until 1901 did British Columbia establish a normal school. Before that, teaching certificates were issued on the basis of examinations following special high school courses.

As the normal schools were unable to train sufficient teachers, inspection was the only way in which the central authority could contact every teacher. James Calder, Goggin's successor in the Northwest Territories and a former student of Goggin's, made a statement which was applicable to all of western Canada: "If any degree of uniformity and unity of purpose are to be secured and maintained in our schools it can only be done under present conditions through our inspectors."[31] And, of course, the inspection itself had to be uniform. Haultain said, "Grants of money meant inspection and control, and inspection could be useful only if it was uniform."[32]

The purpose of uniformity of inspection, method, and content was the achievement of cultural uniformity. In this regard, the large number of immigrants to the prairies from central and eastern Europe posed a special problem, often commented upon in the Northwest Territories. Goggin said that although the newcomers would contribute to Canada's material wealth, it was "unreasonable" to expect much of an immediate contribution in a country's most important wealth, "educated men with refined tastes". Tact, he said, was necessary to secure the co-operation of "alien forces". Teachers with a "missionary spirit" could ensure that the schools would get an "early hold of the children".[33] Haultain declared that the "function and mission" of the school was to "mould and assimilate all families making the prairies their home".[34] Although the federal government permitted ethnic groups to settle in colonies, it is doubtful that it anticipated a Canadian mosaic of diverse cultures.[35] The mosaic concept was absent from the thinking of western school officials; they wanted the Canadian prairies to be a melting pot, and the mosaic that resulted was a mark of their partial failure. The Ukrainians and Doukhobors showed the strongest resistance to education. School inspectors said that the "Galicians" were "violently hostile to schools", and that Doukhobors had "little desire" to have their children learn English.[36]

EDUCATION FOR NATIONALISM AND SOCIAL STABILITY

As the nation state was the father of the common school, it is not surprising that the development of nationalism was one of the chief objectives of the common school. In this regard, educators in Ontario and western Canada in the years following

Confederation went further than Ryerson, who lived most of his active life in pre-confederate Upper Canada. His successors viewed themselves as nation builders. Canadian nationalism differed from that of older countries because of its reliance upon a dual loyalty, to Canada and to Britain. What might be termed "colonial nationalism" developed because of the immaturity of the country and because, for reasons of national defence, it was a means of showing that Canada was essentially different from the United States.[37] The greatness of Canada, it was held, lay in its reliance upon British institutions, its settlement by British people, and its membership in the mighty British Empire. Intensifying this colonial nationalism was the strong imperial sentiment of the 1880s and the 1890s. The textbooks used in western Canada were designed to show the superiority of British institutions and the British "race". Children memorized patriotic poems and songs.[38] They participated in patriotic exercises in the classroom and in public on special occasions, such as Victoria Day, the visits of the Queen's representatives, the Queen's Golden Jubilee in 1887, and her Diamond Jubilee in 1897. The 1893 Manitoba report on schools said that Lieutenant-Governor John Schultz, "so active in the past in endeavouring to encourage the growth of national sentiment," had awarded a flag to the Winnipeg school which excelled in military drill.[39] In 1905, Manitoba ruled that the flag should be flown at every school. When Princess Louise, with the Marquis of Lorne and the Governor General, visited the Victoria high school in 1882, the superintendent, McKenzie, standing beneath a large banner bearing the words "Vivat Regina", assured the visitors that "sentiments of loyalty and attachment to her Majesty's person" were inculcated in the schools.[40] In the same school in 1894, Governor General Aberdeen recited this poem:

> Where are my great men coming from,
>> The men to rule the state,
> When, this old century left behind,
>> We've passed the twentieth's gate:
> My brave, broad-hearted citizens,
>> The strong, the good, the true,
> You're drifting now: rouse up, my boys,
>> They all must come from you!
> Don't let past glories be forgot or patriotism die,
> Let every boy upon the roll shout "Ready—here am I."[41]

Ryerson's first educational principle, according to W. H. Elgie, was that "education is not the mere acquisition of certain arts and knowledge, but that instruction and discipline which qualify persons to live fully as members of the civil community."[42] In other words, education was a means of social control. The relationship between this and education for nationalism is obvious. Goggin said, "The boy who loves his mother and is obedient to her and to his teacher is laying a good foundation for love of country and obedience to its laws."[43] Goggin explained what inspectors looked for upon entering a classroom: promptness of movement, economy of time, simplicity of class tactics, and the arrangement of desks. Then they observed the children to see if they were polite, punctual, interested, orderly, and systematic.[44] The Northwest Territories program of studies said that beginning work silently, co-operating, and obeying the rules of the school were powerful influences in industrial and civic life. Knowledge, the program continued, was subordinate to discipline and culture.[45] Goggin quoted Matthew Arnold with approval: "Conduct is three-fourths of life."[46] All of this emphasis upon character building was clearly aimed at the development of an efficient, obedient, and orderly citizenry. In the United States, the schools were often viewed as a panacea for society's ills.[47] This type of thinking is reflected in statements of Ryerson and of western school officials, although there tends to be more emphasis upon perpetuation and purification of the existing state of affairs than upon the realization of a "Canadian dream". The free, non-sectarian public school, Jessop said, was the "palladium of liberty".[48] William McIntyre, Goggin's successor at the Manitoba Normal School, described the public school as "the most potent and serviceable institution of civilization".[49] Daniel McIntyre, superintendent of Winnipeg public schools, stated bluntly that education was a safeguard against revolution and violence.[50]

PROTESTANT EDUCATION

The Ryerson tradition was distinctive in its emphasis upon non-sectarian rather than secular education. Ryerson believed that religion was, in Elgie's words, "the basis of education and every public school must provide a place for religious training."[51] Ryerson stated, "It is the cultivation of man's moral powers and feelings which forms the basis of social order and the vital fluid of social happiness; and the cultivation of these is the province of Christianity."[52] As Ryerson thought that it was possible to find a common core of belief to which all Christians would subscribe, and as Catholics disagreed with him, it would probably be more accurate to term the type of education which he favoured as Protestant rather than as Christian or non-sectarian.

Separate schools for Catholics are a part of the Ryerson tradition only insofar as Ryerson was prepared to tolerate them. In 1852, he wrote:

> I always thought the introduction of any provision for separate schools . . . was to be regretted and inexpedient; but finding such a provision in existence, and that parties concerned attached great importance to it, I have advocated its continuance,—leaving separate schools to die out, not by force of legislative enactment, but under the influence and enlarged views of Christian relations, rights and duties between different classes of the community.[53]

Thirteen years later, he wrote:

> I think that no one will maintain that Separate Schools are expedient for the interests of the State. . . . Upon public grounds . . . the law for Separate Schools cannot be maintained . . . but the chief injury of such isolation must fall upon the Roman Catholics themselves. Then the youth of those inferior schools are not only excluded from the advantages of the better schools. . . . Then envy, then hatred of the more successful and prosperous classes, then mutual consultations and excitement to revenge their imaginary wrongs, and relieve themselves of their deeply felt but self-inflicted evils. . . .[54]

With regard to religious orientation, the school systems of the west were generally in the Ryerson tradition.

British Columbia was the most consistent, having a strictly non-sectarian system from the outset. Governor F. Seymour said in 1867:

> The Governor believes that the community in which he resides is one where complete toleration in religious opinion exists. . . . Therefore the Government is of the opinion that when the time comes for the establishment of a large Common School, religious teaching ought not to intrude. It is vain to say that there are certain elementary matters in which all Christians,

leaving out the Jews, must agree. It is merely calling upon a man picked up at random, allured by a trifling salary, to do what the whole religious wisdom, feeling and affection of the world has not yet done.[55]

As early legislation made no provision for government assistance to church schools, British Columbia entered Confederation without obligations to maintain separate schools. Considering the popularity of church schools, there may well have been more dissatisfaction at the time than is generally assumed. In 1873, 400 children enrolled in church schools compared with 1,000 in public schools.[56] The public schools were not secular. Jessop recommended that schools open and close with lengthy, prescribed prayers.[57] In 1890, most schools were using the Lord's Prayer.[58]

The Protestant and Catholic sections of the Manitoba Board of Education were largely autonomous, unlike Ontario, where all schools were regulated by a central authority. William Cyprian Pinkham's view on separate schools was somewhat different from Ryerson's:

> Though personally altogether in favor of educating all our children without respect to denomination, yet inasmuch as the majority of Protestants and Roman Catholics never do, and I suppose, never will, agree to have their children educated together in the same school, I would under certain circumstances, allow "separate schools". If people make it a matter of conscience it is quite unnecessary for Government to try to compel them to . . . send their children to a school which they think they ought not to send them to.[59]

Although the Protestant section ruled that there should be systematic religious instruction, little was done in this regard until 1885, when, upon the advice of George Ross, the Ontario minister of education, the section adopted the list of Scripture readings authorized for the Ontario public schools.[60] The section then passed regulations that all Protestant schools open with prayers and a Scripture lesson, use the Bible as a textbook, teach children to memorize the ten commandments and the Apostles' Creed, and close with prayers.[61] John Somerset, Pinkham's successor, reported: "The Board . . . has provided for the most careful inquiry into the character of the teachers, and for such systematic religious instruction in its schools as may be given the object of teaching the principles of Christian truth, contained in the Bible and accepted by all Protestant denominations."[62] The Catholic section, unlike the Protestant section, was closely tied to the church. Although small, it had its own normal schools, examinations for teacher certification, authorized textbooks, and inspectoral system.

In 1870, most of the inhabitants of Manitoba were half-breeds, with Protestants and Catholics approximately equal in number. Ontarians comprised a tiny fraction of the population. The situation changed dramatically after Confederation. Settlers came in great numbers, the large majority of them from Ontario. It is only a slight exaggeration to say that by 1890, Manitoba was a little Ontario in the west. The result, of course, was that now the Protestants greatly outnumbered the Catholics. There were only 90 Catholic school districts compared with 629 Protestant districts.

Agitation from Ontario, led by D'Alton McCarthy, has traditionally been considered a decisive factor in the creation of a non-sectarian system similar to the one in British Columbia. Although this view has recently been challenged[63] it is probably fair to conclude that McCarthy's intervention removed the issue from the realm of rational political debate.

Attorney General Joseph Martin preferred a secular to a non-sectarian system. He informed Premier Thomas Greenway that there should be no religious teaching in public schools.[64] He said that the state had no right to interfere in the matter of religion, that Catholic co-operation was impossible in public schools which retained religious exercises, and that Protestants wanted these exercises merely for reasons of "sentiment".[65] However, Martin was overruled after protests of Protestant clergymen against "Godless schools". The Ryerson tradition was too strong for Martin to succeed.

Instruction in temperance and morals was an important part of the new program of studies.[66] Temperance was a direct import from Ontario and obviously a "Protestant subject." The course on morals was identical to that taught in the old Protestant schools. This fact, combined with the retention of three of the five Protestant inspectors and the Manitoba normal school, caused Bishop Alexander Taché to assert that the non-denominational system was simply a continuation of the Protestant system.[67] But there was a difference. Table 12:4 shows a strong decline in the use of religious exercises in the early years of the non-sectarian system. Inspector D. H. McCalman reported that efforts to establish good moral habits would probably result in more lasting benefits than "the mere perfunctory reading of the Bible, and the formal repetition of the Lord's Prayer".[68] Martin said that many Protestants admitted that the religious exercises were useless.[69] It appears that attempting to find a common core of Protestantism and avoiding all doctrinal differences resulted in the adoption of forms of little value. Manitoba school officials would probably have approved of the view of American educator, Washington Gladden, endorsed earlier by Somerset: "Truth of this kind [morality] must be vitalized by a genuine religious faith. Religion is the inspiration of all highest morality. And while religion cannot be taught in the schools, those teachers who possess this faith may . . . impart it to their pupils."[70] After 1890, it was possible to drop meaningless forms and concentrate upon morals and temperance, taught from a Protestant viewpoint. In doing so, perhaps teachers were able to teach Protestantism more effectively than before, in which case it could be argued that the non-sectarian system was more Protestant than the Protestant system.

The Catholic section in the Northwest Territories was very small and did not have time to develop, the dual-structured Board of Education being abolished only eight years after its establishment. Even in those years, the Catholic section was not as autonomous as in Manitoba. The entire board appointed inspectors, examined and classified teachers, and conducted school examinations. The only important powers held by the separate sections were the rights to cancel certificates and prescribe textbooks.

On three occasions between 1889 and 1892, McCarthy introduced bills before the House of Commons to abolish the separate schools, all of which were defeated. The Territorial Assembly, however, brought all schools under the control of the powerful Council of Public Instruction. In 1901, this control was tightened with the creation of the Department of Education, a body even more closely connected with the government. In Haultain's words, the assembly had "administered the separateness out of the separate schools".[71] When Saskatchewan and Alberta became provinces, the pattern continued: their separate schools were similar to those of Ontario, controlled in all important respects by the central authority.

In the Northwest Territories, as in British Columbia and Manitoba, the same emphasis may be seen on Protestant morality. The program of studies charged the teacher with "the

TABLE 12:4

SCHOOL DISTRICTS GIVING RELIGIOUS AND MORAL INSTRUCTION IN MANITOBA, 1893–1903*
(in percentages)

	closed with religious exercises	closed with prayer	bible used	ten commandments	temperance instruction	moral instruction
1893	63	57	48	48	56	77
1894	79	72	71	36	66	86
1895	55	50	38	26	86	80
1896	43	40	28	24	76	85
1897	40	44	33	28	75	88
1898	35	39	27	27	61	88
1899	37	34	23	26	59	93
1900	33	29	18	24	64	85
1901	23	27	16	24	71	87
1902	23	26	17	23	63	85
1903	23	26	17	27	71	82

*Source: Annual Reports of Schools, Manitoba.

duty to turn the attention of pupils to the moral quality of their acts and to lead them to a clear understanding and practice of every virtue."[72] Goggin agreed with Ryerson that it was possible to maintain a "religious spirit" in the classroom.[73] As in Manitoba, temperance and morals were taught as "subjects".

What were the reasons for opposition to the separate schools? Aside from the obvious variance between the concepts of separate and common schools, the attitude was common in Ontario and the west that a Catholic, because of dual loyalties to Rome and his country, was incapable of being as good a Canadian as a Protestant was.[74] Of greater importance, however, was that the majority of Catholics were French, and what appears as religious strife was in reality racial. McCarthy said, "Let them remain Catholics but not French. That is the object . . . to make the people homogeneous."[75] The first requirement of a Canadian was that he speak English. Goggin said that a common tongue was as important as the common school.[76] In this regard, western Canadian educators were less tolerant than Ryerson, who was prepared to grant a certificate to a teacher trained elsewhere whose native language was German, Italian, or French.[77] The Manitoba Catholic schools were intolerable to the majority because instruction was almost exclusively in French. In the Northwest Territories in 1887, there were apparently only three schools in which French was the sole language of instruction.[78] However, the many bilingual schools were considered to be almost as objectionable. As of 1892, French was permitted only in the primary grades. There was to be nothing special about the French minority; it was a minority like the others, and there were many other minorities in the Canadian west. McCarthy said: "The desire of the Manitoba Legislature [was] . . . to make the people Manitobans and Canadians, not French or Mennonites, not Poles or Jews."[79] Acceptance of dual culturalism, let alone multi-culturalism, was further impeded by the strong British imperialist sentiments of the period.

CENTRALIZED CONTROL AND DECENTRALIZED FINANCING

Ryerson's plan for the administration of the school system was based upon a division of powers. There was to be a strong central authority controlling the "interna": the course of studies, textbooks, examinations, normal-school training, and certification and inspection of teachers. Local authorities were to administer the "externa": care of buildings and grounds, and the appointment and dismissal of teachers. Manitoba and the Northwest Territories followed this plan closely. In the first few years after Confederation, the British Columbia school system was even more centralized. The only power given to school boards there in 1872 was to maintain and develop school buildings and grounds. The next year, they were given the right to appoint teachers, and to dismiss teachers with the approval of the central authority. This need for approval was removed in 1879, giving school boards in British Columbia the same powers as those in Ontario, Manitoba, and the Northwest Territories.

The financing of schools followed a pattern similar to that of administration. Manitoba and the Northwest Territories adopted the Ryerson plan of financing schools through local taxation supplemented by government grants. In the early years in British Columbia, schools were financed entirely by the provincial government. The reasons for this unique system require examination. By 1865, like governments in other parts of the western world, the government of Vancouver Island was convinced of the need for free elementary education. Churches and charitable organizations could not be expected to provide most of the schools as in the mother country. In Ontario, although taxation for school purposes was still not compulsory, Ryerson had been preparing the people for it for a generation, and most local areas had adopted it voluntarily. There had been no such preparation in Vancouver Island, and Ontario was too far away to influence the residents' thinking to any extent. The colony therefore developed this original solution, although later, departure from the free system brought widespread protest resulting in the closure of the Victoria schools. In 1872, anxious to avoid further trouble and aware of large financial reserves, the provincial government reverted to the 1865 pattern, agreeing to pay all educational costs from its own revenue.

School officials often referred to this unique practice. McKenzie told Princess Louise and Governor General Lorne about it.[80] Usually, however, the remarks were not made with pride, as there was an awareness that if people paid a portion of school costs directly, they would take a greater interest in the schools. Jessop said that the common attitude of letting the government attend to all school matters could lead to land taxation.[81] McKenzie said that local responsibility would awaken interest and increase school attendance.[82] The supposed relationship between local taxation and local interest in education is debatable, and in Manitoba and the Northwest Territories, where property was taxed for school purposes, complaints about a lack of interest were as common as in British Columbia. The British Columbia government's expenditures for education were not generous. No money, for example, was provided for janitorial services and teachers were often dismissed for refusing to do this work themselves. Jessop said that, if necessary, the teacher should clean the school.[83]

In 1888, large cities were required to pay a portion of educational costs, an obligation which was extended to all cities in 1901. Nevertheless, by 1905, the government was still paying 62 per cent of the cost of education,[84] a higher proportion than that paid by any other provincial government. The superintendent, Alexander Robinson, complained that government grants to cities were too large. Cumberland, for example, received 90 per cent of its school costs from the government, and levied only a two mill tax. Furthermore, Robinson said, it was unfair that "such prosperous settlements" as Chilliwack, Ladner, Comox, Armstrong, and Kelowna, simply because they were not cities, had the cost "of every cord of wood" and "every box of chalk" provided by the government. "The time has come," he declared, "openly and courageously to revise the Public Schools Act."[85] The change came in 1906. Legislation was passed making all school boards responsible for meeting their expenses in part from local taxation. Defending the bill in the Legislature, F. Carter-Cotton, a former finance minister, said that it was part of a trend towards decentralization.[86] With all other provinces following the Ryerson tradition of sharing costs with local authorities, it proved impossible for British Columbia to maintain its unique system. In 1906, faced with a large deficit,[87] the government was able to cite Canadian precedents to reduce it.

RYERSON AND THE WEST

The similarities between the west and Ontario were so great that one is tempted to conclude that Ryerson was as much the architect of the western school systems as he was of the Ontario system. Yet Ryerson did not visit the west or send any representatives there. Nor is it likely that the politicians, officials, and teachers who migrated from Ontario to the west, even those who had been strongly influenced by Ryerson, considered themselves as his missionaries. They were people who faced an enormous task and sought assistance from all possible sources. William Pinkham favoured the adoption of "what will suit Manitoba from the older provinces, the mother country and the United States."[88] Somerset praised Pinkham for "the wise adaption [sic]" of the best features of the eastern provinces to "the circumstances and conditions" in Manitoba.[89] Of course, most of the assistance came from Ontario, to such an extent that a later western-Canadian educator referred to Ontario as "the Banner Province",[90] but it came from other regions too, such as the Maritimes and the United States.[91] Ryerson's thinking, however, was so attuned to developments elsewhere that the eclecticism of western educators caused their school systems to appear as if they had been fashioned from a mould conceived by Ryerson alone. Egerton Ryerson would have felt at home in the schools of western Canada between 1871 and 1906.

NOTES

1. British Columbia, *Report of the Public Schools of British Columbia, 1875* (Victoria, 1876), pp. 84–87. Cited hereafter as B.C., *Report*, with date.

2. North-West Territories, *Annual Report of the Department of Education, 1903* (Regina, 1904), p. 15. Cited hereafter as NW.T., *Report*, with date.

3. It may be speculated that the resulting schools were more nationalistic than if the federal government had been in charge.

4. B.C., *Report*, 1877, pp. 67–68.

5. Ibid., 1878, p. 180.

6. Ibid., 1881, p. 253.

7. North-West Territories, *Report of Council of Public Instruction, 1898* (Regina, 1899), p. 27. Cited hereafter as NW.T., *Report of Council*, with date.

8. B.C., *Report*, 1875, p. 89.

9. NW.T., *Report*, 1903, pp. 20–21.

10. Minute Book of the Protestant Section of the Board of Education, 1880–1886, Public Archives of Manitoba (PAM), pp. 54–55. Cited hereafter as Minute Book, PAM. Pinkham identified the "leading features": administration by a superintendent rather than by a minister of education, appointment of superintendents by the Board of Education, the power of school trustees to raise money, the lack of a system of "payment by results", and the quality of the proposed program of studies for cities and towns.

11. North-West Territories, *Report of the Board of Education, 1886* (Regina, 1886), p. 27.

12. W. H. Elgie, *The Social Teachings of the Canadian Churches* (Toronto, 1964), pp. 75–76, as cited in N. G. McDonald, "The School as an Agent of Nationalism in the North-West Terri-

tories, 1884 to 1905," (MA thesis, University of Alberta, 1971).

13. Based upon information in NW.T., *Report*, 1904, p. 6; Alberta, *Report of the Department of Education*, 1906 (Edmonton, 1907), p. 13; B.C., *Report*, 1906, p. Aiii; Manitoba, *Report of the Department of Education*, 1906 (Winnipeg, 1907), p. 332. The last reference is cited hereafter as Manitoba, *Report*, with date.

14. In the Northwest Territories, the situation was even worse than the figures indicate, as approximately half of the schools closed from November 1 to April 1. James Brown, Board Secretary, to Sadie Baggett, 18 October 1886, Board of Education Letter Book, 1885–86, Vol. 2, Public Archives of Saskatchewan.

15. B.C., *Report*, 1874, p. 22.

16. In 1876, John Jessop said, "In no instance has the law been put in [*sic*] effect." Ibid., 1876, p. 11.

17. K. Wilson, "The Development of Education in Manitoba", (PHD thesis, Michigan State University, 1967), p. 101.

18. W. L. Morton, *Manitoba: A History* (Toronto, 1957), p. 248.

19. Manitoba, *Report of the Superintendent of Protestant Schools of Manitoba* (Winnipeg, 1876), pp. 26–27. Cited hereafter as Manitoba, *Report of Superintendent*, with date.

20. "It may be doubted whether the compulsory clause has ever been of any real advantage to the cause of education. . . . Many a man has unwillingly sent his children to school because of public opinion, but few because of fear of the law." J. H. Putman, *Egerton Ryerson and Education in Upper Canada* (Toronto, 1912), p. 258.

21. Manitoba, *Report*, 1893, p. 33.

22. NW.T., *Report*, 1903, p. 16.

23. Elgie, *Social Teachings*, pp. 75–76.

24. B.C., *Report*, 1876, p. 88.

25. Manitoba, *Report*, 1893, p. 30.

26. R. S. Patterson, "F. W. G. Haultain and Education in the Early West" (MA thesis, University of Alberta, 1961), p. 59.

27. As quoted in McDonald, "Nationalism", p. 153.

28. Minute Book, PAM, p. 54.

29. Manitoba, *Report*, 1903, p. 366; *1906*, p. 333.

30. NW.T., *Report*, 1903, p. 16.

31. Ibid., p. 21.

32. As quoted in Patterson, "Education in the Early West", p. 84.

33. NW.T., *Report of Council*, 1898, pp. 11–12.

34. As quoted in Patterson, "Education in the Early West", p. 84.

35. Morton says that the federal government permitted the colonies, in part at least, merely to attract prospective settlers away from the United States. Morton, *Manitoba*, p. 159.

36. Reports of A. H. Ball and E. B. Hutchinson, NW.T., *Report*, 1903, pp. 44, 51.

37. McDonald, "Nationalism", p. 70.

38. N. G. McDonald, "David J. Goggin: Promoter of National Schools", in R. Patterson, J. Chalmers, and J. Friesen, eds., *Profiles of Canadian Educators* (Toronto, 1974), p. 158.

39. Manitoba, *Report*, 1893, p. 17.

40. B.C., *Report*, 1882, p. 199.

41. A. Begg, *History of British Columbia from Its Earliest Discovery to the Present Time* (Toronto, 1894), p. 532.

42. Elgie, *Social Teachings*, pp. 75–76.

43. As quoted in McDonald, "Nationalism", p. 138.

44. NW.T., *Report of Council*, 1898, p. 16.

45. Ibid., 1896, p. 29.

46. Ibid., 1898, p. 22.

47. See H. J. Perkinson, *The Imper-*

fect Panacea: American Faith in Education, 1885 to 1969 (New York, 1968)
48. B.C., *Report*, 1875, p. 102.
49. Manitoba, *Report*, 1899, p. 565.
50. Ibid., 1891, p. 17.
51. Elgie, *Social Teachings*, pp. 75–76.
52. As quoted in C. B. Sissons, *Egerton Ryerson: His Life and Letters* (2 vols.; Toronto, 1947), II: 146.
53. As quoted in ibid., p. 254.
54. As quoted in ibid., p. 500.
55. As quoted in D. L. McLaurin, "The History of Education in the Crown Colonies of Vancouver Island and British Columbia and in the Province of British Columbia", (PHD thesis, University of Washington, 1936), p. 85.
56. B.C., *Report*, 1873, p. 5.
57. Ibid., 1874, pp. 37–38.
58. Ibid., 1890, p. 215.
59. Manitoba, *Report of the Superintendent*, 1881, p. 12.
60. Minute Book, PAM, pp. 261–62.
61. Ibid., pp. 269–70.
62. As quoted in L. Clark, *The Manitoba School Question: Majority Rule or Minority Rights?* (Toronto, 1968), p. 69.
63. See J. R. Miller, "D'Alton McCarthy, Equal Rights, and the Manitoba School Question", *Canadian Historical Review* LIV, No. 4 (December 1973), 369–92.
64. Joseph Martin to Thomas Greenway, 6 August 1889, Thomas Greenway Papers, PAM.
65. As quoted in Clark, *School Question*, pp. 76–77.
66. The Women's Christian Temperance Union made representations to the advisory board of education, which was established in 1890, advocating compulsory temperance instruction and adoption of temperance textbooks. Minute Book of the Advisory Board, 1890–98, PAM, II: 88.
67. As quoted in Clark, *School Question*, pp. 67–75.
68. Manitoba, *Report*, 1893, p. 21.
69. As quoted in Clark, *School Question*, p. 76.
70. Manitoba, *Report of the Superintendent*, 1886, p. 27.
71. As quoted in McDonald, "Nationalism", p. 130.
72. NW.T., *Report of Council*, 1896, p. 29.
73. McDonald, "Nationalism", p. 130.
74. Ibid., p. 35.
75. As quoted in Clark, *School Question*, p. 147.
76. McDonald, "Nationalism", p. 3.
77. Sissons, *Egerton Ryerson*, pp. 98–99.
78. M. R. Lupul, *The Roman Catholic Church and the North-West School Question: A Study in Church-State Relations in Western Canada* (Toronto, 1974), p. 31.
79. As quoted in Clark, *School Question*, p. 148.
80. B.C., *Report*, 1872, p. 200.
81. Ibid., 1874, p. 21.
82. Ibid., 1888, p. 179.
83. Ibid., 1877, p. 12.
84. Ibid., 1905, p. A21.
85. Ibid., 1904, p. A64.
86. *The Vancouver Province*, 8 March 1906.
87. M. A. Ormsby, *British Columbia: A History* (Toronto, 1958), p. 337.
88. Minute Book, PAM, pp. 54–55.
89. Manitoba, *Report of the Superintendent*, 1886, p. 6.
90. G. M. Weir, *The Separate School Question in Canada* (Toronto, 1934), p. 119. Weir said that events in the twenty years preceding 1934 had, in the opinion of "certain leading Ontario educators", caused Ontario to be dispossessed of its distinction. He gave as reasons for the dispossession: passive resistance to modern developments, the obscurantism of the official mind,

the inefficiency and economic waste of the small district organization, and the growing influence of the separate schools.

91. Francis Parker, for example, whom John Dewey called "the father of progressive education", was the feature speaker at a Manitoba conference. Manitoba, *Report*, 1891, p. 24.

Ontario at Philadelphia:
The Centennial Exposition of 1876

ROBERT M. STAMP

The year 1976 marked a double anniversary in the history of the Ontario school system. The centennial of Egerton Ryerson's retirement from the position of superintendent of schools was observed in appropriate fashion by the Ontario Ministry of Education. But 1976 also brought the one-hundredth anniversary of another event—one that had equally profound significance for the subsequent development of public schooling in the province. In November of 1875 Ryerson accepted an invitation to enter a Department of Education exhibit in the United States Centennial Exposition, planned for Philadelphia the following summer. It was one of Ryerson's last major policy decisions prior to his retirement early in the new year, and it proved to be a decision that would haunt his successors. The department's interests in Philadelphia were twofold: to learn from the educational experiences of other nations and to boast of the province's own accomplishments in public schooling. These seemingly compatible purposes co-existed uneasily and vied for supremacy, not only during the Philadelphia summer of 1876 but also during at least the next generation in Ontario education. No other Canadian exhibitor was so profoundly influenced by the favourable praise received from the judges and the American press. This euphoria permeated the thinking of department officials until at least the end of the century, making it extremely difficult to implement lessons learned from other nations' exhibits. In the long run, Ontario's presence at Philadelphia retarded rather than advanced educational reform.

"There have been bigger, more spectacular and more profitable world's fairs, but none more indigenous, more *American*, than the Centennial Exhibition of 1876," declared William Randel. "The Exhibition, apart from its foreign exhibits, was intended to put on proud display the manifold achievements of the American people in their first century of independence."[1] At first, devoted almost exclusively to industrial and technological exhibits, the great nineteenth-century fairs gradually began to devote more attention to social development. At the Paris Exhibition of 1867 the American standard of living was reflected in a display of an Illinois rural school, which according to Commissioner Beckwith, "attracted more attention than anything else".[2] The Americans thus saw Philadelphia as an opportunity to present further evidence of their self-proclaimed educational advances. Commissioner Eaton jumped at the chance to flaunt American glories, expressing his desire "that the Centennial should be altogether a school of patriotism, illustrating the excellences of the American system of government by the people, for the people, and that education, as the primary cause of these excellencies, should be fully represented."[3]

Ontario educators were not without doubts as to the wisdom of competing with the American state school systems. "Some hesitation was felt," wrote deputy-superintendent George Hodgins, "when the question was considered as to how we ought, without discredit to ourselves, to enter into a competition with other and more advanced countries, especially the United States, in a subject requiring so many years and such favourable opportunities for development."[4] Canadian departments of education had done little at any of the previous world's fairs, apart from a display of school reports and educational periodicals from Quebec. In part this had been due to the colonial status of the British North American provinces. Lacking nationhood in their own right, their previous participation had been under the wing of Great Britain, part of the "colonial" department of the mother country's exhibits. It was also a function of the modesty and inferiority complexes of the various provincial departments of public instruction. Although Ontario and Nova Scotia could trace the roots of their province-wide, publicly supported school systems as far back as most American states, there had long been a tendency to look south for both inspiration and leadership.

But the situation had changed by 1876. Confederation boosted national pride; perhaps it was time to remind the United States that it did not hold a complete New-World monopoly on social advancement. Ontario especially felt proud of its accomplishments in education. For thirty-two years Ryerson had presided over the steady growth of a comprehensive public-school system. The climax came with the new school laws of 1871, which brought both elementary and secondary schooling under public control, required all municipalities to provide "free" elementary education, and instituted the first compulsory attendance requirements. With Ryerson about to retire, and the subsequent decision to switch from a "non-political" superintendent to a cabinet minister responsible for education, a watershed had been reached. It was time to demonstrate to the world the progress of education in Ontario. The "world" certainly was ignorant of that "progress". As S. P. May regretfully told the province's teachers: "Many of the teachers in the United States did not know where Ontario was. The folk rather laughed at [me] when [I] spoke of the admirable school system of Ontario."[5]

It was time to tell the world. Ryerson at once asked Deputy-Superintendent Hodgins to prepare a detailed scheme of the proposed exhibit, and issued a circular to inspectors and school trustees urging them to contribute specimens of pupils' work and photographs of school buildings. S. P. May, head of the department's book depository, was freed from other duties and assumed full-time responsibility for the Ontario exhibit. Like Ryerson and Hodgins, May clearly saw the public relations potential of the exhibition. He set about to plan "the best method of making the educational exhibits most popular and of most practical value to the educationalists visiting the Exhibition."[6] The Ontario authorities were also aware that lessons might be learned from the other educational displays at Philadelphia. "We could turn the Exhibition to good account for the Department," wrote Hodgins, now deputy-minister, to his new superior, the minister of education, Adam Crooks. "My idea is that an examination of and a comprehensive report on the educational features of the Exhibition . . . would place the Department in possession of most valuable information." Hodgins believed that his own personal account, written "from an Ontario stand point", would be most valuable. There were "many details not embraced in official reports . . . which could only be noted by personal observation and comparison."[7] Hodgins received permission to spend a good part of the summer in Philadelphia, on the lookout for new ideas, but also spreading the gospel of Ontario's accomplishments. Thus the stage was set for the opening of the exhibition in May. Perhaps at that point the Ontario officials hoped to learn as much as to preach; but the balance was soon to be tipped when it became evident that the Ontario exhibit was the envy of other educators.

The Ontario education exhibit occupied 2,750 square feet of floor space in the main display building, in the midst of other Canadian and British displays. There were more than 2,000 separate articles, valued at over $10,000 and enumerated in a sixty-four page catalogue. There were copies of educational reports and school laws; university calendars and examination papers; photographs and models of recently constructed school buildings; school fittings and furniture; examples of pupils' work; textbooks, library books, and teachers' professional books; kindergarten illustrations; and sample visual aids for the teaching of the various subjects of the curriculum. It was this last category that was exhibited at greatest length—geometrical forms and solids, mathematical instruments, plaster models of hands and feet for drawing classes, chronological charts for history classes, globes and maps, geological and biological specimens, and apparatus for chemistry and physics laboratories.

The Toronto press was enthusiastic. *The Globe* commented on "the variety and excellence of the work done by the pupils . . . which reflect credit on both pupils and instructors." Even more striking was "the exhibition of apparatus of every kind", which *The Globe* judged to be "far ahead of any exhibit from any other country and will almost equal the whole of them together."[8] The rival Toronto paper, *The Mail*, fully concurred. "I am happy to say," wrote *The Mail*'s correspondent, "that the Ontario Exhibit in the Educational way takes the shine out of them all."[9] American press reaction was equally favourable. "The Country that exhibits the finest collection of Educational Appliances is Ontario," declared the Philadelphia *Press*.[10] Similar praise for the exhibit and the system behind it came from the New York *Tribune*, the Philadelphia *Herald*, the Buffalo *Advocate* and various American educational journals and reports of state education commissioners. Overseas reactions were even more impressive. British commissioner Sir Charles Reid declared that the Ontario exhibit "transcended all his expectations".[11] M. Buisson of the French ministry of public instruction stated that "to make a brilliant educational exhibition by the side of that of the United States was not an easy thing to do, and for Canada to have succeeded in doing it goes to prove that her schools are in a very prosperous condition."[12] Augustus Morris, commissioner for New South Wales wrote Adam Crooks that "there is nothing which so fully shows the extraordinary progress of Canada as the educational display of Ontario."[13]

This favourable press and public reaction was accompanied by a number of major awards and medals. From the United States Centennial Commission came a bronze medal "for a quite complete and admirably arranged Exhibition illustrating the Ontario system of education; also for the efficiency of an administration which has gained for the Ontario Department a most honourable distinction among Government Educational agencies." There was a gold medal awarded by a committee of British judges and a special award under the category of collective exhibits "for an extensive and attractive collection, illustrative of the growth and extent of the educational system of Ontario."[14] Hodgins' presence at the International Educational Conference held in Philadelphia in mid-July put the icing on Ontario's cake. No other foreign visitor was in such demand as a conference speaker and commentator. He spoke to enraptured audiences at length on whatever they wished to hear about the Ontario system—courses of study, teacher training, or the unity of the system.

One reason for Ontario's rich harvest of awards lay in the peculiar method of judging. Instead of competitive evaluation, the judges—125 American and 125 foreign—considered each exhibit on its own merits. If sixteen exhibits were entered in any given category, all sixteen might be judged worthy of bronze medals; conversely, all sixteen might go unrewarded. The plan made it easy for the judges, who never had to decide between two displays of comparable excellence and could therefore be very generous. The result was a minimum of hard feelings, even though, in the long run, the multiplication of awards robbed each one of any special value. The system made everyone feel good and no doubt contributed to the general opinion that the exposition was a great success. In any case, George Hodgins and S. P. May offered no protest and basked in the resulting glory.

The Ontario and other foreign exhibits—particularly that from Russia—looked especially good when compared with the mediocre efforts of most American state education departments. Of the thirty-eight states in the Union, "perhaps half a dozen should be admitted to have done themselves credit with their educational displays," wrote John Hoyt of Madison, Wisconsin. Hoyt damned some states with faint praise, while others were simply damned. "Of the state of Iowa but little can be said. The Exhibition made by it was comparatively small, and in no way remarkable." Kentucky "made her mark, but not much more," while Missouri showed "just enough to make the deficiency of the State very noticeable."[15] Few Americans expected a comprehensive exhibit from "backwoods" Ontario; yet they were greeted with a display that quantitatively and qualitatively surpassed those of most states and many foreign countries. This "dark horse" candidate became the darling of the judges and was amply rewarded.

But Ontario's impact was also due to the careful thought and planning of Hodgins and May. While most school exhibits concentrated on the "results" of education—copies of pupils' work —the Ontario entry consisted mainly of the "appliances" of education—examples of visual aids designed to lend interest and efficiency to the classroom teaching process. "Other major exhibitors sent volumes and volumes of pupil work," reported former grammar-school inspector George Paxton Young, "while Ontario . . . astonished the natives by an exhibition of the material instruments of education."[16] So the emphasis was placed on the desired process, rather than the end product. Diligent observers might have suspended judgment until they had time to carefully evaluate the product, but diligent observers were in short supply at Philadelphia; there was so much to see that both appointed judge and casual visitor were more likely to be impressed by a glittering array of paraphernalia designed to portray process. Hodgins explained it:

> The Exhibit was so planned and furnished that a stranger . . . would, without difficulty, understand the whole structure and policy of our Educational System and the means employed for making it effective for the purposes which it was designed to serve. . . . An intelligent enquirer at Philadelphia could understand the whole philosophy of our educational plans; take in *at a glance* the outlines of the entire structure of our Educational System, and could understand its practical working.[17]

That the "intelligent enquirers" were so impressed is perhaps more a tribute to the careful planning of Hodgins and May than to the actual working of the school system they represented.

Some visitors did ask if the various kinds of apparatus on display were in general use in the province's schools. The reply of the Ontario personnel was illustrative of a tendency all too prevalent in the late nineteenth century—to ascribe educational progress to the central department and to blame local school boards for any tardiness. As Hodgins wrote:

> Our reply was—the object lessons, maps, charts and globes are in pretty general use; but many of the more expensive kinds of apparatus, or more difficult instruments, are rarely used. Our object is to obtain samples and supplies of all kinds of articles which might be useful in our schools. As the teachers become better trained and the schools more efficient, they require, and should have the very best kind of school material. . . . It is not the fault of the Department, but of the schools, that they are not so generally used as they ought to be.[18]

Nevertheless, most visitors left Philadelphia with the impression that Ontario's schools were very well equipped. And they equated good equipment with good teaching, and good teaching with maximum learning. As the exhibits came down in October, and as educators began to digest the lessons of that Philadelphia summer, officials in the Ontario Department of Education were faced with a dilemma. Could Ontario learn from the rest of the world, or could the rest of the world learn from Ontario?

In common with other jurisdictions, Ontario could and did learn much from the Philadelphia and other world's fairs of the late nineteenth century. This was especially true in the fields of scientific and technical education. The British, for example, traced what they called the "industrial scare" to the great Crystal Palace Exhibition of 1851. This fair was intended to demonstrate to all the world the superiority of British manufactured products. But in those areas of manufacturing requiring superior skill and refined design, it was evident that France, some of the German-speaking states, and other continental countries had surpassed Britain. Subsequent international exhibitions repeatedly revealed remarkable industrial progress on the Continent. Acute observers such as John Mill began to link these advances with the superior education of continental workers. "The whole matter resolved itself into one point— education. Other nations were beating us in artistic and industrial productions, simply because they had been taught how to do it. . . . The matter amounts to this: More than half a century ago . . . it occurred to some educationalists on the Continent to establish trade schools."[19]

The Philadelphia Exposition made the same point for American industrialists and educators. From the beginning the relation of education to national industrial prosperity had been a key theme. It was not surprising that pedagogical innovations associated directly with industrial prosperity came under close scrutiny at Philadelphia. In the end, wrote Lawrence Cremin, "a few displays of tools from Russian schools literally stole the show; for these objects showed the West for the first time that Russian educators had finally scored a breakthrough on the thorny problem of how to organize meaningful, instructive shop training as an essential adjunct of technical education." Cremin concluded that "American education was never the same thereafter."[20] In subsequent years Professor Calvin Woodward of Washington University in St. Louis emerged as the leading American advocate of manual training and vocational education, charging that the schools neither prepared young men for gainful employment nor helped advance the nation's industrial prosperity.

Like Woodward, Ontario's George Hodgins came away from Philadelphia convinced that schooling in his domain was falling behind in the areas of industrial and technical education. The deputy-minister admitted that Ontario was represented at Philadelphia "by many ingenious evidences of industrial skill", but most of them "were rather striking adaptations of what already existed, rather than bold and original inventions . . . they were rather ingenious imitations, rather than as a whole, careful elaborations of scientific principles, indications of enlightened forethought and skill. . . . In this department, Canada —and I am among the last to admit it—is woefully deficient, and is doing very little to ensure progress or practical excellence in the future."[21] This deficiency seemed to stem from the fact that Canadian schools neglected scientific and technical education. "Even in our best Schools the teaching of drawing is the rare exception, not to speak of higher Industrial Training."[22]

Hodgins was critical of a "system of education which would exclude all but the three R's from the primary course of study." To do so was "manifestly unjust to very many boys who have as yet an undeveloped taste for scientific and mechanical pursuits, and a great loss to the interests of the country." Boys were naturally curious and observant, he argued, and "it is a great misfortune to them early in life not to turn such instincts to practical account and utilize them for the benefit of themselves and others." There was also a social argument in favour of vocational education. "Thousands of young men would in later life . . . be saved from many a snare and temptation were their undeveloped tastes and instincts directed into scientific channels while at school. Many an 'idle hand' would be saved from the 'mischief' to which they are prone, and many a valuable contribution to scientific research might thus owe its first idea to the stimulated curiosity of the school boy . . . ."[23]

Hodgins then turned to the educational lessons learned by other countries from the international exhibitions. He spoke of "the thorough awakening which has taken place among the industrial nations of Europe in regard to instruction in industrial and elementary science." Though Britain had temporarily fallen behind in industrial education, now it was "making every effort to recover lost ground and to give industrial training its proper place" in the schools.[24] It was the same with the United States, but unfortunately not so with Canada. "While our immediate neighbours have profited by the example of other nations . . . we have been, to all intents and purposes, idle."[25] The implication for Ontario education was clear: make provision for scientific and technical education within the schools or else be prepared to accept a tail-end position in the worldwide industrial and commercial race.

In the years after 1876 science made gradual inroads into the Ontario school and university curriculum. The sciences, of course, lacked the prestige that centuries of continued recognition had given the literary and classical subjects. University entrance requirements, the lack of trained teachers, the "unscientific" method of much existing science teaching, and the expense involved in outfitting school laboratories all worked against the advocates of the new subjects. Gradually, though, the sciences gained strength through the writings of Herbert Spencer and Thomas Huxley, through public interest in the great scientific discoveries of the day, and through the impact of industrial development. Ontario advocates argued their case on both practical and intellectual grounds. High-school inspector J. A. McLellan related scientific training to future occupations: "It is enough to say that the vast majority of the pupils of the schools go out into one or another of the great industries; and that whether they become farmers or manufacturers, or miners, or mechanics, they are likely to encounter practical questions in which a knowledge of chemistry and physics will prove highly useful."[26] The education minister, George Ross, adhered to the "mental discipline" theory. "The main reason for the introduction of science into our schools is the mental discipline to be obtained therefrom. The training of the reasoning powers and the acquisition of the scienific habit of mind are the objects with special reference to which the method of instruction should be chosen. . . ."[27] In 1885 the Ontario Department of Education required that collegiate institute status be dependent on a high school having a properly equipped science laboratory, and in 1890 the University of Toronto accepted science as a matriculation subject. By the end of the century, almost a full generation after the Philadelphia Exposition, chemistry, physics, botany, and to a lesser extent zoology, were finding their place in most Ontario high schools.

The 1870s and 1880s also saw Ontario take its first halting steps in the direction of technical education. At first, Ross, Hodgins, and other departmental personnel had placed their faith in night-school classes offered by the mechanics' institutes. Ross saw the institutes as aiding "mechanics in becoming acquainted with the branches of science which are of practical application to their various trades."[28] Unfortunately these institutions proved neither hospitable to "mechanics" nor directly correlated with the demands of industrial education. There was an undue emphasis on artistic drawing, to the exclusion of "studies applicable to branches of manufacturing arts other than merely decorative."[29] This emphasis was due in part to Superintendent May's previous connection with the Ontario School of Art and to the fragmentary lessons he had learned at Philadelphia; it was reinforced by the high praise given to exhibits of industrial drawing at the Colonial and International Exposition held in London in 1886.

Although higher technical education went forward at the University of Toronto's School of Practical Science and at Queen's University's School of Mining, it was evident by the 1890s that the lessons of Philadelphia could only be turned to good account through an expansion of industrial and vocational education at the high school level. Here the campaign met with resistance similar to that of the sciences—schooling should not teach "trades"; there was no room in the curriculum; it was too expensive. Again the supporters marshalled counter-arguments—it would make the high school curriculum more

"relevant" to the increasing numbers of non-academically inclined pupils coming from the elementary schools; it would
create a pool of skilled workmen who in turn would aid Canada's industrial progress. The City of Toronto began high
school technical education in 1891 and a few other Ontario
centres followed in the early years of the twentieth century.
Not till the Industrial Education Act of 1911, however, was a
generous provision made for provincial grants. It had taken a
long time for Hodgins's report on the "lessons" from Philadelphia to be translated into action; but there were compelling
reasons why this was so.

"The Ontario exhibitors say that their educational system is
the best in the world," reported the New York *Tribune* shortly
after the opening of the Centennial Exposition.[30] This feeling
of superiority was continually confirmed during the summer
with the winning of numerous awards and the profuse praise
from foreign visitors and the press. Ontario educators returned
from Philadelphia with a feeling of self-satisfaction that proved
a deterrent to future school reform. Politicians and educators
hesitated to make radical departures from a system that had
won such international acclaim. Thus the impetus given to
scientific and industrial education at Philadelphia was balanced
by a streak of conservatism that permeated Ontario's educational establishment throughout the remaining years of the
nineteenth century and well into the twentieth.

Just two years after Philadelphia, at the Paris Exhibition of
1878, the Ontario Department of Education exhibited in six
classes and won awards in each—more awards than Britain
and other parts of the Empire won altogether. Similar results
came at the Colonial Exhibition in London in 1886. The climax
in international praise was reached at the World's Columbian
Exposition in Chicago in 1893. Twenty-one prizes went to
Ontario—for kindergarten and primary work, secondary and
higher education, schools for teacher training, art schools and
mechanics' institutes, schools for the deaf, blind and feeble-
minded, and the University of Toronto's School of Practical
Science. Capping them all was the special award for "a system
of public instruction almost ideal in the perfection of its details
and the unity which binds together in one great whole all the
schools, from the kindergarten to the University."[31]

International acclaim was matched by high domestic regard.
J. G. Bourinot in his *Intellectual Development of the Canadian*

People admitted that "it is to Ontario we must look for illustrations of the most perfect educational system."[32] The *Educational Weekly* magazine was not the least surprised that "the efficiency and worth" of the Ontario system were meeting recognition throughout the Western world. "Whatever defects may be detected by those who scan it in details only, as a whole it challenges the admiration and wins the approval of all who know it."[33] An 1889 publication aimed at the potential British immigrant boasted that "the educational institutions of Ontario are such as to place it in the front rank among the nations of the earth."[34]

Education ministers and senior departmental officials were not reluctant to bask in this national and international acclaim. In fact they continually justified the glowing nature of their annual reports on the basis of this recognition. In the reports from earlier years, strong words had been used to point out faults; Ryerson, for example, in his 1872 report complained that "the internal condition of the schools generally has not improved for years." But the praise gained at Philadelphia resulted in complacent generalities portraying nobler accomplishments. Thus Adam Crooks in the 1878 report: "There are many considerations which enable me to state that the wave of progress flows onward to the maturity of perfection, gradually deepening and widening." Again in 1881: "There are probably no more favourable conditions, in every respect, to be found anywhere, than those which surround the youth of this Province."[35] J. H. Putman summed it up well as he recalled his career as a village schoolmaster in the 1880s. "I was quite content to be a follower," he wrote, "and took for granted that we had in Ontario the best of schools in the world. The Minister of Education, George W. Ross, had said so on many occasions."[36]

On what continuing basis did Ontario justify its superiority in the years following Philadelphia? High school inspector J. A. McLellan enumerated the following points after an 1881 visit to several American states: the unity of aim and method; the unification of educational interests from kindergarten to university; merit rather than political influence as a criterion for senior positions; academic and professional training for all teachers; and a thorough system of school supervision under qualified inspectors.[37] That same year the department produced comparative statistics which showed Ontario to have a higher percentage of pupils enrolled to total school population than the six most "advanced" American states, while at the same time the per pupil costs were lower.[38] Annual provincial expenditures for education more than doubled in the quarter century between 1871 and 1896; when the growth of population is taken into account, this increase amounted to about 50 per cent per capita. By 1893, illiteracy for the whole of the adult population had been reduced to less than 10 per cent and among persons between the ages of ten and twenty, it stood at less than 6 per cent. Little wonder that Ontario expressed its pride and satisfaction by sending a large exhibit to the Chicago World's Fair of 1893 where it was displayed under the motto "Education Our Glory".

And yet the system did have its critics in the years after Philadelphia. As early as 1879 the *Canada Educational Monthly* began raising controversial matters:

> We have the machinery of education, the shafting, the belting, and the motive power,—and the work all goes on from the bottom of the system to the top, with gratifying industry and admirable method. But to a great extent, we fear, it is machine work, marked with the materialism of routine and the elasticity of mechanism. The work, of course, is turned out; but it is done too much in the temper of uniformity and in the methods of a lifeless system. We have the body of educational work without its energizing and liberalizing life—the form but not the fruit.[39]

The following year the journal asked: "Is it not time that we stop patting each other complacently on the back in the belief that no country has a superior or more complete school organization than we have in Ontario?"[40] There was the feeling that the system had not kept pace with changing times. "Our educational system has always been an anachronism and has by no means kept up pace with the social or the intellectual development of the race," charged one high school principal. "Our public school system in respect to its curriculum has never been superior to what ought to have existed in the last century."[41]

The occasional foreign visitor, if not worried about embarrassing his hosts, could also be critical. Thus the following letter came to the *Canadian Educational Monthly* in 1880:

> I am in your country two months now, and at the Paris and Centennial Exhibitions (Philadelphia) attended. I very much astonished was there the display of school apparatus to find

so magnificent. Now I am here, and many schools have visited, and find I nothing as I did intend. In forty-four no globe is there; in thirty-nine no map of Canada itself exhibits; in alone two are there charts like the charts of Paris and Philadelphia, of the body, and of plants, and they the teachers say they find no time to employ. For object-lessons, in all the schools did I discover not one. Philosophical apparatus, most of the teachers do explain they have never heard with. . . .[42]

He asked whether it was "British fair play" to put on a show of superiority at Philadelphia when actually the schools of many European countries were better furnished and taught than those of Ontario.

We, at the exhibitions, were impressed that all the public schools were wholly furnished with all the apparatus exhibited, and so must have been the Commissioners both at Philadelphia and Paris too, who the medals and the honours awarded. As now appears by me, *your exhibit was nothing but a show extracted from a museum.*[43]

But Education Minister Ross would brook no criticism of the Ontario school system. In the years after the Chicago World's Fair of 1893 particularly, he became increasingly more defensive and less willing to listen to criticism of any sort. He reached the pinnacle of self-satisfied smugness in an 1889 political address. "In education I am unable to propound a new policy," he grandly announced, "My contention is that the school laws of Ontario are equal to if not superior to the school laws of any Province." Reflecting on the tributes from Philadelphia, Paris, and Chicago, Ross reminded his critics that "we have proven that our school system is first in competition with the school systems of the world." What of the future? "In the line of general education I think that we have gone about as far as we need to go. All we need to do is to maintain the efficiency of the teaching profession."[44]

During the Philadelphia summer of 1876 a majority of people in Ontario might have agreed that the province's school system was something to boast about. In the latter years of the century, however, as the pace of urbanization and industrialism accelerated, social and vocational problems appeared which could not be handled through traditional approaches to schooling. Indeed, a complete revision of educational philosophy was perhaps needed if Ontarians were to be fitted for the more complex urban-industrial society which was developing. Such an approach was being widely discussed and implemented in the United States through the manual training and new education movements. The Americans traced this reform current back to the Centennial Exposition. Although Hodgins had glimpsed this educational future at Philadelphia, he and other Ontario educators had found it difficult to implement. The forward thrust of reform had been lost in the conservatism resulting from international praise. In the long run, therefore, Ontario's presence at Philadelphia had retarded rather than advanced educational reform.

Fortunately, there was little opportunity for any provincial department of education to mount a comparable display in 1976. The city of Philadelphia did not stage a repeat performance of the Centennial Exposition of the previous century. Its more than 300 smaller commemorative events and projects reflected the decentralized nature of America's current celebrations, with each state and countless cities planning their own ventures. Even if a world's fair had been planned, it is doubtful that a provincial department would have occupied more space or captured more major awards than any other Canadian exhibit. The wheel has come full circle for public education as it has for grandiose international exhibitions. Public pride in the quantitative achievements of public education has receded; in its place are diversity, dissent, and uncertain educational futures. The lack of a major Ontario educational display in the United States in 1976 went completely unnoticed.

NOTES

1. William Pierce Randel, *Centennial: American Life in 1876* (Philadelphia, 1969), p. 4.
2. Merle Curti, "America at the World Fairs, 1851–1893", *American Historical Review* LV (1949–50), 846.
3. United States, *Report of the United States Commissioner of Education, 1874* (Washington, 1875), p. cxxvii.
4. J. George Hodgins, ed., *Documentary History of Education in Upper Canada, 1791–1876* (28 vols.; Toronto, 1894–1910), XXVIII: 47.
5. Ontario Teachers' Association, *Proceedings*, 1876, p. 11.
6. May to Hodgins, 30 June 1876, Education Department Records, Public Archives of Ontario (PAO).
7. Hodgins to Adam Crooks, 17 June 1876; ibid.
8. J. George Hodgins, ed., *Historical and Other Papers and Documents Illustrative of the Educational System of Ontario, 1858–1876* (Toronto, 1911) IV: 311–12.

9. Ibid., IV: 320.
10. Ibid., IV: 323.
11. J. George Hodgins, *Special Report to the Hon. the Minister of Education on the Ontario Educational Exhibit and the Educational Features of the International Exhibition at Philadelphia, 1876* (Toronto, 1877), p. 25.
12. Ibid.
13. Ibid., pp. 38–39.
14. Hodgins, *Documentary History* XXVIII: 60.
15. Quoted by Randel, *Centennial*, pp. 400–01.
16. Hodgins, *Special Report*, pp. 15–16.
17. Ibid., p. 15. Italics added.
18. Ibid.
19. John Mill, *What is Industrial and Technical Education?* (London, 1871), cited in C. A. Bennett, *History of Manual and Industrial Education* (Peoria, 1926), II: 277.
20. Lawrence A. Cremin, *The Transformation of the School: Progressivism in American Education, 1876–1957* (New York, 1961), p. 25.
21. Hodgins, *Documentary History* XXVIII: 219.
22. Ibid., XXVIII: 220.
23. Hodgins, *Special Report*, pp. 241–42.
24. Ibid., p. 248.
25. Ibid., p. 241.
26. Ontario Department of Education, *Annual Report of the Minister of Education, 1882*, p. 222.
27. Ibid., p. 21.
28. Ibid. for 1884, p. 205.
29. Ibid. for 1885, p. 187.
30. New York *Tribune*, 10 May 1876, cited by *The Globe* (Toronto), 12 May 1876.
31. *Report of the Minister of Education*, 1893, p. li.
32. J. G. Bourinot, *The Intellectual Development of the Canadian People* (Toronto, 1881), p. 41.
33. *Educational Weekly*, 5 February 1885, p. 88.
34. E. B. Biggar, *Canada: A Memorial Volume* (Montreal, 1889), Sec. VI, p. 12.
35. *Report of the Minister of Education*, 1878, p. vii; 1881, p. 232.
36. J. H. Putman, *Fifty Years at School: An Educationist Looks at Life* (Toronto, 1938), p. 13.
37. *Report of the Minister of Education*, 1881, p. 239.
38. Ibid., p. 233.
39. *Canada Educational Monthly*, February 1879, p. 65.
40. Ibid., February 1880, p. 125.
41. J. E. Bryant, "Education in the Twentieth Century: A Criticism and a Forecast", Ontario Teachers' Association, 1892, *Proceedings*, pp. 67–68.
42. *Canada Educational Monthly*, February 1880, pp. 100–01.
43. Ibid.
44. George W. Ross, *Great Speech by the Hon. Geo. W. Ross, Premier of Ontario, Delivered at Whitby, November, 1899: Government's Policy* (Toronto, 1899), pp. 24–25.

NOTES ON CONTRIBUTORS

Alf Chaiton

Assistant Professor, Faculty of Education, Memorial University of Newfoundland, St. John's, Newfoundland.

Alan H. Child

Formerly a professor at Notre Dame University, Nelson, B.C., he is presently teaching high school in Fort St. James, B.C.

Ian E. Davey

Lecturer in Education, University of Adelaide, Australia.

Albert Fiorino

Research Consultant with the Commission on Declining Enrollment, Government of Ontario, Toronto.

Goldwin French

President and Professor, Victoria University, Toronto.

R. D. Gidney

Associate Professor, Althouse College of Education, University of Western Ontario, London, Ontario.

Harvey J. Graff

Assistant Professor, Department of History, The University of Texas at Dallas, Richardson, Texas.

Susan E. Houston

Associate Professor, Department of History, York University, Toronto.

D. A. Lawr

Associate Professor, Althouse College of Education, University of Western Ontario, London, Ontario.

Marvin Lazerson

Associate Professor, Faculty of Education, University of British Columbia, Vancouver, B.C.

James Love

Assistant Professor, Department of Education, Brock University, St. Catharines, Ontario.

Neil McDonald

Associate Professor, Faculty of Education, The University of Manitoba, Winnipeg, Manitoba.

Alison Prentice

Associate Professor, Department of History and Philosophy of Education, Ontario Institute for Studies in Education, University of Toronto, Toronto.

Robert M. Stamp

Assistant Dean and Professor, Faculty of Education, University of Calgary, Calgary, Alberta.

J. Donald Wilson

Associate Professor, Faculty of Education, University of British Columbia, Vancouver, B.C.